Foundations of Therapeutic Recreation

Terry Robertson, PhD
Terry Long, PhD

Editors

Human Kinetics

Library of Congress Cataloging-in-Publication Data

Foundations of therapeutic recreation / Terry Robertson and Terry Long (eds.).
    p. ; cm.
  Includes bibliographical references and index.
  ISBN-13: 978-0-7360-6209-1 (hard cover)
  ISBN-10: 0-7360-6209-2 (hard cover)
  1. Recreational therapy. 2. Recreational therapy—Vocational guidance. 3. People with
disabilities—Rehabilitation. I. Robertson, Terry, 1958- II. Long, Terry, 1971-
  [DNLM: 1. Recreation—psychology. 2. Disabled Persons—rehabilitation. 3. Leisure
Activities. 4. Recreation—physiology. QT 250 F771 2008]
  RM736.7.F66 2008
  615.8'5153—dc22
                          2007011903

ISBN-10: 0-7360-6209-2
ISBN-13: 978-0-7360-6209-1

The Web addresses cited in this text were current as of March 2007, unless otherwise noted.

Acquisitions Editor: Gayle Kassing, PhD
Developmental Editor: Ragen E. Sanner
Assistant Editors: Anne Rumery and Carmel Sielicki
Copyeditor: Bob Replinger
Proofreader: Erin Cler
Indexer: Sharon Duffy
Permission Manager: Dalene Reeder
Graphic Designer: Bob Reuther
Graphic Artist: Angela K. Snyder and Tara Welsch
Photo Asset Manager: Laura Fitch
Cover Designer: Keith Blomberg
Photographer (cover): Photo on left provided by the National Center on Physical Activity and Disability; photos on upper and lower right provided by Terry Long
Photographer (interior): Terry Long, unless otherwise noted.
Art Manager: Kelly Hendren
Illustrator: Denise Lowry
Printer: Thomson-Shore, Inc.

Printed in the United States of America   10   9   8   7   6   5   4   3   2   1

Human Kinetics
Web site: www.HumanKinetics.com

United States: Human Kinetics
P.O. Box 5076
Champaign, IL 61825-5076
800-747-4457
e-mail: humank@hkusa.com

Canada: Human Kinetics
475 Devonshire Road Unit 100
Windsor, ON N8Y 2L5
800-465-7301 (in Canada only)
e-mail: orders@hkcanada.com

Europe: Human Kinetics
107 Bradford Road
Stanningley
Leeds LS28 6AT, United Kingdom
+44 (0) 113 255 5665
e-mail: hk@hkeurope.com

Australia: Human Kinetics
57A Price Avenue
Lower Mitcham, South Australia 5062
08 8372 0999
e-mail: info@hkaustralia.com

New Zealand: Human Kinetics
Division of Sports Distributors NZ Ltd.
P.O. Box 300 226 Albany
North Shore City
Auckland
0064 9 448 1207
e-mail: info@humankinetics.co.nz

Contents

PART I   Introduction to Therapeutic Recreation   1

CONTENTS CONTINUED ▶

PART III Trends in Therapeutic Recreation 197

CHAPTER

13

Wellness Through Physical Activity 199

Sheila Swann-Guerrero, CTRS
National Center on Physical Activity and Disability

Chris Mackey, BS
FPG Child Development Institute, University of North Carolina at Chapel Hill

CHAPTER

14

Demographics, Economics, Politics, and Legislation 217

John McGovern, JD
Northern Suburban Special Recreation Association, Northbrook, Illinois

CHAPTER

15

A Global Perspective of Therapeutic Recreation 231

David Howard, PhD, MSW, CTRS
Indiana State University

Rodney Dieser, PhD
University of Northern Iowa

Heewon Yang, PhD, CTRS
Southern Illinois University

Shane Pegg, PhD
University of Queensland, Brisbane, Australia

Julie Lammel, PhD
Lock Haven University

CHAPTER

16

Paradoxes in Leisure Services and Therapeutic Recreation . . 251

Jesse Dixon, PhD
San Diego State University

CHAPTER

17

Envisioning the Future: Therapeutic Recreation as a Profession 267

Terry Robertson, PhD
Northwest Missouri State University

Preface

The purpose of this book is to introduce you, the reader, to the profession of therapeutic recreation. The editors and authors have set out to provide you with an opportunity to explore this topic from both a personal and a professional perspective. As such, the content, format, and layout of the book were designed to provide this opportunity. Not only are you encouraged to examine what therapeutic recreation "is," but also it is critical that you consider what therapeutic recreation can "provide to" you or will "require of" you. Even within the broad profession of therapeutic recreation, there are many career decisions to make. Figuring out where you best fit as a person and a professional is a process you can start right now.

Working in therapeutic recreation is a relatively new occupation, but its roots are as old as civilization. These roots have grown into a diverse array of applications and an equally broad range of potential benefits. To adequately present the diverse body of information, this book draws on the combined wisdom, experience, and technical expertise of 22 contributing authors and leaders within the therapeutic recreation profession. Numerous stories, case examples, professional profiles, vignettes, and other learning tools will help the reader enjoy and personalize his or her exploration of this exciting and rewarding human service profession.

This is the first introductory therapeutic recreation textbook written entirely within this century. Many new or young professionals, as well as a number of seasoned veterans, have collaborated on this book. Much of this information will challenge the status quo. It will push some of the long-established barriers and force people to start thinking outside the box. Through this process, the material will also challenge the expectations of many experienced professionals and educators. At the same time, seasoned educators and practitioners will note that at the heart of the book, there is a call for all of us to make, use, and share our purposeful interventions, our successes, and our challenges.

The book also asserts that these purposeful therapeutic recreation interventions are built on theories of play, leisure, and recreation; therefore, associated interventions should be designed, engineered, and delivered to be enjoyable, beneficial, and rewarding.

The book includes a clear expectation that you will work to develop the appropriate knowledge, skills, discernment, and disposition to be a successful professional. It also challenges those entering the profession to think about their personal, civic, and related professional responsibilities; their ethics; and their level of professional commitment. Times and circumstances have changed and will continue to change at a fast pace, as will our profession.

Stay involved, keep sharing, and keep caring! This profession is not for everyone, but it may be right for you. The challenge to you is to examine your own interests and motivations for a career in therapeutic recreation and then examine the expectations for practicing professionals so that in the end you can decide for yourself whether this occupation, this profession, is right for you. The challenge for the educator is to continue discovering the opportunities and benefits of our profession and to share them with others. Enjoy!

What's Inside

It is important to note that this book is divided into three parts. The first part includes five chapters and presents introductory concepts that are a critical part of orienting the reader to the foundations of our profession. Topics such as career choice and professional opportunities, definition and history of therapeutic recreation, and person-first philosophy are presented. Chapter 5 closes part I with a discussion of potential places of practice, as well as therapeutic recreation models and modalities utilized in therapeutic recreation.

Part II includes seven chapters and takes a closer look at potential areas of practice. In addition to a chapter 6 presentation of the overall therapeutic recreation process, several chapters explore specific areas of application for this process. These chapters address orthopedic and neurological impairments, mental health, developmental disabilities, youth development, and aging. Potential client characteristics, theoretical concepts associated with each area of practice, and specific techniques and modalities that might be utilized are discussed in each of these chapters.

The final five chapters make up part III and consider current trends in therapeutic recreation, as well as mechanisms for engaging and addressing demands associated with such trends. Content includes a chapter dedicated solely to wellness through physical activity (chapter 13), a global perspectives chapter (chapter 15), an exploration of the political process and how to utilize it (chapter 14), a presentation of several professional paradoxes relevant to therapeutic recreation (chapter 16), and a final discussion in chapter 17 on envisioning the future of therapeutic recreation coincides with professional development.

Ancillaries

Three types of ancillaries are available to educators to supplement the information presented in this textbook:

- Instructor guide. The instructor guide includes chapter overviews, chapter objectives, discussion questions, and learning activities.

- Test package. The test package includes a variety of questions, from true/false to short answer. Instructors can create their own tests.

- Presentation package. A Microsoft® PowerPoint presentation package includes key points from the chapters. Instructors may use the presentation package to supplement their lectures. The presentation package may be adapted to suit each instructor's lecture content and style.

For more information and to access these ancillaries, please visit www.humankinetics.com/foundationsoftherapeuticrecreation.

Summary

We hope that you find this book and your journey into the world of therapeutic recreation to be exciting, challenging, and fulfilling. Remember to have fun, and always keep in mind the people you serve. Therapeutic recreation is a profession that will provide you real opportunities to make a difference. We wish you the best!

Acknowledgments

It is with great pleasure and sincere hearts that we are allowed to publicly acknowledge and thank many of those who have encouraged, supported, and helped us in the creation of this book.

First, we would like to thank our spouses (Shelly and Anne). Thank you for your patience, encouragement, and understanding during this process. We could not have done this without you and your support. We also hope that our time away on this project will be far surpassed by time spent with you and our families in the near future.

Second, we want to also recognize the efforts of Human Kinetics, specifically Ms. Gayle Kassing, for her willingness to support us through the initial ideas and formational structuring up to the completion of this text; Ms. Ragen Sanner, who worked day to day with the manuscript and gave us many, many ideas for improvements and for reading drafts of the text. Numerous other HK personnel helped in other ways and we are grateful for their professional commitment to this project.

Next, we would like to thank all of the authors that have contributed their time, thought, and dedication to our profession. Each of the 22 contributing authors is a recognized expert within the area that he or she wrote in and we appreciate their willingness to work with us on the first new introductory, or foundations, text written in this century. We would also like to thank those who submitted personal and professional data to create "Outstanding Professionals" within each chapter. The included individuals represent only a small number of the many professionals willing to share, so we would also like to thank everyone who expressed interest and supplied support information including pictures and case information.

We would be of poor character if we did not also acknowledge those at Northwest Missouri State University who have helped us. This is especially the case for those within the Health, Physical Education, Recreation, and Dance department that have assisted or supported our efforts. Special thanks go to Ms. Cathie Hannigan, Dr. Jeff Ferguson, Dr. Sue Myllykangas, Dr. Alice Foose, and our college dean, Dr. Max Ruhl, for your help! Mr. John Gustafson, Mrs. Gina McNeese, Dr. Janet Reusser, Dr. Matt Symonds, Dr. Loren Butler, Dr. Jim Johnson, and Dr. Rheba Vetter have all also supported our effort in one way or another. Thanks!

Similarly, we want to thank the thousands of students and professionals who have encouraged us over the years to write a book that was more "reader and faculty friendly" and yet maintained high expectations for those who will eventually go into practice. Specifically, we would like to thank the following folks for their professional support, teaching, mentoring, and leadership: Dr. David L. Holmes, Dr. Gerald O' Morrow, Dr. Marcia Carter, Dr. David Compton, Dr. Gary Ellis, Dr. Norma Stumbo, Dr. Gerald Hitzhusen, Dr. David Austin, Dr. Jean Keller, Dr. Syd Post, and Dr. Steven Bell.

We also owe a great deal of appreciation to a number of different professional associations, their elected officials, board members, and staff (i.e., alphabetically, American Therapeutic Recreation Association; Missouri Association of Health, Physical Education, Recreation, and Dance; Missouri Leisure Educators Society; Missouri Parks and Recreation Association; Missouri Therapeutic Recreation Society; National Recreation and Park Association; National Therapeutic Recreation

Society; Nevada Parks and Recreation Association; Nevada Association of Health, Physical Education, Recreation, and Dance; Society of Parks and Recreation Educators; Utah Parks and Recreation Association; and the Utah Recreation Therapy Association).

We would also like to point out the very significant effort put in by the individual who created our supporting instructor's guide, Dr. Susan Myllykangas. Dr. Sue has done a great job in creating activities and specific examples to help clarify and reinforce chapter concepts, as well as creating additional study opportunities that correspond with each chapter in the text.

Finally, I (Terry Robertson) would like to thank Dr. Terry Long for taking the lead on this project. After the initial review and contract signing, he became the primary contact and work horse for this effort due to my battle with cancer. This text would not be a reality without his leadership and work ethic, so thank you, Terry! I would also like to thank God for allowing me to outlive my prognosis and to receive the support, prayers, and encouragement of so many individuals across the United States and from around the world during this time. Thank you all and may God bless you as you read and use this book.

PART

Introduction to Therapeutic Recreation

Considering Therapeutic Recreation as Your Profession

Terry Robertson, PhD
Northwest Missouri State University

Terry Long, PhD
Northwest Missouri State University

LEARNING OUTCOMES

After completing this chapter, learners will be able to demonstrate the following competencies:

- Explain various definitions of therapeutic recreation
- Recognize the importance of leisure in therapeutic recreation
- Appreciate the diverse nature of therapeutic recreation
- Describe various professional opportunities in therapeutic recreation
- Identify basic job skills and responsibilities in therapeutic recreation

Welcome to the challenging and rewarding profession known as therapeutic recreation. You have chosen an area of study that, for the right person, is full of opportunities. That's right—therapeutic recreation is not for everyone. But for those who find themselves drawn to helping others in a dynamic and engaging environment, this may be the perfect career. A lifetime of discovery, creativity, and problem solving awaits the future professional.

The editors and authors associated with this text believe that the presented information can be useful to all students, regardless of major. If you have not committed to an academic major, this book can provide you with information about a potential career choice. If you have committed to a major other than therapeutic recreation, developing a better understanding of disability issues can help you later in your career to provide products, services, and communities that are beneficial to all aspects of society. Finally, if you are a therapeutic recreation major, this text can provide you with a core understanding of your chosen profession. We hope that by reading this book, you will develop confidence in and commitment to your choice of a therapeutic recreation major.

What Is Therapeutic Recreation?

It is important that a definition of therapeutic recreation be provided at this point. The following definition is for the purpose of communicating to the reader basic elements of therapeutic recreation. It is not intended to represent a formal position of any particular professional group or philosophy. Rather, it is meant to be used by students and other interested individuals as a tool for understanding therapeutic recreation from a practical perspective.

Therapeutic recreation is the purposeful utilization or enhancement of leisure as a way to maximize a person's overall health, well-being, or quality of life. To understand this definition, we must carefully consider the chosen terminology.

The first key word in this definition is *purposeful*. Therapeutic recreation professionals should always think about the purpose of whatever ingredients or strategies they include in their programs. What you include is important, of course, but so is how you include it. How you present a challenge, problem, concept, or skill to a client will affect the outcomes of the experience. This purpose should be used to determine the content of every therapeutic recreation session. The purpose is typically described through formally written goals and targeted **outcomes.** Every client or participant has goals that they are expected to achieve through their participation in the program. If a therapist does not intentionally design the work with a client to address these goals, the outcome will depend largely on luck. Such an approach is irresponsible and unethical. In contrast, outcome-driven interventions allow the therapist to maximize client benefits.

SO WHAT'S MY TITLE?

Therapeutic recreation professionals can be called by a lot of names. Job titles such as recreation therapist, recreational therapist, activity therapist, and inclusion specialist might all show up on job advertisements or on your employment contract. These different names are a result of several factors, such as the role of the professional, government-mandated laws and regulations, the rules and guidelines of the agency, and your professional affiliations and philosophy. This mix of names may seem, and sometimes is, very confusing, but you will come to understand these differences soon.

One commonality across all job titles is the fact that they are all more likely to be viewed as more legitimate, or to represent a competent professional, when tied to a credential. In the therapeutic recreation world, the primary credential you can earn is Certification as a Therapeutic Recreation Specialist. This credential may or may not be reflected in your actual job title, but it demonstrates that you possess a certain level of skill and qualification as a professional. It would be a lie to say every job opportunity will require certification, but a significant proportion of agencies do mandate that employees be certified.

Since there are so many title variations in therapeutic recreation, many of which specifically reflect a certain professional role or orientation, the authors of this book will use a single title across all chapters, unless the nature of the discussion requires otherwise. From this point on, *therapeutic recreation specialist* will be used to refer to therapeutic recreation professionals. We've chosen this title because it is not tied to a particular setting or situation, and is commonly understood by all professionals as representing a certain skill set. Ensuring that you attain appropriate and necessary credentials is your responsibility. We've left "certified" off of the title "therapeutic recreation specialist" because some employment scenarios may not require it, but our expectation is that you will pursue certification as part of your professional preparation.

Therapeutic recreation professionals create and implement programs to address client goals, such as here, in which a professional is talking with a young client about the physical and psychological goals that he achieved during a successful hike.

Consistent production of such benefits will, in turn, demonstrate the effectiveness of therapeutic recreation programs.

The next two key words in the definition are *utilization* and *enhancement*. Specifically, this portion of the definition refers to utilizing or enhancing one's leisure. Utilization involves actively engaging leisure interests, choices, abilities, and behaviors to maintain or improve ability levels in both leisure and nonleisure domains. Simply put, recreation is used as a therapy tool. Examples of utilizing leisure in therapeutic recreation could include a person with dementia who regularly participates in memory and object recognition games to exercise his or her cognitive abilities or a stroke patient who works with dominoes to enhance grasp, number recognition, reasoning, and, ultimately, the ability to play games of this nature. In this case, we use the leisure skill or interest to achieve the target outcome. The terms **recreation therapy**, *recreational therapy,* and *therapeutic recreation* are often used interchangeably, but the current authors differenti-

ate recreation therapy and recreational therapy as specific forms of therapeutic recreation involving the purposeful use of leisure-based interventions to improve functional abilities such as strength, attention, basic social skills, or emotional state. Therapeutic recreation is a broader term that refers to both utilization and enhancement of leisure.

Enhancement of leisure focuses on rebuilding lost leisure skills, identifying new interests, learning new skills, or finding alternative ways to perform skills. Examples of leisure enhancement would include working with a substance abuser to develop a drug-free leisure lifestyle or teaching a person with a spinal cord injury how to snow ski.

The most important word of all in this definition is *leisure*. It differentiates therapeutic recreation from other therapies and involves physical, cognitive, social, or emotional activity that is freely chosen and intrinsically motivated. Structured leisure activities are often referred to as recreation, but therapeutic recreation interventions can include any aspect of leisure. Organized sports, creative arts, meditation, outdoor activities, traveling, and bird-watching could all be part of a therapeutic recreation program. Ultimately, developing such leisure abilities allows us to choose and participate in activities that are enjoyable and personally rewarding. Those who lack such leisure abilities will find it difficult to live a healthy, happy life.

Utilization and enhancement of leisure can greatly improve health and well-being, which is the ultimate goal of therapeutic recreation. The extent to which the client achieves this goal depends largely on the care and thoughtfulness applied by the therapeutic recreation professional in planning and implementing interventions that focus on the targeted outcomes (client and program goals).

Criteria for Identifying Therapeutic Recreation

Two criteria can be used to identify whether an intervention or activity can be considered therapeutic recreation. First is ensuring that outcomes are grounded in a leisure context. In many cases, the leisure context is inherent, but not necessarily immediate, because of the current therapy needs of the patient. For example, playing card games can be a useful therapeutic tool when working with stroke patients. Enhancing number recognition or hand grasp may be primary therapy goals when working with such patients, whereas learning to play the game would seem somewhat trivial until those basic skills improve. Still, leisure is embedded in the intervention and separates it from other forms of therapy. Even if playing games is not an immediate concern of the client, the leisure context of this activity may be of use when the client begins to focus on returning home and living a satisfying life. In addition, time spent playing games can provide much needed relief from the physical and psychological strains of therapy. At other times, the therapeutic recreation professional may be more direct in communicating the leisure context of therapy to the client. Later sessions with the same stroke patient might involve direct efforts to develop activity skills or discussion of opportunities for recreation participation through adapted sports organizations.

The second defining characteristic of therapeutic recreation is purposeful intervention. As already mentioned, the therapist must make a deliberate effort to elicit specific, preestablished therapy outcomes. Goals are established through use of client assessment, and therapeutic recreation interventions are built around achieving these goals. Progress is then monitored through periodic evaluation of the client.

Note that using outcome-driven interventions alone is not therapeutic recreation. All legitimate therapies establish and track the achievement of goals, and therapeutic recreation is just one of those therapies. Likewise, all leisure activities that have the potential for enhancing health or well-being are not necessarily therapeutic recreation. Many leisure activities are beneficial to a person, but they may not be purposefully developed and delivered therapeutic interventions. Only when these two characteristics—a leisure context and purposeful intervention—are paired does a true therapeutic recreation intervention exist.

Different Perspectives

Agreeing on a definition of therapeutic recreation has long been a challenge to the profession. This ongoing variation in professional orientation can be seen in many of the conceptual models that have been developed to illustrate the concept *therapeutic recreation*. Rather than aligning solely with one of these existing definitions, this text presents a new applied definition that encompasses the critical elements of several perspectives. We will discuss these perspectives, and the models that accompany them, in detail later in this text.

For now, we view these variations in definition as ideas that represent different schools of thought, all of which are useful within certain realms. This approach is similar to that seen in other professions. For example, psychologists have a common name, but their views on therapy and the mechanisms by which it functions are diverse. Likewise, the effectiveness of these therapy mechanisms varies across different client needs, and no single therapy is the best approach for everyone. As such, the given definition is meant to provide a broad perspective that acknowledges the usefulness of various professional orientations. Its intended purpose is not to replace formal definitional statements that have been put forth by professional organizations such as the National Therapeutic Recreation Society (NTRS) and the American Therapeutic Recreation Association (ATRA), but to illustrate the core ingredients of therapeutic recreation to the enquiring student or layperson (nonprofessional) in a manner that reflects legitimate applications of therapeutic recreation.

A Diverse Profession

Therapeutic recreation has emerged from a dynamic and ever-evolving mix of perspectives, converging schools of thought, borrowed and original theories, and unique interventions and services. This diverse background offers potential for a large variety of service applications. Some have referred to therapeutic recreation as being eclectic in nature. Others have referred to it as a **strength-based approach** to problem solving. Some suggest that therapeutic recreation is unique in that it involves use of nonwork-related or nonobligated time-related interventions (recreation or leisure). Still others say that it is a mix of philosophy, psychology, the arts, and physical therapy and occupational therapy techniques—all used by a trained professional to bring about functional change within another person or group of people.

Regardless of the perspective chosen, therapeutic recreation is a profession that has tremendous potential for growth and evolution. The diverse philosophical positions or perspectives within the profession provide numerous opportunities for flexible application and professional growth. This diversity tends to produce a well-rounded college graduate who is capable of working within, on the fringes, or outside therapeutic recreation. Likewise, therapeutic recreation training programs have tra-

TERRANCE

Terrance is a 62-year-old man who had a left-brain stroke. As a result, he cannot lift his arm above his shoulder and can only hold his arm at shoulder level for a few seconds. He also has difficulty grasping objects, especially small items such as shirt buttons or shoestrings. A few weeks after his stroke, Terrance is still working to regain the skills required to do the basic things necessary to get by in life (activities of daily living).

Terrance works with a certified therapeutic recreation specialist, a professional credential often required by employers of therapeutic recreation professionals (this credential is explained further in chapter 3). The CTRS meets with Terrance for about an hour each day to work on improving grasp, range of motion, and activity tolerance. The CTRS knows what activities to do with Terrance based on an intake assessment that the two completed when Terrance was admitted to the rehabilitation center. The CTRS then works with Terrance to develop goals for treatment. To address these goals, Terrance selects from a variety of activities suggested by the CTRS, all of which involve exercising the targeted functional skills. The activities could include choices such as checkers (grasping skills), model construction (requiring more endurance), or challenges such as stacking blocks (requiring a progressively higher reach).

Leisure Context

The leisure context of Terrance's program can be seen in the nature of the activities that the CTRS provides. By encouraging the client to use these existing leisure interests and abilities, he is able to improve functional limitations associated with the stroke. Also important is the fact that the client is empowered to choose activities that are of interest to him. A core element in providing therapeutic recreation programs is that clients be given as much freedom and control as possible, which ultimately helps ensure that the program is grounded in leisure.

Purposeful Intervention

Because the CTRS identified client needs through an assessment, established goals related to assessment results, and developed activity choices in line with these goals, Terrance's therapeutic recreation program can be considered purposeful. A common error in this area is to choose activities based solely on the interest of the client, or even worse, on the interest of the CTRS. Although choice is important, all program elements should be in line with treatment goals. Remember that therapeutic recreation goals for Terrance may also include enhancing his leisure, even while he stays at the rehab center. As such, some of his program may be oriented around having fun, relaxing, and escaping the worries associated with his condition.

ditionally been ideal for those seeking a bachelor's degree before moving into a graduate degree program in any of a variety of health science–related degree programs. A therapeutic recreation degree has also helped professionals enter community-based recreation and administrative positions within a variety of fields. So, if you are searching for a degree that could prepare you for a wide variety of occupations, or if you are looking for a specific career, then therapeutic recreation may be right for you. Are you still interested?

Choosing a Profession

As a bright person capable of choosing among many occupations, you should think about why you are interested in therapeutic recreation. Are you interested in helping others? Are you interested in physical activity or psychological processes? Do you or any members of your family have a disability? Are you deciding between this major

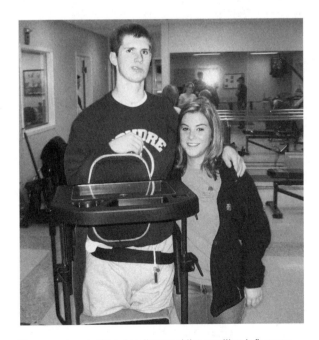

You may have already witnessed the positive influence of therapeutic recreation through the experiences of a family member.

JOHN CONRAD CHAMBERS

Background Information

Education

*AA in Recreation Administration, Los Angeles Valley College, Los Angeles, California *BA in Recreation with an emphasis in Therapeutic Recreation, California State University, Los Angeles *Clinical Therapeutic Recreation Internship, Casa Colina Rehabilitation Hospital

Special Affiliations

*Board member, consumer representative, National Therapeutic Recreation Society *Steering Committee, National Institute Recreational Inclusion *National Recreation Park Association member *National Recreation Park Society member *Executive director, Lakeside Disabled Sports USA

Special Awards

*Nevada Recreation and Parks Society Program Excellent Awards (1992, 1993, 1995, 1996, 1999, 2000, 2001, 2002) *National Therapeutic Recreation Society Presidential Citation (2003) *National Recreation Park Association R.O.S.E. Award (2005)

Position Prior to Retirement

Manager of Adaptive Recreation and Municipal Sports Division for the City of Las Vegas

Job Description

Plan, prioritize, supervise, develop, and implement goals, objectives, policies, and procedures within state and city guidelines in a least restrictive environment for people of all abilities. Oversee and develop $3.1 million budget. Monitor and approve expenditures, administer the department, and oversee evaluation and training programs for 500 full-time employees. Serve as the

city liaison between people with disabilities and state and Federal agencies to negotiate and resolve sensitive and controversial issues. Inspect city facilities for accessibility and make recommendations. Work with other departments and selected architectural and engineering firms to provide access to all.

Career Path

I have worked in the field of parks and recreation for more than 30 years. I started in therapeutic recreation over 27 years ago with the City of Las Vegas and recently retired from the position of manager of the adaptive recreation and municipal sports division for the City of Las Vegas. I currently serve on the boards of directors for the National Therapeutic Recreation Society and National Alliance for Accessible Golf. I am also one of the managing partners for Accent Leisure Inc., a recreation and educational consulting company.

and some other therapy-oriented degree such as medicine, occupational therapy, physical therapy, or nursing? Maybe you are interested in broader topics such as social justice, aging, or health and wellness, or maybe you simply know someone in this major or profession. You may be reading this book because it is assigned reading for a course that you are required to take. You are the only one who can answer the why questions. If you have not done so, try to answer the question for yourself right now—why this profession?

Your interest and motivation in this course and profession will have an effect on what you study, how you study, and whether or not you will succeed in your academic performance. Your motives can also influence who you might study or work with, as well as where you might eventually work and ultimately live. So do you know where or with whom you might want to work? Do you know how this course could benefit you regardless of your major? If you answered no or have other questions, ask the course instructor and your advisor for some individual attention.

If the answer to either question is yes, then we would simply ask that you keep yourself open to more possibilities as you go through this text and course. If you answered no to either or both questions, then we would ask that you try to focus a bit and select a temporary answer that can help you reflect on and understand concepts as you move through the book and explore this profession. In either case (whether you answered yes or no), before you try to finalize your decisions, you should learn the basic **therapeutic recreation process,** understand some of the basic techniques utilized during this process, and become familiar with what therapeutic recreation services have to offer clients who participate in this process (what benefits might come to clients from provision of this service). Later chapters will explore these topics in detail.

Finding a Personal Fit

Success in the therapeutic recreation profession requires commitment, forethought, and a willingness to engage others. The working professional generally has the ability to organize experiences, motivate others, be flexible, and work on several tasks simultaneously. The ability to communicate to a variety of audiences (individuals, groups, other professionals, and so on) in a variety of ways (oral, written, in person, electronically) and to be both understanding and assertive are also important characteristics. In plain words, therapeutic recreation is a people profession; a major job skill for a therapeutic recreation professional is to relate to people in an understanding and accepting way. Because creating effective interactions and experiences requires use of a systematic method, the successful professional must be competent at planning, organizing, solving problems, and managing several tasks and programs at once. To succeed in this profession, a person must be responsible, knowledgeable, and genuinely compassionate.

Occupational Profiles

You will likely find it helpful to look at some examples of where professionals work and what they do as a part of their professional duties.

- Isabelle works at the Veterans Administration in central California with veterans who have disabilities and are homeless. She works with clients to solve or resolve issues such as homelessness, poverty, starvation, substance abuse, violence, stress management, and depression.

- Jerome works for a large municipality in the Midwest that provides programs for school-aged youth with spinal cord injuries who are interested in participating in sport-related activities. Jerome develops and implements recreation-based programs designed to achieve goals related to access to space, adequate coaching, and establishing friendships with nondisabled peers.

- Bernita works in upstate New York at a residential camp that provides temporary or respite services to elderly men and women who are recovering from either stroke or heart-related problems. Bernita's programs are designed to work on regaining strength, range of motion, and coordination, as well as establishing a sense of dignity and respect.

- Hiro works in a small private hospital in the Pacific Northwest that specializes in working with people who have issues with substance abuse. Clients who participate in Hiro's program typically work toward regaining old friendships, healthy leisure activities, and family relationships. Hiro is currently working with several clients on identifying triggers that create stress and lead to further drug use. In his "expressions" group, Hiro provides clients with space, material, and metaphors to express their feelings through music, poetry, art, or creative movement.

- Steve works in a small community center in a suburb of Houston, Texas, that specializes in providing services exclusively for people with disabilities. He is trying to help them resolve issues related to local ethnic discrimination and abuse, which include violence, inadequate access to voting equipment, and being denied access to the local library, pool, and movie theater.

- Greta works in a maximum-security prison in the South. The unit she works in houses criminals with mental illness. Greta is working to help inmates identify and acquire new leisure interests, new activity skills, stress management techniques, and alternative decision-making strategies.

- Charlie works in a Canadian residential care facility designed for elderly people who have significant disabilities. A major goal for his clients is to resolve issues of boredom, apathy, depression, and anger.

- Arlene works at the Olympic training camp with elite-level soccer athletes who use prosthetic devices to ambulate (walk and run). Arlene's programs focus on improving strength and conditioning as well as establishing sport-related strategies for upcoming matches in which the opposing team has different physical abilities than her team does.

Note that these examples do not represent all the potential service arenas available to professionals, nor do they represent the entire list of tasks, duties, or assignments that professionals may be involved with. Finally, they do not convey or represent all the specific methods or methodologies that professionals may use as part of their work.

Therapeutic recreation specialists often use creative and expressive activities as alternative outlets for communication and self-expression. The mask viewed here is an actual casting of a client's face that has been decorated to represent the roles she felt pressured to fulfill in daily life. Notice the symbolism used: a storm in her head, a cloudy future, a broken heart, and the search for spiritual guidance are all apparent.

Summary

Therapeutic recreation is a relatively young profession that has evolved from a long and rich history of people helping other people, of people helping their communities, and of people sharing their knowledge, skills, and insight with others. It is a profession made up of thousands of people around the world who seek to improve the quality and longevity of life.

Just as people and their perspectives change over time, so do professions and their practices and techniques. At present, the broad profession of therapeutic recreation is unified by many concepts, theories, and practices. At the same time, various professional groups or organizations represent differing perspectives. Thus, some viewpoints presented in this book may favor one perspective or another. In all cases, we have tried to be neutral, except where differing viewpoints allow either better student learning or greater potential interaction between instructor and learner. New opportunities and ever-changing approaches are available to the professional. These new ideas, approaches, or innovations are welcomed.

We hope that you have developed an understanding of how the contents of this text and the accompanying course will benefit you. You should also have an idea of typical settings in which a therapeutic recreation professional might work, the clientele whom they might serve, and the type of skills that are necessary for exemplary practice. In particular, you should have a basic understanding of what differentiates therapeutic recreation from other therapy or leisure realms.

As you work through the first section of the book, these concepts will become more complex, enabling a deeper understanding of the overall profession. Open discussion related to the presented topics is critical in mastering these concepts, so take time to read and talk about the following discussion questions with classmates and the instructor. Doing so will help clarify your opinions and understanding of issues that someday you will be required to address.

1. Review the definitions posted on the ATRA and NTRS Web sites. How does the definition presented by the authors compare to those two perspectives? Discuss with your course instructor his or her personal perspective and inquire about influences that led to that viewpoint.

2. What do you think the most important characteristic of a therapeutic recreation professional would be? Do you think that those who work in helping professions are "born with it," or can people learn those skills? Make a list of such skills and apply this question to each.

3. Discuss with a partner or in small groups what your understanding of therapeutic recreation was before you read this chapter. Have your views changed? If so, how? What professional opportunities have you learned about that you were previously unaware of?

4. Review the career examples presented on pages 9–10. Do any of the examples seem like something that you would be interested in doing for a job? Do you have another example that you could share? Is there some combination of the examples that interests you? Are there examples that you would have no interest in? Why or why not? Discuss with your instructor whether he or she believes that all the examples represent something that a therapeutic recreation specialist might do.

5. Review the definition of therapeutic recreation provided on page 4 and consider the following scenario. Is the intervention leisure based? Is it purposeful? Would you consider the program to be utilizing leisure, enhancing leisure, or both?

Jason is a 10-year-old boy diagnosed with attention-deficit/hyperactivity disorder and oppositional defiant disorder. He is impulsive in social situations, often struggling to wait his turn in cooperative play activities or interrupting others in conversations. When adults tell him what to do, he becomes argumentative, frequently throws tantrums, and refuses to comply. Jason also occasionally pushes and shoves other kids when he feels threatened or embarrassed. He is especially sensitive to social play situations in which he fails, or "loses." Because of these behaviors, his peers have rejected him. When he does play, he rarely finishes an activity without incident.

After several behavior-related incidents at the local recreation center, Jason was suspended from participation. When his mother revealed Jason's disability to the recreation center, staff referred the family to Steve, who was the therapeutic recreation staff person responsible for developing inclusion plans for kids with disabilities. Steve met with Jason and his mother to assess Jason's leisure interests and abilities, as well as his current behavior difficulties. To respond to Jason's difficulty with impulsive behavior, Steve worked with the boy to develop ways to remember to take his turn and listen to others. Steve also advised other staff members about strategies to use when communicating with Jason, such as making eye contact before making a request, allowing adequate time for a response, and giving choices whenever possible. Steve also worked with recreation staff to create opportunities for Jason to develop activity skills and experience success in his play, such as by providing appropriate difficulty levels in sports drills. Finally, Steve worked with Jason and his mother to develop a behavior management plan intended to establish not only behavior supports but also behavioral expectations and consequences of inappropriate behavior. Jason's return to the center was contingent on his being able to maintain safe and reasonably appropriate behavior. Over the next 4 weeks, Steve tracked Jason's behavior and his ability to play successfully with others in a fun and rewarding way. Over time, Jason's improved behavior led to his having more friends and being a happier child.

History of Therapeutic Recreation

Rodney Dieser, PhD

University of Northern Iowa

LEARNING OUTCOMES

After completing this chapter, learners will be able to demonstrate the following competencies:

- Articulate why therapeutic recreation students should have a good understanding of the history of the profession of therapeutic recreation
- Demonstrate how medical authority was used to justify leisure experiences
- Identify how the profession of therapeutic recreation developed from both community and medical environments and how various sociological events (e.g., world wars, settlement movement, government legislation) affected the development of therapeutic recreation
- Demonstrate how past (and current) philosophical battles in therapeutic recreation have affected the profession of therapeutic recreation
- Articulate the difference between the leisure orientation and therapy orientation of therapeutic recreation

In the novel *Frankenstein* (Shelley, 1818/2003), the fictional Swiss scientist Victor Frankenstein truly wanted to help people. He was attempting to understand the secrets of heaven and earth so that he could prevent death and the physical and emotional pain associated with it (in the Hollywood movies, Frankenstein is the monster; in the novel, Frankenstein is the scientist). Unfortunately, his ambitions became framed in dangerous extremes and absolutes, resulting in the destruction of his life and any meaningful relationships (Campbell, 1997). In many ways the story *Frankenstein* is relevant to the history of therapeutic recreation. Like Victor Frankenstein, therapeutic recreation leaders (both educators and practitioners) at times cause destructive consequences from genuine intentions. For over 50 years, prominent therapeutic recreation leaders have debated whether therapeutic recreation should have a therapy orientation or a leisure orientation, often using arguments that are extreme, binary, and based on absolutism. These philosophical battles are damaging the professional standing of therapeutic recreation. The aim of this chapter is to explain the development of therapeutic recreation from the late 1700s to the present and underscore the continuing internal struggles regarding the nature and essence of therapeutic recreation.

Importance of History

Students of therapeutic recreation should understand the history of their professional field for three paramount reasons. First, understanding past successes and failures helps professionals avoid repeating past mistakes, learn from past successes, and predict the consequences of individual and organizational actions.

Second, understanding the history of a professional field provides a source of professional identity. According to Sylvester (1989), "A field without history, though, is like a person without a memory . . . without sources of identity drawn from a meaningful past, purposeful direction is unlikely" (p. 19). What makes therapeutic recreation a distinct profession in human services? What are the differences between therapeutic recreation and occupational therapy? How are social work and therapeutic recreation similar? Should therapeutic recreation professionals implement programs that increase self-esteem or well-being? These questions,

and many more, can be answered when a professional identity is in place.

Third, and related to professional identity, historical research creates perceptions of reality in the present (Hutcheon, 1989). That is to say, the present can be affected by how the past is interpreted (Hutcheon). As Dieser (2004a) noted, a historical accounting that interprets the history of therapeutic recreation as being closely aligned to a clinical past (for example, hospital recreation) constructs a contemporary therapeutic recreation identity that makes clinical therapeutic recreation dominant and renders community therapeutic recreation marginal and inferior. In this chapter, I will do my best to follow Sylvester's (1989) proposition that "Historians must be cautious not to force facts that fit their personal views . . . [and should be] aware, though, that their beliefs and values invariably influence their selection and interpretation of facts" (p. 21). In addition, this chapter will not be foolishly optimistic and highlight only the good aspects of therapeutic recreation. Rather, I will attempt to be accurate and inform the reader of the history of therapeutic recreation, even if it underscores certain unsightly and ugly events.

Origins of the Therapeutic Recreation Profession (Late 1700s–Mid-1900s)

Most books that examine the history of therapeutic recreation (for example, Austin, 2002; Carter, Van Andel & Robb, 2003; Crawford, 2001a; Frye & Peters, 1972; James, 1998; Mobily & MacNeil, 2002; O'Morrow & Reynolds, 1989) begin by highlighting how the efforts of various medical experts represent the early history of therapeutic recreation. The "play ladies" of community-oriented settlement houses (e.g., Hull-House), who Bedini (1995) argued were the first therapeutic recreation specialists (p. 32), are simply missing in most therapeutic recreation books that examine history. Rather than follow this rhetoric, which suggests that therapeutic recreation developed from medical and clinical roots, I would like to suggest that the origins of therapeutic recreation developed in both community and clinical arenas. The following section will explain antecedents in medicine and community programs that eventually developed the profession of therapeutic recreation.

European and American Medicine

European medical practices and programs during the later 1700s to early 1900s were antecedents to the eventual development of therapeutic recreation in the United States. This section considers several examples about how medical efforts during this time were embedded in the values of recreation and leisure experiences.

PHILLIPPE PINEL AND WILLIAM TUKE

Phillippe Pinel (1745–1826) of France and William Tuke (1732–1822) of England are often cited as two of the most influential pioneers of the **humanitarian treatment movement** that swept through Europe in the late 1700s and early 1800s (e.g., Davison & Neale, 1990; Minnesota Governor's Council on Developmental Disabilities, 1998). Phillippe Pinel was appointed director of the Bicêtre insane asylum in 1793 (largest hospital for people with insanity in Paris), after which he (1) removed patients from dungeons and chains, (2) allowed patients to reside in sunny rooms, and (3) encouraged patients to exercise and move freely on the hospital grounds. William Tuke, an English merchant and philanthropist, founded the York Retreat (opened 1796), a pleasant country home where people with mental illness worked in a kindly Quaker environment (although William Tuke was not trained as a medical expert, he used a medical and scientific approach to human service work). These two human service pioneers seemed to have no connection; each worked independently of the other, but their ideas and programs were the same. Both reformers influenced medical experts of the time, such as Samuel Hitch (a prominent English medical psychologist) and Benjamin Rush (founder of American psychiatry).

Beyond planting the seeds of humane psychological intervention, Phillippe Pinel and William Tuke are also credited with planting the seeds of therapeutic recreation (Austin, 2002; Carter, Van Andel & Robb, 2003; Crawford, 2001a; Frye & Peters, 1972; James, 1998; Mobily & MacNeil, 2002; O'Morrow & Reynolds, 1989). Carter et al. (2003) noted,

Pinel believed these people [with mental illness] were capable human beings who deserved to be treated with compassion and dignity rather than being chained and locked behind bars. His remarkably successful approach became known as moral treatment and included the use of purposeful recreational activities and work experiences to restore mental and physical health. . . . (p. 33)

By the close of the 1800s the use of humane approaches to treatment, which often used leisure and recreation programs, was widespread in Europe and the United States (Mobily & MacNeil, 2002).

Although it is accurate to say that Phillippe Pinel and William Tuke changed the course of human services and used recreation and leisure in a therapeutic manner, moral treatment interventions had a dark side. Foucault (1965) posited that the end of the great confinement era of people with mental illness during the latter half of the 18th century was not motivated by humanitarian concerns. Rather, it was a stigmatizing response to a myth of a dreaded disease that spread from the houses of confinement. Likewise, the countryside retreat that William Tuke developed "as a quiet country estate where individuals were encouraged to garden, talk with attendants, and take walks in the countryside" (Carter et al., 2003, p. 33) was a method to remove people with mental illness from mainstream society. As Dieser (2002a) suggested, the fathers of "humane treatment" in the 18th century replaced chains of iron with chains of silence and often used recreation in a manipulative manner (e.g., as a reward for assimilation into bourgeois

The hard work of figures like Phillippe Pinel and William Tuke helped to stop the use of cruel restraint devices such as this confinement box.

culture). In this regard, as Rojek (1985, 1995) has suggested, leisure (and therapeutic recreation) has not always been used to help people. At different times throughout its history, "therapeutic" recreation was used as a method to manipulate people into accepting the values of the dominant culture. Hence, the seeds of therapeutic recreation involved using recreation and leisure in both a beneficial and controlling manner.

MEDICAL SPAS AND THERMAL BATHS OF EUROPE

The **medicalization of spas and thermal baths** throughout Europe was another movement that underscored the therapeutic consequences of leisure. According to Mackaman (1998) the development of medical spas throughout Europe, and in particular France, from the early 1800s through the mid-1900s eventually led to an understanding of the therapeutic consequences of leisure. Although medical doctors prescribed different types of spa baths (e.g., cold and hot showers, vapor box bathing, circular showering, hosing and rubbing treatments), the essence of spa and thermal medicine was to experience leisure and freedom during a time in which leisure was not justified (1800s–mid-1900s). That is to say, European medical recreation in the form of spas and thermal baths was rooted in the leisure experience, but needed medical authority to justify it:

> Spa medicine offered precise prescriptions according to which leisure was practiced. Thus medicine let the bourgeoisies have its rest, all the while making the rest impermeable to waste, indecency, excess, sloth, and the other social attributes the still forming bourgeoisies took to be antithetical to the dual guises of productivity and respectability. . . . The medical codification and administration of sea bathing, for example, was effected in both England and France around the middle of the eighteenth century. . . . Now, because of sea-bathing cures, people not only had reasons to go to a beach but also a variety of very specific things to do there. (Mackaman, 1998, pp. 6–7)

Hence, a superficial understanding of European spas and thermal baths located their purpose as recreation therapy or purposeful activity, but the true essence of medical spas was simply to justify leisure experiences. For that reason, medical spas and thermal facilities offered diverse leisure programs and services, such as grand hotels, casinos, musical performances and concert halls, tennis courts, lakes for boating, dance halls, theater houses, libraries, ballrooms, games and billiard rooms, and many other leisure facilities and services (Mackaman, 1998).

Readers are encouraged to see historical pictures of the medical spa and thermal baths at Martigny-les-Bains, which was located in the east part of France, by visiting http://martignylesbains.free.fr/. By viewing the historical pictures from the middle to late 1800s, it is easy to see that these medical facilities were resorts full of leisure experiences and opportunities.

With medical authority to justify leisure, rest cures became popular psychiatric practices throughout the United States in the middle of the 1800s and early 1900s (Shorter, 1997). Silas Weir Mitchell, a nationally respected American psychiatrist who trained in France, created "**rest cures**" based on rest and recreation to help restore mental health. The following medical case study, published by Mitchell in 1904 (as cited in Shorter, 1997), highlights the integration of recreation and rest:

> In January 1874, a Mrs. G from Maine became a patient at . . . the Infirmary for Nervous Diseases. She was suffering from deep exhaustion and was unable to walk upstairs, read, or write . . . [Mitchell realized the patient] . . . needed "exercise without exertion." So he trained a young woman to become a masseuse and rub Mrs. G. . . . In 10 days Mrs. G "blossomed like a rose." (pp. 131–132)

By 1900 rest cures had become a dominant treatment intervention for neurasthenia throughout the United States, "but it soon became apparent to many doctors that the essence of the Weir Mitchell cure was the physician's authority, and not the specific physical components of the cure itself" (Shorter, 1997, p. 133). Just as in European medical spas, the essences of rest cures were simply to justify leisure experiences. The medical spas and thermal baths of Europe and rest cures of America clearly underscore that medical recreation was embedded in the leisure experience.

FLORENCE NIGHTINGALE

Florence Nightingale is often cited as an early medical expert (nurse) who highlighted the therapeutic effects of recreation while working in British hospitals during the Crimean War (1854–1856) (Avedon, 1974; Carter et al., 2003; James, 1998). Nightingale observed that after surgery, patients were left to lie in their cots in dreary hospital environments with little custodial care.

Nightingale also observed that many soldiers were going to bars and using alcohol and other drugs as an unhealthy coping method to deal with the horrors of war. To remedy these issues, Nightingale advocated and provided recreation programs in hospital environments, such as opportunities to listen to and perform music and theater, do needlework, play games (e.g., football and chess), write, and care for pets. In September 1855 Nightingale established the **Inkerman Cafe**—a small wooden hut located at the center of the hospital complex. The cafe had a large recreation room and a coffee house (James, 1998). A safe place where soldiers could escape their problems and find friendship, the Inkerman Cafe gave competition to local bars that profited on the dreadfulness of war. As Nightingale remarked, "Give them books and games, and amusements and they will leave off drinking" (cited in Woodham-Smith, 1951, p. 166).

THE TWO WORLD WARS

Nightingale's ideas that recreation had therapeutic consequences led to the further development of therapeutic recreation programs in the United States during both World War I and World War II. Bedini (1995) noted that the American Red Cross built recreation huts on military bases—homelike structures that provided convalescing soldiers with libraries, movies, entertainment, tables, games, and pianos. Each hut served 2,000 beds staffed by four or five women.

When the United States became involved in World War II, the Red Cross hired a great number of women with college degrees in any area of study and provided them 7 weeks of educational training (4 weeks in recreation leadership and a 3-week internship in military hospitals) for **hospital recreation** (James, 1998). During the period of both world wars there was a consistent pattern of hiring hospital recreation staff during the war and eliminating recreation staff and programs after the war. For example, after the end of World War I the Red Cross staffed only 26 of the original 52 hospitals with recreation leaders. At the conclusion of World War II, the first proposed graduate program curriculum conference for therapeutic recreation, which was requested by the Red Cross in 1945, lost its revenue base and was deleted (James, 1998).

Settlement Houses and Community Therapeutic Recreation

Bedini (1995) suggested that the "play ladies" involved in settlement houses and community schools during the 1800s were some of the first therapeutic recreation professionals in the United States. A **settlement house** was an established human service agency developed purposely in city slums where human service workers provided human services (e.g., education, citizenship classes, community development, immigration protection, recreation) and engaged in social action on behalf of the poor living nearby (Schram & Mandell, 2000). The settlement house movement was at its zenith in the late 19th and early 20th centuries. The primary mission of the settlement workers was to develop a holistic understanding of the conditions and causes of poverty by living with and learning from poor neighborhood residents (Stivers, 2000). By becoming neighbors of the poor, settlement workers developed friendships with them. Friendships and shared experiences would eventually lead to a holistic understanding of poverty, which would then make possible holistic problem solving and community programs to mediate the struggles of poverty. This section will highlight how community social programs in the United States, like the practices in European medicine, represent some of the early efforts to elicit the therapeutic outcomes of recreation and leisure experiences.

JANE ADDAMS AND THE WOMEN OF THE HULL-HOUSE SETTLEMENT

In September 1889 Jane Addams, Ellen Gates Starr, and Mary Keyser opened **Hull-House,** a settlement house in a poor district of Chicago. Hull-House, like most settlement houses of that era, established agencies in city slums where residents provided human services and engaged in social action on behalf of people with special needs (for example, poverty-stricken and homeless immigrants, people with substance dependency) (Schram & Mandell, 2000). Although many leisure academics rightfully underscore Jane Addams' pioneering work in public recreation (Dieser, Harkema, Kowalski, Ijeoma & Poppen 2004; Edginton, DeGraaf, Dieser & Edginton 2005; McBride, 1989), Addams was also a pioneer in therapeutic recreation through her use of recreation and leisure to help improve the health and well-being of people with special needs (for example, people with substance dependency, people living in poverty) (Dieser, 2004a). Like Florence Nightingale, Jane Addams established a coffee shop (in 1893) and provided an assortment of recreation programs and facilities (e.g., gymnasium, music and theatrical groups, art, needlework, creative writing, games) at the center of a poverty-stricken community to promote an alternative meeting place to saloons (Bryan & Davis, 1990). The coffeehouse, which served non-alcoholic beverages, had a men's club, billiards, card tables, baths, food services, and the latest newspapers and magazines so that working immigrants could experience recreation, develop friendships, and be informed about community and national events (Bryan & Davis, 1990). Like Nightingale's Inkerman Cafe, Jane Addams' coffee shop was a safe place where immigrants could escape their problems, find friendship, and become educated citizens. Table 2.1 presents the similarities between Florence Nightingale and Jane Addams (the only real difference was that Nightingale worked in a clinical setting and Addams worked in a community setting). Drawing on the historical research of Dieser (2004a), the following sections underscore how Jane Addams and numerous women of Hull-House (for example, Ellen Gates Starr, Julia Lathrop, and Alice Hamilton) used the recreation programs of expressive arts, bibliotherapy, and leisure education in a therapeutic manner in the later 1800s and early 1900s.

Expressive arts are the employment of visual arts, music, dance, or drama techniques with the intent to produce and achieve a final product (Devine & Dattilo, 2000; Silver, 1989). Numerous Hull-House programs provided expressive arts to people with special needs. For example, Hull-House developed a circulating art program

of pictures and paintings as a method to develop freedom and resilience among tenement residents of Chicago. Regarding this program, Jane Addams (1895/1990) commented,

> Another good mother [using the circulating painting and picture program] . . . who is battling with life against the odds too often found in a tenement-house, of a drinking husband and ever increasing poverty takes the pictures from the collection . . . [as a method] which will enable her to realize for her children some of the things she dreamed out of them. The oldest one of her eight children saw the light in a pretty suburban house. . . . this mother borrowed Mrs. Jameson's "Sacred and Legendary Art" and read the story of St. Genevieve to her children while they had Puvis de Chavanne's St. Genevieve pictures, and she took the Fra Angelico "Paradise" a second time because she thought it gave the children a pleasant idea of Heaven." (pp. 41–42)

This mother used the art program to develop freedom, resiliency, hope, and self-determination in her children. Likewise, Addams (1909/1972) used theater as a medium by which youthful imagination could roam free, in sharp contrast to the otherwise grim lives of most immigrant families (for example, joining gangs or the sex and drug trade). Addams observed young people leaving theaters "with the magic of the play still thick upon them" (p. 75).

Hull-House also used other expressive arts—dances and social events—within the framework of contact theory to bridge cross-cultural differences (Dieser, 2005c). Hilda Satt, a Polish immigrant who worked at Hull-House, highlighted how dances

Table 2.1 Therapeutic Recreation Similarities Between Florence Nightingale and Jane Addams

Florence Nightingale	Jane Addams
• Highlighted how the dreariness of hospitals was counterproductive.	• Highlighted how the dreariness of poverty-stricken communities was counterproductive.
• Explained that the monotony endured by patients affected their recovery and motivation.	• Explained that the monotony endured by poor immigrants affected their motivation.
• Wrote of the benefits of caring for pets, listening to and performing music, doing needlework, and writing.	• Wrote of the benefits of listening to and performing music, doing needlework, and writing.
• Established Inkerman Cafe—a recreation room and coffeehouse.	• Established the coffee shop—a recreation room and coffeehouse.
• Established theatrical groups and social activities (e.g., dances and singing).	• Established theatrical groups and social activities (e.g., dances and singing).
• Recreation centers competed against bars that surrounded the hospital and military installations.	• Recreation centers were to compete against bars, which saturated the community.
• Provided multiple leisure experiences.	• Provided multiple leisure experiences.

and social gatherings at Hull-House built bridges of cross-cultural understanding and developed freedom (Polacheck, 1989).

Beyond art, theater, and dance, other expressive art activities such as therapeutic writing and drama were used to help people with special needs experience the beneficial outcomes of enjoyment, meaning, accomplishment, freedom, and self-determination (Elshtain, 2002; Hackett, 1925/1990; Starr, 1896; Weil, 1913/1990).

Bibliotherapy utilizes reading materials such as novels, plays, short stories, booklets, and pamphlets to help clients (1) become aware that other people share similar problems, (2) become aware of new insights, and (3) structure their lives (Austin, 2004). Jane Addams and Hull-House programs used readings to help people with special needs realize that they were not alone and to gain personal insights. For example, to help Italian immigrants deal with poverty and loneliness, a George Eliot reading group formed in which the first novel selected was Romola, read in Italian (Elshtain, 2002). To help immigrant children deal with poverty and discrimination, Jane Addams held Abraham Lincoln's birthday social celebrations at Hull-House and gave copies of the book *Appreciation of Abraham Lincoln* to immigrant boys who were members of the Hull-House boys club (Addams, 1910/1981). By showing these boys that Abraham Lincoln celebrated cultural diversity by reading books, Jane Addams aimed to help them understand that they should not be ashamed of their cultural backgrounds and that instead they should celebrate them (Addams, 1910/1981).

Furthermore, the reading of poetry and short stories was often used to help Hull-House participants structure their lives (Monroe, 1912/1990; Addams 1905/1990). For example, Carmella Gustaferre (1914/1990), a young Italian immigrant girl, wrote a short story called "What Type of Home I Would Like," in which she explained her life ambition to have a nice house, garden, piano, backyard with a swing, beautiful trees to provide shade to read under, and a parlor full of flowers. This short story provided structure, motivation, and insights to this young immigrant girl.

Leisure education is a developmental process through which a person or group of people increase their understanding of leisure and the relationship among leisure, lifestyle, and society (Mundy, 1998). Jane Addams and Hull-House programs provided leisure-oriented community education to help people with special needs. Community leisure education was offered in literature, the arts, physical activity, and cooking, just to name a few (see Bryan & Davis, 1990; Fischer, 2004). However, the **Labor Museum** exemplifies how community leisure education was a developmental process in which groups of people increased their understanding of leisure and the relationship among leisure, lifestyle, culture, and society.

The Labor Museum developed from Addams' twofold concern for (1) the disdainful attitudes that immigrant children had toward their parents' old-world traditions and culture and (2) the contemptuous attitudes that Americans had toward poverty-stricken immigrants who were living in Chicago (Addams, 1910/1981). Addams wanted to bridge the gap between immigrant parents and children by highlighting how old-world spinning and weaving were a cultural tradition that showcased the leisure skills of immigrant adults and parents (Addams, 1910/1981). By allowing immigrants to display their creative skills through a community leisure education program, the Labor Museum provided people freedom and enjoyment from their depressing lives and educated the masses about the talents of immigrant people. For example, Washburne (1904/1990) reported that an Irish immigrant woman who had experienced physical abuse from a husband and had two children with disabilities commented: "Oh, I can smile and laugh with the best when I am at work here [spindling at the Labor Museum]" (p. 80).

OTHER COMMUNITY ANTECEDENTS TO THERAPEUTIC RECREATION

Other social settlement houses and community settings besides Hull-House also showcased the therapeutic value of play, recreation, and leisure experiences (regarding the role and value of recreation in social settlement houses throughout the United States, see Woods & Kennedy, 1970, and see Gilchrist, 2001, regarding the role of art). For example, in 1919 Ada Sophia McKinley, a retired schoolteacher (who was also a leader in the African American Southside Settlement House in Chicago) volunteered as the head recreational host of the War Camp Club. This club used recreational and civic activities to help returning soldiers and their families make a transition into American society (e.g., dealing with post-traumatic stress syndrome, finding employment and housing; see www.adasmckinley.org).

Bedini's (1995) historical scholarship also demonstrated how various schools used play and recreation as a therapeutic strategy to help children and adults with various illnesses and disabilities during the late 1800s and early 1900s. Community social programs, along with medical practices, planted the early seeds of therapeutic recreation that would later grow into an organized social and professional movement. As the Second World War was ending, therapeutic recreation as a profession was beginning to take shape.

Philosophical Battles in Therapeutic Recreation (1945–1965)

After the end of the Second World War, both medical and community programs and settings began to take a more direct approach to observing and documenting the therapeutic value of leisure and recreation. For example, clinical and medical staff at the nationally known Menninger Clinic in Topeka, Kansas, were explicit in explaining the therapeutic value of providing play, recreation, and leisure experiences to clients who were struggling with psychological disabilities (Carter et al., 2003). Menninger and McColl (1937) stated the following about therapeutic recreation:

> [The patient] is able to begin his renewal of contracts in life by going out for dinner and make shopping trips to town. At the same time these activities are being carried on, other recreational activities attempt to make reality more pleasant . . . to give freedom to phantasy expression; to afford an opportunity to create. (pp. 15-17)

In essence, Menninger and McColl argued that a distinct and distinguishing feature of therapeutic recreation was its clear and direct association to recreation and leisure. The leisure experience was what made therapeutic recreation distinct from occupational therapy and educational therapy.

Likewise, Romney (1945) argued that the essence of therapeutic recreation is its alignment

Prior to its relocation to Houston, Texas, in 2003, the world-renowned Menninger clinic had been based out of this Topeka, Kansas, facility. C.F. Menninger started the clinic with his two sons, Karl and Will, in 1925, and they went on to become pioneers in the development of psychiatry.

with leisure: "[Hospital or therapeutic] recreation is an end unto itself. . . . It does not hide behind the skirts of therapy, nor find only group work reflected in its mirror" (p. 35). Romney further stated: "If the patient is required for curative purposes to weave a basket at a scheduled hour, whether he likes it or not, he is receiving occupational therapy. If he may exercise freedom of choice . . . he is indulging in recreation" (p. 42). Because recreation and leisure are based on choice and freedom, prescribing hospital recreation programs made no sense to Romney—the quintessence of recreation and leisure was freedom and choice.

Beyond Romney, Menninger, and McColl were other like-minded recreation leaders. Carolyn Nice (1948) remarked that the purpose of a recreation program was "to provide opportunities for individuals to do the things of their choice, in their leisure time. . . . Hospital recreation leaders are not therapists whose primary purpose is treatment" (p. 642).

In fact, the **leisure orientation to therapeutic recreation**—the idea that the distinctness of therapeutic recreation is its clear association with programming recreation and leisure services—was the underlying philosophy when hospital recreation became a special interest option or branch of the American Recreation Society (ARS) in 1949 (James, 1998). One of the most powerful founding members, Harold D. Meyer, was able to develop a hospital recreation curriculum that was aligned to recreation and physical education programs (instead of medicine or applied health programs) and pioneered the phrase, "I am a rec-re-a-tor *first!*" (James, 1998).

As the hospital recreation section of ARS was developing, a group of therapeutic recreation professionals who followed the **therapy orientation of therapeutic recreation** began to design a rival organization that stressed the curative aspects of hospital recreation. This group believed that the essence of therapeutic recreation was to use or prescribe recreation and leisure for medical purposes. In 1952 B.E. Phillips (1952a) and a group of like-minded VA professionals eventually formed the Recreational Therapy Section within the Recreation Division of the American Association for Health, Physical Education and Recreation (AAHPER) with "its primary purpose . . . to assist physicians in their treatment of patients" (p. 2). Phillips (1952b) further commented that "[recreational therapy is a] means toward patient recovery rather than an end in itself. This concept dictates the selection of activities primarily on the basis of needs and capabilities, and secondary on the basis of interests" (p. 29). In 1953 Charles Cottle, who shared Phillips' perspective, formed the **National Association of Recreation Therapists (NART)** (1) to dissociate the therapy orientation from the recreation and physical education curriculum of AAHPER and (2) to respond to the lack of attention by ARS to clinical outcomes and the role of recreation in bringing functional improvements to clients (Mobily & Ostiguy, 2004).

Therapeutic recreation was poised to become a respected profession after the end of the Second World War. Instead it became a fragmented and disjointed profession that had no fewer than three organizations claiming to be the voice of therapeutic recreation. (According to van der Smissen [personal communication, June 16, 2005], a fourth voice was the National Association of Recreation Services for the Handicapped, which began in 1953.)

Binary and absolute thinking, the kind of thinking used by Frankenstein, was used to conceptualize therapeutic recreation. In one corner were professionals who followed the philosophy of recreation as therapy, emphasizing the use of recreation and leisure as therapy tools. In the other corner were professionals who believed quality leisure to be the primary goal of therapeutic recreation, recognizing recreation and enjoyment as basic human needs that can be enhanced to allow people with special needs (e.g., people with spinal cord injuries) the opportunity to experience freedom, choice, pleasure, and meaningfulness. In this case, therapy is a by-product to the leisure experience. These differing philosophies, and the professional organizations associated with them, followed separate developmental paths up until the 1960s. As the boundaries of practice between the two camps began to fade, and the political, professional, and social benefits of unity grew stronger, a historical reorganization of the profession was just over the horizon.

SANDRA K. NEGLEY

Background Information

Education

*BS in Leisure Studies with an emphasis in Therapeutic Recreation from the University of Utah Department of Leisure Studies *MS in Recreation and Leisure with an emphasis in Therapeutic Recreation Allied Studies: Social Work from the University of Utah Department of Recreation and Leisure

Credentials

*MTRS *CTRS

Special Affiliations

*ATRA Board of Directors, president (2006–2007) *BCTRC Board of Directors *State of Utah Legislative Special Committee—Recreational Therapy Practice Act

Special Awards

*Outstanding Graduate Scholar, University of Utah Department of Recreation and Leisure (1993) *Outstanding Alumni, University of Utah Department of Recreation and Leisure (1994) *Outstanding Professional, ATRA (1993) *Presidential Award, ATRA (1998) *Distinguished Service, URTA (1992) *Outstanding Program, URTA (1990)

Career Information

Position

*Clinical Instructor, University of Utah College of Health, Department of Parks, Recreation, and Tourism *Manager, Expressive Therapies, University Neuropsychiatric Institution (UNI)

Organization Information

UNI is a 90-bed, freestanding psychiatric hospital, which is part of the University of Utah Health Care System. It services individuals, of all ages, who have acute mental illness. The hospital provides outpatient, day treatment, and inpatient care where recreational therapists, music therapists, art therapists, and challenge course facilitators provide services.

Organization's Mission

The University of Utah Neuropsychiatric Institute is committed to providing excellence in mental health care in the Intermountain West Community.

> I am not late. The bell just rings before I get there.
>
> Levi H. Negley

> Does she not know? You are just my mom.
>
> Joshua W. Negley

Job Description

- **Clinical Instructor**—Teach the clinical-based courses, as well as core courses, in the Department of Parks, Recreation, and Tourism in Therapeutic Recreation and Experiential Education. Serve on the Therapeutic Recreation Faculty Advisory Committee. Serve on the Experiential Education Faculty Advisory Committee. Serve on Master's Thesis and Project Committees. Scholarship chair.

- **Manager, Expressive Therapies**—Provide clinical supervision for over 20 employees. Directly supervise all per diem employees. Human resource duties for all expressive therapists. Organize and provide staff development. Assure competent practice by all services according to perspective standards of practice. Develop and implement department budget. Supervise the coordinator of on-site challenge course. Represent Expressive Therapies to Management Council both within UNI and larger university health care system.

Career Path

In 1977 immediately after graduation, I began my first job in psychiatry and have worked in the area of mental health my entire career. In 1986 I was hired by the Western Institute of Neuropsychiatry (WIN) as the director of activities therapy (AT). The AT program grew to 17 full-time expressive therapists. Through the support of the hospital and staff, I founded and directed the Self-Esteem Institute and a challenge course program called R.O.P.E.S. I later became the director of adolescent services. The University of Utah purchased WIN and renamed it the University of Utah Neuropsychiatric Institute (UNI). In 1996 I was given the rare opportunity to do the two things I enjoy most, teach and practice recreational therapy in mental health.

Advice to Undergraduate Students

This is a service-oriented profession. The work we do is so our clients can have a greater quality of life. Believe in what you do. Advocate for those you serve. Embrace the profession by joining professional organizations. Be involved in practice. Research and write about what you do. Create balance in your life between your work, your relationships, and your leisure.

The Utopian Years of Therapeutic Recreation (1966–1984)

Following the philosophical battles that occurred from 1945 to 1965, a social movement began in the early 1960s to unite all leisure-oriented professionals together into one loosely structured organization (James, 1998; van der Smissen, 2005). In 1965 five organizations began to align to form the **National Recreation and Park Association (NRPA)**, which officially began on January 1, 1966 (van der Smissen, 2005):

* National Recreation Association (NRA), founded in 1906
* American Institute of Park Executives (AIPE), founded in 1898
* National Confederation of State Parks (NCSP), founded in 1921
* American Association of Zoo Parks and Aquariums (AZA), founded in 1924
* American Recreation Society (ARS), with its six sections including therapeutic recreation–hospital recreation, founded in 1938

The **National Therapeutic Recreation Society (NTRS)**, a branch of the NRPA, was also born when NRPA was created. In regard to therapeutic recreation, James (1998) noted,

> The underlying principles supporting such an alliance were so attractive to members of NART and of the Hospital Section of ARS that they put aside their philosophical differences, voted to merge, agreed to a charter and bylaws and elected officials, all within a year. On Sunday, October 9, 1966, the Board of Trustees of NRPA approved the Charter of the National Therapeutic Recreation Society. (p. 25)

In a reflective narrative, Compton (1997) referred to this era as the **utopian years of therapeutic recreation**, because the merger brought together different factions of the leisure field and developed a strong lobbying voice in Washington, D.C. Besides developing a pool of federal dollars that was used to establish therapeutic recreation curricula and professionalism across the nation, the development of both the NRPA and the National Therapeutic Recreation Society (NTRS) brought into focus the social and moral issues of rights for people with disabilities.

Austin's (2002) historical observations confirmed the existence of a utopian era, when therapeutic recreation was a unified profession. Austin also described the benefits of having a unified therapeutic recreation profession:

> For almost 20 years, the National Therapeutic Recreation Society (NTRS) singly advocated for the professionalization of therapeutic recreation in the United States. During these years a number of advances were made by NTRS. . . . the *Therapeutic Recreation Journal* began publication in 1966. Guidelines were published for community-based programs for special populations in 1978, as well as for clinical standards in 1979. . . . University curricula in therapeutic recreation expanded, and accreditation standards were established. . . . Finally, in 1981, the National Council on Therapeutic Recreation Certification was instituted. (pp. 279–280)

Simply stated, the period from the mid-1960s to the mid-1980s was a wonderful time for therapeutic recreation, namely because members of the profession came together, worked in collaboration, and were unified.

As alluded to earlier, this era witnessed a strong focus in community therapeutic recreation programs. In particular, the principle of normalization, which is a conceptual cornerstone in providing therapeutic recreation service delivery (Bullock & Mahon, 2000; Howe-Murphy & Charboneau, 1987; Pedlar & Gilbert, 1997; Searle, Mahon, Iso-Ahola, Sdrolias & van Dyck, 1995, 1998; Sylvester, Voelkl & Ellis, 2001), developed in this era under the framework of recreation inclusion. The heightened focus on the rights of people with disabilities developed a theoretical framework for helping people with disabilities become included in mainstream society. In particular, the **normalization principle** makes "available to persons with intellectual and other impairments or disabilities patterns of life and conditions of everyday living which are as close as possible or indeed the same as the regular circumstances and ways of life of their communities" (Nirje, 1992, p. 16).

Building on the normalization principle and significant acts of legislation (see table 2.2) that were enacted for people with disabilities in the 1960s and 1970s (Halberg, 1997), this era witnessed community-based therapeutic recreation approaches oriented toward **inclusive recreation,** which created recreation opportunities so that people with disabilities could experience leisure in mainstream society (Dattilo, 2002). Therapeutic recreation programs developed in various community and human

Table 2.2 Legislation and Other Events Affecting Recreation for Special Populations

1932	**Bill of Rights for the Handicapped.** Adopted by the White House Conference on Child Health and Protection, it provided an important endorsement of recreation for children with disabilities.
1936	**Social Security Act.** A compilation of laws, including numerous amendments over the last several years related specifically to older adults and people with disabilities, the Social Security Act includes provisions for physical education and recreation through formal procedures for review of professional services, establishes funds in states for self-support services for people, and gives grants to states to provide community-based care.
1963	**Vocational Rehabilitation Act.** This act provided training and research funds for recreation for those who are ill or handicapped. This act was the first recognition by a specific federal agency of the importance of recreation services in rehabilitation.
1963	**National Outdoor Recreation Plan,** PL 88-29. Directing the formulation and maintenance of a comprehensive nationwide outdoor plan, this plan was completed in 1973 and included an emphasis on compliance with PL 90-480 (see later entry). Concerns for those with handicaps were listed as a priority area.
1967	**Education for Handicapped Children Act,** PL 90-170. This law established the unit of physical education and recreation for children with handicaps within the Bureau of Education for the Handicapped; it became the largest federal program for training, research, and special projects related to recreation for special populations.
1968	**Architectural Barriers Act,** PL 90-480. Simply stated, this law indicates that "any building or facility, constructed in whole or part by federal funds, must be accessible to and useable by the physically handicapped."
1971	**Developmental Disabilities Services and Facilities Construction Act,** PL 91-517. Developmentally disabled persons are specifically defined, and recreation is listed as a specific service to be included as a fundable service in this federal law.
1973	**Rehabilitation Act,** PL 93-112. This act was a comprehensive revision of the 1963 Vocational Rehabilitation Act that included an emphasis on the "total" rehabilitation of the individual.
1974	**Rehabilitation Act Amendment,** PL 93-516. This law authorized the planning and implementation of the White House Conference on Handicapped Individuals. The final report noted the importance of recreation for people with disabilities and called for the expansion of recreation services and an increase in the number of professionally trained people employed in the field of recreation.
1975	**Education for All Handicapped Children Act,** PL 94-142. By mandating free and appropriate education for all handicapped children, this law identified physical education as a direct service and recreation as a related service to be offered to those with disabilities. Mainstreaming in the school system is usually viewed as an outgrowth of this act, which provides the legislative leverage for children with disabilities and their families to gain access to often denied educational services.
1978	**Rehabilitation Act,** PL 95-602. As with many federal programs, the 1973 Rehabilitation Act and the programs it authorized expired at the end of 5 years. In 1978, legislation was introduced to extend and amend the 1973 act. This renewal called for recreation and leisure services to be part of the rehabilitation process.
1981	Designated by the United Nations as the **International Year of Disabled Persons,** 1981 had as its theme "the full participation of disabled persons in the life of their society."
1990	**Americans with Disabilities Act,** PL 101-336. Probably the best known of all the laws protecting those with disabilities, the ADA provides comprehensive guidelines banning discrimination against people with disabilities. It is an omnibus civil rights statute that prohibits discrimination against people with disabilities in sectors of private and public employment, all public sectors (including recreation), public accommodations, transportation, and telecommunications.

Reprinted, by permission, from M.E. Crawford, 2001. Organization and formation of the profession. In *Therapeutic recreation: An introduction,* 2nd ed., edited by D.R. Austin and M.E. Crawford (Boston: Allyn & Bacon), 22-44.

service organizations, such as public recreation and park programs, voluntary nonprofit organizations (e.g., YMCA and YWCA), outpatient programs in hospitals and rehabilitation centers, group homes and transitional living facilities, youth services, community councils, and consortiums of public agencies that represented community needs (see Carter & LeConey, 2004; Kennedy & Montgomery, 1998; Kraus & Shank, 1989; Scholl, Smith & Davison, 2005). According to Sylvester and colleagues (2001), within a therapeutic recreation framework, inclusive recreation can be provided in three ways: community reintegration programs (e.g., providing therapeutic recreation services to recently discharged rehabilitation patients during the period of transition from hospital to home or community), community integration programs (e.g., helping people with disabilities develop leisure skills so that they can experience interdependent or independent leisure participation), or the community development approach (e.g., building accessible and inclusive community recreation facilities and services). To this end, community development inclusive recreation occurred during the early 1970s with the creation of numerous special recreation programs (e.g., Special Olympics) and special recreation associations throughout the United States, which provided recreation programs and services specifically for adults and children with disabilities (Bullock & Mahon, 2000). For example, the Northern Suburban Special Recreation Association (NSSRA) of Chicago, which formed in 1970 and was the first special recreation association in Illinois and among the first of its kind in the United States, was, and still is, an intergovernmental partnership of 10 park districts, one city, and one village. NSSRA provides year-round recreation programs and services for over 5,000 people with various disabilities per year (see www.nssra.org).

Furthermore, the utopian years of therapeutic recreation also witnessed the development of the **National Council for Therapeutic Recreation Certification (NCTRC)** in 1981. The NCTRC is an independent credentialing agency that oversees the national certification program in therapeutic recreation. NCTRC has identified through years of research (e.g., Anderson & Stewart, 1980; Smith, 1976; Stein, 1970; Stumbo, 1986) minimal competence skills that a certified (or competent) therapeutic recreation specialist should possess (Stumbo & Folkerth, 2005). The NCTRC was able to trademark the title *certified therapeutic recreation*

specialist (CTRS) in 1993 in the United States and today has over 17,000 active certificants of therapeutic recreation (NCTRC, 2004).

The Fragmentation Years of Therapeutic Recreation (1985–Present)

During the utopian years (1966–1984) therapeutic recreation was a promising and emerging profession under a unified banner, but tension still existed between the recreation therapy approach and the leisure orientation approach. For example, in the early 1980s, Meyer (1980) argued that there were two subspecializations to therapeutic recreation—the therapist and the special recreator. As such, Meyer suggested that the two subspecializations functioned in different worlds, with different purposes, work settings, and accountability structures. Meyer predicted that it would only be a matter of time before one of these specializations would seek its independence from the other.

Compton's (1997) personal reflections provide additional understanding of the tension that was occurring during this era. He described the growing unrest between the NTRS and the NRPA during the early 1980s, notably the doubts that many NTRS leaders had about the commitment that NRPA made to NTRS. Furthermore, Compton explained how nasty allegations were thrown back and forth between NRPA and NTRS, and he can still "vividly remember sitting in the office of NRPA refereeing a shouting match between the president of NTRS and the executive director of NRPA over the relationship of NTRS and NRPA and some other rather seminal issues. It was not a pretty sight and affected the relationship of the 'parent' and 'child' for years to come. The marriage seemed to be coming apart" (p. 43).

In an attempt to develop a philosophical statement and mission for therapeutic recreation, Meyer (1980) articulated the following four possible positions (see table 2.3). Positions 1 and 2 represented a resurfacing of the historical conflicts between ARS and NART. Positions 3 and 4 were attempts to maintain unity while acknowledging a broader purpose or set of purposes.

After spirited and ugly debate, the NTRS membership turned toward a democratic method and allowed its therapeutic recreation membership to

Table 2.3 Four Positions of Therapeutic Recreation

Approach	Definition
Recreation services approach	The primary purpose of therapeutic recreation was to provide recreation services to people with special needs. The role of a therapeutic recreation specialist was to help or enable people with disabilities to experience leisure and its benefits.
Therapy approach	The primary purpose of therapeutic recreation was to treat and ameliorate the effects of illness and disabilities. Therapeutic recreation was a means to a curative end.
Umbrella, or combined, approach	The primary purpose of therapeutic recreation involved two roles. Therapeutic recreation could be shifted to provide recreation services to people with special needs and shifted to ameliorate the effects of illness. Hunnicutt (1980) posited that "therapeutic recreation is unique because it rests on recreation's subjective quality (the individual's own state of mind, his fun) at the same time it provides tangible evidence that real medical and health goals are served through recreation" (p. 132). That is, therapeutic recreation may be used both as a medium for therapeutic change and simultaneously as an enjoyable outcome that is pursued for its own sake.
Leisure ability approach	According to the academic work of Gunn and Peterson (1978) and Peterson and Gunn (1984), the primary purpose of therapeutic recreation was to integrate three phases—therapy or treatment, leisure education, and recreation participation—along a continuum, and the ultimate goal was to help people with disabilities establish an independent leisure lifestyle. A therapeutic recreation specialist would choose which phases to work within based on the context and needs of the client.

vote on the four positions. The results were decisive: 62.9% voted for the leisure ability approach, 22.9% for the therapy approach, 10.6% for the umbrella, or combined, approach, and 3.7% for the recreation service approach (NTRS, 1982, cited by James, 1998). In May 1982 NTRS adopted the leisure ability approach as its official philosophical position (for more information on the leisure ability approach, see p. 68 in chapter 5).

But this decision did not end the tension within NTRS. Although 77.2% of the NTRS membership voted against a strict therapy-oriented approach to therapeutic recreation and believed that the leisure ability approach maintained unity while acknowledging a broader purpose or set of purposes (both therapy and leisure), members who followed the therapy orientation continued to believe that NRPA was too controlling, and they eventually developed a **separatist mentality.** James (1998), one of the leaders of the separatist movement, explained that in the late 1970s and early 1980s

> NRPA became more centralized . . . [and] was not directly involved in the arenas in which health care issues were being resolved. For example, while the American

Occupational Therapy Association and the American Physical Therapy Association were involved in writing the home health care legislation, NRPA legislative staff was preoccupied with the Land and Water Conservation Fund and the Bureau of Outdoor Recreation. (p. 29)

Peterson (1984), another leader of the separatist movement, provided her rationale:

> The basic mission of NRPA is to advocate for and promote the public park and recreation movement. Since the role of clinical therapeutic recreation is quite different from public recreation it becomes somewhat easier to see why controversy exists. Clinical therapeutic recreation is substantially outside the purview of public parks and recreation. (p. 12)

Moreover, James (1998) reported that NTRS made a motion that NRPA become less centralized and study alternative organizational structures. After NRPA officials defeated the motion, James and other like-minded therapeutic recreation specialists began a separatist mentality and ". . . earnestly pursue[ed] the feasibility of establishing an independent [therapeutic recreation] organization" (p. 30). During the 1983 NRPA Convention in Kansas City, the separatist group met in the hotel room of David Park, a former executive secretary and past president of NTRS, and made a formal commitment to start an independent therapeutic recreation organization focused on the therapy approach and clinical practice. Although some therapeutic recreation leaders opposed creating an independent therapeutic recreation organization that focused solely on a therapy orientation, and others called for an umbrella, or combined, approach, David Park (1983, as cited in James, 1998) argued that "another organization with an 'umbrella' orientation will not be any more successful than the present one" (p. 30).

On June 12, 1984, followers of this movement formed the **American Therapeutic Recreation Association (ATRA).** As was the case with the NART, the early ATRA leaders felt that therapeutic recreation should emphasize that therapeutic recreation is a treatment for therapeutic change and should separate from its historical roots with parks and recreation and its distinct association with leisure (Austin, 2002). Within a year the membership of ATRA had grown to 300 (James, 1998), and by 1999 ATRA had over 4,000 members (Crawford, 2001b). But many therapeutic recreation leaders had concerns about the possible short- and long-term negative consequences of ATRA. During the formation of ATRA, Nesbitt (1984) reflected that "the ATRA may be a vain, ill-timed, in some way self-serving, futile effort that will serve to dissipate limited resources, widen professional schism. . . and do irreparable damage to the future of recreation therapy" (p. 15).

Although ATRA membership was growing, internal conflicts and problems plagued the organization. In particular, early ATRA leaders had difficulty agreeing on a statement of purpose before they eventually created one that underscored that therapeutic recreation had "two functions: treatment services and recreation services. Denoting them both as therapeutic recreation, however, reverted the [purpose] statement to the umbrella dilemma" (James, 1998, p. 31). In short, the original statement of purpose that ATRA drafted did not align with a therapy focus—rather, it aligned with an umbrella, or combined, focus, similar to the leisure ability model.

NTRS clearly suffered when ATRA was formed, with membership falling slightly below 2,000 in 1999 (Crawford, 2001b). Today NTRS membership is still slightly less than 2,000 (Terry Robertson, personal communication, June 7, 2004) (and in 2002 ATRA's membership had dropped to 3,200 [Austin, 2002]). Despite this change, NTRS main-

tained its goals to (1) unite therapeutic recreation personnel, (2) encourage the professional development of therapeutic recreation personnel, (3) be an advocate for the leisure rights of individuals with disabilities, (4) encourage research to improve the quality of therapeutic recreation practice, and (5) promote the relationship between therapeutic recreation and other professions concerned with the health and well-being of people with disabilities (Mobily & Ostiguy, 2004). To bolster its commitment to health and rehabilitation in 1992, NTRS became an associate member of the Commission on Accreditation of Rehabilitation Facilities (CARF) and joined the Joint Commission on Accreditation of Healthcare Organizations (JCAHO) Coalition of Rehabilitation Therapy Organizations (see the NTRS Web site at www.NRPA.org).

In 2000 NTRS, following its parent organization NRPA, developed the "Therapeutic Recreation—The Benefits Are Endless" training program, which is a communication medium to stakeholders regarding the beneficial outcomes of therapeutic recreation, recreation, and leisure (see the NTRS Web site at www.NRPA.org). Broida (2000) prepared the "Therapeutic Recreation—The Benefits Are Endless" training program and resource guide to enable therapeutic recreation specialists to (1) promote therapeutic recreation programs in terms of benefits and outcomes produced, (2) develop and justify programs based on documented benefits and outcomes, and (3) manage programs in a manner that highlights efficacy.

A problematic aspect of Broida's (2000) work is its suggestion that therapeutic recreation always produces benefits and never produces harmful outcomes. Dieser, Magnuson, and Scholl (2005) have posited that NTRS has done well in openly communicating the beneficial outcomes of therapeutic recreation but distances itself from studies or reports that indicate that therapeutic recreation programs, like all human service programs, can unknowingly harm participants and clients (see Dieser, 2002a, 2005a; Voight, 1988; Caldwell, Adolph & Gilbert, 1989; White, 1997 for examples of how therapeutic recreation can unintentionally harm people).

Some Positive Steps During the Fragmentation Years

During this era, therapeutic recreation became a fragmented profession (Compton, 1997). Still, ATRA and NTRS worked in partnership on special

It is important that organizations that govern therapeutic recreation continually come together to monitor treatment practices and standards so that patients can experience the greatest benefits—including a sense of accomplishment and fun.

1980s and early 1990s, one of the most complete and wide-ranging attempts to consolidate research findings took place—the National Conference on the Benefits of Therapeutic Recreation, sponsored by the therapeutic recreation program at Temple University and National Institute on Disability and Rehabilitation Research (NIDRR) of the United States Department of Education (Malkin, Coyle & Carruthers, 1998). The result of this conference was the development of an extensive and precise typology of therapeutic recreation benefits (Shank, Kinny & Coyle, 1993), which appeared in the lengthy publication *Benefits of Therapeutic Recreation: A Consensus View* (Coyle, Kinney, Riley & Shank, 1991). The typology of therapeutic recreation benefits highlighted that therapeutic recreation influenced health care outcomes in (1) physical health and health maintenance, (2) cognitive functioning, (3) psychosocial health, (4) growth and personal development, (5) personal and life satisfaction, and (6) societal and health care system outcomes (Coyle et al., 1991; Shank et al., 1993). Since then, numerous publications have underscored how therapeutic recreation programs provide health and well-being benefits (e.g., Broida, 2000; Dieser, Fox & Walker, 2002; Malkin et al., 1998; Mobily & MacNeil, 2002; Mobily & Ostiguy, 2004).

Summary

The purpose of this chapter was to explain the development of therapeutic recreation from the late 1700s to the present and describe the continuing internal struggles about the nature and essence of therapeutic recreation. In this last section I would like to make some summary remarks based on historical observation and return to where I began the chapter—the story of Frankenstein.

When Victor Frankenstein created his monster his intentions were good; he wanted to help society by overcoming death. But the result was tragic—both Victor Frankenstein and the monster became binary thinkers who followed the doctrines of absolutism and constantly battled each other. Both died a cold death (Shelley, 1818/2003). Frankenstein's "quest for a grand achievement . . . [became] his own undoing" (Kelly, 2000, p. 80).

In my mind, this absolutism has limited our ability to thrive as a profession by creating confusion in external stakeholders regarding the profession (Skalko, 1997). More important, absolutism limits

events. For example, in 1996 ATRA and NTRS established the Joint Task Force on Credentialing to assist agencies in becoming recognized health care providers in their home states (James, 1998), and in 1998 the organizations mutually developed a resolution and a letter of agreement acknowledging that two national organizations represent therapeutic recreation professionals (Wenzel, 1998). In 1998 ATRA and NTRS created the **Alliance for Therapeutic Recreation,** an entity that brings together board members of both organizations to communicate and work in partnership on certain issues (Carter et al., 2003). Likewise, in 2005 NTRS and ATRA worked together to develop the Therapeutic Recreation Educators Conference (TREC) in Chicago to examine the academic concerns of therapeutic recreation and to plan the future of therapeutic recreation education.

One of the most positive events during the fragmentation years was the production of solid qualitative and quantitative research that showed that therapeutic recreation programs affect the health and well-being of people. During the late our ability to serve the many people who might benefit from therapeutic recreation services. In short, the quest for grand achievement has become our own undoing. Although other important economic, social, and political factors have hurt the profession of therapeutic recreation (e.g., fiscal conservatism, Proposition 13; see Compton, 1997; Crawford, 2001b), collectivistic actions of conflict have marred the profession from its very beginning. Likewise, economic, social, and political forces helped therapeutic recreation flourish during the utopian years (1966–1984), but I also believe that a paramount reason why therapeutic recreation flourished was the unified efforts of leaders who were able to demonstrate high collectivistic ego development by having a solid understanding for the needs of others, welcoming and thinking in diverse ways, and acting for the common good (see Hauser, 1991, regarding ego development). As Mobily and Ostiguy (2004) remind us "part of the explanation for why therapeutic recreation has less impact on healthcare legislation and the health insurance industry is that we have taken a growing but small field and divided it into two cultures of care" (p. 182). Therapeutic recreation is a wonderful and important profession with a solid body of research regarding its beneficial outcomes in both community and clinical services (Coyle et al., 1991; Mobily & MacNeil, 2002; Mobily & Ostiguy, 2004), but internal conflicts have challenged its legitimacy and credibility.

Perhaps the Alliance for Therapeutic Recreation can begin a unified movement. Cohesive action occurred once in the history of therapeutic recreation, and if we can learn from past successes, we may be able to make it happen again. As Sylvester et al. (2001) noted, "The current ATRA and NTRS definitions share much in common, including the goals of independence, health and well-being" (p. 23). Mobily and Ostiguy (2004) posited that the umbrella, or combined, approach to therapeutic recreation, which Hunnicutt (1980) outlined over

20 years ago, "accurately represents how therapeutic recreation is actually delivered in real world settings" (p. 161). In fact, Dieser and Peregoy (1999) argued that the umbrella, or combined, approach has broad application in a multicultural and diverse world in which the cultural background of the client should determine philosophical orientation. I would also assert that the umbrella approach should be rooted in leisure theory and the leisure experience (see Sylvester et al., 2001, for an excellent justification regarding therapeutic recreation being rooted in leisure theory).

At the end of the *Frankenstein* novel (Shelley, 1818/2003), Victor Frankenstein is close to death somewhere in the cold Arctic when another ambitious scientist and explorer, Robert Walton, attempts to save him. Walton is a kindred spirit who is also driven by a quest for grand and glorious achievement. But Walton is in grave danger because his boat is stuck in ice and his rebellious men want to turn back to England. Even so, Walton wants to continue pursuing his extreme and absolute professional and scientific mission. Frankenstein shares his story with Walton and urges him to "learn of my miseries and do not seek to increase your own" (p. 200). On his deathbed, Frankenstein urges Walton to "seek happiness in tranquility and avoid ambition, even if it be only the apparently innocent one of distinguishing yourself in science and discoveries" (p. 208).

In writing this chapter my desire was that young therapeutic recreation students and professionals (and all readers) would come to know their professional history and learn from past mistakes and successes. My suggestion is to follow the advice of the fictional Victor Frankenstein and seek professional development in tranquility by avoiding ambition focused in absolutism. Do not destroy something good. As future leaders in therapeutic recreation, you can help manage or resolve the damaging conflict that has harmed the credibility of this wonderful profession.

DISCUSSION QUESTIONS

1. Explain why students of therapeutic recreation should understand the history of their profession.

2. In regard to medical spas, thermal baths, and rest cures, explain why medical authority was needed to justify a leisure experience. To this end, do you agree

or disagree with the following statement: A distinct feature of therapeutic recreation is its clear and direct association to recreation and leisure? Support your answer.

3. In regard to the history of therapeutic recreation, how are Jane Addams and Florence Nightingale similar? How are they different?

4. How did both world wars (as sociological events) affect the development of therapeutic recreation?

5. How did the development of Hull-House and other settlement houses affect community-based therapeutic recreation?

6. What conclusions can you draw about the philosophical battles in therapeutic recreation from 1945 through 1966? Do these past philosophical battles exist in the profession of therapeutic recreation today?

7. Explain why the utopian years of therapeutic recreation occurred from 1966 through 1984?

8. In your opinion, after the NTRS membership turned to a democratic method to identify its philosophical position, was it ethical for therapy-oriented therapeutic recreation specialists to break off and develop ATRA? Further, has the creation of ATRA helped or harmed the profession of therapeutic recreation?

9. In your interpretation of the history of therapeutic recreation, who is Victor Frankenstein and who is the monster? To this end, do you agree or disagree that the quest for grand achievement in therapeutic recreation has become the undoing of the profession?

Professional Opportunities in Therapeutic Recreation

Michal Anne Lord, PhD, CPRP, TRS/TXC
Executive Director of Texas Recreation and Park Society

LEARNING OUTCOMES

After completing this chapter, learners will be able to demonstrate the following competencies:

- Accurately explain terminology associated with careers and professionalism
- Accurately describe the characteristics of a profession
- Communicate the importance of and mechanisms for professional development
- Accurately describe primary mechanisms of professional credentialing
- Identify, explain, and use ethical concepts and decision-making models
- Differentiate between professional and nonprofessional occupations
- Accurately describe mechanisms of accreditation
- Accurately explain the potential range of therapeutic recreation services and clientele
- Identify professional organizations relevant to the therapeutic recreation profession

Therapeutic recreation is a profession. Certainly, if you ask those who have made a career of delivering therapeutic recreation services and programs, most will respond that therapeutic recreation is indeed a profession. A **career** is an occupation or profession followed as a life's work. But what is it that makes the practice of therapeutic recreation a profession as opposed to just a job? How does therapeutic recreation go beyond being an occupation? A **job** is a regular remunerative position; a person is paid for the completion of assigned tasks. A person with a **profession** directs his or her efforts toward service rather than only financial remuneration. A person's profession is a personal choice and reflects his or her personality, creativity, interests, and goals.

Characteristics of a Profession

A profession is a calling that requires specialized knowledge and often long academic preparation. A profession can also refer to the collective body of persons engaged in a "calling." All professions include several common elements: a systematic body of knowledge, professional development, professional authority, professional credentialing, and a code of ethics.

Body of Knowledge

A primary prerequisite of a profession is that it must have a distinct set, or systematic body, of knowledge. Edginton et al. (2005) noted that the unique body of knowledge in the field of recreation and leisure is considered professional knowledge and consists of information drawn from three sources. These three sources, which apply to therapeutic recreation as well, are the following:

- Scientific disciplines—areas of study that provide the theoretical notion of man, the environment, and how the two relate (e.g., sociology, psychology, biology, botany)

- Values that we profess and subscribe to—belief among therapeutic recreation professionals that all people have the right to recreation and leisure experiences or that recreation is the medium used to bring about physical, cognitive, emotional, or social behavioral changes in the individual

- Applied and engineered skills—skills required by the professional to perform the job, such as leading an activity to assess client functionality or writing goals and objectives

Professional Development

Professional development is the exchange and transmission of professional knowledge through professional associations' conferences, workshops, and publications. A critical responsibility of being a therapeutic recreation professional is to maintain one's skills and knowledge base within the field of therapeutic recreation. A therapeutic recreation professional should be committed to professional development. Moreover, employers generally expect their employees to engage in professional development. Professional development includes continuing education, professional and civic contributions, research, and evaluation.

The therapeutic recreation professional should take advantage of continuing education opportunities available through conferences, workshops, and

Service is a key aspect of the individual's professional development and personal growth.

KIERA'S JOURNEY IN THERAPEUTIC RECREATION

One of the biggest challenges for therapeutic recreation professionals is helping clients deal with behavior management problems. Kiera, a 42-year-old woman with intellectual impairment, was one such client. Kiera lived in a group home, worked in a sheltered workshop, and regularly went with her home mates to organized recreation events such as Special Olympics and movie night. A number of people worked with Kiera, including several certified therapeutic recreation specialists (CTRS, which will be explained later in this chapter) who were on staff at the group home.

Current Challenge

A problem developed when Kiera started stealing things on a daily basis. Typically the items were small things. She would steal her roommate's lunch at work, another person's soda at home, or small items from the mall. Frustrated by the disturbances that her behavior was causing at work, the group home administrator threatened to terminate Kiera's employment unless the behavior changed. Other residents at the group home started to act out toward Kiera because of her continued disregard for other people's stuff. Although Kiera had always had a history of helping herself to things that were not hers, the stealing had escalated to the point that

her living situation and employment were threatened. Reprimands from the staff were becoming ineffective, and Kiera was at risk of losing her job.

Changes

When Kiera's CTRS attended a conference, she was able to speak with other specialists who were helping clients with similar problems. In fact, she found that problems like Kiera's were commonly discussed at conferences. At one presentation, she learned that negative behaviors are typically inappropriate ways of achieving some type of goal. She also learned that providing an alternative goal, or reward, is an effective way of discouraging negative behavior. Finally, she learned that a token economy can be used to delay final reward and sustain behavior over time. After talking with the presenter at the evening social, she took some ideas back to the group home staff. The staff decided to try a token economy system. For every day that Kiera refrained from stealing, she received a coupon signed by the minister at her church. Because Kiera was religious, she viewed the coupon as an especially valuable reward. After Kiera earned 10 coupons, she was rewarded with dinner at a restaurant of her choice (food was also a major motivator for her stealing). After implementation of this system, Kiera's stealing became almost nonexistent, with only one incident over the following 2 months.

publications sponsored by professional associations. A responsible and committed professional attends conferences and workshops, reads professional journals and books on related topics, advocates for in-service training opportunities within his or her agency, and willingly participates in them.

Professional behavior speaks to professional involvement. Involvement in professional and civic organizations provides leadership development opportunities for the professional. Opportunities may include serving on committees or boards of professional associations and organizations. Community involvement with civic organizations demonstrates professional behavior, which moves the professional beyond just doing the job. Service is a key aspect of professional development and often is an avenue to career advancement.

Responsible professionals use research related to therapeutic recreation and recreation. Therapeutic

recreation professionals regularly read research in the *Therapeutic Recreation Journal* of NTRS, the *Annual in Therapeutic Recreation* of ATRA, or other related professional journals or magazines. When appropriate, they conduct or participate in research projects. They cooperate on applied research programs within their agencies or programs. Although a faculty member or graduate student from a university or college may approach a therapeutic recreation professional to participate in research, the therapeutic recreation professional should not hesitate to initiate a research idea with university personnel. Likewise, the therapeutic recreation professional should consistently carry out evaluative research on his or her own programs and services. Evaluations and research findings can provide greater credibility of therapeutic recreation services and document the value of programs and their effect on consumers.

CAREER RESILIENCE

Career resilience is an emerging aspect of professional development. The therapeutic recreation professional should take control of his or her future by seeking out appropriate training, at his or her own expense if necessary, to be in the best position for a desired career track. A person's willingness to take planned risks, to guide his or her future rather than react to it, will potentially provide a win–win outcome. Career resilience as outlined by Joseph A. Bucolo (2003) is the ability to

- initiate or respond to changes in the workplace,
- initiate new learning,
- reinvent oneself,
- take past successes and experiences and leverage them into future successes that will help the organization meet its anticipated goals, and
- determine one's value-added ingredient.

BUILDING CAREER RESILIENCY IN THERAPEUTIC RECREATION

People can create added value and career resilience for themselves by assessing their value, just as a therapeutic recreation specialist would assess a client's needs, by asking themselves, What is it that I do better than others in the organization? What are my specific talents or my areas for future development? As individual professionals assess their value, they should consider not only their perspective but also that of their employers or prospective employers. For example, if an agency or organization needs the therapeutic recreation specialist to do more with less, what can the therapeutic recreation specialist offer or do that will not only satisfy the immediate business needs of the employer but also advance his or her personal career objectives? Career resilience is the result of being able to deal with change positively, to use it as an opportunity for skill development and knowledge transference that can enhance the person's capabilities and future career prospects.

For example, a therapeutic recreation specialist in a Chicago rehab facility recognized that the administration was cutting staff in all departments because of financial challenges (reduced income). Noting that the chief administrator had stated that all unnecessary, non-revenue-generating services would be cut first, the therapeutic recreation specialist began to consider how he could create value as a therapeutic recreation specialist for the agency. During a subsequent staff meeting, the administrator noted that the facility had received a donation of a car, with adapted driving controls, from a local car dealer who hoped that the facility would start a driving program as part of its rehab services. But the administrator noted that although a driving program could generate some income for the facility, the budget included no money to hire an instructor. The therapeutic recreation specialist realized that if he volunteered to do the driving program in addition to performing his therapeutic recreation service responsibilities, he would be creating value by generating income while enabling the rehab facility to carry out the wishes of a donor. Additionally, the therapeutic recreation specialist would be adding to the menu of therapeutic recreation services, as well as to his own resume and skill set. Because of the therapeutic recreation specialist's initiative, the driving program was implemented, a critical need of consumers was met, a donor's wish was recognized, the value of therapeutic recreation services was enhanced, and the therapeutic recreation specialist kept his job despite the downsizing of the rehab facility.

Professional Authority

Professional authority is the ability of a profession to hold its members accountable. Professional authority generally starts with a dialogue on professional values and acceptable tenets of practice, which ultimately translates into professional standards. Professional authority is how a professional responds in light of shared socialization (the norms of accepted practice) and internalized expertise (knowledge and personal expertise—individual skill and judgment). Professional authority depends on a person's technical skills rather than position or office. Edginton et al. (1989) said that professional authority "is created and exists when an occupation is, generally speaking, free from the consequences of its actions and has monopolized services" (p. 55).

Therapeutic recreation specialists tend to be the sole providers of therapeutic recreation services (monopolized services). In a few settings, other health care providers may endeavor to offer activities, but they usually lack the philosophical or theoretical background necessary to provide effective services. In contrast, therapeutic recreation as a profession has had professional standards of practice for the past 30 or more years and more recently added standards of practice for paraprofessionals and guidelines for internships.

Professional Credentialing

Professional credentialing serves to document the fact that society accepts the authority of a profession; the profession thus has the sanction of the community. A profession (through professional organizations or associations) defines who it is or what it does, and credentialing bodies establish the minimum standards required to perform the professional duties and responsibilities. The basic purpose of a professional association is to improve the level of practice within the profession. Promoting professional competence is extremely important.

The purpose of credentialing is multifaceted. Credentialing provides evidence that a professional has acquired a body of knowledge that includes theory, philosophy, and practice within a given field. It also provides insurance that an individual has met specific standards or criteria with regard to education, experience, and continuing professional development. Finally, credentialing is a strategy of risk management in that services provided by a credentialed professional offer reasonable protection of the consumer, safeguarding the public from incompetent, unauthorized people claiming to be within the profession. Thus, credentialing enables the public, government, or third-party payers to distinguish between those who have attained some qualifying level of competency from those who have not. Credentialing enhances the credibility of the individual and the profession. Another benefit of credentialing is that it, in the case of licensure, establishes a legal definition of the profession within state law.

REGISTRATION, CERTIFICATION, AND LICENSURE

Professional credentialing can occur at the state or national level. The recognized certifying body for therapeutic recreation professionals is the National Council on Therapeutic Recreation Certification (NCTRC), which oversees the national certification program for certified therapeutic recreation specialists (CTRS). Some states have therapeutic recreation credentialing bodies and processes as well. As of 2006, Utah, North Carolina, and New

Hampshire had state licensure requirements for practicing therapeutic recreation professionals. Additionally, a therapeutic recreation professional may seek to become a certified parks and recreation professional (CPRP), which is governed by the National Certification Board (NCB) and affiliated with the National Recreation and Park Association (NRPA), either through the direct national program or through the certification program of the state association.

The three main types of professional credentialing are registration, certification, and licensure. **Registration** and **certification** are forms of voluntary credentialing, whereas **licensure** is a legal requirement that must be met by anyone who wishes to practice the profession in a particular state. Professional credentials are generally in effect for a specified period (2 to 5 years) and are maintained or renewed by completing a required number of continuing education units (CEUs), submitting verification of CEUs or other professional contributions (professional presentations or publications, or leadership service), and paying a fee. Some credentials, such as the CTRS, require the certified professional to pay an annual maintenance fee. Table 3.1 shows the similarities and differences among the types of credentialing.

Professionals can take two professional credentialing paths, academic or equivalency, to document their ability to meet minimum knowledge, skill, and experience standards. Eligibility requirements for the CTRS may be met through the academic path or one of two equivalency paths (see table 3.2).

Code of Ethics

A **code of ethics** represents the official moral ideology of the professional group. In the helping professions, a code of ethics is a basic requirement for recognition as a professional body. An ethical code governing professional behavior is a characteristic shared by the majority of human service occupations and symbolizes autonomy of the professional body.

Ethics deals with the duties and obligations of professionals to their consumers (service recipients), the profession, and to the wider public. Professional ethics considers **moral conduct,** or how one should act; **moral character,** or what sort of person one ought to be; and **moral community,**

Table 3.1　Types of Professional Credentialing

Aspects	Registration	Certification	Licensure
Purpose	Provides a record in official directory	Authorization of adequate training, ensures minimum competencies	Gives permission to practice
Responsibility	Created and monitored by professional organization	Monitored by state board by law or an autonomous board	State board created by law
Effects	The person—voluntary	The person—voluntary	The practice—required by state law
Process	Application and fee, optional exam	Application and fee, required exam	Application and fee, required exam
Criteria	Minimum standards met through application, tend to be flexible and reflect constantly changing criteria	Minimum standards set regarding education and experience, specified criteria for changes through policies and procedures or by-laws	Specific standards set regarding minimum competencies, specified criteria for changes through legislative amendments
Outcome	Directory or list of professionals registered	Professional certificate	License to practice
Renewal	May be contingent on professional development (CEUs)	Contingent on professional development (CEUs)	Contingent on professional development (CEUs)

or how society should be constructed to enable ethical people to act ethically. Moral conduct, character, and community make ethical behavior possible and sustain moral acts. Ignorance or lack of knowledge of professional ethics may well be the primary cause of misguided, inappropriate professional behavior.

Ethical principles (norms) prescribe responsibilities for the individual. They allow for professional discretion and judgment. They do not necessarily determine what ought to be done in a given situation. Instead, they serve as a guide to decision making, which may require a person to weigh and balance multiple principles, one against another.

Five ethical principles are common to human services:

- Principle of beneficence—the duty to promote good to further a person's health and welfare. A therapeutic recreation professional ought to do good to others.

The five ethical principles of human services should be followed to ensure the client has a positive and healthy experience.

Table 3.2 CTRS Eligibility Paths

	Academic path	Equivalency path A	Equivalency path B

Education: baccalaureate degree or higher	• Major in TR or recreation with TR emphasis
	• Minimum of 18 hours in TR or recreation with a minimum of 12 hours specifically in TR
	• 18 hours of support course work to include anatomy or physiology (3), abnormal psychology (3), human growth and development throughout the life span (3), and remaining hours from approved human services.
		• Degree (area of degree is not specified by NCTRC)
		• 18 hours of upper-level or graduate TR or recreation with no fewer than 12 hours in TR
		• 24 hours of support course work in three of six areas:
		  – Adaptive physical education
		  – Related biological and physical sciences
		  – Human services
		  – Psychology
		  – Sociology
		  – Special education
			• Degree (area of degree is not specified by NCTRC)
			• 18 hours of upper-level or graduate TR or recreation with no fewer than 12 hours in TR
			• 18 hours of support course work to include anatomy or physiology (3), abnormal psychology (3), human growth and development throughout the life span (3), and remaining hours from NCTRC-approved human services (i.e., adaptive physical education, human biological or physical sciences, psychology, sociology, special education, education, ethics, health-related issues, communication, human behaviors and problems, allied health, and other disciplines that support TR practice

Experience: work or internship	Internship under an on-site CTRS to include 480 hours over 12 consecutive weeks	Minimum of 5 years' full-time paid experience (minimum of 32 hours per week in direct TR services)	1 year of full-time paid experience (minimum of 1,500 hours or 52 weeks) under supervision of a CTRS and no more than 5 years before applying

Note: All hours above reflect semester hours. Refer to NCTRC regarding quarter hour requirements.

- Principle of nonmalfeasance—relates to beneficence and means that one has a duty not to injure or harm another person. One should not knowingly inflict harm and must strive to remove or reduce risk of harm in all situations.

- Principle of autonomy—concerns the right of people to be respected and make their own choices. A person has the right to determine his or her own course of action in accordance with a plan designed or directed by him or her.

- Principle of justice—requires one to treat others fairly and to be fair in distributing burdens and benefits from the point of view of the least advantaged.

- Principle of fidelity—includes faithfulness as well as obligations to be truthful and keep promises. The statement "I promise" establishes a moral relationship that signifies that one has accepted a self-imposed obligation, whereby the other party has the right to have that obligation fulfilled. Note that truth telling and promise keeping are fundamental building blocks for trust.

The therapeutic recreation profession and agencies or institutions have a responsibility to demonstrate that the community can trust the profession and that the behaviors of its workers will not injure consumers. Ultimately, only the internalization of the value and application of ethics by the professional will result in meaningful validation of a written code of ethics. By working to understand the ethics of the profession, a person can better understand what a therapeutic recreation professional does and what it means to be a therapeutic recreation professional.

ETHICAL DECISION MAKING

One of the more challenging aspects of any profession is identifying and addressing ethical dilemmas. At first, this task seems to be simply a matter of doing the right thing, of following the formal codes written by NTRS, ATRA, or the service-providing agency. In truth, making real decisions is rarely this simple. For example, accepting valuable gifts from a long-standing client in a mental health facility would typically not be seen as ethical. Essentially, a client–therapeutic recreation specialist relationship is different from a friendship because the balance of power is not equal. This fact opens the door for the professional to manipulate and take advantage of the client. At the same time, accepting a token of appreciation, such as a framed photo of the client and therapist on an outing together, may be acceptable if the meaning of the gift is clear. The challenge in this example is determining when a gift becomes an ethical compromise. Does this judgment rest on the value of the gift, the context in which it is given, or both?

In addressing such dilemmas, structured codes of ethics, as well as guidelines for decision making, can be helpful. Figure 3.1 illustrates an example of an ethical decision-making model (Long, 2000). Note that the model focuses on identifying all available information and repeatedly reviewing the consequences of any potential action to be taken. The model assumes that the most ethical decision is to be determined by the amount of positive or negative consequences resulting from each possible action. Even with a structured guide for gathering and analyzing information, determining what is best requires honest, objective consideration of difficult scenarios. Thus, a competent professional becomes familiar with available sources of information, including the advice of other professionals.

Consider the ethical scenarios that follow. Is enough information provided to make a decision? Besides the provided information, what other information would you want to consider before making a decision or judgment? Which of the five ethical principles listed earlier apply to each scenario? The first is a hypothetical situation, whereas the last three are real-life scenarios that have been reported in the past.

- A CTRS has been working with a client who is recovering from an automobile accident that caused a severe injury to both of his legs. After 4 months of intense rehabilitation, the client and CTRS began attending adapted sports clinics and events together as part of an outpatient leisure education program. They also spent several scheduled sessions in the community participating in leisure activities to identify and address physical and environmental barriers related to the client's injuries. On their last outing, the client invited the CTRS to attend a jazz concert at a local night club. When the therapist said that she didn't work on that particular night, the patient stated, "I know, that's why I'm asking."

- A CTRS working in a substance abuse program was asked on occasion by the substance abuse counselor to fill in as the lead therapist during group therapy sessions. Because the CTRS demonstrated that she could adequately run the group, the counselor asked the CTRS to cover one particular group on a full-time basis. When the substance abuse counselors all received pay adjustments, the CTRS filed a complaint with the administrators that she had not received the same adjustment despite her work with the program.

- A mental health patient complains to hospital administrators that one of her therapists has been using "lap hugs" as an intervention during self-esteem groups. The client reports that the therapist periodically instructs patients to sit on his lap, or the lap of a fellow client, for hugs of encouragement during sessions. When approached about the issue, the therapist says that the technique is legitimate and that he tells clients that the activity is voluntary.

- A professional working with a depressed 22-year-old homosexual male tells his client that most of his problems stem from his living a gay lifestyle and that his family is likely to continue to reject him unless he "changes." The professional tells the client that unless he finds God and gives up his sexual lifestyle, his family will never accept him. Two weeks after breaking up with his boyfriend, the man is admitted to a residential therapy program for depression.

ENFORCEMENT OF ETHICAL CODES

Both NTRS and ATRA have developed formal codes of ethics for therapeutic recreation professionals. These codes are generally accepted by the profession, and violation of such codes can result in reprimands from credentialing organizations such as state certification boards or the National Council on Therapeutic Recreation Certification. Possible reprimands could be as severe as loss of license or certification but more often would involve probationary periods and requirements for additional participation in various continuing education efforts. As an example, in reference to the fourth case study, the therapeutic recreation professional may be asked to take a sensitivity training course regarding homosexual issues or

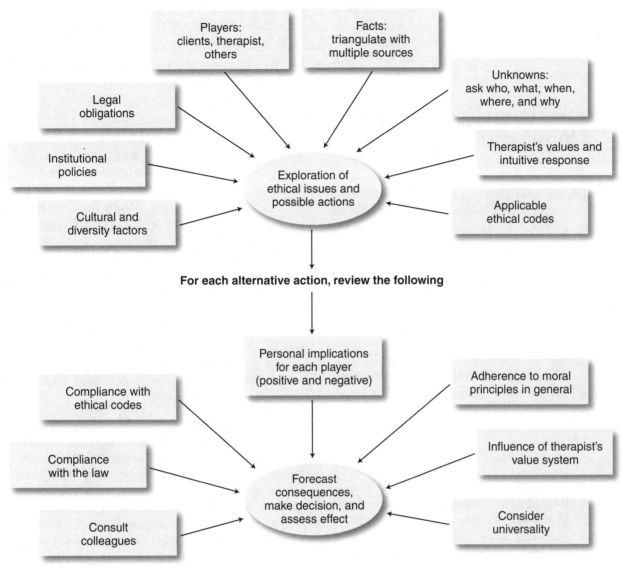

Model for Ethical Decision Making

Figure 3.1 Problem-solving model for ethical decision making.

a class on current counseling considerations for homosexual clients. In addition, service-providing agencies may develop internal codes of ethics and enforce additional reprimands such as probation, training, and termination. Finally, ethical code violations that violate laws or harm others may leave the therapeutic recreation professional open to criminal or civil legal action.

Professional Culture

A **professional culture** is made up of the customary beliefs, norms, or traits of the profession. Professional associations often define the professional culture. The typical professional culture of a therapeutic recreation specialist is consumer focused. Serving as an advocate on behalf of the person with disabilities is an important responsibility of a therapeutic recreation specialist, whatever the setting or delivery system. Therapeutic recreation professionals believe that leisure and recreation are basic human rights and critical to the health and well-being of people, to their quality of life and life satisfaction. Therefore, therapeutic recreation professionals are committed to providing services that are beneficial, dignified, and empowering. Therapeutic recreation specialists are committed to making a difference in the lives of those whom they serve through a continuum of care. Therapeutic recreation professionals believe that only professionals with training, education, and credentials in therapeutic recreation should provide therapeutic recreation services.

Professional Preparation in Therapeutic Recreation

Those who want to work at the professional level in therapeutic recreation must complete a program of study at an accredited college or university. Those seeking certification may also choose to attend a college or university that offers an accredited curriculum in therapeutic recreation or an accredited curriculum in recreation with a therapeutic recreation emphasis. (Ask your instructor or advisor about which type of program your school offers.) Professional preparation programs generally require students to complete an internship under qualified supervision (a certified therapeutic recreation specialist). Ultimately, those who complete a professional preparation path will receive a bachelor's degree or, for teaching or administrative positions in therapeutic recreation, a master's or doctoral degree.

Accreditation

Accreditation is the credentialing of an academic institution and specific curriculum that meets or exceeds prescribed criteria of educational quality with regard to professional preparation curricula and is often closely associated with professional associations in the field. The National Recreation and Park Association (NRPA)–American Association for Leisure and Recreation (AALR)–American Association for Physical Activity and Recreation (AAPAR) Council on Accreditation is the accrediting entity for park, recreation, and leisure services curricula, including therapeutic recreation professional preparation programs.

Accreditation is a voluntary process and has two fundamental purposes: (1) to assure program quality and (2) to assist in program improvement (see NRPA Web site, Overview of Accreditation). Although an accredited program or curriculum cannot guarantee the quality of individual graduates, the institution can affirm that the quality of the education offered has conformed to established minimum standards of knowledge and competencies required for entry-level positions.

NRPA–AALR–AAPAR accreditation standards address several points:

- Organization and operation of the academic program, focusing on characteristics, philosophy, and goals of the academic unit, as well as aspects of the faculty, students, administration, and instructional resources
- Program content, which includes foundations of understanding, professional competencies, and specialized accredited options (leisure services management, natural resources recreation management, leisure and recreation program delivery, and therapeutic recreation)
- Professional competencies, that is, conceptual foundations assessment, planning and evaluation, legislative and legal aspects, leisure services delivery systems, programming strategies, administration and management, and field experiences
- Foundations of understanding, which are the general education requirements of the higher education institution

Only undergraduate baccalaureate programs in parks, recreation, and leisure services are eligible to apply for accreditation from NRPA. No mechanism is in place to accredit 2-year or postgraduate programs in the field. Students who graduate from accredited parks and recreation curriculums, including therapeutic recreation curriculums or curriculums with an emphasis in therapeutic recreation, are immediately eligible to sit for the certified park and recreation professional (CPRP) exam, whereas those who graduate from nonaccredited programs must be employed full-time in the field for a minimum of 2 years before they are eligible to take the exam. The CPRP is an increasingly recognized professional credential for park and recreation professionals. Although the CPRP is not the primary credential for therapeutic recreation specialists, professionals who work in community settings often seek and obtain this additional credential.

Gaining Experience in Therapeutic Recreation

Professional preparation is more than just academic course work. Experience is a valuable teacher. Students and new professionals should seek volunteer opportunities to gain knowledge and experience, as well as build their resumes. Volunteer experience is often as marketable as work experience. Volunteer experience can help students or new professionals gain experience with other special population groups and complement their work experience. The goal is to gain experience with a variety of disability groups, ages, and delivery systems. If a person works or interns in a clinical setting, he or she should seek volunteer opportunities in the community. If a person serves an adult clientele during work or an internship, he or she should consider volunteer experience with children. For example, perhaps the therapeutic recreation professional or student's first job or internship is with a physical rehab facility that serves primarily patients who have experienced a stroke. The person could seek volunteer opportunities with Special Olympics (for those with intellectual disabilities) or Easter Seals (youth with disabilities), coach a beep baseball team (for those who are visually impaired), or assist with a community wheelchair basketball or wheelchair tennis program.

Certainly, a depth of experience with one disability group or age group is valuable when seeking a job in that particular area, but having volunteer experience with other disability groups, ages, and delivery systems will help prepare the student for other available therapeutic recreation positions. Additionally, a person can glean program activity ideas, instructional techniques, and behavioral management strategies from volunteer experiences that could have application in future internship positions or work settings.

Professional Opportunities

After graduating from an accredited program and obtaining professional certification or becoming certification eligible (application in process), diverse employment opportunities are available. As mentioned earlier, therapeutic recreation specialists may work with numerous disability groups, ages, and delivery systems. Some delivery systems focus only on a specific disability or age group (for example, an adolescent drug treatment program). Other delivery systems, such as community parks and recreation departments or VA hospitals, provide services to people who represent a range of ages and disabling conditions.

Service Delivery Systems

Therapeutic recreation uses recreation and leisure as a way to help people function independently and enjoy life. The various delivery systems for therapeutic recreation services offer a variety of employment opportunities. Delivery systems fall along several axes—a clinical–community axis, a public–private axis, and a profit–nonprofit axis (see figure 3.2).

Therapeutic recreation services could be delivered by a private for-profit clinical organization, such as a psychiatric facility. But a psychiatric facility could also be a public nonprofit agency in a state hospital or a community-based psychiatric service such as a mental health outreach program, which could be public nonprofit-based or private for-profit oriented.

Physical rehabilitation services could be provided to people with head or spinal cord injuries in a clinical setting (rehabilitation hospital) or a community program (wheelchair sports programs in a parks and recreation department). The rehabilitation facility could be a for-profit organization or a nonprofit entity like the Scottish Rite Hospital.

Populations Served

Therapeutic recreation specialists serve a variety of populations with special needs. The purpose of therapeutic recreation services is to improve functioning and independence as well as reduce or eliminate the effects of illness or disability; to improve health and well-being; and to facilitate the development, maintenance, and expression of appropriate leisure lifestyle for people with physical, mental, emotional, or social limitations. Table 3.3 summarizes therapeutic recreation services for specific populations, noting possible delivery systems and the potential effect of therapeutic recreation on each group. The table provides information about the most common diagnostic groups, so it does not include all disability groups or delivery systems that employ therapeutic recreation specialists. Although the table includes general statements regarding diagnostic groups and populations served, each person is unique and requires individualized services.

New Horizons

The Bureau of Labor Statistics projected in 2005 (United States Department of Labor) that the

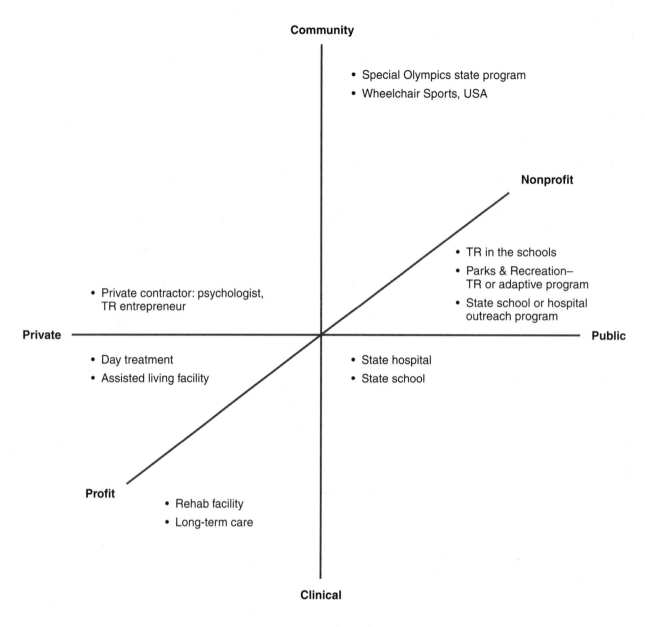

Figure 3.2 Therapeutic recreation delivery systems axes—potential employment options.

overall employment of "therapeutic recreation specialists" and "recreational therapists" was expected to grow more slowly than the average for all occupations. But employment of therapists who work in community care facilities for the elderly and in residential intellectual impairment, mental health, and substance abuse facilities should grow faster than the average. This projection was based on the traditional definition of recreational therapists or therapeutic recreation specialists who provide treatment services and recreation activities to people with disabilities or illnesses through acute health care settings or community-based service delivery

systems. Most people with disabling conditions or special needs live in the community. The "social responsibility" emphasis is on inclusive experiences rather than segregated or specialized services. Medical advances, increasing health care costs, the rapidly increasing number of seniors in the population, and the escalating pace of change offer new opportunities for therapeutic recreation specialists. These opportunities include newly evolving areas of practice such as life transitioning (young and elderly), inclusion services, home-based care, trauma and emergency care, and youth intervention programs.

Table 3.3   Summary of Therapeutic Recreation Services

Population served	Potential delivery systems	Focus of TR	Effect and comments
PHYSICAL IMPAIRMENTS			
Amputations	• Adapted sports program (i.e., Winter Park skiing) • Municipal TR program (such as a city, county, or state park and recreation agency) • Physical rehab facility • VA hospital	• Well-balanced program of body awareness activities • Activities that promote constant change • Increase endurance and balance to promote better physical conditioning	• Acceptance of prosthesis • Improved gross motor skills • Minimization of trauma to stump
Arthritis	• Aquatic therapy through wellness centers • Municipal TR program • Arthritis Foundation program • Physical rehab facility	• Safe and nonstrenuous activities, individual or dual sports such as swimming • Use of arts and crafts (e.g., clay)	• Development of confidence in motor skills • Exercise for hands or feet to develop fine motor skills
Neuromuscular (e.g., cerebral palsy, muscular dystrophy, multiple sclerosis, Parkinson's disease)	• Aquatic therapy through wellness centers • Municipal TR program • Easter Seals • Physical rehab facility • Specialty camps or associated nonprofit groups (e.g., MDA, UCP)	• Gross motor movement • Maintenance of physical well-being • Relaxation techniques • Foster social interaction and support, self-expression • Use of assistive devices, when appropriate	• Maintenance of muscle tone and range of motion • Enhanced endurance, strength, balance, muscle tone • Improved voluntary muscle control • Improved self-esteem • Increased involvement and enhanced independence
Spinal cord injury	• Adapted sports program (i.e., Winter Park skiing, wheelchair sports, and fitness center) • Aquatic therapy through wellness centers • Municipal TR program • Physical rehab facility • VA hospital	• Build on remaining ability, not loss • Strengthen and stretch upper-extremity muscle groups • Develop body image • Develop recreation and sport-related knowledge and skill	• Functional independence • Improved endurance and conditioning (well-being) • Improved self-esteem • Provide a balanced wheelchair sports program (recreational versus competitive)
Stroke	• Aquatic therapy through wellness centers • Municipal TR program • Stroke Club through American Heart Association • Physical rehab facility	• Gross and fine motor activities • Incorporate active with cognitive skill components (e.g., sequencing, recall) • Promote social interaction	• Improved functional use of affected limbs • Improved locomotion, balance, range of motion, and muscle tone • Increased self-confidence • Improved memory and speech • Enhanced socialization skills and sense of self-worth

TABLE 3.3 CONTINUED

TABLE 3.3 CONTINUED

Population served	Potential delivery systems	Focus of TR	Effect and comments
SENSORY IMPAIRMENTS			
Visual impairments or blindness	• Commission for the Blind rehab facility or school • Municipal TR program	• Develop positive attitude toward self and others • Enhance mobility, physical well-being, and conditioning • Maintain residual vision • Increase socialization skills	• Improved self-esteem • Use of active sports and games to enhance confidence • Maintenance of hand–eye coordination • Facilitation of inclusion opportunities
Hearing impairments or deafness	• Municipal TR program • State facility or school • Independent living centers • Deaf clubs	• Facilitate socialization • Enhance communication skills • Develop self-concepts and physical motor skills • Enhance self-direction	• Reduced isolation between hearing and nonhearing, reduced social naivete • Increase curiosity and mastery of environment • Facilitation of inclusion opportunities
COGNITIVE IMPAIRMENTS			
Alzheimer's and dementia-related disorders	• Adult day care • Municipal TR program • Long-term care facilities • VA hospital	• Exercise and gross motor activities • Facilitate social interactions through outings and family gatherings • Promote independent functioning • Provide opportunities to share previous life experiences and instruction if needed	• Improved health and conditioning • Maintenance of contact with community and family • Enhanced activities of daily living • Appropriate to person's functioning level
Learning disabilities: attention-deficit/ hyperactivity disorder	• Municipal TR program • School districts and special education • Specialty camps and residential facilities (e.g., Star Ranch in Texas)	• Determine accommodation needed • Promote involvement in active and passive pursuits	• Individualization through observing, questioning, setting limits and boundaries • Enhanced use of compensatory skills, increased socialization
Intellectual impairment	• Adult day care • Municipal TR program • Group homes • School districts and special education • Special Olympics • State facility or school	• Enhance motor development and physical conditioning • Develop new skills and interest through a variety of activities • Increase social interaction and social skills	• Increased activity level, reduced tendency to be overweight, outlet for energy, enhanced sense of accomplishment and self-worth • Reduced isolation and recidivism rate, improved communication skills

Population served	Potential delivery systems	Focus of TR	Effect and comments
Traumatic brain or head injury	• Adult day care • Municipal TR program • Group homes • Physical rehab facility or specialty residential facility • School districts and special education • VA hospital	• Social and affective difficulties • Sensory and psychomotor problems • Cognitive and intellectual problems	• Improved self-image, reduced aggression or withdrawal, enhanced ability to cope • Assistance with sensory integration; improved perception, balance, and locomotion • Increased attention span and reduced impulsivity and distractibility; increased short- and long-term memory; enhanced problem-solving skills

PSYCHOLOGICAL IMPAIRMENTS

Population served	Potential delivery systems	Focus of TR	Effect and comments
Eating disorders	• Outpatient psychiatric services, day treatment programs, or community mental health agencies • Psychiatric rehab facility or specialty residential facility	• Assess leisure lifestyle skills and behaviors • Assist in identifying and understanding feelings and emotions • Provide healthy balance and perspective about physical activity and fitness	• Provision of more specific diagnostic information and thus more effective treatment • Improved self-esteem and self-concept or self-image
Organic, functional, psychogenic, depression	• Adult day care • Municipal TR program • Group homes • Psychiatric rehab facility or specialty residential facility • VA hospital • Acute care hospitals	• Assess functional abilities • Assess leisure lifestyle skills and behaviors • Assist in identifying and understanding feelings and emotions • Teach skills related to successful personal living (e.g., relaxation, stress management, time management, health and fitness, assertion)	• Provision of more specific diagnostic information and thus more effective treatment • Identification of needs for treatment focus and assurance of successful community reintegration and adaptation
Substance abuse	• Experiential, outdoor, or wilderness treatment programs • Outpatient psychiatric services, day treatment programs, or community mental health agencies • Psychiatric rehab facility or specialty residential facility • VA hospital	• Assess functional abilities • Assess leisure lifestyle skills and behaviors • Focus on leisure education including teaching skills related to successful personal living (e.g., relaxation, stress management, time management, health and fitness, assertion)	• Promotion of social, physical, mental, and emotional growth and development • Identification of needs for treatment focus and assurance of successful community reintegration and adaptation

TABLE 3.3 CONTINUED

TABLE 3.3 CONTINUED

Population served	Potential delivery systems	Focus of TR	Effect and comments
		SOCIAL IMPAIRMENTS	
Corrections	• Criminal justice facilities (i.e., detention centers, prisons)	• Reduce stress and provide outlet for energy • Provide leisure education • Encourage positive use of free time and recreation alternatives	• Reduced personal and environmental tension • Increased levels of self-awareness, leisure awareness, leisure skills, decision-making skills, and social skills • Enhanced self-concept and sense of accomplishment, increased quality of life
HIV and AIDS	• Acute care hospitals or hospice • Municipal TR program	• Quality of life and dignity in death • Reduce isolation • Promote exercise and nutrition	• Outlet for self-expression • Increased motivation • Maintenance of health
Homeless and victims of trauma	• Municipal TR program • Outpatient psychiatric services or day treatment community mental health agencies • Domiciliary care for homeless veterans	• Create a natural setting or safe environment that affirms experiences • Social and affective difficulties • Reduce isolation and assist in meeting person's basic needs • Facilitate social interactions through outings and family gatherings	• Improved self-image, reduced aggression or withdrawal, enhanced ability to cope • Increased motivation • Maintenance of contact with community and family, creation of sense of belonging

Professional Organizations

Professional organizations exist to support professionals within a chosen field. Their purpose is to articulate the practice and benefits of the profession, to promote and foster the advancement and growth of the profession, and to improve services by those who practice it. People in therapeutic recreation, in both clinical and community settings, are supported by and can become involved in national and state professional organizations. Many state park and recreation associations have branches or sections with a specialized focus such as therapeutic recreation. In some locales, state or national organizations have local or regional units. For example, state associations may have geographic regions or districts that serve the function of sharing informa-tion and networking, providing professional development, advocating for public policy, or enhancing public awareness at a grassroots level.

Benefits of professional association membership may vary to some degree, but associations generally offer benefits in five areas:

- Sponsoring informative meetings and educational programs—Training and educational development is central to fulfilling the mission of the professional organization.

- Publishing literature that reflects the body of knowledge of the profession and could contribute to improving practice within the profession—Professional organizations may commission research projects that will contribute to the body of knowledge, but more often they distribute findings and other relevant information through their publications, conferences, and meetings.

- Providing for credentialing or maintenance of professional credentials—Organizations promote and support credentialing through continuing education units (CEUs) for CTRS, CPRP, and so on.

- Defining professional behavior—Professional organizations develop, monitor, and enforce codes of acceptable conduct. Professional behavior, also known as **professionalism,** occurs when professionals perform competently and demonstrate high moral character in fulfilling obligations to their constituents.

- Recognizing change factors that could influence the profession of parks and recreation and therapeutic recreation and the careers of those within the field—Professional organizations strive to keep the profession current and relevant.

Several organizations provide services to those in the field of parks, recreation, and leisure services, including therapeutic recreation. Among these organizations are the National Therapeutic Recreation Society (NTRS), the American Therapeutic Recreation Association (ATRA), and the American Alliance for Health, Physical Education, Recreation and Dance (AAHPERD).

National Therapeutic Recreation Society

The National Recreation and Park Association (NRPA) is the largest and broadest based of the professional organizations, boasting 22,000 members. The association includes both professional members and citizen members. A 70-member board of trustees governs the organization, although this number will be reduced to 21 in October 2009. The diverse interest areas and disciplines within the parks and recreation industry are represented by 10 individual branches and sections, including the National Therapeutic Recreation Society (NTRS) and eight regional councils. The mission of the National Recreation and Park Association is "to advance parks, recreation and environmental conservation efforts that enhance the quality of life for all people."

The National Therapeutic Recreation Society (NTRS) is one of two national organizations with the specific focus of promoting therapeutic recreation. NTRS, a branch of the National Recreation and Park Association, is the leading membership organization of practitioners, educators, students, and consumers in advancing the belief that leisure and recreation are basic human rights and are critical to health, quality of life, and happiness. As basic rights, leisure and recreation must be available to all people, including those with illnesses, disabilities, or other conditions that may restrict health, independence, and quality of life. NTRS supports its members in their informed endeavors to serve the consumers of therapeutic recreation in a way that is helpful, empowering, inclusive, dignified, and just (NTRS Web site: www.nrpa.org/ntrs).

During its 40 years as a professional organization, NTRS has articulated what therapeutic recreation is and what its benefits are. It established standards and guidelines about how therapeutic recreation services are to be provided in both clinical and community settings. NTRS has and will continue to support research and efficacy efforts, provide professional development opportunities, and advocate for appropriate public policy development and greater public awareness of therapeutic recreation services.

American Therapeutic Recreation Association

The American Therapeutic Recreation Association (ATRA) is the largest national membership organization representing the interest and need of the recreational therapist (recall the distinction in terminology mentioned in chapter 1). ATRA was incorporated in 1984 as a nonprofit grassroots organization in response to growing concern about dramatic changes in the health care industry and because of philosophical conflict over the nature of therapeutic recreation. It was formed specifically to respond to the lack of financial support for the treatment aspect of therapeutic recreation by NRPA management. Therapeutic recreation specialists, many of whom had served in leadership positions within the National Therapeutic Recreation Society, were instrumental in the establishment of ATRA. The organization defines therapeutic recreation as "the provision of treatment services and the provision of recreation services to persons with illnesses or disabling conditions" (ATRA, 2006).

The vision of the interim board included an organization that was accountable to the

TRACEY CRAWFORD

Background Information

Education
BS degree in Therapeutic Recreation, University of Iowa

Credentials
*CPRP *CTRS

Special Affiliations
*Illinois Park and Recreation Association *Ethnic Minority Section Board of Directors *ITRS *IPRA *Special Recreation Association of Northern Illinois *Illinois Park and Recreation Foundation *NTRS *Great Lakes Regional Council

Special Awards
*Presidential Award, National Therapeutic Recreation Society (2001) *Meritorious Service Award, National Therapeutic Recreation Society (2004) *Member of the Year Award, National Therapeutic Recreation Society (2004) *IPRA Chairman's Award, Illinois Park and Recreation Association (2005)

Career Information

Position
Superintendent of Recreation, Northern Suburban Special Recreation Association (NSSRA)

Attitudes are contagious...is yours worth catching?

Organization Information
As a partnership of twelve municipalities in the northern suburbs of Chicago, NSSRA provides and facilitates year-round recreation programs for adults and children with disabilities who reside in the partner communities.

Organization's Mission
NSSRA provides and facilitates year-round recreation programs for adults and children with disabilities who live in the partner communities.

Likes and Dislikes About the Job
I love working with professionals to help them grow individually, helping them to define their leadership styles. I also enjoy working on the agency's public relations and marketing efforts, fund-raising, and developing the programs and services offered at NSSRA.

Advice to Undergraduate Students
I feel that the field of parks and recreation is one of the most rewarding professions. It is a career and not a job. I encourage those new to the field to experience different avenues and gain maximum exposure. This exposure is what will help students make those future career choices. I also encourage students to seek mentors.

membership and had a decentralized organizational structure responsive to membership needs rather than organizational expediency. With that end in mind, ATRA established a chapter affiliates program.

American Alliance for Health, Physical Education, Recreation and Dance

The American Alliance for Health, Physical Education, Recreation and Dance (AAHPERD) has a long history of supporting the efforts of therapeutic recreation professionals and promoting educational and recreational programs for people with special needs. The organization dates back to 1885, when William Gilbert Anderson, a medical school graduate and an instructor of physical training in Brooklyn, invited a group of people who worked in the gymnastics field to gather to discuss their profession. AAHPERD, an alliance of five national associations and six district associations, supports members with resources and programs to help practitioners improve their skills and further the health and well-being of the American public (AAHPERD Web site, www.aahperd.org, 2006).

The American Association for Physical Activity and Recreation (AAPAR), one of the five national associations within AAHPERD, supports a broad range of community-based programs, issues, and populations, such as aquatics, adapted physical activity, outdoor recreation, lifelong recreational sport, fitness for older adults, wellness, professional recreation services, and others. AAPAR promotes public awareness and understanding of lifelong physical activity and recreation through continuing education for professionals who serve diverse audiences throughout the life span. AAPAR and the National Recreation and Park Association have jointly sponsored the Council on Accreditation since its establishment in 1974.

Professional Networking

Networking, an important tool for advancement, leadership, power, and influence, is related to organizational variables such as socialization, motivation, commitment, and innovation. Networking, as an individual skill, is the ability to create and maintain an effective and diverse system of resources, made possible by using relevant information, having good working relations, and maintaining and communicating a good track record. The professional should know the players within a network and their different responsibilities, perspectives, personalities, and sources of power. The professional should be able to identify and articulate the goals of each group and person involved in the network, as well as their willingness to act on goals.

As a critical strategy in the field of therapeutic recreation, networking serves several useful purposes:

- To develop skills and accomplish activities
- To bridge the gaps between or within functions of a job or organization
- To foster communication, both formal and informal
- To gather and manage information
- To facilitate exchange or interchange of resources

Professionals working within the field of therapeutic recreation and recreation are often masters of networking, because collaboration with others is a prerequisite to getting projects, programs, and events accomplished. Collaboration is particularly important for the one- or two-person therapeutic recreation work unit within an agency or institution. Networking is a process of sharing information, resources, or technical assistance for the purpose of achieving common goals. Information sharing

eliminates the need to reinvent the wheel and often strengthens a person's resolve to pursue a cause or innovative idea; knowing that others share similar thoughts can foster increased confidence within a professional entity. Through the sharing of information and resources by professionals or agencies, a professional association can voice concerns and identify issues to policy makers or regulatory bodies, demonstrate the effect and value of service delivery, or heighten public awareness. Through networking, organizations or groups can demonstrate that many people are involved and that the scope of involvement—geographic, professional preparation, financial, political, social—is broad.

Organizational networking is either **intraorganizational,** that is, operating within an organization to reach a shared goal and ultimately advance the organization, or **interorganizational,** that is, operating among organizations that share similar characteristics, such as populations served, service delivery system, goals, or issues.

For example, a therapeutic recreation specialist might network intraorganizationally (share information) with nursing staff, food service, and transportation to ensure the success of a community reentry outing. A therapeutic recreation specialist needs

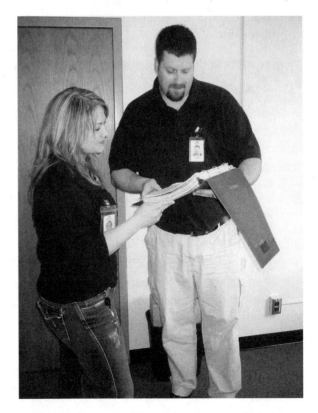

Networking is important in learning new ways to help clients.

the cooperation of these support services to have consumers ready for the outing—meds given, meals concluded or perhaps prepared for the outing, and transportation provided. Through collaboration, all services contribute to the goal of quality service and care of clientele. A therapeutic recreation specialist might also share resources to assist another service unit, such as recruiting or scheduling volunteers for a fund-raiser or recruiting carnival booths and games from community parks and recreation peers for the hospital's employee picnic.

On an interorganizational level, all therapeutic recreation specialists within a community, both clinical and community-based, might work together to promote Therapeutic Recreation Week during the second week in July. They would not only work within their own agencies but also persuade the city council to make a proclamation and encourage the media to run stories focused on therapeutic recreation during the week. Another example would be for therapeutic recreation specialists to join their parks and recreation agency peers in visiting their state or federal legislative representatives. The goal would be to increase the lawmakers' awareness of the importance of the reauthorization of IDEA and the inclusion of therapeutic recreation and recreation as a related service or the need for increased Land and Water Conservation Fund appropriations.

Summary

Therapeutic recreation is a profession. Like other allied health professions, therapeutic recreation embraces the distinguishing key elements of a profession: a systematic body of knowledge, professional development, professional authority, professional credentialing, and a code of ethics. A therapeutic recreation specialist may provide treatment or educational services and recreation activities to people with disabilities or illnesses in health care settings, community-based delivery systems, or through combinations or variations of both. Emerging professional career opportunities within therapeutic recreation will tend to be in one- or two-person work units, such as a therapeutic recreation specialist in the schools or emergency care intervention or an inclusion specialist, rather than in a larger service department. A professional association often dictates the professional culture, provides professional development or continuing education alternatives and networking opportunities, and defines the profession for professional credentialing at state or national levels. Ultimately, therapeutic recreation specialists are committed to making a difference in the lives of those whom they serve through a continuum of care.

DISCUSSION QUESTIONS

1. When and why should a therapeutic recreation specialist begin addressing career resilience?

2. Does having a professional credential make a therapeutic recreation professional more qualified or a better practitioner? Why or why not?

3. What are the benefits of professional credentialing for the individual therapeutic recreation specialist? For the employer? For the consumer?

4. How does the therapeutic recreation profession determine, that is, define and measure, professional competence?

5. Maintaining client confidentiality is an ethical responsibility of the therapeutic recreation specialist. Is confidentiality absolute or situational? Why?

6. How does the professional (moral agent) contend with consumers' choices that are immoral in nature?

7. Why and how are professional organizations important to the vitality of the profession? How and why are organizations beneficial to the individual specialist?

Person-First Philosophy in Therapeutic Recreation

Mary Ann Devine, PhD, CTRS
Kent State University

LEARNING OUTCOMES

After completing this chapter, learners will be able to demonstrate the following competencies:

- Describe the person-first concepts related to people with disabilities
- Explain the role of person-first terminology as it relates to reflecting a person-first philosophy
- Discuss the issues of multidimensionality of barriers relative to a person-first philosophy
- Explain the role of attitudes toward people with disabilities as they relate to embracing differences
- Identify the factors that influence one's attitude toward people with disabilities
- Describe various philosophical models of service delivery and their relationship to therapeutic recreation

Our differences make us interesting, but our humanity makes us the same. This chapter will explore, discuss, and challenge you to view in a positive way the differences between people with and without disabilities. All too often, society places people with and without disabilities at opposing ends of a spectrum. This notion has lead to a collective focus on how we are different from one another rather than on what we have in common. This emphasis on differences has led to stereotypes and stigmas about those with disabilities that have prevented their full participation in community life.

Therapeutic recreation specialists have often served as agents of change. By adopting an attitude that celebrates rather than discourages differences, we can continue to advocate for the rights and full participation of people with disabilities in our communities. This chapter will explore person-first, attitudinal, and service delivery aspects of disability. The emphasis will be on our perceptions and belief systems about those with disabilities and how those beliefs affect our profession. The chapter will conclude with a discussion about the role of therapeutic recreation relative to people with disabilities.

Who Is the Person With a Disability?

Over the years, people with disabilities have been stereotyped as limited in potential. This generalization is based on a comparison of them with people who do not have the same characteristic. Labels drive such stereotypes, and these labels can originate from several sources, some of which were originally intended for good. Labels referring to disabilities have been medically based, such as the labeling of a person as blind because he or she cannot see. Labels can be socially based. For example, a person who uses a wheelchair may be assumed to be disabled in ways that exceed his or her actual impairments. Labels can even be legally based and are often required for the provision of supportive services in school and recreation. For example, to qualify for certain special education services, a child must fall into specific diagnostic categories such as autism or attention-deficit/hyperactivity disorder. Regardless of the mechanisms through which a person is labeled, the person with a disability is someone who has a limitation in some aspect of his or her functioning according to our social norms.

Whether they are good or bad, all people tend to be identified by and associated with characteristics that really are only superficial indicators of who they are. Society worships celebrities based solely on public personas that are crafted by Hollywood moguls and music industry executives. Likewise, society has a history of ridiculing and ostracizing those who do not meet these unrealistic standards. This superficial idea of perfection leads to judgmental standards built on trivial characteristics that have no relationship to the essence of a person. The labeling of people, and the stereotypical assumptions that we make based on such labels, discounts the true value of the person. In other words, labels and inaccurate stereotypes of society often overshadow the strengths, potential, and accomplishments of persons with disabilities.

To be fair, labels can serve a valuable purpose because they facilitate communication of the nature of a particular condition to others. This message in turn allows for the provision of appropriate care, access to resources or accommodations, and program enrollment. The danger of labels comes from the misuse and misunderstanding, as well as the tendency to generalize impairment, of one particular area of functioning to the overall abilities of the person. An example of such a generalization would be assuming that a person has difficulty solving problems because he or she cannot hear. Even worse, we begin to focus so much on the disability that the differentiating characteristic overshadows the person.

According to the Americans with Disabilities Act (ADA) (U.S. Department of Justice, 1991), legally a person with a disability is someone who

- has a physical, mental, or cognitive impairment that substantially limits one or more major life functions or activities;
- has a record of such an impairment; or
- is regarded as having such an impairment.

This legal definition requires the disability to result in a substantial limitation in one or more major life activities such as walking, breathing, seeing, thinking, performing tasks, speaking, learning, working, driving, and participating in community life. Although this definition is clear, it goes beyond how well a person can function and the degree to which he or she can be independent. The spirit of the ADA also embraces a philosophy or belief system that the person should not be taken out of the equation. In other words, the person is much more than his or her disability. People with disabilities have the right to be treated as a person first, not as their disability. Beyond the individual's physical, mental, or cognitive limitations, the constant factor is our humanity (Bogdan & Taylor, 1992). Thus, the humanity should be our first consideration.

Each of the hundreds of disabilities has a differing degree of severity. Chapters 8 to 13 discuss characteristics and aspects of various disabilities from the perspective of disability-related characteristics and programs. Here we will explore the idea of viewing a person with a disability as a person first, with the focus not on the person's limitations but on the individual as a person. This perspective is a key element in the prevention of handicaps. A handicap is a situation in which a person can be disadvantaged not by the disability but by other factors. These disadvantages may result from a preventable or removable barrier to performance of a particular activity or skill. Handicaps can include physical barriers but also can come from society's negligence or from negative personal attitudes, beliefs, or knowledge. This chapter focuses on the social issue of how society perceives and interacts with people with disabilities. In particular, we discuss person-first aspects of disability, the effect of negative perceptions of disability, and the role of therapeutic recreation relative to people with disabilities.

Person-First Philosophy

Considering our humanity first is predominately the philosophy or belief system of therapeutic recreation. This philosophy means that we treat each other as unique human beings with the potential to grow and develop. We respond to each other first according to our human needs and second in terms of individual characteristics (Bogdan & Taylor, 1992). For instance, we address the person who has a cognitive impairment as a person first, not as a person who has trouble making decisions or recalling information.

The foundation of a person-first philosophy involves believing that each person is unique and that his or her uniqueness is a positive attribute, not a negative one. This philosophy is founded on the belief that each person is made up of many different qualities, such as possessing a sense of humor or being good at card tricks, not only his or her disability. A person-first philosophy embraces the belief that all persons have the potential to grow and develop as human beings. Regardless of one's limitations, a person can learn new things, engage in activities, participate in reciprocal relationships, and have a fulfilling quality of life. We can embrace a person-first philosophy in several ways. One is through the terminology or language that we use when referring to, speaking to, or talking about people with disabilities. Another indicator of a person-first philosophy is an understanding of the multidimensionality of barriers that people with disabilities face.

Person-First Terminology

Words are powerful. They convey meaning, attitudes, philosophical beliefs, and personal perspectives. So, being aware of words that we use when speaking with or about a person with a disability is important in embracing a person-first philosophy. **Person-first terminology** requires the use of respectful language when referring to those with disabilities. Specifically, terminology should focus on the person first, not the disability. For example, it would be more appropriate to state that "Joe is a child who has autism"

Each person is unique and has the potential to grow. Focus on this humanity rather than on marginalizing characteristics.

rather than "Joe is autistic." This distinction seems minor, but the former approach acknowledges Joe as a person first, whereas the latter does not. A broad example is in the preference for using "people with disabilities" instead of "disabled people," "the disabled," or "handicapped." Furthermore, it is important to refer to a disability only when relevant and necessary. Person-first terminology also requires us to avoid referring to someone with a disability as a "special child" or a "challenged person" because those terms focus on the disability as the identifying characteristic that makes someone unique. Terminology should reflect respect for the person by not referring to adults with disabilities as kids or referring to them in a childlike manner. Eliminating from our vocabulary words such as *imbecile, psycho, lunatic, moron,* and *spaz,* whether referring to someone with or without a disability, is another way to communicate respect.

Understanding the Multidimensionality of Barriers

To embrace a person-first philosophy, we need to understand that people with disabilities encounter barriers not only because they have functional limitations. We understand and view problems, limitations, deficits, boundaries, and constraints as resulting from a number of causal factors rather than simply a person's disability (Howe-Murphy & Charboneau, 1987). This perspective requires that constraints and limitations to participation in community life should focus not only on characteristics of disabilities but also on the design of programs, accessibility of buildings, and training of staff. For example, if a woman with a developmental disability is not participating in her community's recreation programs, the cause may be that the programs are beyond her financial means, are inaccessible by public transportation, are not designed with her abilities in mind, or are unwelcoming to her. This principle requires looking beyond disabilities and taking into account environmental factors such as negative attitudes held by the public, accessibility of buildings, or program design.

Using Person-First Philosophy

Promoting a person-first philosophy means that we need to serve as change agents by modeling and insisting on actions that empower rather than demean people with disabilities (Dattilo, 2002). As a profession, we have an ethical responsibility to promote the dignity and rights of those whom we serve. By modeling person-first behavior, we demonstrate to others that we respect the uniqueness of each person, that we welcome differences between people. We provide opportunities that challenge myths and stereotypes that can reduce barriers to community involvement.

Therapeutic recreation specialists can play an important role in teaching skills to participants that help them be more independent or interdependent in their leisure. Learning skills and new ways of thinking about leisure can empower those with disabilities and is a strong reflection of a person-first philosophy.

One service model that has been useful in delivering therapeutic recreation services has been the leisure ability model (Stumbo & Peterson, 2004). The components of this model are discussed more thoroughly in chapter 5. One component of this model is leisure education, a process based

Therapeutic recreation specialists work with clients to achieve maximum independence in recreation and leisure.

on the idea that people with disabilities can be taught how to make leisure choices, learn new recreation skills, and use community resources like park and recreation services. A therapeutic recreation specialist can facilitate the examination of leisure values and attitudes to identify interpersonal barriers to leisure. By applying this model, a therapeutic recreation specialist can also teach new leisure-related skills such as how to socialize in large groups, ski using adaptive equipment, or make decisions when faced with multiple choices. Framing services from the recreation engagement segment of this model, a therapeutic recreation specialist could refer people to accessible community services, assess a recreation program for inclusive participation with peers without disabilities, or implement an adapted recreation program.

Social Inclusion

Besides teaching skills and examining leisure values or attitudes, therapeutic recreation specialists can facilitate social inclusion in promoting a person-first philosophy. **Social inclusion** involves sharing common experiences, valuing the participation of all people, and providing support for participation (Devine, 2004; Goodwin, 2003). When a therapeutic recreation specialist facilitates social inclusion, he or she is concerned with more than the number of friends that someone with a disability may have. Instead, he or she focuses on creating a sense of belonging to a group, a feeling that participation is valued. For instance, skills would not be ridiculed when they look different from those performed by peers without disabilities, the interests of participants with disabilities would be actively sought, and the atmosphere would be welcoming (Devine & Lashua, 2002).

Social inclusion is critical because lack of social acceptance in inclusive recreation environments is more constraining than are architectural or programmatic barriers (Bedini, 2000; Bedini & Henderson, 1994; West, 1984). Moreover, studies have found that people with disabilities take an emotional, social, and psychological risk when they choose to participate in inclusive rather than separate (i.e., disability only) recreation programs (Bedini & Henderson 1994; Devine & Lashua, 2002). Thus, social inclusion is a way to break down barriers so that people can feel comfortable and welcomed in a recreation environment.

Least Restrictive Environments

In promoting a person-first philosophy, therapeutic recreation specialists should create an environment that is least restrictive. These environments provide maximum support to people with disabilities for engagement in recreation or therapy without over-reliance on adaptations if they are not necessary. **Least restrictive environments** are situations in which adaptations would be made only when evidence indicates that a person with a disability needs changes to function. The goal of a least restrictive environment is to make changes based on the person's individual strengths and limitations. Making changes or adaptations that are beyond the person's needs may actually make the environment more restrictive. As people learn and change, their skills and knowledge may change, eventually rendering adaptations no longer necessary (Dattilo, 2002).

Interdependence

When therapeutic recreation specialists foster interdependence among all participants, a person-first philosophy can develop. **Interdependence** implies relationships of cooperation and reciprocity among participants with and without disabilities, as well as the staff, to accomplish tasks and achieve common goals. For example, participants could work together to paint a wall mural, with those who use wheelchairs painting the lower parts of the wall and those who do not painting the upper sections.

Attitudes Toward People With Disabilities

Attitudes have the power to create either positive forces for change or major barriers. Thus, our attitude toward differences between people is one point that distinguishes positive and negative interactions. Historically, society's attitude toward people with disabilities has been predominantly negative. This way of thinking has resulted in such actions as segregation (separating people based on a personal characteristic that is different) and discrimination (actions that devalue a person based on a personal characteristic).

Society at times has also treated those with disabilities as superhumans, resulting in perceptions that people must be extraordinary, that they must

Phoebe is an 11-year-old girl with Prader Willi syndrome, a chromosomal disorder that results in hypotonia (poor muscle tone), speech problems, and developmental delays. Like a typical 11-year-old, Phoebe has many recreation interests, such as painting, riding her bike, dancing, playing basketball, and spending time with friends. Phoebe has some cognitive delays that are not typical of an 11-year-old, such as difficulty remembering things, recalling sequences of tasks, reading, writing, verbally communicating her ideas, recognizing cause-and-effect situations, and problem solving. Her poor muscle tone sometimes makes it difficult for her to control motor functions such as grasping things and kicking actions, and she has low stamina for activities that require endurance.

PHOEBE'S LEAST RESTRICTIVE ENVIRONMENT

As we learned, Phoebe likes to paint. Because of her cognitive impairment she tends to forget what supplies she will need and how to prepare the area or herself for painting. The goal for Phoebe is to teach her to paint independently, with friends, or in a class. In keeping with the tenants of a least restrictive environment, a therapeutic recreation specialist would develop a way for her to remember what supplies she needs to gather, how to lay them out, and how to begin using them independently. Because Phoebe has difficulty reading, the recreation therapist determines that pictorial charts would be a useful way to show her how to go about painting independently. Additionally, to address her problems of grasping and holding small objects, the recreation therapist enlarges the handles of her paintbrushes with fabric and padded tape so that Phoebe will be able to use them more easily. Because Phoebe needs adaptations only for recall, sequencing, reading,

and holding small objects, these modifications will be the only ones made to this activity, in keeping with the principles of a least restrictive environment. The therapeutic recreation specialist develops one chart that has pictures of all the supplies that she needs and another chart that has step-by-step pictures that show Phoebe the sequence of preparing the area and herself for painting. The therapeutic recreation specialist first teaches Phoebe how to look at the chart and use a step-by-step process to gather items. He then teaches Phoebe how to use the pictures on the second chart to prepare herself and her area to paint. As Phoebe learns these skills, the therapeutic recreation specialist would stop providing assistance. Later, the charts can be withdrawn because Phoebe would no longer need them. Withdrawing modifications when they are no longer needed is the second principle of a least restrictive environment.

Down the Road

As Phoebe develops an interest in other recreation activities, she will need different modifications to meet her needs. This need is especially legitimate because she is at an age when she faces rapid changes emotionally, physically, cognitively, and socially even without added concerns of her developmental delays. Her therapeutic recreation specialist will watch for components of recreation participation that involve fine motor activities, reading, sequencing, short-term and long-term recall, problem solving, and activities that require multiple pieces of equipment for which she may need an adaptation. When Phoebe needs these skills, adaptations will be made to help her. For example, if Phoebe wants to participate on a basketball team, frequent breaks will help compensate for her poor physical stamina. Activities that require problem solving, such as board games, may require modified rules to allow Phoebe to participate.

have capacities beyond those of typical humans, to live with a disability. After interacting with people who hold this attitude, some people with disabilities have felt that they have been treated as heroes simply because they have a disability.

Some people with disabilities experience a neutral attitude toward them, leaving them feeling invisible. One man who has a spinal cord injury described that neutral attitude as people looking past him or through him as though he were not present. What all of these ranges of attitudes have

in common is their focus on the disability first, instead of the person first.

Influence of Society, Community, and Family

Our society as a whole is a strong influence on individual belief systems, attitudes, and perceptions toward people, events, language, and objects. Because most human beings do not live in social isolation, our beliefs are a reflection of many variables.

Various institutions in society such as schools, governmental agencies, laws, and families play a role in shaping beliefs, attitudes, and perceptions of many things including those related to people with disabilities. In particular, looking at our attitudes toward and perceptions of people with disabilities is important because they are a mirror to our beliefs about those with whom we will work.

As young children we may have learned not to stare at someone who uses a wheelchair or to avoid people who talk differently than we do. Historically, schools segregated children with disabilities from their peers without disabilities, teaching students that their peers with disabilities didn't belong with them. Segregation in schools sent a message that the difference between people with and without disabilities was not a positive difference but a devalued negative difference. Our family members taught some of us to feel blessed or privileged to be born without a disability. Children were often taught that not having a disability was a stroke of luck or divine intervention and that we should be grateful for not having been born with such afflictions. The inadvertent consequence of such a belief is that it leads to the assumption that having a disability makes you less of a person.

During adolescence our peer groups have a significant influence on our behavior, because, by nature, we want to gain and maintain a sense of belonging (Witt & Caldwell, 2005). In this life stage, our peers influenced our attitudes toward those with disabilities by expecting us to go along with behaviors such as making fun of disability characteristics or name calling each other using derogatory disability-related language. A perception of superiority can also hold sway in adolescence. For instance, one study that examined perceptions of youth toward inclusive recreation found that adolescents without disabilities felt that competing in sports or other recreation activities was unfair to their peers with disabilities because they were not as good at those activities as were those without disabilities (Devine & Wilhite, 2000).

In our play or leisure, we received the message from many sources that people with disabilities were less able, less capable, and inferior in their abilities to those of us without a disability. The loud message is that they are not like those of us without disabilities. The prevalence of segregated recreation options sends the message that only in these contexts can people with disabilities engage in recreation because their abilities are less than ours.

Research has found that people without disabilities perceived that recreation participation with peers with disabilities would result in a watered-down experience that would be less challenging or enjoyable (Archie & Sherrill, 1989; Wilhite, Devine & Goldenberg, 1999). We also have been taught that recreation skills must all look the same and that skills performed differently are inferior and result in a less enjoyable experience.

Even manufacturers of sport apparel and equipment continue to send the message that people with disabilities can't be athletes or enjoy participating in recreation. Take the case of an advertisement for a running shoe by one sport-apparel company. In 2000 an advertisement appeared in magazines around the world warning would-be purchasers that they risked slamming into a tree if they did not buy a particular running shoe. The commercial graphically showed the creator's idea of the result of running without the right type of shoes. The would-be runner becomes a drooling, misshapen husk of his former self, forced to roam the earth in a motorized wheelchair with his name embossed on one of those cute license plates found at carnivals or state fairs, fastened to the back—all for not wearing the proper shoes.

Clearly, what is being communicated is that a disability is a sentence to a poorer quality of life compared with the quality of life experienced by persons without disabilities. From this perspective, a disability is perceived as more than a loss of functioning resulting from impairment; it is disqualification from a full life as well as an enjoyable recreation experience (Devine & Sylvester, 2005).

Influence of Language on Attitudes

Another indicator of attitudes is language. As the example in the previous section indicates, the words that we use can create a vivid picture of our stereotyped image of someone with a disability. Our language is a gauge of our beliefs about people with disabilities. For example, if we believe that they are inferior to the rest of us, we may say, "He can't play checkers, he's retarded." We believe that the person cannot play the game because he is less intelligent than we are. If we believe that we should have pity for people with disabilities, we may say, "That poor woman is a victim of polio." Although some disabilities are more difficult to live with than others, referring to someone as a victim because he or she has a disability places the person in a helpless position.

Some attitudes toward people with disabilities are reflective of them as objects. This viewpoint is evident when we use terms like *the blind, the deaf,* or *the retarded,* words that place them in a category, reflecting an attitude that they are things, not people. Sometimes people with and without disabilities are referred to as *them* and *us.* This distinction portrays an attitude that we are opposites; we are focusing on differences rather than similarities. The language that we choose to use is a mirror of our attitudes toward people with disabilities. Stereotypes or inaccurate reflections can create tension and lead to significant barriers for those with disabilities.

Influence of Laws on Attitudes

Chapter 14 discusses legal and political issues as they relate to therapeutic recreation. Here we will explore the influence of laws related to people with disabilities and attitudes toward those people. Clearly, the law enacted in the past 25 years that had the greatest effect on society as a whole as related to people with disabilities has been the Americans with Disabilities Act (ADA). This law requires private and public organizations to include people with disabilities in all aspects of services provided and amenities offered and to provide full and equal access to all services and programs.

Another law that has influenced services as well as attitudes is the Individuals with Disabilities Education Act (IDEA), which mandates that all children with disabilities have access to free and appropriate public education. Although laws mandate what recreation organizations and others can and cannot do when providing goods and services to people with disabilities, laws cannot mandate attitudes. Since the passage of the ADA and IDEA, an entire generation is growing up in nonsegregated classrooms. The expectation of those with disabilities in this generation is to be included in all aspects of daily life, including recreation opportunities. An important question remains: What is the attitudinal response by society to the laws that govern goods, services, and programs and to the expectations of the next generation of people with disabilities regarding inclusion in community life?

Supporters and critics of the ADA appear to agree that since the adoption of this law, attitudes toward people with disabilities have advanced in some areas but regressed in others. The legal nature of providing services to people with disabilities is one concern. Specifically, the idea of being mandated or required by law to make changes and provide services to a statistically small percentage of the population has left some feeling resentful. They believe that providing equal access is extremely costly and more trouble than it is worth. But research has shown that people with disabilities are among the most discriminated groups of people in our society (Burgstahler & Doe, 2006). Service providers face complications in complying with the ADA. In fact, some recreation service providers have felt unprepared to accomplish some of the more complex tasks related to meeting the mandates of the ADA, leaving them with a negative attitude toward the law (Devine & McGovern, 2001).

On the other hand, some feel that the ADA has empowered people with disabilities to seek a variety of recreation options and to request inclusion in community life. Therapeutic recreation specialists have found that the law provides specific parameters for service provision, eliminating the guesswork of how to include people with

© Vegas Adaptive Recreation

Inclusion maximizes the potential growth opportunities that leisure can provide.

disabilities in their communities. Although the jury may be out on specific influences on attitudes toward people with disabilities because of the ADA and IDEA, one way to judge the current attitude of society is through people's behavior.

Behaviors are observable and measurable acts or responses by people, and these actions tend to reflect attitudes. Historically, behaviors toward people with disabilities occurred in the form of stereotyping, discrimination, stigmatizing, segregation, and inaccessibility, to name a few. Earlier in this chapter, stigma and stereotypes were mentioned as being the opposite of a person-first philosophy. Behaviors can also reflect negative attitudes toward people with disabilities. One hope that people with disabilities had about the ADA and other laws was that they would feel less stigmatized and negatively stereotyped. Although attitudes cannot be subject to laws, behavior can. Thus, behaviors that may reflect negative attitudes, such as discrimination in recreation access, building of inaccessible parks, and segregation of people with disabilities in sport activities, can be subject to scrutiny under the ADA. By challenging stereotypes that may lead to segregation, the law can reshape people's attitudes. For example, the ADA mandates access to equal benefits of recreation participation. If people with disabilities have access to sport competition, then the belief that they cannot be athletes may change.

Service Delivery

Therapeutic recreation has viewed people with disabilities in various ways over the history of the field. In the early years, therapeutic recreation took a social reform perspective where recreation was used to keep children who lived in poor and often unhealthy environments off the streets (Duncan, 1991). Over the years we have used medical, social, and ecological models or perspectives, all which recognize and celebrate differences. Although therapeutic recreation has viewed disability with multiple models, the major ones are the medical model, the social model, and the ecological model.

Medical Model

The **medical model of disability** views disability as a variation from the physical norm that can disadvantage the person physically and in quality of life (Koch, 2001). This model of disability is based on a number of assumptions. One assumption is that disability is a physical condition in that something is physically different about a person as compared with the norm. This physical condition is less desirable than the norm and can be treated or changed through medical or therapeutic intervention. This model applies the idea that it is the responsibility of society to use resources, such as therapies, to try to cure

OUTSTANDING PROFESSIONAL

DAVID DONALDSON

Background Information

Education
*Emphasis in Recreation Therapy, Department of Recreation, Parks, and Tourism *MS in Rehabilitation Counseling

Career Information

Position
Recreation therapist for the Comprehensive Combat Casualty Care Center at the Naval Medical Center in San Diego, California

Job Description
Serve patients who have experienced amputations or traumatic brain injuries while serving in Iraq or Afghanistan

Career Path
I completed my academic work after a 20-year career as a Navy Hospital Corpsman (medic) and a physical therapy technician. I have worked and volunteered in a variety of clinical and community recreation settings, but my real passion has always been providing therapeutic recreation services to our military personnel. My military experience and my preparation in recreation therapy gives me a special ability to relate to the soldiers and sailors serving in our armed forces.

disabilities, with the medical profession having the greatest responsibility (Devine & Sylvester, 2005). In addition, services received by people with disabilities must be prescribed by someone in a medically authoritative position. This model regards all services received by people with disabilities, including recreation participation, as therapy (Wehman, 2001). Barriers experienced by people with disabilities arise from individual functional limitations resulting from disability instead of social factors that limit individuals (Fine & Asch, 1988; Oliver, 1996).

Therapeutic recreation has applied this perspective in the treatment and functional improvement components of our service delivery models. The focus is on the illness or disability of the person to address limitations in coordination, endurance, mobility, strength, hand–eye coordination, emotional or social functioning, and cognitive limitations as well as sensory limitations. With this model, recreation is used in a prescriptive way to correct or improve negative effects of a disability.

Social Model

The **social model of disability** views disability as a result of social discrimination toward people who are different from the norm. Rather than being a problem with the individual, disability occurs when society does not accommodate physical, cognitive, social, or emotional differences (Koch, 2001). Society has prescribed a set of standards for and values of functional independence, capabilities, and social reciprocity. When people cannot function at those standards or when they have a biological composition below those standards, they are assumed inferior and are subject to social exclusion (Allen & Allen, 1995; Bogdan & Taylor, 1992; Hahn, 1988). For example, the fact that a person uses a wheelchair to ambulate tells little about his or her physical condition, but it offers a great deal of information about how buildings, curbs, and parks are designed and built to exclude people who use this equipment. As such, disability or handicaps arise out of society's failure to accommodate its members who have impairments.

Therapeutic recreation has long embraced the role of being advocates for the rights of people with disabilities. Advocacy involves commitment to a cause, taking risks, and challenging norms (Wolfensberger, 1977). This role reflects the social model of disability. Therapeutic recreation service models provide guidelines through leisure education services in promoting the teaching of skills and accessing of community resources. Some service models have embraced the social model of disability by viewing a person with a disability as someone who could have an active healthy lifestyle (see chapter 5) (Stumbo & Peterson, 2004; Wilhite, Keller & Caldwell, 1999).

Ecological Model

The **ecological model of disability** is based on the idea that people and their environments are interconnected. That is, reciprocity and interaction occur among systems within which we live (Howe-Murphy & Charboneau, 1987). Systems can be defined as social organizations (e.g., family, schools, religious affiliations, society) that people interact with directly and indirectly. The ecological model asserts that if a change occurs within the community, the change will affect not only that system but also individuals, directly or indirectly. In addition, if something occurs to an individual, a reciprocal influence will occur in another system (e.g., family). For instance, when the ADA was written into federal law, the change affected state and local governments, communities, families, and individuals with disabilities. On the other hand, when a person acquires a disability, this event affects his or her family, the school system, and the community by virtue of the person's changing needs.

Evidence of the ecological model can be seen in therapeutic recreation services. For instance, when a therapeutic recreation specialist consults a patient's family members, schoolteachers or employers, or other members of a therapy team, or surveys the person's home and community environment when composing a discharge plan, then he or she is applying the ecological model. Some of the service delivery models have included this perspective by taking a person's life course (where a person is in his or her life span) into consideration when providing services and evaluating the parts of services and needs in the person's life (Wilhite, Keller & Caldwell, 1999).

Summary

Sadly, society in general has been slow to respond to the rights of people with disabilities to participate actively in all that communities have to offer. By embracing person-first philosophies, being aware of our role as change agents, and knowing the various models of disabilities, therapeutic recreation professionals can become more informed and competent as practitioners. Person-first philosophy not only provides a framework from which to influence societal attitudes but also serves as an internal compass that helps professionals keep sight of the true potential of every client.

DISCUSSION QUESTIONS

1. How can labels be detrimental to people with disabilities?

2. What characteristics legally constitute a person with a disability according to the ADA?

3. A foundation of person-first philosophy is the belief that each person is unique and that his or her uniqueness is a positive attribute, not a negative one. In your own words, describe what this means.

4. In what ways is social inclusion an important component of recreation participation for individuals with disabilities?

5. Identify and discuss the two primary components of a least restrictive environment.

6. In the story of Phoebe, you learned of two ways to make her environment least restrictive. Identify other ways that would reduce the restrictiveness of her environment.

7. What suggestions can you provide that could foster a positive attitude toward Phoebe's participation in her community?

8. What effect have the ADA and IDEA had on the inclusion of people with disabilities in community life?

9. How does the social model of disability differ from the medical model of disability?

Places, Models, and Modalities of Practice

Richard Williams, EdD, CTRS
East Carolina University

LEARNING OUTCOMES

After completing this chapter, learners will be able to demonstrate the following competencies:

- Identify potential places of practice for therapeutic recreation professionals
- Describe elements of predominant models of practice
- Identify philosophical differences and similarities across such models
- Identify conceptual differences and similarities across such models
- Identify commonly used therapeutic recreation modalities
- Identify potential applications of various modalities within specific client populations

A tremendous variety of services and programs can be accurately labeled therapeutic recreation. Diverse programs such as animal-assisted therapy, adaptive sports, and reminiscence therapy are made available to an equally diverse range of clients in just about every conceivable human-services setting. To make matters even more complex, therapeutic recreation specialists use several different service delivery models in the planning, organization, and delivery of their services. Although entire books could be devoted to a single piece of this rich tapestry of settings, practice models, and service modalities, this chapter was written broadly to help students learn some fundamental distinctions between these elements of the profession.

Settings

Therapeutic recreation specialists can be found practicing in a wide variety of service settings. Despite this variety, most therapeutic recreation specialists work in either a hospital or a nursing home. According to the National Council for Therapeutic Recreation Certification (NCTRC, n.d.), 41.6% of certified therapeutic recreation specialists (CTRSs) work in hospitals and an additional 19.3% work in nursing homes. The remaining 39.1% work in one of the many other settings that offer therapeutic recreation services including community parks and recreation departments, residential facilities, schools, and corrections facilities. This section contains general descriptions of several of the more common settings where therapeutic recreation specialists offer services, but it is important to remember that therapeutic recreation is practiced in many other places other than those described here.

Hospitals

According to the American Hospital Association (2005), there are 5,764 hospitals in the United States. The type of hospital that is most familiar to many people is the **acute care hospital.** This type of facility offers many different health care services, typically focusing on short-term care for serious health concerns. Increasingly, patients remain in acute care only long enough to become medically stable, after which they receive treatment through **outpatient services.** Typically, acute care hospitals offer both inpatient and outpatient psychiatric

care. In addition, freestanding psychiatric hospitals offer inpatient and outpatient care. Similarly, although acute care hospitals often offer inpatient and outpatient physical rehabilitation services, there are also freestanding **rehabilitation hospitals.**

ACUTE CARE HOSPITALS

Acute care hospitals are so named because their primary mission is to treat acute conditions, that is, conditions (e.g., injuries, severe illnesses) that require immediate medical attention. These hospitals vary greatly in size and scope of services offered. For example, some large urban hospitals encompass several city blocks and are housed in skyscrapers, whereas many smaller community hospitals are single-story buildings that offer a limited range of services. A teaching hospital is an acute care hospital associated with a medical school that includes in its mission the training of medical personnel.

The expense of providing health care in acute care hospitals has grown tremendously in recent decades. As a result, the average length of time that a patient stays in the hospital has dropped to an average of 4.8 days (National Center for Health Statistics, 2005). With such short stays, health care providers often begin discharge planning for patients as soon as they are admitted to the hospital. Because of the relatively short length of stay, many therapeutic recreation specialists in acute care settings will see some clients only long enough to conduct an initial assessment and to recommend outpatient and follow-up services. Patients with more critical conditions will have longer lengths of stay, providing increased opportunities for therapeutic recreation specialists to provide inpatient treatment before discharge.

Because patients in acute care hospitals present a variety of medical conditions, therapeutic recreation specialists must provide an equally large variety of services. Some of the more common therapeutic recreation services offered in acute care hospitals include general physical rehabilitation (often co-treating with occupational and physical therapists), aquatic therapy, community reorientation outings, community skills development, patient education, fitness education, and teaching stress and coping skills. Depending on their diagnoses, patients are commonly referred to longer-term treatment through outpatient services. Alternately, patients may be referred to long-term treatment in a specialty hospital (e.g., psychiatric hospital, rehabilitation hospital).

OUTPATIENT CARE

Often an acute care hospital will offer both inpatient and outpatient therapeutic recreation services. The advantages of outpatient services for clients are primarily the cost savings and the comfort of living at home. Therapeutic recreation specialists and other health providers appreciate outpatient services because these services allow longer-term access to clients, thus facilitating greater client progress. Outpatient program offerings typically coincide with inpatient offerings and are determined by the needs of the clients. For instance, a therapeutic recreation specialist who provides physical rehabilitation services on an inpatient basis may move clients to an outpatient adaptive sports skills development program.

PSYCHIATRIC CARE

Traditionally, a significant proportion of therapeutic recreation specialists have provided psychiatric care, and this trend continues today. According to the NCTRC (n.d.), 34.2% of all CTRSs provide services to clients receiving psychiatric care. Kinney, Kinney, and Witman (2004) reported that 32% of therapeutic recreation specialists primarily serve people with mental health care needs. These services are offered in both psychiatric units of acute care hospitals and freestanding psychiatric hospitals. The American Hospital Association recognizes 477 registered nonfederal psychiatric hospitals in the United States (American Hospital Association, 2005). This number does not include psychiatric services offered through acute care hospitals or through other facilities such as Veterans Administration hospitals.

Many therapeutic recreation specialists who work in psychiatric facilities are members of treatment teams that include other health care personnel such as psychiatrists, psychologists, nurses, occupational therapists, and social workers. Members of a treatment team work together with clients to achieve therapeutic goals related to individual diagnoses. To help clients reach their goals, therapeutic recreation specialists in psychiatric settings offer programs such as (a) expressive arts including art, crafts, and music; (b) stress and coping skill development; (c) behavior management skills; and (d) physical fitness.

The most common source for psychiatric diagnoses is the *Diagnostic and Statistical Manual (DSM)* of the American Psychiatric Association, which details the symptoms of an enormous variety of psychiatric conditions. Two of the most common reasons that people seek psychiatric treatment are (a) mood disorders such as various forms of depression and bipolar disorder and (b) anxiety disorders such as generalized anxiety disorder, phobias, and obsessive-compulsive disorder.

Besides working with those who have mood and anxiety disorders, therapeutic recreation specialists often work with clients who have personality disorders that coincide with other conditions. Personality disorders are generally understood to be entrenched beliefs and behavior patterns that render people relatively inflexible in their dealings with other people and with changes in their environments. Examples of personality disorders include antisocial personality disorder, borderline personality disorder, and avoidant personality disorder.

Although not as common as the psychiatric conditions discussed so far, schizophrenia is a serious disorder characterized by symptoms such as delusional and disorganized thinking and hallucinations. Although people may go years without treatment for many disorders, schizophrenic symptoms are often serious enough to warrant hospitalization.

Clients from Madonna Rehabilitation in Lincoln, Nebraska, take part in an out-patient golf clinic at their state-of-the-art and all-accessible community fitness center. This center is designed to close the gap between inpatient care and home life.

Most people who receive psychiatric care and psychological counseling do so on an outpatient basis, but acute cases can require hospitalization. According to the American Psychiatric Association (2005b), people are not hospitalized when they can benefit from services offered in a less restrictive environment. Additionally, a large percentage (88%) of adults receiving inpatient psychiatric care were admitted to the hospital voluntarily (Association Task Force on Consent to Voluntary Hospitalization, 1992). Involuntary hospitalization may be necessary in extreme circumstances, but states have instituted procedures designed to protect the rights of patients (American Psychiatric Association). Hospitalization (both voluntary and involuntary) often follows an incident such as a suicide attempt or a psychotic episode.

REHABILITATION HOSPITAL

Freestanding physical rehabilitation hospitals also offer inpatient and outpatient physical rehabilitation services. These facilities specialize in the long-term rehabilitation of people with acquired disabilities that often result from a trauma such as a stroke or accident. Typically people who have experienced a serious injury first receive treatment in an acute care facility before transferring to a rehabilitation facility.

Therapeutic recreation specialists who work in rehabilitation hospitals use treatment modalities such as aquatic therapy and community outings to help clients regain skills and develop new skills. Quite often, therapeutic recreation specialists in these facilities provide cotreatment, working closely with occupational therapists, physical therapists, and others in the delivery of services.

Nursing Homes

The average life span of Americans continues to increase because of a number of factors including improved medical care, reductions in infant mortality, and safer workplaces. In 1900 the average life expectancy of Americans was about 45 years. By 2000 life expectancy had grown to 78 years for men and 84 for women. Consequently, the number of older adults is much larger than it used to be. More than 70,000 Americans are older than 100, and this number is expected to grow rapidly in the coming decades. Although there have always been unconfirmed reports of extremely old people, the oldest person with reliable birth records was Jeanne-Louise Calment, a French woman who died in 1997 at 122 years old (see the sidebar "Oldest Living Person").

As the population ages, demand for therapeutic recreation specialists in facilities offering services to older adults will likely increase (U.S. Department of Labor, Bureau of Labor Statistics, 2005). The types of services offered to older adults by therapeutic recreation specialists will vary according to the needs of clients and the type of facility where the services are offered. **Long-term care facilities** are generally classified according to the level of care that they provide to their residents. Although there are different ways of defining and classifying the various types of long-term care options, the Centers for Medicare and Medicaid Glossary (n.d.) categorizes facilities for older adults in the following way:

- Nursing home: "A residence that provides a room, meals, and help with activities of daily living and recreation. Generally, nursing home residents have physical or mental problems that keep them from living on their own. They usually require daily assistance."

- Long-term care: "A variety of services that help people with health or personal needs and activities of daily living over a period of time. Long-term care can be provided at home, in the community, or in various types of facilities, including nursing homes and assisted-living facilities. Most long-term care is custodial care."

OLDEST LIVING PERSON

Jeanne-Louise Calment was 122 years old when she died in a nursing home in France in 1997. Remarkably, she smoked until she was 119, quitting only because she had lost her vision and was too proud to have others light her cigarettes for her. After her death, CNN reported, "Calment credited her longevity to Port wine, a diet rich in olive oil, and her sense of humor. 'I will die laughing,' she predicted." According to *Guinness World Records* (2005), Ms. Calment learned the sport of fencing at age 85, continued riding her bicycle until she turned 100, and even starred as herself in a movie at 114.

- Skilled-nursing facility: "A facility (which meets specific regulatory certification requirements) which primarily provides inpatient skilled-nursing care and related services to patients who require medical, nursing, or rehabilitative services but does not provide the level of care or treatment available in a hospital."

- Custodial care facility: "A facility which provides room, board, and other personal assistance services, generally on a long-term basis and which does not include a medical component."

Because therapeutic recreation specialists in long-term care facilities have extensive contact with clients, they have the opportunity to develop deep and meaningful therapeutic relationships. With such extensive contact, these therapeutic recreation specialists are ideally suited to help their clients lead more meaningful and happier lives.

Municipal Therapeutic Recreation Settings

By this point, readers should be well aware that the Americans with Disabilities Act requires that recreation facilities provide services to persons with disabilities in the least restrictive environment. To ensure that this requirement is fulfilled, **municipal therapeutic recreation settings** are becoming more common. Municipal parks and recreation agencies are hiring therapeutic recreation specialists to work as inclusion specialists or to work with adapted recreation programs. Some municipal agencies even provide community-based support services for people who are reintegrating into the community following hospitalization. The gap between community and clinical setting is shrinking every day, as rehabilitation centers begin to sponsor and organize community-based programs. For example, Madonna Rehabilitation Center in Lincoln, Nebraska, opened the Madonna ProActive in 2005, which is intended to provide health, fitness, and wellness services to persons with disabilities and the general community.

Other Settings

Several less common but equally valuable service settings exist in therapeutic recreation. These settings include correctional facilities, camp settings, wilderness therapy settings, and schools. Some therapeutic recreation professionals maintain a private practice and provide assistance with issues ranging from accessibility to program development. As long as the professional practices therapeutic recreation in line with standards of practice, models, processes, and modalities associated with therapeutic recreation, virtually any setting that serves people with illnesses and disabilities is a potential home for a CTRS.

Practice Models

Models of therapeutic recreation practice are designed to provide frameworks for the delivery of services and for conducting research (Carruthers, Hawkins & Voelkl, 1998). As described by Austin (1998), practice models "provide specific frames of reference to describe and direct professional practice" (p. 109). Starting in the late 1970s, numerous models have been proposed, and therapeutic recreation specialists continue to use several different models and individual adaptations of models.

With little question, most discussions of therapeutic recreation practice models begin with the **leisure ability model**, identified not immodestly as "one of the oldest, most widely used, and most often critiqued therapeutic recreation practice models" (Stumbo & Peterson, 1998, p. 82). The leisure ability model has had a lasting and deep influence on the profession and has served as a "guiding force for therapeutic recreation and has fostered most needed consistency" (Yaffe, 1998, p. 103), yet the model seems to have nearly as many critics as it does adherents.

Although the leisure ability model has received the majority of attention and criticism, no therapeutic recreation practice model has been described that satisfies the needs of all therapeutic recreation practitioners. Part of the difficulty of identifying a satisfactory practice model lies in the struggle to "wed therapeutic outcomes to leisure without losing the essence of the leisure experience" (Mobily, 1999, pp. 176–177). The field has always faced difficulty in describing the often-quixotic benefits of leisure with the practical demands of reimbursable health care provision.

In an ongoing effort to refine the organization of services and research and to address perceived limitations of the leisure ability model, scholars have proposed and debated numerous additional service delivery models. Austin (1997) described the **health protection–health promotion model** in an effort to align therapeutic recreation practice more specifically with health and health care delivery than the services described in the leisure ability model. More recently, Burlingame (1998) proposed the **recreation service model** in an effort to align therapeutic recreation practice with the World Health Organization's suggested practice model.

Leisure Ability Model

The leisure ability model has been described in numerous publications, perhaps most fully in Peterson and Gunn's (1984) *Therapeutic Recreation Program Design*. More recently Stumbo and Peterson (1998) presented an updated explanation of the theoretical foundations of the model, yet the essential elements of the model have remained unchanged through the years.

For therapists who use the leisure ability model, the ultimate goal of therapeutic recreation is "improved independent and satisfying leisure functioning, also referred to as a 'leisure lifestyle'" (Stumbo & Peterson, 1998, p. 83). According to Peterson and Gunn (1984), a leisure lifestyle is "the day-to-day behavioral expression of one's leisure related attitudes, awareness, and activities revealed within the context and composite of the total life experience" (p. 83). The model organizes therapeutic recreation services into three components: (a) functional intervention (b) leisure education, and (c) recreation participation. Depending on individual needs, clients might be engaged in only one or as many as three of the components concurrently.

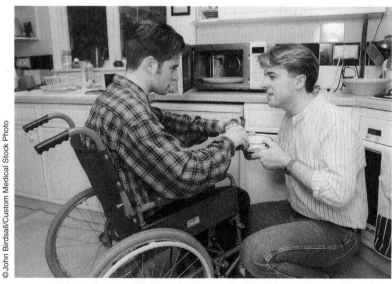

Functional deficits related to memory, strength, and coordination make it difficult for this patient with a traumatic brain injury to prepare an evening snack.

FUNCTIONAL INTERVENTION

Therapeutic recreation services delivered in the **functional intervention (FI)** component focus on correcting functional deficits related to leisure-related activity in the physical, mental, emotional, and social domains. The general goal of FI services is the elimination of, improvement in, or adaptation to functional deficits that constrain participation in leisure. During FI, the therapeutic recreation specialist maintains a high level of control (e.g., assigning clients to programs), while client behavior is relatively constrained, dependent, and motivated by extrinsic rewards.

LEISURE EDUCATION

Therapeutic recreation services delivered in the leisure education component focus on helping clients acquire "leisure-related attitudes, knowledge, and skills" (Stumbo & Peterson, 1998, p. 89) and are organized into four subcomponents: leisure awareness, social skills, leisure activity skills, and leisure resources. A therapeutic recreation specialist who uses the leisure ability model might offer a single leisure education program that addresses the concerns of the four components of leisure education, or separate leisure education programs may address those four items. Generally, the goal of leisure education services is to help clients understand the importance of leisure and learn ways to participate successfully in leisure. Although therapeutic recreation specialists maintain some control during leisure education services and assume the roles of instructor, advisor, and counselor, clients have opportunities for choice and experience more freedom than they do during treatment services.

RECREATION PARTICIPATION

The final component of the leisure ability model is recreation participation. Therapeutic recreation services delivered within this component are "structured activities that allow the client to practice newly acquired skills, and/or experience enjoyment and self-expression" (Stumbo & Peterson, 1998, p. 91). During these services, client behavior is intrinsically motivated, and therapeutic recreation specialists exert relatively little control beyond acting as facilitators.

USING THE LEISURE ABILITY MODEL WITH MR. NELSON

Mr. Nelson was an 82-year-old man living in a skilled-nursing facility. His wife died 5 years ago, and after living independently in his home for 2 years, he began to experience symptoms of Alzheimer's disease. As his cognitive symptoms grew progressively more pronounced, Mr. Nelson had an increasingly difficult time caring for himself, and he recently agreed with his adult son and daughter-in-law that he should move into Tall Oaks Center, a long-term-care facility in his hometown. Marcy, a CTRS at Tall Oaks, consulted Mr. Nelson's chart and then met with him to perform an assessment. After her assessment, Marcy and Mr. Nelson met to set goals and then chose several therapeutic recreation programs for him to attend that would help him address his goals. Most of Mr. Nelson's goals centered on maintenance of existing skills.

Functional Intervention

Because Mr. Nelson had experienced cognitive declines, Marcy recommended that he attend reality orientation sessions each morning following breakfast. In these sessions, residents and staff members sit around a large table and discuss the date, season, weather, and items in the news. Newspapers and news magazines are made available to the clients, and a large chalkboard with current information helps cue clients. Additionally, because Mr. Nelson had gained a substantial amount of weight since the loss of his wife, Marcy recommended a low-impact exercise class to help him control his weight.

Leisure Education

Mr. Nelson's son and daughter-in-law came for occasional visits, but otherwise he was socially isolated. To help him gain social support through other residents of Tall Oaks, Marcy recommended that Mr. Nelson attend a program called Circle of Friends, a daily support group facilitated by staff members and residents. Additionally, Mr. Nelson began to participate actively in the many community outings offered by Marcy and the other CTRSs. Both programs helped Mr. Nelson become more socially involved and prevented isolation.

Recreation Participation

As a child Mr. Nelson lived on a farm, and he and his wife were avid gardeners. Since his wife's death, Mr. Nelson had quit gardening, but when Marcy told him about the Tall Oaks residents' garden and small greenhouse, he immediately expressed interest in helping with the garden. Additionally, Mr. Nelson enjoyed attending occasional special events put on by the therapeutic recreation staff and others.

Health Protection–Health Promotion Model

Drawing on theories related to humanism, wellness, and self-actualization, Austin (1997) designed the health protection–health promotion (HP–HP) model. According to Austin (1998), for those practitioners using the model, the goals of therapeutic recreation services are to assist clients "to recover following threats to health (health protection) and to achieve as high a level of health as possible (health promotion)" (p. 110). With its focus on health, the HP–HP model has been described as more in line with the goals of modern health care than the leisure ability model is (Ross, 1998). But the HP–HP model is similar in structure to the leisure ability model in that it organizes therapeutic recreation services into three components: (a) prescriptive activities, (b) recreation, and (c) health.

PRESCRIPTIVE ACTIVITIES

According to Austin (1998), "When clients initially encounter illnesses or disorders, often they become self-absorbed. They have a tendency to withdraw from their usual life activities and to experience a loss of control over their lives" (p. 112). Thus, therapeutic recreation specialists may have to prescribe activities that will help clients regain control of their lives and begin progressing toward health and actualization. The therapeutic recreation specialist largely directs activity during this component, and one of the main goals of treatment is simply to help clients stabilize.

RECREATION

As clients gain stability, begin to assume some control, and move toward health and actualization, they move into the recreation component of the HP–HP model. Relying on the naturally restorative powers of recreation, therapeutic recreation specialists provide opportunities to gain valuable skills, knowledge, and values. As clients become healthier and more actualized, they take more control over their lives and their health.

LEISURE

The first two components of the HP–HP model focus on health protection, but the third component focuses on health promotion. Through engagement in leisure, clients have the opportunity to become self-determined and ultimately self-actualized. After threats to health have been largely eliminated in the first two components of the model, the third component provides the opportunity for clients to become healthier and begin reaching their potential.

Recreation Service Model

Burlingame (1998) based the design of the recreation service model on a comprehensive model of health care service proposed by the World Health Organization (WHO). As such, the recreation service model represents an attempt to integrate therapeutic recreation services into the wider system of health care delivery. Rather than organizing therapeutic recreation services into domains, the recreation service model mirrors the WHO's organization of services into levels of care.

The WHO model describes four levels of care: (a) disease, (b) impairment, (c) disability, and (d) handicap. According to Burlingame (1998), "Each level has its own definition of the scope of disease/trauma contained within that level, character of the types of treatment provided within that level, codes to use for billing and research, as well as descriptions of qualities required of the testing tools and treatment protocols used" (p. 87). Thus, the descriptions contained within each level serve as a guide for health care practitioners.

The recreation service model describes each of the levels of the WHO model within the context of therapeutic recreation services, and it adds three additional levels: education, organized recreation services, and independent activities. According to Burlingame (1998), the recreation service model "provides the therapist with a taxonomy which organizes practice into a scientific model" (p. 95) that matches therapeutic recreation assessments and interventions into criteria pre-established by the health care community.

All three models presented offer structure and guidance for therapeutic recreation specialists when working to provide the best services for clients. Often the choice of model reflects the mission of the agency, characteristics of clients served, and personal philosophy. In addition, specialists may choose different elements from a variety of models. Although no consensus about a service model for the field has been reached, all high-quality therapeutic recreation services are organized to respond efficiently to the specific needs of individual clients.

Therapeutic Recreation Treatment Modalities

Therapeutic recreation specialists use the term **treatment modality** to describe recreation or other activities used to help clients meet therapeutic goals (Austin, 2001). Considering the wide variety of settings in which therapeutic recreation is practiced and the equally broad spectrum of desired client outcomes, therapeutic recreation specialists must become proficient in using many different interventions.

Kinney, Kinney, and Witman (2004) conducted a nationwide survey of therapeutic recreation specialists and identified the most common treatment modalities across settings and populations. In order, the most common modalities reported were (1) games, (2) exercise, (3) parties, (4) arts and crafts, (5) community reintegration activities, (6) music, (7) problem-solving activities, (8) sports, (9) self-esteem, and (10) activities of daily living. The authors also reported the most common activities used by population (see table 5.1). Besides these frequently used modalities, many other equally useful therapeutic activities are available to therapeutic recreation specialists. This chapter reviews some of the more common modalities, and later chapters will present modalities viewed as especially useful for particular client populations or settings. In addition, table 5.2 presents a more comprehensive list of therapeutic recreation modalities. Within this table, modalities are arranged by "invention categories" developed by Shank and Coyle (2002). The suitability of any one of these methods will depend on the nature of the clientele and the targeted goal area. The therapeutic recreation specialist must identify potential modalities, ensure that they are appropriate for client goals, and implement them in a competent manner.

Table 5.1 Most Common TR Modalities by Population (Kinney et al., 2004)

Physical rehabilitation	Mental health	Older adults	Other populations
Community reintegration	Games	Music	Sports
Games	Self-esteem experiences	Parties	Community reintegration
Arts and crafts	Problem solving	Games	Games
Problem solving	Exercise	Exercise	Arts and crafts
Exercise	Arts and crafts	Arts and crafts	Parties/special events

Table 5.2 Examples of Modalities Falling Within Shank and Coyles' (2002) Intervention Categories

Modality (reading resources)	Modality category (Shank & Coyle, 2002)	Mechanism for change	Possible client populations or conditions	Possible client goal areas
Aquatics	Physical activity	Buoyancy, increased resistance, and water temperature facilitate participation and goal achievement.	Arthritis, cerebral palsy, multiple sclerosis, limb deficiencies	Learn to swim, strength, balance, endurance, physical activity
Exercise	Physical activity	Education and participation programs provided to clients	Senior populations, mood disorders, substance abuse, physical rehabilitation	Strength, mobility, endurance, and physical and psychological health
Sports	Physical activity	Skill development and organized sport programs	All disability groups, with opportunities for inclusive participation	Sport skills, psychomotor skills, self-concept social skills
Tai chi	Mind-body	Various styles utilize movement sequences for physical and mental development.	Senior populations, anxiety disorders, physical rehabilitation, intellectual disabilities	Balance, coordination, stress, anxiety, physical activity
Sensory stimulation	Mind-body	Senses stimulated with pleasurable or meaningful stimuli, such as home videos	Clients with limited or no responsiveness (coma) or with advanced dementia	Increased arousal and responsiveness to stimuli
Medical play	Mind-body	Play is used to help children cope with fears and anxieties about medical care.	Children receiving medical care	Educate child about his/her condition, reduce related fear and anxiety
Dance and movement	Creative-expressive	Utilizes physical, social, and emotional expression through dance	Intellectual disability, psychiatric care, physical disability	Social interaction, self expression, psychomotor skills

TABLE 5.2 CONTINUED

TABLE 5.2 CONTINUED

Modality (reading resources)	Modality category (Shank & Coyle, 2002)	Mechanism for change	Possible client populations or conditions	Possible client goal areas
Storytelling	Creative-expressive	Oral narratives read, created, and presented by clients as meaningful to personal goals	Family counseling, psychiatric care, coping with change, hardship, or abuse	Creativity, memory, social anxiety, self-expression
Arts and crafts	Creative-expressive	Clients are taught skills related to art or craft, both process and product applied to therapy goals	Substance abuse, physical disability, psychiatric care, intellectual disability	Self-expression, leisure skill development, self-efficacy, personal achievement
Adventure/ challenge	Self-expression and discovery	Adventure/challenge experiences are related to client goals.	Psychiatric care, substance abuse, victims of abuse, youth at risk	Courage, empowerment, problem solving, relationships
Reminiscence	Self-expression and discovery	Past memories evoked by prompts are discussed to reaffirm self-worth.	Late life transitions, terminal illness	Self-worth, dignity, come to terms with past life issues and mortality
Values clarification	Self-expression and discovery	Writing tasks, worksheets, and discussion of personal value system	Substance abuse, family counseling, career planning, youth and adult criminal offenders	Identify values and examine choices and actions in light of value system
Assertiveness training	Social skills	Group work built around games, role play, rehearsal	Intellectual disability, victims of abuse, family counseling	Social aggression, social passivity, self-advocacy
Anger management	Social skills	Thinking strategies are learned, rehearsed, and applied in social situations	Violent offenders, family counseling, various mental conditions	Expressing and coping with anger in acceptable manner
Reality orientation	Social skills	Environmental cues and verbal reminders used to reorient client	Disorientation from stroke, traumatic brain injury, or Alzheimer's disease	Reduce disorientation, confusion, and resulting distress
Animal-assisted therapy	Nature-based	Utilizes animals to enhance goal areas	Autism, orthopedic injury, depression	Depression, initiative, balance, coordination, personal care
Horticulture	Nature-based	Utilizes gardens/ plants to enhance goal areas	Stroke, traumatic brain injury, intellectual impairment	Endurance, coordination, concentration, planning, and decision making
Assistive technology training	Education-based	Education about assistive devices available to clients	Physical or communication-related disabilities of all types	Eliminate barriers to communication and participation
Community reintegration	Education-based	Education about and practice of activities in the community	Physical rehabilitation, psychiatric care, substance abuse	Identify resources and barriers, make adaptations, maximize participation

Games and Parties

Kinney et al. (2004) noted that although therapeutic recreation specialists commonly use games and parties, not all modalities need to be taught to therapeutic recreation students. Most games are relatively simple to learn, and therapeutic recreation students will have played many of them before enrolling in college. Instead, therapeutic recreation students could make better use of their time and tuition by learning about the therapeutic processes relevant to client change and the ways in which games and parties can activate or enhance such mechanisms. Furthermore, simply facilitating a game or planning a party does not fit within the scope of **active treatment.** To serve our clients in the best way possible, to be taken seriously as practitioners, and to gain access to the resources readily available to similar professionals (e.g., occupational therapists), therapeutic recreation specialists must be sure that the activities they use have measurable outcomes that address the therapeutic needs of clients.

To be sure, games can be used as an effective treatment modality, but therapeutic recreation specialists must be sure that therapeutic outcomes of a particular game can be clearly documented. For example, many educational games can be used to teach community skills such as the use of money. Additionally, therapeutic recreation specialists frequently adapt commercially available and familiar games (e.g., Jenga, Uno) to help clients reach therapeutic goals. For instance, children can learn colors and numbers playing Uno, and Jenga might be used to help people with a variety of disorders (e.g., attention-deficit/hyperactivity disorder) practice frustration tolerance, logical thinking, and social skills such as cooperation. As such, therapeutic recreation specialists should consider and choose games and parties based on their potential to affect client goals.

Community Reintegration Outings

Therapeutic recreation specialists and other health care practitioners frequently use community reintegration outings with clients who have acquired life-altering disabilities such as spinal cord injuries and with clients who have been institutionalized for a long period. As reported by Kinney et al. (2004), community reintegration outings were the most commonly used therapeutic recreation treatment modality in physical rehabilitation settings.

Typically, community reintegration outings are planned visits to local businesses (e.g., restaurants) and public facilities (e.g., museums, post office). The risk management issues associated with outings are too numerous to cover, but outings clearly require extensive planning to ensure the safety of clients. For instance, when facilitating such an outing, therapeutic recreation specialists must determine the appropriate ratio of health care personnel to clients, and they must recognize that this ratio will vary greatly depending on the nature of the outing and the characteristics of the clients.

The purposes of community reintegration outings include (a) reducing the stigma associated with an acquired disability, (b) practicing in a real-world setting the skills that have been learned in treatment, and (c) gaining familiarity with community resources. Surprisingly little research has been conducted into the effectiveness of community reintegration outings, but many therapeutic recreation specialists believe this modality to be an effective treatment option for a variety of clients including people with physical disabilities, people with addictions, people with psychiatric disabilities, and older adults.

Arts and Crafts

Participation in arts and crafts activities provides clients with opportunities for self-expression. Learning skills such as painting or needlework can lead to continued, meaningful participation in these activities outside treatment. For clients who are unable or unwilling to express themselves verbally, creative activities provide an important outlet. Manipulating paintbrushes, clay, and other art supplies can help clients develop fine motor skills. Additionally, successfully completing projects can contribute to the self-esteem, self-image, and overall psychological well-being of a client. From a practical perspective, many therapeutic recreation specialists value arts and crafts because the supplies needed are relatively inexpensive and easily stored, and the activities are often popular with clients.

Therapeutic recreation specialists can use group arts and crafts projects like murals to facilitate appropriate social skills such as sharing and teamwork. Although many group activities (e.g., sports, games) rely on competition that can cause undue tension among participants, group art projects often facilitate cooperation and prosocial communication.

HELENE M. FRENI-ROGERS

Background Information

Education
BA in Recreation Administration with an emphasis in Recreation Therapy from San Diego State University

Credentials
CTRS

Special Affiliations
*ATRA *NRPA-NTRS
*HAPT (Hawaii Association of Play Therapy)

Career Information

Position
Recreation Therapy Manager, Shriners Hospitals for Children-Honolulu

Organization Information
Shriners Hospitals for Children is a network of 22 hospitals throughout the United States that provide specialized medical care at no cost to children up to 18 years old. Shriners Hospitals for Children-Honolulu has provided free, world-class orthopedic care to children from Hawaii and the Pacific Basin since 1923. The hospital is supported by the Shriners fraternal organization and by donations from the people of Hawaii. At Shriners Hospitals for Children-Honolulu, expert orthopedic medical care is combined with outstanding teaching and research programs. Shriners Hospitals are among the very best children's hospitals in the world.

Job Description
Work directly with pediatric patients who come to the hospital for various orthopedic conditions. Work with the kids individually and in groups following their surgery to assess and involve them in a wide variety of treatment options. Manage the department, which includes program planning and coordinating with other departments. Plan many fun and exciting special events involving the entire hospital that allow the children to work on their rehabilitation, relaxation, pain management, self-esteem building, developmental stimulation, and leisure skill building, and become more independent.

Career Path
I started out at Sharp Memorial Rehabilitation Center in San Diego, California and had various jobs in between, including mental health and geriatrics. I initially worked on-call at Shriners Hospitals and then quickly realized that my true passion was to work with children. Luckily they had a full-time position open and I gladly accepted it. All the different populations that I've worked with have given me the exposure to appreciate each individual's needs, thus teaching me to be a better recreation therapist today.

Likes and Dislikes About the Job
I absolutely, with no doubt, love working with the kids. They have tons of energy and such a positive outlook on life. They really don't focus on their disability, but rather they focus on what they can do. I just feel lucky to be a part of helping them achieve their goals. I can honestly say that my job is a lot of fun. We're a small hospital, where everyone is part of our "ohana" (family in Hawaiian). When we plan our big special events, everyone gets involved, even our administrators and physicians. It's obvious that people here have the same goal in mind, to help our keiki (children).

Advice to Undergraduate Students
Take the time to volunteer in a variety of settings and then find an internship with the population that you love. This way you'll have experience in finding the job of your dreams. Believe that you can make a difference if you put your heart and soul into it. I believe that we have to practice what we preach, and in our field we have the privilege to do so. It's very rewarding to be able to see that what you do for patients while they are in your facility can make a difference in their lives. I believe that we have to give 110%. I aim to make every event, activity, outing, or treatment plan something that will make people say, "Wow!" This way I know that I did my best and only hope that it will impact a patient in a positive way.

> Pain is temporary, quitting lasts forever.
>
> Lance Armstrong

Self-Esteem Activities

Therapeutic recreation specialists use a variety of programs to facilitate enhanced self-esteem and self-image of clients. Almost any recreation activity that provides the opportunity for success and self-exploration can be used to address goals related to self-esteem. Clients often list self-esteem as a goal without the proper context. Remember that people develop a positive opinion about themselves when they have accomplished something. Poor self-esteem results from failure. Thus, to facilitate self-esteem, therapeutic recreation specialists must create programs that provide an opportunity for clients to succeed. Dattilo (2002) and others have pointed to the need to provide alternatives to competitive activities such as sports and winner-take-all games, and cooperative activities are particularly effective at helping clients develop positive self-esteem.

Adventure programming entails many types of cooperative activities that therapeutic recreation specialists and others have successfully used to promote self-esteem. These activities include wilderness activities such as camping, rafting, and hiking. Other activities within this category include challenge courses, also sometimes called ropes courses. Therapeutic recreation specialists structure these activities so that clients must depend on and cooperate with one another to succeed in progressively more difficult tasks. As the group meets with success, people gain confidence, and ultimately, their self-esteem increases.

Exercise

Considering the well-documented physical and psychological benefits of exercise for practically all people, it is no surprise that therapeutic recreation specialists identify exercise as a common treatment modality for a variety of clients (Kinney et al., 2004). Benefits of exercise include improved cardiovascular fitness, improved strength, increased bone density, decreased incidence of connective tissue disorders (e.g., arthritis), and improved mood.

©Vegas Adaptive Recreation

Adventure programs involve the use of physical and mental challenges, both man-made and natural.

Despite the benefits, many therapeutic recreation clients are hesitant to engage in exercise for a variety of reasons. For instance, people from different generations and cultures have different beliefs about appropriate behavior. Although practically no population could reap more benefits from resistance training than older women because of its positive effects on bone density, connective tissue, and muscle mass, some older women resist such exercise because they were reared at a time when many forms of exercise were considered unladylike. Other clients may resist engagement in exercise because of unhealthy body images or unpleasant past experience with exercise. Therapeutic recreation specialists must help clients understand the benefits of exercise and use some creativity to help clients find a form of exercise that they can enjoy. Although an older female client may not enjoy lifting weights, she may enjoy other activities that can provide similar benefits such as a water aerobics class or gardening. As with any strenuous activity, therapeutic recreation specialists should carefully consider any medical or other restrictions that a client may have.

For clients with physical disabilities, adaptive sports are a common and effective intervention used by therapeutic recreation specialists. Clients who commonly receive physical rehabilitation are young people who have acquired a disability such as a spinal cord injury. Adaptive sports such as wheelchair basketball, wheelchair tennis, or quad rugby offer the opportunity for clients to engage in physical activities that may have been an important part of their lives before they acquired their disability. Almost any sport can be an adaptive sport. Although the list is far from complete, people with disabilities commonly engage in adaptations of the following sports: snow skiing, water skiing, rock climbing, horseback riding, golf, tennis, basketball, rugby, scuba diving, archery, and even hunting. Therapeutic recreation specialists must consider the interests and abilities of clients when programming adaptive sports and be creative to facilitate active participation (see chapter 13 for more information on exercise for people with disabilities).

Summary

Therapeutic recreation services are offered in many different types of facilities to a wide variety of clients. As a result, the programs offered by one therapeutic recreation specialist may not resemble (at least on the surface) the services offered by any other. Several therapeutic recreation service models, however, help therapeutic recreation specialists organize the various programs that they offer, and all high-quality therapeutic recreation programs have features in common. Perhaps most important, high-quality therapeutic recreation services are designed to provide active treatment based on the clinical needs of individual clients. The many excellent and exciting modalities available provide the opportunity for therapeutic recreation specialists to create programs that help clients gain knowledge, increase skills, and ultimately improve quality of life.

DISCUSSION QUESTIONS

1. Why have many different therapeutic recreation service models been proposed?

2. Which therapeutic recreation service model presented in this chapter appears to be the most useful?

3. In which therapeutic recreation setting would you most like to work?

4. With the large number of therapeutic recreation treatment options available, how does a therapeutic recreation specialist choose which interventions to use with her or his clients?

5. What is the difference between the implementation of a therapeutic recreation intervention such as arts and crafts and a client's choice to do a crafts project in her free time?

PART

Potential Areas
of Practice

The Therapeutic Recreation Process

Terry Long, PhD
Northwest Missouri State University

LEARNING OUTCOMES

After completing this chapter, learners will be able to demonstrate the following competencies:

- Identify the four parts of the therapeutic recreation process
- Identify basic assessment methods and potential applications of each
- Identify critical considerations for planning therapeutic recreation programs
- Competently conduct activity analysis, task analysis, and activity modification
- Differentiate between comprehensive program planning, specific program planning, and individualized client or session planning
- Identify planning and implementation considerations related to technical skills and counseling skills
- Identify and explain various aspects of briefing and debriefing therapeutic recreation-based experiences
- Identify techniques for and potential applications of client and program evaluation

The therapeutic recreation process consists of four parts, each of which will be reviewed in this chapter. **Assessment,** the first part of the process, involves identification of the client's current level of functioning as it relates to therapeutic recreation services. The second part is planning, which includes developing a plan of care for the individual client, placing the client into appropriate therapeutic recreation programs, and structuring those programs in a manner that best addresses targeted goals. Implementation involves delivery of planned programs and facilitation of related experiences before, during, and after the program occurs. **Evaluation** comes in many forms, but the ultimate purpose is to document client progression or regression. This information can then be used to fine-tune various aspects of the ongoing therapeutic recreation process.

The therapeutic recreation process, at first glance, may appear to be a linear movement through the four stages, but this is not the case. After the initial assessment has been conducted and the client is engaged in the therapy process, each of these four stages can occur and reoccur. A therapeutic recreation professional who never considers the need to revisit assessment results, revise treatment goals, or alter the manner in which he or she delivers programs or the content of those programs is practicing in an incompetent and unethical manner. Using structured protocols and curricula for service delivery is good, but so is observing best practices (doing things according to the best known procedures). If professionals never revisit the overall process, advancements in the quality of our services do not occur for either individual clients or our overall programs and profession. Thus, understanding how the therapeutic recreation process works is a fundamental skill that all practicing therapeutic recreation professionals must master.

Assessment

An endless number of definitions have been provided for assessment, most of which are fancy ways of saying the same thing over again. Put simply, assessment is the information-gathering process that occurs when clients enter the therapeutic recreation program. The nature of this information and how it is used will vary based on the purpose of the program. In most cases, this information is used to identify needs or issues to be addressed (current level of functioning), as well as any information relevant to the process of addressing those needs (e.g., financial limitations, family support).

Stumbo (2002) provided a more formal conceptualization of assessment by classifying the purposes of therapeutic recreation assessment into four areas:

- To gather client information to establish a baseline for client functioning and to monitor and summarize client progress
- To determine overall program effectiveness
- To communicate with other professionals inside and outside therapeutic recreation
- To meet the requirements for assessment by administrators and external agencies such as the Center for Medicare and Medicaid Services (CMS), the Joint Commission on the Accreditation of Healthcare Organizations (JCAHO), and the Commission on the Accreditation of Rehabilitation Facilities (CARF), agencies that oversee issues such as financial reimbursement (CMS) and agency accreditation (JCAHO, CARF)

The basic information gathered for each of these purposes may be the same, but it is used in different ways, all of which are directed toward providing the best service possible to clients. Assessment is the starting point for the therapy process. All actions of therapeutic recreation professionals should be grounded in some form of assessment. As noted in the standards of practice of both the National Therapeutic Recreation Society (NTRS) and the American Therapeutic Recreation Association (ATRA), assessment is a critical skill for all therapeutic recreation professionals and a necessary component of the therapeutic recreation process (see appendixes A and B).

Assessment Methods

When dining at a nice restaurant, choosing a dish is a critical part of determining how enjoyable the evening will be. Personally, I like to read each menu item carefully, ask for the specials, think back on past meals, ask other people for their opinions, and even look at plates being served at other tables (my wife says that this is rude). I have even sampled food off a plate that somebody else left behind (my wife doesn't know about this one). Based on the gathered information, I devise a plan for a quality meal. Conducting an assessment is similar in that we use multiple sources of information to devise a plan for helping the client. The more that we can learn about the client's current situation, the more likely it will be that we can assist him or her.

To ensure a true and complete understanding of the client's situation, several specific data-gathering strategies can be used. These methods include a review of existing documents, observation, interviewing, and use of standardized assessments and interest inventories. Exactly which method should be used depends on various situational factors including the functional level of the client, the purpose of the program, and available resources such as time and money.

EXISTING DOCUMENTS

The most useful existing, sometimes called historical, document is typically the intake **assessment report.** This document comes from a psychiatrist, psychologist, social worker, doctor, or other approved professional who is responsible for identifying and developing a plan to address the client's needs. This report will contain a substantial amount of information including the presenting problem, related history, precautions or standing orders from the lead doctor, results from various specific assessment procedures, and a summary that includes the overall goals and objectives for the client. When therapeutic recreation specialists conduct a therapeutic recreation assessment, they will create a similar report that pertains specifically to therapeutic recreation goals and objectives. Reviewing the intake assessment helps identify appropriate lines of questioning for interviews and ensures that already available information isn't needlessly gathered (although some instances might require verification of facts). This process also helps ensure that therapeutic recreation goals are congruent with the overall treatment goals of the client, as specified by the lead doctor. Other historical documents that might be useful include long-standing charts or medical histories of clients. These charts often include periodic case summaries that are helpful in identifying critical issues in what may otherwise be an overwhelming collection of information.

The following list represents commonly reported information that should be noted when reviewing intake information in preparation for assessment and planning a program for a client. This list is not all inclusive, and some items may be irrelevant in certain settings.

- General information such as name, age, and family members
- Presenting problem or reason for referral
- Results from previously conducted assessments (e.g., intellectual functioning)
- Any reported leisure-related interests, attitudes, behavior patterns, or barriers
- Limitations regarding physical activity
- Medication precautions
- Dietary requirements
- Any other standing orders (requirements) from the lead physician
- Facility restrictions and privileges such as requirement to be in a secured ward
- General behavioral patterns such as self-injurious behaviors, aggression, and sexual behaviors
- General client goals

In community settings, the therapeutic recreation professional is likely to be the lead service provider; therefore, a general assessment conducted by a doctor typically will not exist. Registration forms would take the place of a general intake assessment as the primary source of existing information. Quality registration procedures and paperwork can help focus therapeutic recreation services and identify any need for additional assessment. Records from ongoing or past programs, such as incident reports or other forms of documentation, may also be useful in understanding client needs. Although not present in every case, information may also be provided by medical professionals with regard to the nature of a particular client's condition. For example, the therapeutic recreation program might require medical clearance for certain known medical risks such as atlantoaxial instability (a condition involving instability of cervical vertebrae that sometimes coexists with Down syndrome).

Regardless of the setting or clientele, confidentiality of information from historical documents should always be maintained. When gathering this information from existing documents, be sure to monitor these files appropriately and return them as quickly as possible. Always keep in mind that information pertaining to an illness or disability should not be disclosed to parties outside the immediate treatment team or service providers without client or guardian permission.

STANDARDIZED ASSESSMENTS AND INTEREST INVENTORIES

Various standardized instruments have been developed for use in therapeutic recreation settings. Burlingame and Blaschko (2002) provided a comprehensive review of therapeutic recreation assessments in the "Red Book," including details pertaining to the development, psychometric properties, and intended use of each assessment. These instruments are too numerous to discuss individually, but mentioning a few of the more commonly used assessments will be helpful. The first is the leisure diagnostics battery, developed by Witt and Ellis (1989) as an indicator of perceived freedom in leisure and leisure barriers. This instrument can be administered through pencil and paper or computerized procedures, producing five subscale scores for perceived freedom (perceived competence, perceived control, needs, depth of involvement, playfulness) and three subscale scores for leisure functioning (barriers, leisure preferences, knowledge of leisure opportunities).

Another therapeutic recreation specific instrument is the leisure competence measure, or LCM (Kloseck & Crilly, 1997). The LCM measures current levels of functioning in eight leisure domains:

- Leisure awareness
- Leisure attitudes
- Leisure skills
- Community integration skills
- Community participation
- Cultural and social behaviors
- Interpersonal skills
- Social contact

Each domain is rated based on observations of the therapeutic recreation professional. The client's functioning within each domain is rated with a seven-point rating system that is modeled after the functional independence measure (FIM). Scores range from 1 (complete dependence) to 7 (complete independence) and are individually developed to represent a continuum of independence within each leisure domain. The original FIM is a standardized rating procedure implemented in various health care settings, most notably physical rehabilitation; therefore, the LCM is especially useful because of consistency with agency-wide assessment procedures.

A third frequently used assessment tool is the comprehensive evaluation for therapeutic recreation (CERT). The CERT comes in two versions (see Burlingame & Blaschko, 2002). The CERT psych/R is designed to determine one's ability to integrate successfully into society through social interaction, whereas the CERT–physical disabilities examines functional abilities related to leisure skills. Both scales are formatted to allow the CTRS to track changes over time. The CERT psych/R assesses social interaction skills across 25 items scored on a scale of 0 to 4 based on the observations of the CTRS. The CERT–physical disabilities consists of 50 items related to the following functional domains.

- Gross muscular function (9 items)
- Fine movement (4 items)
- Locomotion (4 items)
- Motor skills (5 items)
- Sensory (6 items)
- Cognition (11 items)
- Communication (5 items)
- Behavior (6 items)

Besides assessments developed specifically for the therapeutic recreation setting, several general assessment systems used in certain health care systems or settings are important. Because therapeutic recreation professionals are part of treatment teams within these systems, they must be aware of how these assessments function. The first is the inpatient rehabilitation facility–patient assessment inventory (IRF–PAI). This instrument is used in inpatient rehabilitation settings to assess client functioning in domains such as self-care, locomotion, communication, and social cognition. The Centers for Medicare and Medicaid Services (CMS) requires that this assessment be completed for all patients receiving fee-for-service Medicaid funding (part A). The IRF–PAI rates the client's level of functioning with the earlier mentioned FIM system. A simple decision-making tree is used to determine the score for each rated functional area.

The second system-specific assessment is the resident assessment inventory–minimum data set (RAI–MDS). The RAI–MDS is a computer-based assessment designed by CMS for use in long-term care facilities. A team of care providers works to complete the assessment based on observation of the client's functional level. One area particularly relevant to therapeutic recreation services is activity pursuit patterns. Information relevant to this area is often provided by therapeutic recreation professionals and relates to issues such as time awake, average time involved in activities, and preferred activities. Gathered information is entered into the computer, which then generates guidelines for appropriate treatment plans and determines cost of care.

Both the RAI–MDS and the IRF–PAI are comprehensive assessments that are, at most, only partially completed by the therapeutic recreation specialist, but the results of these assessments can still influence the nature of the services that we provide. As noted earlier, such assessments can be valuable sources of information when developing individualized program plans for therapeutic recreation services (treatment plans). In the case of the IRF–PAI, the LCM can be integrated into the assessment process to ensure that recreation and leisure needs are addressed. Likewise, the RAI–MDS consists of domains directly relevant to leisure and can serve as a major resource for establishing therapeutic recreation goals and objectives.

An interview will help you to gauge the client's interests and identify therapy goals.

INTERVIEWING

Interviewing clients is a critical part of the assessment process. Questions should focus on leisure functioning (leisure interests, behaviors, desires, barriers, resources) as well as physical, social, emotional, cognitive, and spiritual considerations related to this area of function. Understanding the relationship between leisure and other aspects of functioning is a critical competency for therapeutic recreation professionals. When conducting interviews, the therapeutic recreation specialist who has this knowledge can ask the right questions, identify areas that need further questioning, and determine the importance or meaningfulness of responses. See the sidebar on page 85 for examples of questions that an interviewer might present to a client.

When practicing interviews, students often make the mistake of asking good questions that elicit a significant response from the client but then failing to follow up with additional questions about the issue. They are, therefore, unable to integrate relevant information into treatment plans. Instead, students stick to the comfort of their list of questions and prematurely move on to the next topic. These shallow interviews typically result in vague or random recommendations that do not have a logical relationship to client needs. Knowing how therapeutic recreation services can help clients and then recognizing information relevant to this process during an interview is a key component to successful interventions. In other words, the professional must be good at finding common ground between the purpose of the therapeutic recreation programs offered and the client's presenting problem.

The quality of the interview depends heavily on preparation. Reviewing available existing documents and results from standardized assessments can be tremendously helpful in appropriately focusing the interview content. Equally important is allotting adequate time for the interview and conducting the interview in a location without distractions. To ensure preparation, the therapeutic recreation specialist should address the following questions before conducting the interview.

- What documents should I review before the interview?
- Have I made arrangements for needed space and time?
- How should I start the interview?
- What behaviors should I be watching for during the interview?

- What questions do I want to ask related to the presenting problem?
- What questions do I want to ask related to recreation and leisure?
- When do I want to ask these questions (beginning, middle, or end of the interview)?
- When I'm finished questioning, how will I close the interview?

The first of these questions has already been addressed, but it is listed here because reviewing documents will help identify information pertinent to the rest of these issues. The second question, related to how to open the interview, is equally important. Goals for opening the interview should include informing the client about the purpose of the interview and therapeutic recreation in general. The therapeutic recreation professional should also introduce him- or herself and explain his or her role within the organization. If the interviewer is an intern, he or she should not hide this fact if it comes up. The intern should be honest with the client, inquire about any apprehensions that the client has, and assure the client that more experienced professionals are also part of the team. This initial conversation is also critical to establishing some level of rapport with the client. Casual conversation can be used to relax the client and inform him or her of the interviewer's intentions. A casual (but still professional) tone should be carried into the early stages of the interview, meaning that questioning should be oriented toward nonthreatening topics and information that is not too personal. As the interview progresses, the interviewer can move to higher levels of intimacy regarding the topics being discussed. Bringing discussion back to casual conversation before ending may also be necessary, especially if the conversation is emotionally challenging for the client. In closing, the interviewer should provide the client with information pertaining to the next step. When will the interviewer be back? What does the interviewer intend to do with all the information that the client has provided? What will the interviewer and the client do next time? The interviewer should address these questions before leaving the client.

The one question listed earlier that has yet to be addressed is related to observing behavior during the interview. The level of orientation of the client should be noted, because it is relevant to a variety of presenting problems (e.g., dementia, traumatic brain injury, stroke), as well as the validity of information gathered during the interview. Orientation refers to whether the client knows what day, month, and year it is (time), where they are (place), and who they are (person). Time disorientation is usually the first lost. More severe disorientation will progress to place and then person. The interviewer should note posture, eye contact, tone of voice, and overall demeanor of the client, because those observations may also be relevant to client condition, assessment results, and appropriateness of certain activities.

OBSERVATION

Observation is a useful assessment tool during the interview, but it also can be used in a variety of other ways. One of the major benefits of observation is that it documents actual behavior. Interviews, on the other hand, may be misleading when it comes to differentiating between what people say they do, what they desire to do, and what they actually do. The second major advantage to observation is that is does not depend on the client's communication skills. Many illnesses, injuries, or disabilities may not allow effective interviewing or use of standardized, self-report assessments (although parents, partners, siblings, or friends can serve as information resources). Likewise, some clients may not wish to cooperate with interviews; therefore, observation provides an alternative source of information. In some cases, observation is combined with a standardized assessment, such as the case with the two versions of the CERT. Note that observation cannot measure **constructs,** or internal states, such as motivation, depression, or intelligence. Rather, observation focuses on documenting behavior patterns.

Therapeutic recreation professionals should closely examine the quality and intended purpose of any assessment procedure that they are considering for use in practice. In particular, evidence that a particular assessment strategy is producing reliable (consistent) results and providing valid (accurate) assumptions about the client should be considered. This information should also be directly relevant to the client's presenting problem and the potential service areas of the therapeutic recreation program. Assessing areas of function that are irrelevant to either the client's needs or the corresponding intervention will result in information that is not usable. Valid, reliable, and usable assessment results are the foundation for developing goals and objectives for the client, and any threat to assessment legitimacy can compromise the entire therapeutic recreation process.

ASSESSING HUYEN

Huyen is a 47-year-old woman who is receiving treatment in a residential drug and alcohol program. After a recent DUI arrest and conviction, Huyen was sent to the 8-week program by the courts as part of her sentence.

Historical Documents

The intake assessment report conducted by Huyen's lead counselor reported that this was her third DUI and that her life has been significantly affected by drinking over the last 10 years. Most notably, she has lost custody of her 9-year-old daughter, who now lives with Huyen's parents. Huyen also took part in an outpatient counseling program after her husband divorced her. A summary from these counseling sessions (referred to as a chart summary) indicated that Huyen was drinking heavily at the time, but the summary also stated that her husband left because he didn't want to be a father. Huyen also indicated that her drinking at the time was temporary and her way of coping with the divorce. Despite a previous diagnosis of alcohol dependence, Huyen denied during the intake interview that she had any problem with drinking. As part of the intake assessment Huyen had completed a substance abuse subtle screening inventory (SASSI), which produced results that supported the previous diagnosis. Huyen's explanation for her current situation was that she "just liked to have a good time" and that she "wasn't even drunk this time, the alcohol limits are just set low to trap people." Huyen did indicate a strong desire to participate in the 8-week program because she wanted to make the judge happy and regain custody of her child. She did not, however, see the program as being useful to her.

Standardized Assessment

Huyen's therapist had her complete the leisure diagnostics battery, which suggested that Huyen had high levels of perceived competence in leisure but reported limited perceived control in leisure. Results from the LDB also indicated barriers related to money, opportunities, time, and decision making.

Interview

With this information from the historical documents and the standardized assessments in hand, Huyen's therapist constructed the following questions for an interview with Huyen.

- Tell me about yourself.
- How do you like to spend your free time?
- Who do you typically spend your free time with?
- Have you always done these things, or have your interests changed over time?
- What about when you were a kid, in high school, or even before? Were you into sports, drama, hanging out?
- I know from reading your chart that one of your goals is to regain custody of your daughter. Can you tell me about that situation? Do you currently have any contact with her?
- When you are with her, what do you two like to do?
- What about your parents? How is your relationship with them?
- Let's go back to your current interests and pastimes. You mentioned that you like to hang out at Joe's Pub and to play softball. How often do you hang out at the pub?
- When you play softball, do you drink there too? Does everyone on your team drink, or are there some who don't?
- Why do you think that alcohol is such an important part of hanging out with friends?
- Can you think of any negative consequences that drinking has caused for you?
- Would you consider drinking to be a problem for you?
- Do you have any friends who don't drink? What do they say about your drinking?
- Can you think of any activities that you enjoy that don't involve drinking?
- What activities would you like to try that you don't currently do?
- Can you think of anything else related to our conversation that you can tell me?

Observation

Although Huyen reported during both her intake interview and her therapeutic recreation assessment interview that drinking alcohol was not a problem, her therapist observed that she was, in fact, experiencing problems related to persistent drinking during free time. With the answers from the documents, standardized assessments, interview, and careful observation, the therapist was able to form a more accurate picture of Huyen and her needs so that a plan could be formed to help her reach her goals. Note that during the interview, the line of questioning focused specifically on how Huyen's leisure choices both fed into and were being driven by her drinking. Huyen's therapeutic recreation program would most likely focus on these choices and the importance of finding alcohol-free activities and friends, as well as how making better choices could help her regain access to her daughter.

Planning

Planning occurs at multiple levels in therapeutic recreation. The broadest form of planning is called comprehensive program planning (see Stumbo & Peterson, 2004). This process refers to the development of the overall therapeutic recreation department, program, or agency. Developing a mission statement, setting goals for the comprehensive program, and identifying specific programs to be implemented within the comprehensive program are all part of this process. The second tier of planning is specific program planning, which involves the detailed planning of the chosen specific programs to be implemented within the department. Different clients may require different specific programs, so a comprehensive program or agency typically has several specific programs. The third tier of planning relates to planning for the individual client. Because comprehensive and specific program planning are a major focus of other courses and corresponding textbooks, this section focuses primarily on planning for the individual client. The concepts presented are, however, analogous to many of the tasks associated with the other planning realms, and the lines drawn between these three tiers are less apparent in real practice.

After a therapeutic recreation assessment has been conducted, the resulting information is placed into a therapeutic recreation specific assessment report and **individualized program plan (IPP)** that complement the general assessment report and treatment plan (remember that a doctor typically conducts the general assessment, and in community settings, such documents may not be available). The assessment report refers to a summary of results from the assessment, whereas the IPP is a statement of the client's strengths, limitations, goals, and objectives. Although the therapeutic recreation assessment report and the IPP are developed as separate documents, they are often integrated into a single report. No standardized procedure for reporting assessment results is used across all therapeutic recreation departments or programs, but every organization should require some form of standard assessment report and plan. In addition, the IPP may be referred to by many other names, including treatment plan or individualized intervention plan, but they all serve essentially the same purpose. This purpose, to specify appropriate client goals and objectives based on assessment results, is the start of the planning process for individual clients.

Goal Development

Therapeutic recreation **goals** are the general accomplishments that the client should achieve through participation in the therapeutic recreation process. Goals should be directly tied to the assessment results and should be developed in collaboration with clients whenever possible. In fact, thorough assessment reports are like the trail of bread crumbs that Hansel and Gretel left to find their way home. Every goal listed in the treatment plan should be detectable in both the raw data from the assessment and in the assessment report. Likewise, any significant need identified through the assessment process should be addressed in client goals and objectives. Essentially, a trail of evidence should support each stated goal and objective throughout the assessment report and IPP.

Objectives are measurable criteria for determining when a goal has been met. A correctly written objective consists of three parts, referred to as condition, behavior, and criterion. The condition refers to the circumstances under which an objective is intended to be achieved (during social leisure activities, when given instructions to complete it, upon request). The behavior specifies the measurable behavior to be performed and is represented by an action verb and associated noun (throw a ball, balance the body, greet a stranger, identify coping strategies). The criterion specifies the measurable indicator of goal achievement (at least 75% of the time, three out of five times, meeting 8 of the 10 following criteria). To illustrate the elements of an objective, consider the goal and objective in the sidebar. This example is typical of what might be included in the IPP of a 12-year-old child with cerebral palsy who is participating in a sports day-camp program.

Because goals are typically broad, several objectives (three to five) are typically listed under each of the client's goals. Notice in the example in figure 6.1 that the objective addresses only one element of the goal. In practice, additional objectives would be needed to address this goal adequately. In addition, goals should be prioritized. The potential areas of intervention that might arise during an assessment are often broad. Identifying where the majority of time and resources should be dedicated helps focus

ANATOMY OF GOALS AND OBJECTIVES

Sample Goal

Improve motor skills related to throwing, kicking, and catching.

Sample Objective

When given the cue "throw the ball in the bucket," the client will throw a tennis ball into a 24-inch (60-centimeter) bucket within 30 seconds, at a distance of at least 3 feet (90 centimeters), four out of five times, at least once a day during 4 of the 5 camp days.

Considerations

- What part of the goal does the objective address, and what parts still need attention?
- Would it be possible to have additional objectives related to throwing?
- What would be the benefit of including additional throwing objectives?

Condition, Behavior, Criteria

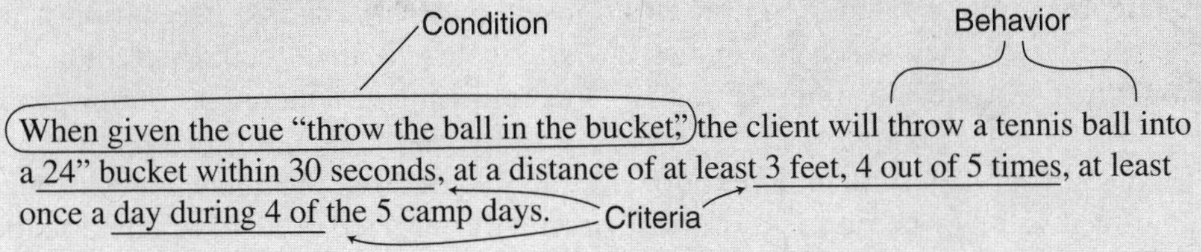

Condition

Behavior

When given the cue "throw the ball in the bucket," the client will throw a tennis ball into a 24" bucket within 30 seconds, at a distance of at least 3 feet, 4 out of 5 times, at least once a day during 4 of the 5 camp days.

Criteria

Figure 6.1 In this example, written notes indicate elements of condition, behavior, and criteria.

---

therapeutic recreation services on goals that are critical to client functioning.

Placement of Clients

After establishing goals and objectives for a client, the therapeutic recreation specialist must then determine the best way to help the client achieve these goals. Besides considering the client's goals, the professional must also be concerned about program goals. These are the goals of the various programming options available to clients (e.g., leisure education, social skills group, self-esteem, problem solving, strength training, adapted aquatics, and so on). Such programs are usually delivered in separate sessions, or "groups," that the therapeutic recreation specialist implements throughout the day. Establishing a match between client goals and specific program goals ensures that the client is placed in the right programs.

The overall therapeutic recreation program (the therapeutic recreation department) will typically provide a variety of specific programs (whether participatory, educational, or therapy oriented) designed to address a certain set of outcomes that are commonly beneficial to the agency's clientele. No one program can address every client need.

For example, a social skills group for adults with intellectual impairment is unlikely to address fitness-related goals adequately. The therapeutic recreation professional's job is to match clients with specific programs that address their personal goals. This means that

- not every client needs to participate in every program,
- the groups that a client participates in should provide outcomes consistent with his or her goals, and
- therapeutic recreation specialist is likely to be planning several specific programs at the same time.

The third bulleted item is notable because therapeutic recreation specialists must be careful not to abandon this purposeful philosophy for a "whatever is easiest" approach. To prevent this from happening, planning must be seen as a necessary aspect of every group, session, or activity.

Other Considerations for Planning

Program planning is a complex responsibility. Working with multiple clients with diverse needs and multiple ongoing programs designed to address those needs presents a challenging work environment. In addition, therapeutic recreation specialists often try to plan programs for the long term, but daily planning for each session of a program based on various client factors and environmental factors is also necessary. These challenges make it easy to lose sight of the therapeutic recreation process and the importance of developing programs that consistently address client goals.

Stumbo and Peterson (2004) make several recommendations related to activity selection that can help address this challenge. These authors emphasize the importance of developing therapeutic recreation programs that will produce predictable and replicable outcomes among clients. Outcomes are defined as "observed changes in a client's status as a result of our interventions and interactions" (Stumbo & Peterson, p. 85). This approach is consistent with the concept of purposeful intervention presented in chapter 1 as a key component of the definition of therapeutic recreation.

Considering that Stumbo and Peterson (2004) advocate outcome-driven planning, it is not surprising that the first area they identify for consideration when selecting activities is "activity content and process" (p. 174). Stumbo and Peterson use the term *activities* to describe "the methods by which therapeutic recreation specialists help clients change their abilities, knowledge, and attitudes" (p. 174). Specific considerations for identifying appropriate activities include the following:

- "Activities must have a direct relationship to client goals" (p. 174).
- Activity characteristics can influence successful activity implementation.
- Client should be able to place the activity in the context of overall therapeutic recreation goals (outcomes).
- Activities should be interesting and engaging for the client, as well as enjoyable.

Except for the first, the items in this list are presented in abbreviated form to focus on concepts most relevant to this chapter. As such, a brief discussion is provided to clarify the latter three concepts.

Examples of characteristics that might support successful completion of an activity include factors such as client-to-staff ratio, the physical environment, and the presence or absence of skills necessary to participate successfully in the activity. Conducting an activity in a distracting environment or at a level that is above the developmental level of clients will negatively affect outcomes, regardless of whether the initial intent of the activity was directly tied to targeted outcomes.

The third bullet in the list refers to the need for clients to understand why they are being asked to participate in an activity. Some therapeutic recreation modalities or activities involve extensive problem solving on the part of clients, so the therapeutic recreation specialist should not be overly helpful during these activities. But this guidance does not mean that professionals should hide the targeted outcome from clients. Presenting a task without adequate explanation and watching clients wallow in confusion and failure is counterproductive. The activity may be counterproductive even if clients succeed because they may not associate the activity with the targeted outcomes. Therapeutic recreation specialists should fully inform clients about how the activities pertain to their therapeutic recreation goals and objectives. This task relates to planning in that it reinforces the need to plan activities oriented toward client needs and to be prepared to deliver such activities in a useful way.

The fourth bulleted consideration is associated with the critical second aspect of therapeutic recreation (see chapter 1), which was an inherent relationship with recreation and leisure. When describing the need for interesting, engaging, and enjoyable activities, Stumbo and Peterson (2004) suggest that the planning process should identify activities that clients would participate in even if they were not part of treatment or rehabilitation. In other words, programs should provide activities that are congruent with the client's recreation and leisure preferences. For this to happen, therapeutic recreation specialists should collaborate with the client as much as possible. When clients are unable to take part in the planning process, family involvement can help ensure that the IPP is consistent with the client's needs and interests (Shank & Coyle, 2002).

Tools for Planning

Besides describing activity content and process, Stumbo and Peterson (2004) also pointed out that client characteristics and available resources need to be considered. The following section describes several procedures or tools that the professional can use to identify and organize relevant factors related to client characteristics, required activity skills, and the potential application of various resources (e.g., number of staff needed and equipment needed).

Two commonly used tools for planning activities in therapeutic recreation include the **activity analysis** and the **task analysis.** Sherrill (2004) described these terms as interchangeable, with activity analysis most commonly used in therapeutic recreation and task analysis most commonly used in education. Stumbo and Peterson (2004) refuted this point, arguing that the two tools are inherently different and useful in different ways. The distinction drawn by these authors will be used here to illustrate this point.

TASK ANALYSIS

Task analysis involves breaking down a specific skill into its component parts. How basic, or minute, these parts need to be depends on how the task analysis will be used. As an example, bending over to pick up an item, such as a pencil, off the floor is a behavior that could be task analyzed. The task analysis might look something like this:

- Step 1: Flex neck into downward position.
- Step 2: Visually locate pencil.
- Step 3: Position body so that pencil is next to foot, directly below hand.
- Step 4: Bend at knees, keeping back straight, until hand touches floor.
- Step 5: Grasp object.
- Step 6: Rise to standing position.

More detailed steps or elements of the task could be added if necessary, but for the sake of this discussion, the example is sufficiently comprehensive. Note, however, that the gaps between steps must not be too large or overlook critical aspects of the behavior.

After the task analysis is completed, it can be used as an assessment tool to identify aspects of the skill that the client is able or unable to perform. For example, step 4 may be difficult for a particular client because of difficulties with balance. Thus, appropriate adjustments, or adaptations, could be made. Examples would include use of a cane for balance or use of a grasping tool that would

allow the client to pick up objects from a standing position. Task analysis can also be used to identify appropriate increments of skill or information when teaching complex behaviors in incremental steps.

ACTIVITY ANALYSIS

Activity analysis systematically identifies the skills necessary to participate in an activity through the comprehensive analysis of various areas of functioning. Typically, these areas correspond with the functional domains categorized as physical, social, cognitive, and emotional. Stumbo and Peterson (2004) identified this broad approach as differentiating activity analysis from task analysis, and pointed out that this comprehensive approach contributes to the task analysis by further exploring the skills necessary for each sequential step. For example, activity analysis typically would consider various aspects of physical ability and could help isolate the reason that step 4 (bending down) of the task analysis was so difficult for the client. What might appear as a balance problem may be further complicated by flexibility limitations or vestibular disturbances (dizziness when tilting the head). Task analysis alone does not provide such details.

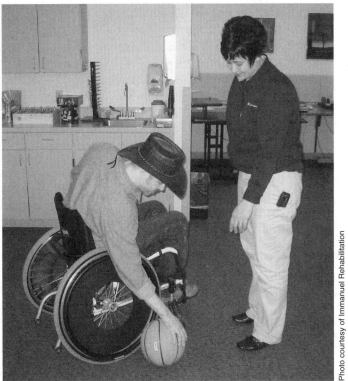

Photo courtesy of Immanuel Rehabilitation

The certified therapeutic recreation specialist depicted here utilizes activity analysis to evaluate basic activity skills and identify necessary adaptations.

ACTIVITY MODIFICATION

Task analysis and activity analysis allow for appropriate activity modifications. Activity modifications involve adjusting the activity or activity environment to meet the ability characteristics of the client. Activity modifications are commonplace in everyday life, and many common products or services cater to commonly needed modifications. Video games offer different difficulty levels, car seats adjust to accommodate individual differences in height, and sporting equipment comes in all shapes and sizes to fit individual needs. The game of golf is one massive modification machine. A golfer can walk or ride, tee off from different distances to meet his or her ability level, and even use oversized clubs and "far-flying" golf balls to turn an average drive into a 300-yard monster. Golf is one big adjustable mechanism for finding an appropriate balance between skill and challenge, which is a critical element of any adaptation.

In therapeutic recreation, activity modifications are used to circumvent impairments that are barriers to participation. These modifications often come in the form of specialized equipment but can also involve adjusting how an activity is performed or the rules and procedures of the activity. A softball with a beeper inside, a bowling ball with a retractable handle, a rule change that allows two bounces in tennis, a reduction in the size of a soccer field, or use of a "sip and puff" device to play a video game are all considered modifications. In any case, modification should allow participation while minimizing the effect on the inherent nature of the activity. In other words, modification should not occur unless it is necessary. As mentioned in chapter 4, removing such modifications when they are no longer needed is also important, although some modifications will be permanent. Enabling independent and successful participation is the primary goal. As long as the client is engaged in the activity in the most rewarding, normalized, and independent manner, the modification is appropriate.

Activity Plan

Whenever possible, professionals should develop an activity plan, or session plan, that outlines exactly what will occur during a particular therapeutic recreation program. This process addresses many logistical concerns that should be considered during the planning process. Addressing these issues before implementation is critical to successful programming. Issues to be addressed include

- equipment needed,
- safety precautions,
- targeted program and client goals,
- rules and procedures,
- potential modifications, and
- activity time line.

Whether the activity plan is a formally written document or just a checklist for planning, the professional should consider each of these issues. The last bullet, activity time line, should include a rough estimate of how long each aspect of the activity will take. This includes the actual activity and any discussion that might be necessary (briefing, leading, and debriefing are described later in this chapter).

Activity plans are often developed and kept on record for future sessions, but the plan should be reviewed and considered within the context of the current client or group of clients. What may have been appropriate for last year's group of clients may not be suitable for the current group. Within an overall group, individual clients may require certain safety precautions or a change in the manner in which the professional presents or discusses an activity.

Implementation

Mental health professionals often describe counseling as a profession that is as much art as it is science. Although therapeutic recreation and counseling are not the same, this artistic aspect of counseling is definitely present in some therapeutic recreation situations. Ask any intern who works in a mental health facility what it was like to process a group experience with real clients for the first time, and they will tell you that no predetermined list of questions or activities can ensure that the professional will "say the right thing." Every therapeutic recreation setting presents opportunities to facilitate personal growth through skilled dialog.

Developing this artistic element of helping others takes practice. A thorough knowledge of theoretical frameworks and practical counseling skills is necessary, but just as a person doesn't become a great

CORINNE NORMAN

Background Information

Education

*BS in Recreation and Leisure Studies, concentration in Therapeutic Recreation from James Madison University, Department of Kinesiology *MA in Exercise, Leisure, and Sport, concentration in Therapeutic Recreation from Kent State University, School of Exercise, Leisure, and Sport

Credentials

CTRS

Special Affiliations

*National Therapeutic Recreation Society *National Recreation and Park Association

Career Information

Position

Recreation Specialist I, Therapeutic Recreation Programs for the Virginia Beach Department of Parks and Recreation

> Go confidently in the direction of your dreams. Live the life you have imagined.
>
> Henry David Thoreau

Organization Information

Virginia Beach Parks and Recreation is located within the city of Virginia Beach, Virginia. Various recreation centers (all equipped with natatoriums, gyms, locker rooms, weight rooms, and meeting rooms) and beautiful parks are located throughout the city.

Organization's Mission

The Department of Therapeutic Recreation Programs works to enhance the quality of life in Virginia Beach by providing for the recreational needs of the community through parkland, facilities, and programs.

Job Description

Supervise and coordinate various therapeutic recreation programs. Develop marketing materials and present programmatic information at local educational clinics, meetings, and events. Oversee programming aspects of each sport activity by conducting registration, coordinating staff and volunteers, formulating program plans and skill sheets, purchasing and providing needed equipment, supervising and facilitating the actual program, documentation, and conducting evaluations. Hire and train part-time staff; secure equipment and materials, and facility space; arrange transportation; write individualized recreation plans (which include functional goals) for each participant; document weekly participant progress; coordinate volunteer opportunities for participants and vocational job site visits; plan team building activities; and facilitate leisure education sessions for various programs run by the Department of Therapeutic Recreation Programs.

Career Path

Through college, I held various jobs and internships that have led me to this particular career. I was a lifeguard and swimming instructor for Virginia Beach Parks and Recreation for many years and also supervised an after-school program for Rockingham County Parks and Recreation. After assisting with a therapeutic recreation swim class as a swimming instructor, I developed a passion for working with individuals with various disabilities and special needs. I completed a therapeutic recreation internship with Virginia Beach Parks and Recreation as well as a therapeutic recreation internship at St. Thomas Hospital in their Behavioral Health Unit in Akron, Ohio. Both of these experiences provided me with the knowledge and confidence to obtain my current position here with the City of Virginia Beach.

Likes and Dislikes About the Job

One aspect I love about my job is directly facilitating programs. Being able to work with participants on developing a healthy leisure lifestyle and seeing them grow and expand their recreational skills are incredibly exciting! I dislike many of the administrative responsibilities; however, I accept them as they are a part of the job.

Advice to Undergraduate Students

My advice is to find your passion in the field and make sure what you will be doing for your career is something you have pride in and will enjoy doing.

painter from painting by numbers, no one becomes a great therapeutic recreation professional solely from reading a book. Learning how to counsel clients effectively is the most difficult part of working in a helping profession. Genuine moments occur when what the professional says (or doesn't say) can significantly affect a person's experience, day, month, or lifetime. These moments can range in content from figuring out how to get a camper out of his wet sleeping bag without embarrassing him, to persuading a client to talk about how her unwillingness to take risks has affected her and her family, to responding to a physical rehabilitation patient with a severe injury who says, "Why should I play a stupid game when my life is ruined?" These intimidating situations present the professional with an opportunity to have either a positive influence on clients or a negative one. Dealing with these situations is a skill that comes with practice, but the key to success is the ability to focus on the task at hand and recognize opportunities for meaningful discussion. To be prepared for these critical situations, the therapist should have taken care of other tasks or responsibilities beforehand so that he or she can facilitate this dialogue. These preparatory tasks are referred to here as technical skills.

Technical Skills

Technical skills, sometimes referred to as hard skills, include physical tasks associated with job responsibilities. Examples include filling out paperwork, using and maintaining equipment correctly, planning sessions, and demonstrating an activity skill correctly. **Facilitation skills,** or soft skills, are related to the interpersonal interactions that therapists have with clients. Facilitation skills are maximized when technical skills are mastered and performed in a competent manner. To put it bluntly, if the "professional" pulls a random activity out of a book 20 minutes before a session, fails to understand activity rules and prepare for equipment needs adequately, and neglects to think through how the session relates to the current needs of clients, he or she will almost certainly fail to facilitate beneficial activities or sessions. Adequate preparation and practice, on the other hand, allow the professional to focus on the one thing that he or she should be thinking about during the group: how to facilitate therapeutic growth. As such, the ability to use technical skills successfully during a session depends on whether they were addressed in the planning stage (and included in the activity plan).

One simple technical skill related to both planning and implementation that can significantly increase the likelihood of success in any therapeutic recreation environment is sequencing. The sequence of activities should be specified in the time line portion of the activity plan. **Sequencing** is arranging the elements of a session or series of sessions in an order that facilitates successful performance. Everyone benefits from sequencing when learning new tasks. A small child learns to walk a balance beam that is extra wide and 6 inches (15 centimeters) off the ground. As skills develop, the beam becomes higher and narrower. This graduated difficulty, if started at an appropriate level, encourages early success, builds confidence, and provides a consistently attainable goal for the client. The experience of succeeding can itself be therapeutic, especially among those who lack self-confidence or have been discouraged in the past. Such people are sensitive to failure, and creating a few simple early successes can greatly affect willingness to participate and take risks.

Sequencing can be planned ahead of time, but the therapeutic recreation specialist must also be able to identify appropriate times to move to the next level of participation and modify activities in midstream to meet the client's needs. Likewise, progression through sequential stages can occur over several months or within a few minutes. The challenge for the therapeutic recreation specialist is to provide the appropriate level of challenge that both engages the client and allows improvement.

Another important skill associated with implementation is the ability to monitor all clients at all times. This responsibility includes staying in tune with not only what clients are doing but also how they are doing. In some cases, therapeutic recreation specialists monitor from an outside perspective, observing and facilitating the activity without participating. In other cases, they may participate in an activity with clients. Active involvement can sometimes increase the ability to facilitate successes (note that success does not mean performing a skill or creating a solution *for* clients), but this approach can also be a distraction for inexperienced or incompetent professionals who focus on their own game instead of facilitating the experience for the client. Professionals must never lose sight of their purpose. Maintaining this awareness represents a transition from technical skills to facilitation skills.

Being an excellent glass blower (a technical skill) is much more valuable if one is also an excellent listener and facilitator.

Facilitation Skills

Facilitation skills are what create and maximize a therapeutic relationship or experience. They represent the humanistic side of therapeutic recreation. Observation skills, active listening, and counseling skills all work together to enable personal growth. Because facilitation occurs within the context of technical tasks, the following section will present a mixture of the two. Specifically, three stages of implementation will be discussed. The professional should address these stages during the planning stage but also be ready to react to events as they occur. In reading this section, keep in mind that sequencing should be present across and within the stages.

BRIEFING

Briefing involves informing clients of what is about to happen, describing associated behavioral expectations, and establishing goals related to the session activities (Schoel, Prouty, & Radcliffe, 1988). Briefing can occur many days before a session or immediately before the session starts. Whenever possible, establishing session goals should involve clients. Established goals typically focus on session activities (swimming at least 10 laps, identifying five new leisure interests) but also may be related to issues that go beyond the immediate activity (walking to the store, communicating with family). These latter examples are referred to as **spiral goals,** and generally tie the immediate activity to the overall therapeutic recreation and general treatment goals of the client. They focus on how the activity relates to the daily life of the client and may include goals such as improving the ability to control anger or increasing self-esteem. Activity goals are typically shared by the group, whereas spiral goals are more likely to be client-specific (such as Huyen regaining custody of her child).

Briefing is also a time to maximize interest of clients in the activity. At this point the therapeutic recreation professional begins to engineer an experience that is engaging but not overwhelming. Many factors can influence this balance, including clearly defined expectations, appropriate levels of novelty, verbal persuasion, appropriate use of modeling (demonstration), and appropriate sequencing (Ellis, Morris & Trunnell, 1995). Appropriate briefing focuses clients on goals and creates motivation and arousal levels that optimize performance.

LEADING

When leading a session, the therapeutic recreation specialist works consistently to ensure that the events that take place relate to the targeted goals. In physical rehabilitation settings, this task might involve encouraging clients to exercise choice in activities or to continue participating in an especially challenging task. In psychiatric facilities, the task might involve skilled questioning that encourages clients to consider alternatives independently and choose a plan of action. Many inexperienced therapeutic recreation specialists struggle with this skill. Asking leading questions such as "What would happen if you made a net out of the rope and then carried Joe across the gap?" provide solutions that clients should be allowed to discover

Skilled facilitation empowers clients to reflect upon and understand the meaning of therapeutic experiences.

independently. Another common mistake involves growing impatient with clients and providing hints or other forms of assistance that make the activity too easy. Maintaining balance between too little and too much assistance is an important skill to have when leading sessions. In working to develop this talent, the therapeutic recreation professional may profit by considering the following questions after facilitating therapeutic recreation sessions.

- What role was I playing during the session?
- Where was I physically? How did my location and movement affect the group?
- Where was I emotionally? Was I nervous, frustrated, impatient, or distracted?
- How was I communicating (verbal, nonverbal)? Listening? Directing? Facilitating?
- Was I anticipating problems such as victimization or isolation?
- What were my successes and mishaps? Did I facilitate any specific successes? Did I help too much?
- Was I monitoring goal achievement and making adjustments?
- Did I take notes? Mentally or written? What were they, and what is their relevance?

Therapeutic recreation specialists who answer "no" to this last question will probably be unable to answer any of the previous ones. Failure to take note of significant events is a problem because the facilitator will be unable to process the experience appropriately. As such, the ability to facilitate a group while identifying and remembering significant events that occur during the session is a critical skill.

DEBRIEFING

Debriefing therapeutic recreation sessions, otherwise known as processing, includes reviewing the events that occurred during the session, the experiences and emotions of clients, the progress made toward session goals, and the relevance of this progress to overall therapy goals (spiral goals when relevant). Many structured techniques have been developed for processing experiences. One of the most widely used is the "What, So What, and Now What" approach, often referred to as the Outward Bound approach (see Schoel, Prouty, & Radcliffe, 1988). The *What* involves reviewing concrete events that occurred during the session. This

discussion helps clients remember what occurred and encourages open discussion by focusing on comfortable topics. The *So What* involves reviewing activity goals that were established for the session, as well as emotional reactions to the events that occurred and the effect on the individual or group. The *Now What* consists of relating the content of the session to issues outside the therapy environment (the real world). Questions such as "How is your unwillingness to help the group similar to the challenges that you have faced with your parents?" would be useful during this stage. It focuses on how experiences related to the activity can translate to the client's spiral goals. This discussion is the most personal and most difficult to facilitate. Also in the *Now What* stage would be discussion related to the next session and how the therapeutic recreation process will continue.

A more directed processing strategy developed by Jacobson and Ruddy (2004) involves five stages of questioning. According to these authors, the five questions follow the natural processing tendencies of the human mind, easing the movement from stage to stage and the resulting insight of clients. The first question is "Did you notice . . . ?" followed by "Why did that happen?" "Does that happen in life?" "Why does that happen?" and "How can you use that?" The similarity between the two techniques is not coincidental because both are meant to achieve similar results, but there are also differences.

One of the most notable is the fact that the first of the five questions, "Did you notice . . . ?" is not open ended, requiring the facilitator to refer to a significant observation made during the leading stage. Jacobson and Ruddy believe this to be critical in setting up the rest of the discussion and avoiding large gaps between what has happened and what can be learned. In contrast, the *What* stage is less specific about appropriate discussion content and relies on the facilitation skills of the professional. Jacobson and Ruddy's process provides a more open-ended approach for the final four questions, but they are still much more specific in nature than the questions asked in the Outward Bound approach.

Important in both approaches is the sequencing of discussion from the immediate experience to the overall therapeutic goals of the client. The therapist must determine how simplistic, complex, directed, or open ended this discussion should be for any particular client or group. For more information on specific debriefing skills and strategies, refer to Jacobson and Ruddy's affordable book *Open to Outcome* (2004).

These two approaches are general guidelines for processing therapeutic recreation sessions, so not all parts will be relevant in every situation. For example, a leisure education program for adults with intellectual impairment may focus on reviewing events and reinforcing lessons learned with "What would you do if?" questions, demonstrating learned skills, and offering positive reinforcement for successes. In any case, therapeutic recreation specialists should think about the processing strategy before the session ever starts and adjust accordingly to fit the clientele.

Besides the general format for processing described here, several strategies that are more specific have been developed. These methods focus more on how to ask rather than what to ask and can typically be used in conjunction with the two approaches presented earlier. A brief description of some of these strategies is provided in table 6.1.

Regardless of the technique used, the therapeutic recreation specialist should be facilitating the discussion rather than lecturing clients. In fact,

clients should do most of the talking. The role of the facilitator is to ensure that discussion stays focused on targeted goals or other relevant concepts and to help clients make connections between the session and their goals. In addition, the facilitator works to ensure constructive discussion and addresses attacking or avoidant comments.

With regard to programs that are more participatory in nature, extensive debriefing may not be necessary or appropriate. Still, discussion should occur about the extent to which activity goals are being achieved with the client, even if the goal is simply to have fun. This process ultimately leads into the fourth aspect of the therapeutic recreation process, which is evaluation.

Evaluation

As with the other three aspects of the therapeutic recreation process, evaluation techniques vary based on clientele and setting. This section will briefly summarize some of the general concepts of evaluation. Specific methods of evaluation will be explored later in this text.

Table 6.1 Commonly Used Debriefing Techniques

Technique	Description
Go Around	Each client contributes a descriptive sentence or word regarding the activity or a portion of the activity. ("Can each of you share an emotion you experienced during the session?")
Whip	Similar to Go Around, but each client completes a sentence stem presented by the facilitator. Examples include "One thing we did well today was . . ." or "I feel good about . . ."
Memory Game	Clients recall the events of a session in chronological order, with each client taking up where the previous one left off. The facilitator indicates when to pass off the story to the next person.
Gestalt	The client closes his or her eyes, recalls an event, and describes it as if he or she is actually going through the event again. Essentially, the client mentally relives the experience. The facilitator questions the client about the experience when appropriate. "What do you see as you stand in front of the group?"
Props	Props can be used to stimulate discussion, including "talking sticks," playing cards, and other commercially produced processing products.
Artifacts	Physical items created or related to the experience can be used to stimulate discussion. Examples would include T-shirts, medals, craft projects, and self-assessments such as the colors personality test.
Videos or photographs	Videos, photos, or audio recordings made during a session can later be used as a prompt for recollection and discussion of the experience.

Stumbo and Peterson (2004) defined evaluation as "the systematic and logical process of gathering and analyzing selected information in order to make decisions about the quality, effectiveness, and/or outcomes of a program, function, or service" (p. 364). Everybody wants to see quality documented in therapeutic recreation programs. Insurance companies, government funding programs, accreditation agencies, professional therapeutic recreation organizations, and internal administrators all request documentation of outcomes. This documentation justifies the cost of services by demonstrating outcomes, which in turn justifies our existence.

The group most entitled to quality assurance and accountability is the client population. Cost is important to this group, but what they really want is quality care. For the individual professional (and for the organized profession), this should be the motivating factor in meeting demands for quality evaluation. As such, the first aspect of evaluation to be considered is client evaluation.

Client Evaluation

One of the big challenges in conceptualizing an evaluation protocol (procedure) is determining what outcomes should be measured. Logic suggests that evaluating an individual client's progression or regression should be built around his or her pre-established therapeutic recreation goals and objectives. If the client's goal was to participate successfully in an adapted ski program, evaluation should focus on associated skills and participation rates. If the client's goal was to remove leisure barriers, evaluation should focus on the presence or absence of these barriers. Data can be collected in an ongoing manner (formative evaluation), which allows for changes to be made as necessary. Data can also be gathered at the end of the program (summative evaluation). Summative evaluation does not help identify needed midstream program changes, but it is cleaner in terms of documenting the outcomes of a specific treatment protocol or program. Fortunately, the therapeutic recreation process allows clients with similar needs to be placed in similar programs. Because clients within these programs are likely to have similar goals, the data collected to evaluate these goals can be pooled. This approach allows evaluation of specific programs as a whole.

Program Evaluation

Evaluation of a specific program can involve information sources other than pooled outcomes of multiple clients. Financial reports can be combined with outcome data to analyze the cost-to-benefit ratio. Various reporting forms can be used to track the nature and content of individual activity sessions. This type of form is helpful in ensuring that professionals are planning and implementing sessions in a manner that is consistent with client goals and objectives.

Besides looking at specific programs, the evaluation process should review the overall comprehensive therapeutic recreation program. Individual client evaluation and specific program evaluation usually are conducted internally, but internal or external parties can mandate comprehensive program evaluations. Most notably, insurance providers and accreditation agencies may mandate certain evaluation procedures. External agencies such as the Centers for Medicare and Medicaid Services and the Joint Commission on the Accreditation of Healthcare Organizations regularly audit health care agencies to ensure quality of care and accountability. These audits include verification that the health care provider is following appropriate assessment, documentation, and evaluation procedures. In cases when external evaluation does not occur, the agency should consider an internal evaluation of the overall program. Such evaluations help document quality programs and justify requests for funds from public or private funding sources.

Evaluation Tools

Before considering specific strategies for evaluating clients, a review of what areas should be evaluated will be useful. Attendance and participation are two of the easiest areas to evaluate but are probably the least informative. Simple checklists typically can be used to record this information, possibly with notations about the level of involvement. Another outcome to consider is participant satisfaction levels. This item is most commonly targeted in participatory programs, but it is relevant to all therapeutic recreation settings. This information can be gathered from participants, spouses, guardians, or parents. The third major area is, again, client goals (targeted outcomes). These goals might focus on client behaviors, emotional states, attitudes, knowledge, or skills and abilities. Methods for measuring each of these areas will vary, but procedures are analogous to those used for assessment. Interviews, observation, standardized assessments and interest inventories, and existing documents can all provide useful evaluative information. Assessment also frequently involves use of mailed surveys or phone interviews to gather information after programs have ended or after the client has departed.

Even in settings that do not involve interventions, all aspects of the therapeutic recreation process should be implemented. Adjustments must be made to make the process responsive to client needs. Assessment, planning, implementation, and evaluation in a community-based inclusive recreation program will be much different from those that occur in physical rehabilitation or mental health settings. This reality does not change the fact that the therapeutic recreation process is necessary to ensure that services produce the desired outcomes. Moreover, therapeutic recreation professionals must have a thorough understanding of how this process works, how it relates to different client groups, and how it interacts with other aspects of the overall therapeutic recreation agency or department.

Evaluation Systems

Many systems have been developed to provide a structured mechanism for evaluation. Two creative approaches worth mentioning here are goal attainment scaling and SMART goals (Conzemius & O'Neill, 2002). Goal attainment scaling was first described by Kiresuk and Sherman (1968) as a general method to evaluate the outcome of mental health treatment. Goal attainment scaling (GAS) takes a measurable objective and establishes various levels of achievement. The client is then scored based on his or her level of achievement. This scoring system provides a consistent mechanism for evaluating agency effectiveness in achieving individual or program goals.

The creators of GAS provided a system that allows clients to be compared with one another, even when the targeted goals are different (Kiresuk, Smith & Cardillo, 1994). The current author has used GAS on several occasions as an evaluation tool for a therapeutic recreation camping program for adjudicated youth (referred to as the Empower Me program). The example in table 6.2 illustrates how five goal areas were operationalized into different levels of attainment.

Various sources of documentation from the Empower Me program were used to determine the extent to which these goals had been met. In this case, the same goals were used for all participants, but the system can be tailored to use goals of the individual client. For stage 2 of the Empower Me program (which occurred after camp), clients worked with counselors to establish individual goals under each goal area. One of the most attractive characteristics of GAS is that the evaluation of an overall program can be based on the unique goals of individual clients.

SMART goals provide another method of evaluation. The acronym SMART refers to goals that are specific and strategic, measurable, attainable, results oriented, and time bound. Tree diagrams are used as a tool for operationalizing SMART goals (see figure 6.2). This approach is less complex than the GAS approach but can be equally useful in ensuring that individual and departmental goals and objectives are being developed and evaluated.

Summary

Up to this point, the duties associated with the therapeutic recreation process have been presented in regard to helping individual clients achieve their therapeutic recreation goals. Note that therapeutic recreation specialists are also responsible for developing the comprehensive therapeutic recreation program. This responsibility includes developing the overall mission and goals of the therapeutic recreation department, as well as the specific programs mentioned earlier. Clients can then be introduced to specific programs that fit their needs.

In most cases, specific therapeutic recreation programs are already in place, but the professional should always be looking to make adjustments and upgrades. There is no guarantee that an existing program is adequately aligned with the needs of the agency clientele. Development of comprehensive and specific programs is somewhat beyond the scope of this class, but gaining an understanding of how the therapeutic recreation process functions within the context of organized frameworks is important.

All professionals, regardless of where or with whom they work, must be competent in delivery of

Table 6.2 GAS Worksheet and Scoring for Empower Me Program

Level	Scale 1 Self-concept	Scale 2 Social competence	Scale 3 Planning and decision making	Scale 4 Constructive use of time**	Scale 5 Activity skills***
Much less −2 than expected	Regression in self-esteem.	Average score on CC* social ratings was less than 2.5.	Average score on CC* ratings was less than 2.5.	Appropriately participated in one Empower Me bonus opportunity.	Average score on activity ratings was less than 3.0.
	Three or fewer completed journal entries.	Five or more behavioral violations.			
Somewhat less −1 than expected	Self-esteem scores improved by less than 5%.	Average score on CC* social ratings was 2.5-2.99.	Average score on CC* ratings was 2.5-2.99.	Appropriately participated in two Empower Me bonus opportunities.	Average score on activity ratings was 3.0-3.49.
	Four completed journal entries.	Four or fewer behavioral violations.			
Expected level 0 of outcome	Self-esteem scores improved by 5-7.5%.	Average score on CC* social rating was 3.0-3.49.	Average score on CC* ratings was 3.0-3.49.	Appropriately participated in three Empower Me bonus opportunities.	Average score on activity ratings was 3.5-3.99.
	Five completed journal entries.	Three behavioral violations.			
Somewhat more +1 than expected	Self-esteem scores improved by 7.6-10%.	Average score on CC* social rating was 3.5-3.99.	Average score on CC* ratings was 3.5-3.99.	Appropriately participated in four Empower Me bonus opportunities.	Average score on activity rating was 4.0-4.49.
	Six completed journal entries.	Two behavioral violations.			
Much more +2 than expected	Self-esteem scores improved by more than 10%.	Average score on CC* social rating was 4.0 or greater.	Average score on CC* ratings was 4.0 or greater.	Appropriately participated in five Empower Me bonus opportunities.	Average score on activity ratings was 4.5 or greater.
	Seven or more completed journal entries.	One or no behavioral violations.			
Score					
Comments					

*CC refers to challenge course ratings conducted by counselors that corresponded to the goal area.

**Empower Me bonus activities were free-time choices made by the campers.

***Every camp activity involved a 1 to 5 rating of the level of camper engagement.

the therapeutic recreation process. Lack of skill and knowledge in any one of the four areas can threaten the well-being of clients. In truth, the therapeutic recreation specialist has an ethical responsibility to master these skills to the best of his or her ability. At this point, the prospective professional should start to think about being the best therapist possible rather than just getting through college. The foundation of being an outstanding therapeutic recreation specialist lies in making a personal decision to master the therapeutic recreation process. Your personal commitment must be not only to academic preparation but also to the individual people that you will one day help.

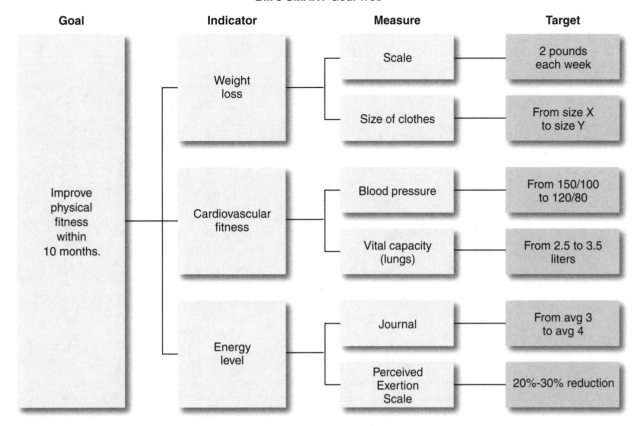

Bill's SMART Goal Tree

| Goal | Indicator | Measure | Target |

Goal: Improve physical fitness within 10 months.

- **Weight loss**
  - Scale → 2 pounds each week
  - Size of clothes → From size X to size Y
- **Cardiovascular fitness**
  - Blood pressure → From 150/100 to 120/80
  - Vital capacity (lungs) → From 2.5 to 3.5 liters
- **Energy level**
  - Journal → From avg 3 to avg 4
  - Perceived Exertion Scale → 20%-30% reduction

Figure 6.2 This tree diagram helps operationalize SMART goals.

Courtesy of Dr. Terry Robertson

DISCUSSION QUESTIONS

1. What pros and cons do you see regarding each of the assessment methods presented in this chapter (interviewing, observation, standardized assessments)?

2. Discuss the relationship between assessment and planning. What does it mean to target a particular outcome, and how are these outcomes identified or established?

3. How can task analysis assist a therapeutic recreation specialist in determining appropriate sequencing for an activity? Perform a task analysis of a recreation-related behavior and give an example of how the activity could be sequenced for a particular client group.

4. How does sequencing relate to the two debriefing strategies presented in this chapter? What might happen if a therapeutic recreation specialist skipped stage 1 of either approach? What might happen if the therapeutic recreation specialist failed to proceed past stage 1 of either approach?

5. What is the difference between assessment and evaluation? What similarities do you see? How is writing goals and objectives related to these two aspects of the therapeutic recreation process?

Allied Professions

Frederick P. Green, PhD
University of Southern Mississippi

Tanya E. McAdory-Coogan, MS, CTRS, CPRP
National Recreation and Park Association

LEARNING OUTCOMES

After completing this chapter, learners will be able to demonstrate the following competencies:

- Identify various professions that may work within the same realm as the certified therapeutic recreation specialist
- Explain the range of services and settings associated with each profession
- Identify education and credentialing requirements for each profession
- Identify potential opportunities for collaboration between a certified therapeutic recreation specialist and other professionals

A therapeutic recreation specialist will rarely work in a vacuum, alone and isolated from other professionals. In most cases, he or she will be working as part of a team in order to ensure that individuals receiving care (whether patients, clients, members, or participants) receive the most comprehensive and appropriate services. Thus, it is important that all team members develop an understanding and respect for the professions of their colleagues.

Therapeutic recreation specialists often state that our fellow professionals know little about what we do and really do not understand the intent and purpose of our profession. We often note that we do not get the respect that we deserve—respect that we have earned through our education, our commitment to our profession, and our dedication to the health and well-being of the people we serve. But how much do we know about the professionals whom we work with? We may be stymied in our efforts to enlighten our colleagues about the purpose and benefits of therapeutic recreation, but we have no legitimate excuse for our failure to understand the role that our colleagues in **allied health professions** play in the health care system.

Knowledge of our colleagues' professional qualifications and responsibilities is critically important to the care of the people we serve. Many of us will serve on a team. In some cases the team will be well defined, such as an interdisciplinary team in a rehabilitation setting. In this case, the team will have representatives from allied disciplines who will meet, share information, and work together to plan and provide the best level of care for the individuals served. In other cases, the boundaries of the team will not be as well defined, but each member of the team will have specific responsibilities. In these situations, the success of the program or services will depend on collaboration among team members. For example, a certified therapeutic recreation specialist working as an inclusion facilitator for a community park and recreation program serves as a member of the staff. Staff meetings, like team meetings, are regularly scheduled to ensure the most efficient, effective, and safe way to deliver recreation services to the community.

Understanding of the qualifications and responsibilities of colleagues across the health professions is more than just a professional courtesy. We are ethically bound to stay within the limits of our professional qualifications and training. Although we may at times believe that we are able to contribute much more to the health and well-being of our clients, we must understand, respect, and rely on the contributions of our colleagues to ensure comprehensive care. Understanding the allied health professions and appreciating their contributions will help us offer the best possible therapeutic recreation services.

The purpose of this chapter is to present introductory information about some of the more common allied health professions with whom therapeutic recreation specialists will most likely work. The list is incomplete because it focuses on the more common collaborative disciplines. For each discipline we have provided a brief description of the purpose and nature of the work, the range of services offered by the discipline, the settings in which they may be found, education and credentialing requirements, and the potential for collaboration with therapeutic recreation specialists.

Child Life Specialist

Child life specialists are professionals who are specially trained to help both children and their families understand and manage stressful health care experiences and challenging life events. They provide developmental, educational, and therapeutic interventions for children and their families under stress. Child life specialists support growth and development while recognizing family strengths and individuality, and respecting different methods of coping (Child Life Council, 2005a).

Range of Services and Settings

Child life specialists are typically found in hospitals. They work with patients and families in areas such as the emergency department, patient rooms, surgical areas, the neonatal intensive care unit, and the pediatric intensive care unit. In each of these areas, child life interventions focus on the individual needs of the patient and family. Child life specialists can also be found in other settings (Child Life Council, 2005a).

Educational Requirements and Credentialing

Certified child life specialists (CCLS) have earned a bachelor's or master's degree, with an educational background that includes human growth and development, education, psychology, and counseling. Students who wish to become a CCLS explore the scientific study of human development from birth through adolescence with an interdisciplinary focus that includes psychological, educational, and social-behavioral perspectives (California State University at Northridge, 2005). They are required to complete an internship program and a rigorous application and examination process. Child life specialists are certified through a program administered by the Child Life Council (Child Life Council, 2005b). In some cases, professionals achieve certification as both a CCLS and a certified therapeutic recreation specialist. They work toward both certifications because the Child Life Council does allow course work in therapeutic recreation to count toward CCLS certification. As long as course work includes the associated course requirements, students who major in therapeutic recreation can do a second internship under a CCLS and be eligible for both certification exams.

Potential for Collaboration With Therapeutic Recreation

In hospitals that employ both child life specialists and therapeutic recreation specialists, some initial confusion may result because members of both disciplines have a similar scope of services. But therapeutic recreation professionals should focus on the potential for collaboration with various pediatric therapies such as child life specialists. Therapeutic recreation specialists and child life specialists could offer an expanded range of options for stress management, or they could collaborate in programming special events. Both disciplines may select play and recreation as a modality, but therapeutic recreation specialists can focus on leisure education and the development of self-determination, lifelong leisure interests and skills, and strategies that clients could use to pursue their interests long after discharge.

Art Therapy

Although art therapy is a relatively new field, the American Art Therapy Association has a membership of 4,000 professional art therapists (CtArtTherapy.org, 2005). **Art therapists** are psychotherapists who are trained in both psychology and art. The purpose of art therapy is to address a person's inner conflicts, abilities, personality traits, interests, and concerns by using art media, images, the creative process, and patient responses to artwork (American Medical Association, 2004a).

©Pattie Rouse

As a therapeutic recreation specialist, you may collaborate with a Child Life Specialist to help your client.

Range of Services and Settings

Art therapists work in hospitals, rehabilitation centers, nursing homes, prisons, and private offices. Populations served by art therapy include people with physical or cognitive limitations, patients who are receiving psychiatric services (all diagnostic categories), and individuals, couples, and families who are seeking to improve self-awareness and form stronger relationships (CtArtTherapy.org, 2005). Art therapists use art materials with a therapeutic application to help people develop improved communication and self-expression; increase self-awareness; integrate physical, affective, cognitive, and social functioning; and facilitate healthy life changes.

Educational Requirements and Credentialing

Educational requirements established by the American Art Therapy Association include a 4-year college degree that includes 15 semester hours of studio art and 12 semester hours of psychology, a master's degree in art therapy, and a 1-year clinical internship under the supervision of a registered art therapist (ATR). Art therapists who complete degree requirements are granted registration (ATR) after completing the board examination administered by the Art Therapy Credentials Board, Inc. (Ct.ArtTherapy.org, 2005).

Potential for Collaboration With Therapeutic Recreation

Therapeutic recreation specialists and art therapists have some potential areas for collaboration. Artwork produced by clients in the therapeutic recreation program may present an opportunity to assess potential client problems, conflicts, or inner turmoil. Therapeutic recreation specialists should be careful not to overstep the limits of their professional training by interpreting client artwork, although they can use client artwork as a way to trigger discussion and expression of emotions. Artwork can also be used as a metaphor to represent client goals and change. To clarify, therapeutic recreation specialists do not interpret artwork, but they do use the process and meaning of the artwork as expressed by the client. Therapeutic recreation professionals can also confer with art therapists for interpretation, refer clients to art therapists for assessment and psychotherapy services, and provide clients who express an interest in art with the opportunities and resources they need to enjoy art as a lifelong leisure pursuit.

Music Therapy

Music therapy is the use of music as a modality to treat the health needs and improve the quality of life of both well people and people with illnesses and disabilities (American Medical Association, 2004c). The purpose of music therapy intervention is to promote health and wellness, manage stress, improve communication, facilitate movement and exercise, increase social interactions, and serve as a foundation for the expression of feelings. Modern applications began as musicians played music to ameliorate the physical and emotional effects of trauma of veterans of the two world wars (American Music Therapy Association, 1999).

Range of Services and Settings

Music therapists are musicians who are also trained as therapists. Intervention techniques may include singing, creating, or playing music; dancing or moving to music; listening to music; and applying music and imagery. Music therapists are often employed in psychiatric hospitals, physical rehabilitation facilities, nursing homes, and substance abuse centers. Recipients of music therapy include people with developmental disabilities, dementia, brain injuries, drug and alcohol addictions, acute and chronic pain, and mothers in labor (American Music Therapy Association, 1999).

Educational Requirements and Credentialing

The music therapist–board certified (credential) is required for practice as a music therapist. To be eligible for certification, individuals must complete baccalaureate requirements for a degree in music therapy and successfully complete the national exam administered by the Certification Board for Music Therapists. Qualified music therapists are registered through the National Music Therapy Registry (NMTR) (American Music Therapy Association, 1999).

Potential for Collaboration With Therapeutic Recreation

The potential for collaboration between music therapists and therapeutic recreation specialists is tremendous. A therapeutic recreation specialist could make a referral to music therapy if a client expresses an interest in music. Music could be identified as a program option in a comprehensive therapeutic recreation program. In some cases, music therapists and therapeutic recreation specialists could offer an expanded range of options for stress management, or they could collaborate in programming special events. Finally, a client's interest in music can be developed by the music therapist and incorporated into a healthy leisure lifestyle by the therapeutic recreation specialist.

Dietetics

Dietitians assess the nutritional needs of their clients, plan and manage dietary intake, and promote sound eating habits to aid in the prevention and treatment of illness (United States Department of Labor, 2004a). A dietitian who meets specific prerequisites is eligible to be registered with the Commission on Dietetic Registration.

Range of Services and Settings

Registered dietitians work on the treatment and prevention of disease in hospitals, **HMO**s, long-term care facilities, community and public health settings, home health agencies, and schools. They assess patient's nutritional needs, implement nutrition programs, provide counseling, and provide instruction on grocery shopping and food preparation to the elderly and people with special needs (United States Department of Labor, 2004a).

Educational Requirements and Credentialing

Four years of university study and a dietetic internship or master's degree in nutrition or a closely related field is required for eligibility as a registered dietitian. Additionally, successful completion of a national exam is required, and registered dietitians are expected to participate in continuing education to maintain their credentials. By meeting these strict standards, a dietitian is awarded a license to work using the title of registered dietitian (RD) (United States Department of Labor, 2004a).

Potential for Collaboration With Therapeutic Recreation

Therapeutic recreation specialists often do not work directly with dietitians. From time to time, however, therapeutic recreation interventions involve outings in which food is included. In these cases, the specialist would work closely with the dietitian to plan a menu that offers healthy food choices and accommodates patients on a restricted diet. Additionally, if the therapeutic recreation staff notice that a patient's poor eating habits are negatively affecting his or her health and subsequently negating the benefits earned from therapeutic recreation intervention, the therapeutic recreation staff could refer the person to the dietitian for assessment and assistance.

Kinesiotherapy

Kinesiotherapy is the application of therapeutic exercise to improve the strength, endurance, and mobility of people with physical injuries or limitations (American Kinesiotherapy Association, 2005). Kinesiotherapy as a professional discipline originated during World War II as therapy provided by corrective physical conditioning specialists to aid the recovery of injured service personnel and speed their return to active duty. After the war, the discipline continued service primarily in Veterans Administration hospitals as corrective therapy. The profession became known as kinesiotherapy in 1987.

Range of Services and Settings

The primary role of the kinesiotherapist is to employ physical exercise to improve a patient's physical conditioning following stabilization. Kinesiotherapists also employ exercise programs designed to stabilize physical capacity following injury or loss of functioning. Because of an early association with the military, kinesiotherapists work primarily in Veterans Administration hospitals, although a growing number of kinesiotherapists work in private hospitals and rehabilitation facilities, nursing homes, and sports medicine and exercise facilities (American Medical Association, 2004b).

Educational Requirements and Credentialing

A bachelor of science degree from an accredited program, including a 1,000-hour clinical internship, is required for kinesiotherapy eligibility. Candidates who graduate from an accredited academic program are eligible to take the kinesiotherapy registration exam. After successfully completing the exam, a registered kinesiotherapist is listed on the kinesiotherapy registry contingent on completion of annual continuing education requirements.

Potential for Collaboration With Therapeutic Recreation

The services provided by a registered kinesiotherapist and a therapeutic recreation specialist have some similarities. Professionals from both disciplines assess functional limitations and plan and implement activities or exercises to improve functioning. The potential for collaboration, however, is excellent. For example, in a rehabilitation setting the registered kinesiotherapist would take the lead role in stabilization by providing exercises to improve physical functioning. The role of the therapeutic recreation specialist would be to work with patients to identify desirable activities after discharge that would allow them to continue the growth initiated by kinesiotherapy.

WORKING WITH HAYDEN'S KINESIOTHERAPIST

Hayden had finally turned 16 and gotten his license when he was involved in a car accident. Before his accident, Hayden had played baseball, was on the school wrestling team, and enjoyed camping and hiking with his family. Hayden experienced a traumatic brain injury during the car wreck and was nonresponsive for the first 3 months of his rehabilitation. One day while playing tapes of Hayden's high school wrestling matches, his dad noticed that Hayden had opened his eyes. Over the next 3 months, Hayden gradually improved. He spent much of his time working with both a kinesiotherapist and a certified therapeutic recreation specialist.

Certified Therapeutic Recreation Specialist

The CTRS worked with Hayden from day 1 of his rehabilitation. Early on, sensory stimulation was used to encourage brain activity and responses from Hayden. After Hayden "woke up," the CTRS used games and other recreational activities as a way to encourage Hayden to speak, exercise cognitive skills, and use motor skills. By the third month, Hayden was walking with assistance. The CTRS implemented games and activities involving gross motor skills, balance, and coordination into Hayden's program. Many of these activities took place in the pool, where Hayden could maneuver more easily. Over time, the CTRS introduced additional activities that required Hayden to stand and ambulate on his own.

Kinesiotherapist

After Hayden gained consciousness and demonstrated some ability to use motor skills, the kinesiotherapist developed an exercise program congruent with Hayden's needs. This process continued throughout Hayden's rehabilitation and ultimately allowed him to recover most of his motor abilities.

Working Together

During Hayden's rehabilitation, the kinesiotherapist worked with the CTRS to identify games and activities that would allow Hayden to perform the exercises in a more enjoyable way. This approach was critical to Hayden's rehabilitation because of the extensive time and effort that would be required. Early on, these were simple activities such as block stacking, three-dimensional puzzles, and gardening in indoor flower boxes. Six months after the injury, Hayden was able to ambulate independently and started to take part in an inpatient fitness and wellness program developed by the CTRS and the kinesiotherapist. By the ninth month of Hayden's rehabilitation, the two colleagues began working with him to develop a plan for achieving strength and endurance levels necessary to participate in strenuous physical activity such as hiking and baseball. Two years after his injury, Hayden regularly participated in strenuous physical activity. On Hayden's 21st birthday, the two colleagues attended an adult amateur wrestling tournament, during which Hayden competed in his first match since his injury (with clearance from his doctor). He was pinned in the first 30 seconds, but losing the match was the greatest victory of his life.

Athletic Training

The athletic training profession began as a service to school sport teams as team managers that served water and passed out towels to athletes. Today athletic trainers are medical professionals who are responsible for the prevention, assessment, treatment, and rehabilitation of injuries related to participation in physical activities. The small group of professionals who began with college sport teams now includes over 30,000 members who provide training services to many levels of active people (Board of Certification, 2004). Although most trainers work with people without permanent disabilities, awareness of the need for trainers with disability-specific knowledge is growing. Such people would be especially useful for providing services to Paralympic athletes, Special Olympians, and others with disabilities who are interested in sport activities.

Range of Services and Settings

Athletic trainers provide injury prevention; clinical evaluation and diagnosis of athletic injuries; immediate care following injury; and treatment, rehabilitation, and reconditioning services for injuries that result from physical trauma. Athletic trainers work on-site at professional sport activities, collegiate athletic events, and secondary school athletic events for the primary purpose of providing immediate care for injuries. Additionally, athletic trainers are employed by hospitals, sports medicine clinics, and fitness centers (Board of Certification, 2004).

Educational Requirements and Credentialing

Athletic trainers are certified as athletic trainer certified (ATC) by the National Association of Athletic Training–Board of Certification (Board of Certification, 2004). Eligibility requirements for certification include successful completion of the national certification exam. Eligibility requirements for the exam include a bachelor of science degree in athletic training from a CAAHEP-accredited athletic training program, endorsement from the program director of university athletic training, and current certification in emergency cardiac care.

Potential for Collaboration With Therapeutic Recreation

Athletic trainers are an invaluable addition to the team, especially for special events in the community. Although most recreation staff members are certified in first aid and other emergency procedures, the athletic trainer's extensive training in immediate

©Human Kinetics

Athletic trainers are important during sport and athletic events.

care and treatment of injuries is invaluable during sport and athletic events.

Nursing

Nurses assist individuals, families, and communities in attaining, reattaining, and maintaining optimal health and functioning (Answers.com, 2005). Specifically, the purpose of the nursing profession is to promote health, prevent disease, and help people cope with sickness. Registered nurses observe patients, assess their symptoms, and document their reactions and progress (Medical-Central.org, 2005).

Range of Services and Settings

When providing direct patient care, nurses observe, assess, and record symptoms, reactions, and progress in patients; assist physicians during surgeries, treatments, and examinations; administer medications; and assist in convalescence and rehabilitation. Registered nurses also develop and manage nursing care plans, instruct patients and their families in proper care, and help individuals and groups take steps to improve or maintain their health. As the largest health care occupation, registered nurses held about 2.3 million jobs in 2002. Almost three out of five jobs were in hospitals, in inpatient and outpatient departments. Others worked in offices of physicians, nursing-care facilities, home health care services, employment services, government agencies, and outpatient care centers. The remainder worked mostly in social assistance agencies and educational services, both public and private (United States Department of Labor, 2004e).

Educational Requirements and Credentialing

A nursing candidate's education is grounded in anatomy, physiology, pharmacology, the cause and treatment of disease, the intricacies of nutrition and diet, surgical skills, and a variety of techniques pertaining to patient care. Training includes both classroom study and actual hospital practice (Answers.com, 2005). After completing educational requirements, candidates must take a written licensure examination, administered by the National Council of State Boards of Nursing, to become a licensed registered nurse (RN) (Discovernursing.com, 2005).

Licensed practical nurses (LPNs) usually have 18 to 24 months of training in anatomy and physiology, medications, and practical patient care. They must pass state or national boards (such as NCLEX–PN in the United States) and renew their licenses periodically. Typically LPNs provide basic bedside care, take vital signs, prepare and administer injections, and monitor patients to report adverse reactions to medications or treatments. They may also evaluate patients' needs, develop care plans, and supervise the care provided by nursing aides (United States Department of Labor, 2004e).

Potential for Collaboration With Therapeutic Recreation

The professional responsibilities of the nurse and the therapeutic recreation specialist are clearly different. This contrast can be helpful in promoting therapeutic recreation in health care facilities. Nurses may identify conditions in which patients would benefit from therapeutic recreation services. For example, patients may exhibit signs of boredom, low self-esteem, or an external locus of control and lack of internal motivation to participate in therapy. As a result, nurses may recommend therapeutic recreation services to alleviate these conditions. Conversely, nurses who serve as case managers may notice that patients have responded well to treatment, have attained a level of stability, and are ready to develop healthy life skills. Nurses who are aware of and appreciate the potential contribution of therapeutic recreation services can refer patients to leisure education programs.

Occupational Therapy

Occupational therapy is similar in many ways to therapeutic recreation, especially therapeutic recreation services that are designed to improve functional skills of clients. According to *Health Professions Career and Education Directory, 2004–2005* (American Medical Association, 2004d), **occupational therapy** is "the use of purposeful activity and interventions to achieve functional outcomes" (p. 280). The intended purpose of occupational therapy intervention is to help clients achieve independence in all life activities and across all health domains (American Occupational Therapy Association, 2005).

Range of Services and Settings

Occupational therapists work with people who have temporary or permanent physical, emotional, or cognitive impairments (OccupationalTherapist.com, 2005). Occupational therapy interventions focus on activities of daily living including play, self-care, work readiness and school readiness skills, leisure, interpersonal skills, self-management, and family care. Similar to the therapeutic recreation specialist who employs the therapeutic recreation process, the occupational therapist assesses individual functioning; develops and implements intervention strategies including direct service to clients; and consults with clients, families, agencies, and educational services (Sharp, 2005). Occupational therapists are employed in hospitals, rehabilitation clinics, schools, nursing homes, private industry, and other health-related agencies.

Educational Requirements and Credentialing

A bachelor's degree from an accredited program and successful completion of the national exam is the current minimum requirement for occupational therapy practice. As of 2007, a master's degree represents the entry-level academic requirement (United States Department of Labor, 2004b). The curriculum in occupational therapy includes work in human development, anatomy and physiology, health, psychology, sociology, sciences, and the humanities, and 6 months of fieldwork (American Medical Association, 2004d). Occupational therapists are certified by the National Board of Certification of Occupational Therapy after graduation from a program accredited by the Accreditation Council for Occupational Therapy Education, completed fieldwork, and successful completion of the national certification exam. All states regulate the practice of occupational therapy, and each state has additional requirements for licensure.

Potential for Collaboration With Therapeutic Recreation

In agencies that employ both an occupational therapist and a therapeutic recreation specialist, some initial confusion may result because members of both disciplines focus on the similarities in professional mission. Although similarities are present, therapeutic recreation specialists should employ their stronger background in leisure and leisure education. Both disciplines may select play and recreation as a modality for improving functioning, but therapeutic recreation specialists should be better equipped to address areas such as leisure education and the development of self-determination, lifelong leisure interests and skills, and strategies for pursuing those interests long after discharge. In addition, therapeutic recreation specialists should focus on the potential for collaboration with occupational therapists and keep in mind the best interest of clients rather than engage in turf wars (an issue that should be dealt with outside the immediate treatment environment). Educating colleagues about therapeutic recreation is encouraged, but this process should not create barriers to patient care.

Physical Therapy

The purpose of **physical therapy** is to reduce pain, improve strength and mobility, and prevent or treat permanent physical disabilities. Physical therapists provide a wide range of preventative and rehabilitative therapies including assessment and evaluation of muscle strength and functioning, joint motion, and the need for braces and prosthetic devices (American Medical Association, 2004e). The profession is served by the American Physical Therapy Association (APTA), an organization that originated in 1921 as the American Women's Physical Therapeutic Association, an organization that was open only to women until 1930 (American Physical Therapy Association, 2005).

Range of Services and Settings

Physical therapists work with a variety of patients, including those with acute or chronic injuries, people with permanent disabilities, older people, and athletes who are striving to achieve maximum performance. Services may include physical exercises, massage, relaxation exercises, and other techniques that promote the attainment of a person's ultimate physical functioning (Physical-Therapist.com, 2005). Physical therapists are employed in many settings, most notably in rehabilitation centers, nursing homes, private physical therapy centers, schools, and sport and exercise facilities (American Medical Association, 2004e).

Educational Requirements and Credentialing

Physical therapists are subject to state licensure, and requirements for licensure vary from state to state. To be eligible for licensure, a person must graduate with a minimum of a master's degree in physical therapy from an academic program accredited by the Commission on the Accreditation of Physical Therapy Education (CAPTE) and successfully complete a state-administered national exam (American Medical Association, 2004e). Course work requirements include basic sciences (biology, chemistry, and physics), and specialized course work in biomechanics, kinesiology, anatomy, and human growth and development. Continuing education is required for maintaining licensure in most states. Additionally, a voluntary clinical specialization program that reflects a physical therapist's clinical knowledge and expertise in a specialized area of practice is administered by the American Physical Therapy Association (2005).

Potential for Collaboration With Therapeutic Recreation

The techniques used by therapeutic recreation and physical therapy overlap to some degree, although physical therapy appears to be more similar to kinesiotherapy. The potential for collaboration does exist. In facilities that employ both physical therapists and therapeutic recreation specialists, therapeutic recreation services may be most effective after stabilization because therapeutic recreation focuses on leisure education and facilitating the development of a repertoire of leisure interests that will allow the patient to maintain the functioning achieved through physical therapy and continue to improve after discharge.

Psychiatry

Psychiatry is the branch of medicine that deals with the diagnosis, treatment, and prevention of mental and emotional disorders (MedicineNet.com, 2005). The recognition of the significance of emotions in mental disorders has been around since ancient Greece. Today, psychiatrists are licensed physicians, specially trained to treat patients with mental disorders and prescribe medications (HealthyMinds.org, 2005).

TERRI JOHNSON

Background Information

Education
*Bachelor's degree in Recreation and Leisure, Southwest Missouri State University (now Missouri State University) *Master's degree in Business Administration from Fontbonne College

Credentials
*CPRP *CTRS *MBA

Special Affiliations
*National Recreation and Park Association/National Therapeutic Recreation Society *Missouri Parks and Recreation Association *Therapeutic Recreation of Greater St. Louis Association

Special Awards
*Associate Fellow Award, Missouri Parks and Recreation Association (1991) *Employee of the Year Award, Alliance for Inclusion, Missouri Governor's Council on Disability (1996) *Outstanding Therapeutic Recreator Award, Missouri Therapeutic Recreation Society (2003) *Outstanding Service Award, Recreation Council of Greater St. Louis (2005) *Presidential Citation, National Therapeutic Recreation Society (2006)

Career Information

Position
Executive director, Municipal Partners for Inclusive Recreation

Organization Information
On October 1, 1997, seven municipalities in southwest St. Louis County, Missouri, joined forces to create a governmental agency known as Municipal Partners for Inclusive Recreation (MPIR). The agency's board consists of directors of parks and recreation for Ballwin, Crestwood, Des Peres, Ellisville, Kirkwood, Manchester, and Sunset Hills; and they employ an executive director.

Organization's Mission
Municipal Partners for Inclusive Recreation's purpose is twofold: to welcome and facilitate the inclusion of people with disabilities into existing programs offered by the participating departments, and to assist with

Americans with Disabilities Act (ADA) compliance when participating municipal facilities and parks are newly created or renovated.

Job Description
Plan, develop, and implement a marketing strategy to promote and publicize inclusive recreation programs. Prepare and present information to target populations, parents, care providers, and social service organizations for people with disabilities. Write news releases, promotional literature, advertisements, and pamphlets encouraging people with disabilities to utilize their local parks and recreation department programs. Initiate, manage, and coordinate the inclusion of people with disabilities into existing recreational and leisure programs. Monitor the effectiveness of inclusive recreational programming in order to ensure success and quality services. Recruit support staff and volunteers for participants with disabilities who need assistance in order to successfully take part in activities and programs. Assist participants in securing needed services and adaptive equipment. Maintain program statistics and written records, assist with grant writing, and prepare reports and documentation as required by the Recreation Council and the Productive Living Board.

> Wake each day with the thought that something wonderful is about to happen!

Career Path
I worked with people with physical disabilities in a community-based recreation program right out of college for 8 years before I was hired to create my current job.

Likes and Dislikes About the Job
I love that I was able to create my job by borrowing bits and pieces from several of the best departments and agencies across the country that were pioneering the inclusion movement and that I can change the way I do my job as I learn from others around the country. I learn something every day and I love seeing the smiles and hearing the giggles from the kids I am serving. I sometimes wish there was someone to help me get everything ready for the extremely busy springs and summers, but I manage.

Advice to Undergraduate Students
Be prepared to try and do tasks that you did not think you would do or never planned to do—you just may like them! Every day is different and you can always try new approaches to see if they will enhance your experience and the experiences of those around you.

Range of Services and Settings

Psychiatrists assess and treat mental illness through a combination of psychotherapy, psychoanalysis, hospitalization, and medication. They often regularly talk with patients about their problems in order to help them find solutions through changes in their behavioral patterns. They explore their patients' past experiences and facilitate group and family sessions. In many cases, medications are administered to correct chemical imbalances that may be causing emotional problems (United States Department of Labor, 2004c). Psychiatrists work in group or private practice, general and state hospitals, community health centers, and in the public sector such as the Veterans Administration (American Board of Psychiatry and Neurology, 2005).

Educational Requirements and Credentialing

In the United States, psychiatrists are board certified as specialists in their field. After completing 4 years of medical school, physicians practice as psychiatry residents for 4 years. Requirements for certification by the American Board of Psychiatry and Neurology (ABPN) are the completion of an MD or a DO degree from an accredited school of osteopathy, at least 4 years of accredited postgraduate (residency) training, and successful completion of both written and oral examinations (American Board of Psychiatry and Neurology, 2005).

Potential for Collaboration With Therapeutic Recreation

In both inpatient and outpatient mental health settings, therapeutic recreation specialists may work with psychiatrists as members of a team. The psychiatrist is often the head of this team and will expect input from the therapeutic recreation specialist to develop and monitor an interdisciplinary plan. The psychiatrist will rely on the therapeutic recreation specialist to carry out elements of the team's plan that relate not only to leisure-oriented goals but also to social and behavioral goals that may arise during therapeutic recreation interventions. For example, a person diagnosed with bipolar disorder in a community treatment program may become increasingly depressed if he or she is no longer involved with group activities. In this case the role of the therapeutic recreation specialist might be to help that person learn about and participate in individual activities that provide the same satisfaction and enjoyment as the group activities did.

Psychology

A **psychologist** is a social scientist who studies the human mind, thought, and human behavior. Psychologists are usually categorized under a number of different fields, with the most well recognized being clinical psychologists, who provide mental health care (United States Department of Labor, 2004d). Although psychologists are not medical doctors, they do have doctoral degrees, either a PhD or a PsyD. Clinical psychologists generally are not allowed to prescribe medication; however, two states (Louisiana and New Mexico) currently allow this practice and other states are considering the same (United States Department of Labor, 2004c).

Range of Services and Settings

Psychologists work in a variety of settings including health and human services, management, education, law, and sport. Besides working in a variety of settings, psychologists typically specialize in one of a number of areas.

Clinical psychologists constitute the largest specialty. They often work in counseling centers, independent or group practices, hospitals, or clinics. They help patients with mental and emotional disturbances adjust to life and may help medical and surgical patients deal with illnesses and injuries. Some clinical psychologists work in physical rehabilitation settings, treating patients with spinal cord injuries, chronic pain or illness, stroke, arthritis, and neurological conditions (United States Department of Labor, 2004d). Counseling psychologists help people recognize their strengths and draw on the resources necessary to cope with their problems, and they employ counseling or psychotherapy, teaching, and scientific research with individuals, families, and organizations (e.g., schools, hospitals, businesses) (American Psychological Association, 2003).

Educational Requirements and Credentialing

A PhD degree in psychology can be obtained in research areas such as behavioral neuroscience, clinical, cognitive systems, developmental, quantitative, and social psychology. A minimum of 60 semester hours of course credit beyond the bachelor's degree and 24 semester hours of credit in research and dissertation are required. Besides completing a core curriculum, students take courses related to their area of interest, such as psychobiology and human factors seminars, as determined in consultation with their supervisory committees (Arizona State University, 2005).

Potential for Collaboration With Therapeutic Recreation

Psychologists work in many environments in which therapeutic recreation specialists work, most commonly mental health and physical rehabilitation settings. A good psychologist welcomes input from all disciplines including therapeutic recreation to produce assessments and individualized plans. A clinical psychologist might help a person with a newly acquired disability adjust to a new lifestyle. As part of this person's overall treatment, he or she might be involved with the therapeutic recreation specialist to learn new activities and activity skills. A psychologist might evaluate a client's adjustment based on his or her commitment to developing a new leisure lifestyle.

Social Work

Social work is practiced in many countries. The profession provides a myriad of services and accepts many responsibilities. Responsibilities are often culturally specific because they reflect the norms of the society in which the profession is practiced. **Social workers** help people function in the healthiest way possible in the environment, manage their relationships, and solve personal and family problems. Social workers often see clients who face challenges such as inadequate housing, unemployment, serious illness, a disability, or substance abuse. Social workers also assist families that have serious conflicts, often involving abuse of children or a spouse (United States Department of Labor, 2004f).

Range of Services and Settings

Charity organizations, social service organizations, welfare administrations, and poverty agencies employ many social workers. Social workers are also employed in mental health services as psychothera-

pists or counselors. The role of the social worker is to advocate for better living, economic, social, and political conditions for individuals, groups, families, and organizations. Specific responsibilities may include administering welfare, coordinating community shelters, providing counseling and education sessions, running social services such as food banks and outreach programs, and providing community support (United States Department of Labor, 2004f).

Educational Requirements and Credentialing

The practice of social work requires a bachelor's or master's degree in social work. People with a bachelor's degree, who are considered generalists, carry the designation of bachelor of social work (BSW). The equivalent for social workers with a master's degree, who are considered specialists, is master of social work (MSW), although the titles of master of science in social work (MSSW) and master of social service (MSS) are also used. Some social workers carry the title of licensed clinical social worker (LCSW), a title granted through individual states (CWSE Online, 2005). The Association of Social Work Boards (ASWB) regulates social work licensure. Eligibility for an LCSW title includes a master's degree in social work from a program accredited by the Council on Social Work Education (CWSE), 2 years of practice post master's degree, successful completion of the ASWB exam, and other requirements specific to each state.

Potential for Collaboration With Therapeutic Recreation

Opportunities for social workers and therapeutic recreation specialists to collaborate are plentiful, especially in community settings. Social workers who advocate for a better quality of life for their constituents often recognize the importance of a healthy leisure lifestyle and active participation in recreation activities. The purposeful nature of therapeutic recreation also allows social workers to refer their constituents to our programs to improve functioning across the domains. Finally, therapeutic recreation in the community can serve as a nonthreatening means of attracting members of the community who may not participate in other social services. After community members are in the program, the therapeutic recreation specialists

Collaboration among health professionals is essential to holistic care.

can identify problems and refer the person to the professionals in social work.

Speech-Language Pathology and Audiology

Audiologists and speech-language pathologists work with children and adults who have impaired ability to communicate (American Speech-Language-Hearing Association, 2005a). **Audiologists** are trained in the area of hearing processes and hearing loss (American Medical Association, 2004f). Audiologists assess hearing loss and recommend hearing aids or other assistive listening devices. **Speech-language pathologists** are trained in disorders related to speech, language, cognitive communication, and swallowing skills (American Medical Association, 2004f). The purpose of speech-language services is to improve the person's ability to understand and use language appropriately (American Speech-Language-Hearing Association, 2005a).

Range of Services and Settings

Audiologists and speech-language pathologists work in a variety of settings including schools, hospitals, rehabilitation centers, nursing-care facilities, public health departments, and private practice (American Speech-Language-Hearing Association, 2005b). Responsibilities of audiologists include assessing hearing ability and identifying problems, determining the appropriateness of hearing aids and other amplification devices, providing consultation on practical solutions for reducing hearing problems, and teaching lip reading. Speech-language pathologists help people learn proper speech sounds, reduce stuttering and increase fluent speech, develop correct voice production, and minimize the effects of aphasia.

Education Requirements and Credentialing

Audiologists and speech-language pathologists are eligible for ASHA's Certificate of Clinical Competence (CCC). The CCC is required of ASHA members who provide independent clinical practice or supervise other professionals in their field. To be eligible for the CCC in speech-language pathology, applicants must have a master's degree, demonstrate required knowledge and skills, complete 375 clock hours of supervised clinical practice, and complete a 36-week (minimum) clinical fellowship. As of 2007, applicants for the CCC in audiology must possess a doctoral degree (typically the AuD or doctor of audiology degree), demonstrate appropriate knowledge and skills, and complete 1 year of clinical externship. As with therapeutic recreation, applicants for certification must successfully complete a national examination (American Speech-Language-Hearing Association, 2005c).

Potential for Collaboration With Therapeutic Recreation

Therapeutic recreation specialists who notice that a program participant is having difficulty hearing or responding to oral cues should refer the person to an audiologist for a hearing test. Conversely, therapeutic recreation specialists can augment the treatment efforts of speech-language pathologists by recommending leisure activities that allow children the opportunity to use speech.

Summary

Collaboration can occur at many levels. Some of the professions described in this chapter, such as art therapy, music therapy, and occupational therapy, are likely to represent areas of direct program collaboration. In other words, the therapeutic recreation specialist will work with these people in daily planning and implementation of programs. Other professions are likely to collaborate with a therapeutic recreation specialist at the team level but not in program development and delivery. For example, psychiatrists often supervise several facilities or programs at once. They may show up in rounds, ask questions about how clients are doing, make recommendations for services, and adjust medications based on feedback from the team, but the therapeutic recreation specialist rarely works within the same therapy environment. Psychologists are much the same. As health care has become financially strained, these professionals often supervise professionals at the master's and bachelor's level, who oversee daily care. Similar workforce structures exist within acute care, rehabilitation, and long-term facilities, where a single physician oversees a large number of patients or residents. These situations make it essential that the therapeutic recreation specialist be familiar with the roles that other professionals play, as well as the terminology and procedures that they use. Whether the therapeutic recreation specialist sees a member of the team for 60 minutes a week or throughout every working day, he or she must be prepared to take full advantage of team resources.

DISCUSSION QUESTIONS

1. What benefits does collaboration offer? What challenges do you see associated with collaborating, especially with other agencies?

2. Of the professions discussed in this chapter, which might offer good cross-training opportunities for a therapeutic recreation specialist?

3. What other professions or specialties not listed in this chapter might be potential collaboration partners, either within or outside typical therapeutic recreation-providing agencies? List them and provide ideas for how such collaborations might work.

4. In addition to becoming a CTRS, what other credentials might be of use to you as a professional? What would acquiring these credentials require?

5. Explain the differences and similarities between a psychiatrist, a psychologist, and a social worker. Also differentiate between an occupational therapist, a physical therapist, a therapeutic recreation specialist, and a child life specialist.

6. What dangers come from confusing or overstepping the job roles and responsibilities associated with the professions described in this chapter?

7. What strategies can you take as a professional to develop a full understanding of those professions you work with and to educate other professionals about therapeutic recreation?

Orthopedic and Neurological Impairment:

From Rehabilitation to Community Reentry

Terry Long, PhD
Northwest Missouri State University

Terry Robertson, PhD
Northwest Missouri State University

LEARNING OUTCOMES

After completing this chapter, learners will be able to demonstrate the following competencies:

- Recognize common orthopedic and neurological conditions experienced by therapeutic recreation clients
- Explain the role that therapeutic recreation plays in providing services to people with such conditions
- Understand modalities typically used to address orthopedic and neurological conditions in both rehabilitation and reintegration settings
- Identify appropriate application of these modalities to various orthopedic and neurological conditions
- Describe best practice mechanisms for the delivery of such modalities, including use of protocols and critical pathways

Physical rehabilitation services are designed to address disturbances or deterioration of physiological functions, but the nature of impairments that can result from such disturbances can go far beyond the physical realm. Physical rehabilitation services often involve programs that address impairments of social, emotional, cognitive, and physical functional skills. Likewise, causal factors and pattern of progression can vary widely even within specific diagnostic categories. As such, rehabilitation programs must provide for a broad range of client needs. As an example of the diverse needs of patients who are receiving rehabilitation services, consider that a person with a traumatic brain injury is likely to experience not only physical challenges but also a variety of other impairments related to cognitive processing, emotional stability, and social interactions. Furthermore, the need for support or additional rehabilitation does not end when patients are discharged from the hospital (see chapter 5 for a description of the types of hospitals that might provide rehabilitation services). A gradual community reentry with continued involvement in community-based programs is often a necessary component of recovery.

Therapeutic recreation can be a significant part of physical rehabilitation programs and is uniquely capable of addressing this broad range of client needs. Approximately 16% of certified therapeutic recreation specialists work in rehabilitation hospitals or in the rehabilitation department of general medical hospitals (NCTRC, 2004). These professionals work to develop and implement therapeutic recreation interventions that address the affected functional skills, notably those necessary for successful participation in recreation and leisure activities. In addition, leisure skill development and reintegration into the community are major goal areas that therapeutic recreation specialists commonly address during the rehabilitation process. After patients have achieved appropriate levels of function and independence, the provision of therapeutic recreation services can shift to community-based professionals who provide adapted and inclusive forms of recreation and leisure.

Common Diagnostic Groups in Rehabilitation

Patients find themselves in need of rehabilitation services for a variety of reasons. Some people may have been in an accident; others may be experiencing deficits caused by genetic conditions or transmittable diseases. Many need rehabilitation services because they have simply worn out part of the body (joint replacements). Other patients are receiving care for impairment that has resulted from an unhealthy lifestyle (smoking, poor diet, drug use). This broad array of causal factors naturally results in an equally broad list of diagnostic groups representing people who potentially could receive services in a physical rehabilitation program. The following section identifies some of the more common patient categories, but many other conditions are likely to be observed in practice. More important than patient classification is the use of a competent assessment procedure to identify deficits in client functioning. Care plans can then be built around individual client needs.

Orthopedic Impairments

Orthopedic impairments refer to conditions caused by disruption of the skeletal–muscle system. Such disturbances are common in rehabilitation, and a substantial portion of care is provided to people who receive joint replacements. Typically, **osteoarthritis** leads to deterioration of joint cartilage, requiring replacement of a knee or hip with an artificial joint. Osteoarthritis, the most common form of arthritis, results from wear and tear on joints over a person's life span. Genetics can play a role in how quickly such deterioration occurs, but lifestyle is a major factor in determining progression. In all, there are over 100 known types of arthritis, with osteoarthritis and **rheumatoid arthritis** accounting for the majority of cases (Sherrill, 2004). Rheumatoid arthritis involves inflammation of the lining of joints and is believed to be related to an attack on the body by the immune system. In some cases, rheumatoid arthritis is systemic, affecting vital organs and causing **pericarditis** (inflammation of the lining of the heart).

Other conditions such as degenerative bone diseases or severe fractures can lead to the need for joint replacement, but more common is the general rehabilitation of hip fractures, multiple bone fractures, or soft tissue injuries (muscle, ligaments, tendons). Rehabilitation following limb amputation is also common. Common goals for therapy include mastery of ambulation techniques, use of **prosthetic devices,** therapy for phantom pain, mastery of activities of daily living (ADLs), and mastery of recreation and leisure skills.

The Arthritis Foundation estimates that 1 in 3, or 66 million, Americans had arthritis in 2005. For more information on the effects of arthritis, go to www. arthritis.org.

Neurological Impairments

Neurological impairments include injuries or diseases that originate in the nervous system. The two most common neurologically based injuries observed in rehabilitation are spinal cord injury and traumatic brain injury. These two classifications include a broad array of potential impairments.

SPINAL CORD INJURY

Spinal cord injuries (SCI) involve trauma to the spinal cord that creates disturbance of either motor functions or sensation. The spinal cord is actually a bundle of nerves that carries information back and forth between the brain and the rest of the body. A series of hollow bone structures referred to as the spinal column protects the spinal cord. The bones that make up the spinal column are called vertebrae. The extent of impairment from an SCI depends on the location of the injury, with higher injuries resulting in greater impairment. The nervous system functions much like a telephone line. When the line is damaged, service beyond the damaged area is affected, but customers that precede the fallen line still receive service.

Spinal cord injuries are classified in several different ways. **Paraplegia** refers to an injury that affects only the lower limbs of the body, whereas **quadriplegia** (also called tetraplegia) affects all four limbs. A common misconception is that people with quadriplegia have no use of their arms. In truth, the nervous system is extremely complex, so certain aspects of upper-limb function can be affected while others remain intact. Depending on the location of the injury, upper-limb function can be disrupted to various degrees. A second classification to consider is whether an injury is complete or incomplete. Complete SCI involves loss of all functions below the location of the injury, whereas incomplete SCI involves partial loss of function. This classification depends on the severity of the injury. A complete severing or destruction of the spine results in a complete injury. In about half of cases, incomplete injury occurs, leaving some functions below the injury area intact. Likewise, about half of spinal cord injuries involve paraplegia, and the other half involve quadriplegia.

TRAUMATIC BRAIN INJURY

Because the brain is responsible for controlling virtually every function of the human body, rehabilitation from traumatic brain injury (TBI) requires a comprehensive approach to recovery that is equipped to address functional deficits across all domains. Unlike many other conditions being addressed through rehabilitation, TBI typically disrupts interpersonal and social functioning. Patients may be extremely self-centered, display socially inappropriate behaviors, and experience outbursts of anger or other extreme emotional states. Executive functions can also be affected, leaving the patient with difficulties in planning and carrying out self-initiated behaviors. The severity of a TBI can range from mild concussion to coma, but those relevant to this discussion typically involve a long-term rehabilitation program with significant deficits in all areas of functioning. The relatively advanced areas of functioning mentioned earlier may not even be relevant to treatment until after weeks or months of therapy.

LINDA OHNOUTKA

Background Information

Education
BS in Therapeutic Recreation from University of Nebraska-Lincoln

Credentials
CTRS

Special Affiliations
*National Therapeutic and Recreation Society *Nebraska Amputee Golf Association Board

Special Awards
Employee of the Month

Career Information

Position
Recreation Therapist, Madonna Rehabilitation Hospital

Organization Information
Madonna has national CARF accreditation for both inpatient and outpatient spinal cord and brain injury, adolescent and child rehabilitation programs, plus all inpatient rehab programs, including stroke and orthopedic. Madonna Rehabilitation Hospital is one of the few rehabilitation facilities in the nation to offer a true continuum of care, allowing patients to efficiently progress from LTACH to specialized rehabilitation or subacute rehabilitation programs, to a rehabilitation day program without ever leaving the facility.

Organization's Mission
Madonna Rehabilitation Hospital is a Catholic organization that exists to provide medical and physical rehabilitation services to children and adults throughout the nation.

Job Description
Complete assessments; plan and lead individual treatment sessions and groups; provide leisure skills training, education, and community training individually or in a group setting; supervise volunteers. Serve as program leader for the Madonna Adaptive Sports and Recreation Program; co-leader for Spinal Cord Injury support group; and student internship coordinator.

Career Path
My student internship was at Madonna Rehabilitation Hospital, and I was able to get a recreation therapy position after completion of the internship.

Likes and Dislikes About the Job
I like working with people and teaching them ways to return to recreation when they didn't think it was possible and using leisure opportunities to enhance their rehabilitation. In addition, I enjoy being part of a team that continues to develop and move the adaptive sports and recreation program forward. I wish inpatient's length of stay would be longer in order to have more time to work with the patients, but I am glad that Madonna's continuum of care provides the opportunity for recreation therapy through outpatient services.

> God grant me the serenity to accept the things I cannot change; courage to change the things I can; and wisdom to know the difference.

Advice to Undergraduate Students
Be flexible to meet the needs of your clients and adaptable to the ongoing changes in health care. Working with patients in assisting them to achieve their highest level of functioning through leisure activities and sports is a rewarding experience.

TBI can be the result of a penetrating injury (gunshot) or a closed head injury (boxing, football collision). Closed head injuries can involve impact from an external force or an internal shifting of the brain (a common example is a shaken baby). Brain injuries can also occur from extended periods without oxygen, extreme temperatures, or toxins such as methamphetamine. A TBI is differentiated from conditions such as intellectual impairment, cerebral palsy, and Alzheimer's disease because it is neither **degenerative** nor **congenital.** TBIs are typically graded with the **Glasgow coma scale.** This scale evaluates patient functions in the areas of eye response, motor response, and verbal response. The TBI is then classified as mild, moderate, or severe.

Following are some additional deficits associated with a TBI:

- Physical—can affect speech, vision, hearing, eating, swallowing, mobility, and gait; can cause headaches, seizures, paralysis, and sensitivity to light and noise.
- Cognitive—can cause disorientation; can affect memory, concentration, judgment, problem solving, perceptions, academic skills, and task-oriented behavior.
- Psychological—can cause depression, anxiety, frustration, anger, egocentricity and insensitivity toward others, low self-esteem, socially acting out, setting inappropriate limitations, and self-destructive behaviors such as stealing, gambling, promiscuity, and spending sprees.

CEREBRAL VASCULAR ACCIDENTS

Cerebral vascular accidents (CVA) is a term used to describe conditions that involve disruption of blood flow to the brain. **Aneurism, stroke,** and **multi-infarct dementia** are examples of conditions that would be considered CVAs. Stroke, the most common form of CVA, typically involves blood clot blockage (ischemia) or bleeding (hemorrhage) within the brain. The former cause is most commonly associated with heart disease or high cholesterol, whereas the latter is related to high blood pressure and the structural integrity of arteries and veins (Sherrill, 2004). Strokes typically occur as either a left-brain stroke or a right-brain stroke, with symptoms manifesting on the opposite side of the body.

Possible Consequences of Stroke— Right Brain

- Weak or paralyzed left side
- Literal thinking
- Lack of insight and denial of disabilities
- Distractible and inattentive
- Impaired judgment and memory
- Left-side neglect
- Quick and impulsive behavioral style
- Dysarthria—oral muscle weakness

Possible Consequences of Stroke—Left Brain

- Weak or paralyzed right side
- Slow and cautious behavioral style

- Aphasia—impaired language structure
  - Word order
  - Sentence length and complexity
  - Vocabulary
  - Speech sound productions
- Impaired comprehension

Most people are left-brain dominant, but if a patient is right-brain dominant the symptoms associated with each side of the brain will be opposite those listed. Key to the potential extent of recovery from a stroke is immediate provision of treatment. Likewise, the most significant gains in function come within the first 6 months of rehabilitation.

Hemiplegia, a common consequence of stroke, involves loss of sensation or movement on one side of the body. Stroke patients in rehabilitation typically face impairments related to **ambulation,** upper-limb functions, and speech. Speech impairments can be associated with aphasia (left-brain CVAs) or dysarthria (right-brain CVAs). **Aphasia** involves disruption of speech patterns, whereas **dysarthria** involves impaired speech motor functions (Auxter, Pyfer & Huettig, 2005).

Aneurism, another form of CVA, involves the bursting of a blood vessel within the brain. Aneurisms are much more likely to be fatal than strokes, but when patients survive, the challenges are analogous to those associated with stroke. A more subtle but equally threatening condition is the occurrence of multiple infarctions occurring over an extended period. This condition results in gradual loss of function. This gradual process often leads to a failure to notice early symptoms. Long-term consequences include a condition referred to as multi-infarct dementia, which causes **dementia** because of multiple ministrokes. A similar condition is **transient ischemic attack** (TIA), which also involve ministrokes. The differentiating factor is that TIA typically involves full recovery after several hours of impairment. TIAs can be a warning sign of impending major strokes.

Other Notable Conditions

Several other conditions that are likely to be observed in rehabilitation settings should be briefly mentioned. Those that are neurological in nature include multiple sclerosis, **Parkinson's disease, Guillian Barre syndrome,** and **ALS** (Lou Gehrig's disease). **Cardiovascular** and **pulmonary** impairments may also be observed, and many hospitals provide specialized pulmonary or cardiac rehabilitation programs.

Some rehabilitation centers have specialized programs for **thermal injuries** and treatment of open wounds such as decubitus ulcers (also known as pressure sores), whereas others address those conditions as part of their general services. Finally, many patients with cancer participate in rehabilitation services following surgeries associated with their treatment.

Common Therapeutic Recreation Modalities in Rehabilitation

Chapter 5 presented several of the more commonly used modalities in therapeutic recreation. This chapter points out modalities commonly used as part of rehabilitation and reintegration of persons with injuries or illnesses of a physical nature. Again, a physical cause does not ensure that impairments will be limited to the physical realm.

Functional Interventions: Recreation as Therapy

In both the leisure ability model (Stumbo & Peterson, 2004) and the health protection–health promotion model (Austin, 1998) that are discussed in chapter 5, a specific realm of therapeutic recreation services is designated as involving treatment, therapy, or functional intervention (three terms referring essentially to the same thing). This is the entry point of services for patients in rehabilitation programs. Functional skills are the primary concern. Other secondary therapeutic recreation services (e.g., leisure education, wellness programs) are provided simultaneously or after functional skills improve. Essentially, recreation and leisure are used as tools for therapy (recall the definition of therapeutic recreation in chapter 1, which specified that recreation skills could be utilized as a means of enhancing functioning). To illustrate this potential application, the following sections discuss how "recreation therapy" can be applied toward the improvement of cognitive, physical, and socio-emotional functions.

COGNITIVE REHABILITATION

Cognitive rehabilitation services refer to a comprehensive therapy effort implemented by a team of professionals to restore cognitive functions in persons with TBI, stroke, or other conditions that cause deficits in cognitive functions. Therapeutic recreation professionals contribute to this effort by planning and implementing games, activities, and other cognitive tasks that exercise areas of cognitive functioning identified in the treatment plan. The therapeutic recreation specialist can present daily recreation and leisure tasks that require people to use their memory, recognize shapes and colors, place items in order, develop strategies, and perform other increasingly complex tasks.

PHYSICAL REHABILITATION

The method used to address the physical deficits experienced by patients is similar to the approach taken with cognitive deficits. Therapeutic recreation specialists plan and implement activities that correspond with deficits identified through assessment procedures. As such, the process is individualized. To illustrate how this process works, this section will discuss several specific physical areas of functioning, including ambulation, sensory–motor functions, strength, and endurance. The application of the therapeutic recreation process to address ambulation is illustrated by a program that encouraged patients recovering from stroke to maintain a walking pace that corresponded with the tempo and beat of a standardized piece of music. This process was intended to encourage program adherence

Games can serve as a means to an end in helping patients regain functional skills.

and maintain maximal effort. The program was a collaborative effort between music therapists and therapeutic recreation specialists working in the rehabilitation department of St. Francis Hospital in Topeka, Kansas. Sensory–motor functions are a common area of intervention and frequently involve games or puzzles that require the manipulation of objects in space. Jenga is an example of a game that requires coordination of senses and motor skills (both fine and gross).

Strength and endurance are areas of significant concern for persons who have had a stroke. Many activities have been created to work on strength, endurance, and range of motion in affected limbs. One of the most simplistic, but also motivating, activities involves the use of clothespins and a yardstick (graduated measuring stick). The yardstick is attached to a table in a vertical position. The patient is asked to place clothespins on the yardstick, starting at the bottom and working upward. This simple activity provides immediate feedback because the number and height of the clothespins are easily determined, allowing the patient and therapeutic recreation specialist to monitor progress from day to day in a concrete way.

SOCIO-EMOTIONAL

As mentioned earlier, this domain is probably most relevant to those with TBI, but other conditions can also affect social skills and emotional state. For example, stroke and multiple sclerosis can both affect emotional functions. Understanding that physical impairment may cause these deficits is important in determining appropriate interventions and expectations. Likewise, sessions should be planned at an appropriate social or emotional level, allowing room for improvement without overwhelming the patient with unreasonable demands. Loved ones should be educated about the nature of such social behaviors and emotional states. For many families, the injured loved one seems like a completely different person. As such, the effect of injury has social and emotional implications for the patient's entire family system.

Other Modalities

The modalities described in this section may also fall under the recreation as therapy realm, but they are mentioned separately because of their distinct purpose or function. In addition, some of these modalities, pet therapy for example, might be used in settings outside the rehabilitation setting.

Because the editors of this text have attempted to avoid redundant listings of each modality in every chapter, you are encouraged to consider how each might be applied to other populations or situations.

SENSORY STIMULATION

Sensory stimulation is a technique used with people who have severe brain injury and demonstrate limited responsiveness to stimuli. Sensory stimulation is designed to engage clients who are in unconscious (coma) or subconscious states, thereby reducing the depth and length of unconsciousness (Austin, 2004). This technique can be implemented in a multimodal or unimodal fashion (Austin, 2004). Multimodal sensory stimulation involves engaging all senses during each treatment session, and unimodal sensory stimulation focuses on a single sense during each session. For both techniques, stimulation is usually applied at the lowest level that is still capable of eliciting a response (eye responses, muscle contractions).

PAIN MANAGEMENT AND RELAXATION TECHNIQUES

Pain management and relaxation strategies can be useful for patients who are dealing with severe and persistent pain. Training clients to use **biofeedback, meditation, progressive relaxation,** and other pain management techniques can be a significant part of therapeutic recreation programming and can have important implications for the patient's ability to control pain in the long run. Patients who may find such programs particularly beneficial include those with thermal injuries (burns), **chronic** conditions such as rheumatoid arthritis or fibromyalgia, and **terminal** conditions such as acquired immune deficiency syndrome (AIDS) and some forms of cancer. Massage may also be used to manage muscle pain and **spasticity,** but therapeutic recreation specialists should ensure that those providing such services are appropriately qualified. In addition, massage can be harmful for people with soft tissue injuries or recent thermal injuries.

Aquatic Therapy

Certified aquatic therapists or physical therapists typically implement aquatic therapy, but therapeutic recreation specialists can also gain certain water certifications or help facilitate such sessions. For example, the Arthritis Association offers certification programs for therapeutic aquatics instructors.

These programs are often offered in community-based settings but are specifically designed for people who have conditions of **rheumatism,** or arthritis. Such people may also use aquatic-based programs for fitness and exercise, because exercising in the pool reduces impact on joints and muscles. Therapy pools, that is, pools with temperatures typically ranging from 88 to 92 °F (31.1 to 33.3 °C), can be used to reduce spasticity, increase flexibility, and encourage blood flow to injured areas. In addition, specialized strategies, such as the **Halliwick method,** have been developed for teaching persons with significant disabilities to swim.

Animal-Assisted Therapy

Animal-assisted therapy, or pet therapy, is commonly used in rehabilitation, especially in facilities that involve extensive stays. True therapy animals are certified through organizations such as the Delta Society (deltasociety.org) or Therapy Dogs International (tdi-dog.org) and have gone through an extensive process to ensure that their tempera-

Therapeutic recreation specialists at Truman Medical Center in Lee Summit, Missouri, include pet therapy as part of their therapeutic recreation program.

ment is appropriate for the therapy environment. Because certified therapy animals require extensive time and care, they are typically brought in by outside persons who volunteer their time and services to the rehabilitation centers. Some facilities, however, have in-house animals that the therapeutic recreation staff might care for. These animals might include birds, fish, or rabbits. In some cases uncertified dogs and cats may be present (this is more likely to be the case in long-term care facilities). Certified service animals can be used in various ways. They may be used as motivators to encourage persons with disabilities to engage in what would otherwise be unattractive or discomforting therapy activities. They may be used as a form of sensory stimulation for people with severe brain injuries. They may be used as calming agents for patients who are experiencing substantial discomfort or anxiety. Finally, they may be used to improve the quality of life of patients by simply being there.

Another area of animal-assisted therapy involves the use of horses. Two primary types of horse-based therapies exist. The one most likely to be tied to orthopedic or neurological conditions is **hippotherapy.** This approach uses the movement of a walking horse to relieve muscle contractures; build trunk stability; and increase strength, flexibility, and range of motion. Only certified hippotherapists should provide services, but therapeutic recreation specialists can be instrumental in arranging and supporting such a program. The second type of horse-based therapy is **therapeutic riding.** These programs are less directly related to physical rehabilitation but do provide an avenue for community reentry, as well as cognitive and socio-emotional functions. Therapeutic riding involves more than just riding the horse. The process includes caring for the horse, grooming the horse, saddling the horse, and forming a relationship with the horse that involves both responsibility and trust. Therapeutic riding can be used in a variety of therapeutic recreation realms including mental health, youth development, programs for people with developmental disabilities, and aging populations. The same can be said for pet therapy in general. Such programs exist in virtually every type of therapeutic recreation setting.

Horticulture

Horticulture therapy uses plant life as a means of therapy. This technique uses the tasks associated with horticulture and metaphors related to the experience of caring for plant life. Horticulture therapy is used in a variety of therapeutic settings but is specifically relevant to physical rehabilitation for several reasons. First, planting and caring for plant life provides an opportunity for exercising a variety of cognitive, motor, and sensory–motor functions. Strength, endurance, kinesthetic awareness, hand–eye coordination, and controlled motor movements are all potential areas of functional intervention that horticulture therapy can address. Horticulture therapy can even engage social competencies through mechanisms such as the development of a community garden. Second, horticulture provides purposeful and satisfying leisure activities that can help clients cope with the psychological challenges of rehabilitation and use cognitive functions such as memory, planning, and executive functions. Third, this modality provides the potential to develop a leisure skill that will continue after the patient returns home. Finally, horticulture therapy requires relatively limited resources and space, which is often a consideration for therapeutic recreation programs.

Community Reintegration

Community reintegration programs, sometimes called community reentry, are designed to assist patients with the adjustments associated with returning home. The goal is for patients to be able to participate in ADLs and continue with a satisfying and healthy lifestyle. As such, therapeutic recreation specialists work with patients to identify barriers to reentry, master skills necessary for home life and community involvement, and develop strategies for involvement in recreation and leisure activities at home and in the community. In many cases, services will include field trips into the community and home visits intended to assess and address real-world functioning.

Leisure Education

Leisure education, as conceptualized in the leisure ability model (Stumbo & Peterson, 2004) addresses issues related to leisure awareness, leisure resources, social skills, and activity skills. Any of these four content areas might be relevant in the rehabilitation environment depending on the nature of the

patient's impairments. Patients with TBI are likely to experience social deficits and challenges with cognitively processing information related to leisure decisions. Persons who have a life-changing injury such as SCI, heart disease, or a limb amputation may not recognize the importance of recreation and fitness in maintaining health. Furthermore, they may be unaware of the resources available for becoming involved in such activity. These examples illustrate the importance of leisure education in making a successful transition to living with a disability. Therapeutic recreation specialists must be familiar with the content and process of delivering leisure education services to patients.

Exercise and Fitness

One potential modality that can be part of rehabilitation and is directly tied to leisure education is an exercise and fitness program. Because the dangers of sedentary living are even greater for those with a disability than for those without one, people with physical injuries can gain particular benefit from living an active lifestyle. Patients should be informed of proper exercising techniques and activity precautions associated with their particular condition. For example, high-impact activities can exacerbate symptoms of arthritis, and therapy pool (warm-water) activities would be inadvisable for a person with multiple sclerosis. Chapter 13 provides an in-depth look at designing fitness and exercise programs for persons with disabilities.

Community-Based Services

To this point, the described modalities have been at least partially grounded in what can be described as clinical settings. As the title of this chapter implies, the needs of people with extensive injury or permanent disability rarely end with the conclusion of an inpatient rehabilitation program. Thus, community-based services can be an inherent aspect of making the transition from the rehabilitation setting to a maximal level of independence and quality of life. The diversity noted within each disability category described earlier is even more present in community-based programs, where adapted and inclusive recreation services are provided to a broad array of participants. The task of finding the best way to engage each participant requires that therapeutic recreation specialists be competent in applying the therapeutic recreation process to a variety of participant circumstances. The general concept of community programming is not itself a specific modality, but this element is discussed here because of the importance of ensuring that the opportunity for therapeutic recreation services continues beyond formal rehabilitation services.

Best Practices Issues

Typically, those who work with people with physically disabling injuries or illnesses will serve as part of a treatment team. The therapeutic recreation specialist can be a critical part of this team. As pointed out in chapter 7, team members must understand the nature of each other's work and collaborate to maximize patient benefits. As part of this team, the therapeutic recreation specialist must follow standardized procedures associated with the therapeutic recreation process.

In addition, this process must occur within the context of a larger system. Many rehabilitation facilities follow **clinical pathways,** which map out the role of each department within an agency in providing care to a particular client. Within these pathways are **treatment protocols.** These protocols outline the standard practices and procedures for care within each department. As such, treatment protocols for providing therapeutic rec-

CLIENT PORTRAIT

EZRA

Ezra is a 17-year-old high school junior who wrecked his motorcycle into a telephone pole while street racing with a group of other riders. He received a partial spinal cord injury at the C5 vertebra resulting in complete loss of sensation and movement in his legs, and partial loss of movement in his arms. His doctors informed him that he would not regain function in his legs and that he would need to use a wheelchair for the rest of his life.

Ezra's Rehabilitation

A CTRS began working with Ezra within days of his admission into rehabilitation. Following an assessment of Ezra's functional abilities and leisure needs and interests, the CTRS and Ezra established therapeutic recreation goals and objectives. Immediate goals focused on maximizing range of motion, strength, and endurance in Ezra's upper body, and also assisting the rehabilitation team in teaching Ezra about prevention of secondary health conditions, using his wheelchair, and living with a spinal cord injury. To address these goals, the CTRS encouraged Ezra to participate in a variety of activities and games that encouraged him to push his limits in the goal areas. These sessions involved activities such as gardening, cooking and nutrition, card and board games, painting and sculpture, air hockey, playing fetch with the therapy dog, aerobic and anaerobic exercise, swimming, and a variety of customized games and activities designed to work on the targeted goal areas.

Ezra's Reintegration

Once Ezra had begun to make some of these life adjustments, the CTRS suggested that they broaden Ezra's therapy goals to include leisure education and community reintegration. At this point, Ezra began participating in a leisure education program that included leisure awareness and activity skill development. Content focused on ensuring Ezra was aware of the benefits of maintaining his previously active and satisfying leisure lifestyle, and the identification of barriers and resources associated with this goal. Ezra also learned about adapted sports opportunities and available equipment that could be used by a person at his ability level. As Ezra's health, knowledge, and independence increased, a plan for community re-entry was developed. Ezra was fortunate that he had regained enough strength, mobility, and trunk control during his rehabilitation that he did not require an electric wheelchair. Still, he openly questioned how he could ever have a satisfying life with his injury.

Before his discharge from the rehabilitation center, the CTRS developed a weight training program for Ezra that could be conducted at home and at the local fitness center. He accompanied Ezra to the center on several occasions until the client was ready to go on his own. He also accompanied Ezra on a visit to a local paralympic sports competition, where Ezra met several wheelchair basketball players. Finally, the rehabilitation center sponsored an adapted sport and activity clinic that introduced Ezra to several activities including golf, rugby, scuba diving, hunting, and even dancing. After his discharge, Ezra continued to participate in sports and recreation events sponsored by the rehabilitation center, as well as other organizations in the community. He was also able to return to school for his senior year, graduate with his friends, and dance with his girlfriend at senior prom.

reation services are likely to exist within a particular rehabilitation hospital.

Following such structure serves multiple purposes. First, it provides a mechanism for ensuring quality care of the client. The therapeutic recreation specialist has an ethical obligation to provide quality care, regardless of whether internal and external agencies are monitoring performance. This process of purposeful intervention is also necessary to maintain accreditation with the Commission on Accreditation of Rehabilitation Facilities (CARF) and the Joint Commission on Accreditation of Healthcare Organizations (JCAHO) (see chapter 3 for additional discussion of the purpose of accreditation). These procedures also allow for fiscal accountability within prospective payment system (PPS) used in health care today. A PPS designates anticipated costs of services associated with a specific health care procedure or service. Insurance companies pay agencies based on this preestablished expense, regardless of how much the agency spent on the patient. As a result, therapeutic recreation services must be provided in a competent yet cost-effective manner.

Summary

This chapter has focused on the nature of orthopedic and neurological conditions that require rehabilitation services, as well as therapeutic recreation modalities that can be implemented within the context of a rehabilitation program. These commonly observed conditions are only a sample of what the therapeutic recreation specialist may encounter. On any given day, a therapeutic recreation specialist might be exposed to a patient who broke a hip in a fall, who received a TBI from a motorcycle wreck, who has brain damage from oxygen deprivation, or who has a condition that he or she has never even seen before. Regardless of what physical injury or illness is occurring, the responsibility of the therapeutic recreation specialist is to determine how to address cognitive, physical, or socio-emotional deficits that might manifest. This task may sound intimidating, but adhering to the therapeutic recreation process and the associated standards of practice can guide the adequately trained therapeutic recreation specialist through this challenge.

DISCUSSION QUESTIONS

1. Differentiate between a neurological injury and an orthopedic injury. What commonalities and differences do you see between these two diagnostic areas?

2. Discuss the role of the therapeutic recreation specialist as the client moves through the recovery process. Do you think that this role would change as the client progresses? How is this concept reflected in the therapeutic recreation models presented in chapter 5?

3. Can you think of other modalities that could be integrated into the therapeutic recreation process for any of the described conditions? State your case about why you believe that this particular modality would be useful for the chosen condition (client group).

4. Why is the use of standardized procedures outlined in protocols or critical pathways important? Do you see any drawbacks to using such a system?

5. Of the described modalities, which do you currently feel most comfortable with, and which are most intimidating? What steps can you take to ensure that you are professionally capable of using these modalities? Do you think that any of these modalities have the potential to harm a client if used inappropriately?

Therapeutic Recreation and Developmental Disabilities

Alice Foose, PhD
Northwest Missouri State University

Patricia Ardovino, PhD, CTRS, CPRP
University of Wisconsin at La Crosse

LEARNING OUTCOMES

After completing this chapter, learners will be able to demonstrate the following competencies:

- Describe the commonalities and differences in diagnoses of the described developmental disabilities
- Identify the main knowledge areas that a therapeutic recreation specialist should possess when working with a person with a developmental disability
- Explain the importance of age-appropriate interventions and give at least two examples
- Explain why taking the life-span approach is important when working with people with developmental disabilities
- Describe the best practices for working with people of different ages and different developmental disabilities
- Explain what precautions need to be taken for contraindications associated with at least five types of developmental disabilities

What do all these people have in common?

- Mary is a petite, bright-eyed woman in her mid-50s. She enjoys gardening, playing rummy, and being with her cat, Sara. Mary lives with her mother, Ruth, who is in her late 90s and whose eyesight is failing. Mary worries that her mother will soon need to move to a nursing home.
- Jordan is a rambunctious 5-year-old who loves skipping stones with his older brother and is excited about starting his new school.
- Laura is a beautiful but shy 16-year-old. She's interested in a guy in her high school class and is afraid to ask him out.
- Domico loves to hang out after work with his friends at the local park.

They are all involved in social networks, they are all dealing with life issues—illness, transitions, sexual attraction, friendship—they all have unique strengths and weaknesses, and each has a developmental disability.

What Are Developmental Disabilities?

Developmental disabilities (DD) are lifelong impairments that occur before adulthood. Because they originate during early development, these disabilities often affect multiple aspects of life including physical and mental abilities. Public Law 101-496 describes the current criteria for having a developmental disability as having a severe, chronic disability of the following characteristics:

- Resulted from mental or physical impairments
- Is manifested before age 22
- Is likely to continue indefinitely
- Results in substantial functional limitations in two or more of the following areas of major life activity:
  - Self-care
  - Receptive and expressive language
  - Learning
  - Mobility
  - Self-direction
  - Capacity for independent living
  - Economic self-sufficiency

- Reflects the person's need for a combination and sequence of special interdisciplinary, or generic, services, supports, or other assistance that is of lifelong or extended duration

People with DD include people who have intellectual impairment, autism, cystic fibrosis, cerebral palsy, spina bifida, deafness, blindness, or any other condition meeting the criteria described earlier. Common to all forms of DD is an extended delay in development of one or more adaptive areas. Although rates of development vary considerably, people with DD have at least one area in which the delay in adaptive life area hinders their ability to live independently. With facilitation and training, many people with DD are able to adapt or gain the skills needed to live independently or semi-independently.

For most of the 20th century, people with DD have been treated as children. This view led to low expectations and minimal intervention, which in turn fostered high levels of dependence. Only within the past 30 or so years has society viewed people with DD with a holistic, **life-span development** approach. Fortunately, the past four decades have brought legislation (see table 9.1), advocacy, research, and service programs that reflect a definitional shift away from the simplistic categorization and toward a holistic view of individuals and their environment.

In 2001 the surgeon general issued a national blueprint to improve the health of persons with intellectual impairment (U.S. Public Health Service, 2002). The report outlined six focuses for integrated teams of self-advocates with intellectual impairment and their families, scientists, health care providers, professional training institutions, advocacy organizations, and policy makers. The six goals are the following:

- Integrate health promotion into community environments
- Increase knowledge and understanding
- Improve quality of health care
- Train health care providers
- Ensure effective health care financing
- Increase sources of health care

Professionals within therapeutic recreation are well suited to address these goals because they are trained to focus on the whole of life. In particular, integration of therapeutic recreation techniques

Table 9.1 Abbreviated Public Laws (PLs)

Public law	Description
PL 91-517	Disabilities Services and Facilities Construction Amendments of 1970 defined developmental disabilities to include people with intellectual impairment, cerebral palsy, epilepsy, and other neurological conditions closely related to intellectual impairment that originated before age 18 and constituted a substantial disability.
PL 101-336	Americans with Disabilities Act, 1990.
PL 101-476	Individuals with Disabilities Education Act (IDEA) of 1990, amended in 1997 (PL 101-476), includes autism as a disability category.
PL 108-446	Individuals with Disabilities Education Improvement Act of 2004 (IDEA); this revision adds further requirements for qualified professionals and appropriate assessments.
PL 103-203	Developmental Disabilities Act of 1994 emphasized the need to address the cultural and ethnic needs of the person served and promote dignity.
PL 105-17	Individuals with Disabilities Education Act (IDEA), formerly PL 94-142, or the Education for All Handicapped Children Act of 1975 provides free and appropriate education to all children.
PL 106-402	The Developmental Disabilities Assistance and Bill of Rights Act Amendment of 2000, extended the definition of a developmental disability to infants and young children from birth to age 9.

within the community is an ideal way to address these goals.

This chapter will explain how to implement the goals related to improving the health of a person with a DD. When working with someone with a DD, the therapeutic recreation specialist must have a fundamental understanding of how to enhance a person's life context by taking an integrative approach to therapy. Understanding life context is vital for working with a person with a DD. Unlike many other diagnoses, a developmental disability is lifelong and directly affects an entire social network. A wide range of career opportunities are open to those who have knowledge of DD.

Understanding the Developmental Process

Because DD involves impairment during the early stages of life, understanding the potential effect of a particular condition requires knowledge of the developmental processes that occur over the life span. Therapeutic recreation specialists must understand the early-life effects of a particular condition and also have insight into implications that may or may not manifest in later stages of life. This understanding must be holistic, considering all domains of function. Developmental delays are typically identified by examining three main developmental domains: physical, cognitive, and socio-emotional (the latter is sometimes broken down into a third and fourth domain). Table 9.2 provides a description of typical developmental progression across these functional domains. With enhanced development in each domain comes an increase in leisure needs, interests, and capabilities. Likewise, barriers or limitations in each domain can manifest in barriers or limitations for leisure.

Acknowledging Strengths

Vital to working with any person with a DD is the recognition that, in most cases, not all areas of functioning are delayed. For instance, in the example at the beginning of the chapter Laura has spina bifida. Her disability is mainly physical. She has learned to adapt in many areas. She uses a wheelchair to get around and has learned to catheterize herself, but she is also self-conscious about her disability. Like her classmates, she would like to start dating. Although Laura has a developmental disability that will affect her throughout life, her disability is only part of who she is. She has the same social and emotional needs as other teenagers her age do.

Human development varies greatly, even for people without a disability. While reading the rest of this chapter, keep in mind that the information in table 9.2 is a rough overview of development. Recognize that in many cases of people with DD, only a few developmental areas are affected and that it is common to excel in other areas, even within the same functional domain. An adult with intellectual

Table 9.2 Physical, Cognitive, Socio-Emotional, and Leisure Development

Development	Physical	Cognitive	Socio-emotional	Leisure focus
INFANCY				
0–4 months	Raises head, grasps and shakes toys, follows faces and moving objects, responds to loud noises, and pushes down with legs when placed on firm surface.	Begins to babble and imitate sounds, and begins to respond to "No."	Imitates facial movements of others and shows affection toward caregiver.	Explores the environment by responding to and imitating environmental stimuli (things that move or make noises), such as by playing peek-a-boo, shaking a rattle, or imitating simple noises; play is often solitary.
4–7 months	Supports whole weight on legs and reaches with one hand.	Finds objects that are partially hidden, tries to get objects that are out of reach, and turns head when called.	Responds to emotional expressions of others and enjoys social play such as peek-a-boo.	
7–12 months	Uses and imitates simple gestures (waving, clapping), develops beginning walking skills, and uses crude pincer grasp (picks up objects with thumb and one finger).	Makes basic words and sounds (ma, da-da), responds to own name, and responds to basic commands that are accompanied by gestures (come, get, and so on).	Trusts and bonds with caregiver.	
TODDLER OR PRESCHOOLER				
2 years	Walks (heel to toe) alone, begins to run, kicks a ball, carries large toy while walking, walks up and down stairs while holding on for support, scribbles, and builds block towers of four or more blocks.	Links two to four words together to communicate ideas (more milk, no bed), follows simple instructions, can identify by pointing to named objects, begins to sort by color and shape, and begins make-believe play.	Begins to show independence through defiant behavior, shows separation anxiety, and imitates behaviors of others.	Play is imitative of others; still initiates little or no interaction (parallel play); play is mainly home based.
3 years	Climbs stairs alternating feet; kicks ball; runs easily; pedals tricycle; bends over without falling; can manipulate small objects (turns book pages one at a time, holds pencil); can make up-and-down, side-to-side, and circular marking with a pencil or crayon; turns rotating handles.	Follows a two- or three-part command, recognizes most common objects and pictures, understands placement in space (in, below, above), and uses four- or five-word sentences; speech understood by strangers.	Expresses emotions openly, separates easily from parent, and spontaneously shows affection toward familiar playmates.	Plays in presence of others with little to no interaction (egocentric–cooperative play); engages in pretend play and exploratory play; play is still mainly in the home environment.

Development	Physical	Cognitive	Socio-emotional	Leisure focus
TODDLER OR PRESCHOOLER (CONTINUED)				
4 years	Goes up and down stairs with no support, throws ball overhanded, catches ball, moves forward and backward, can hop on one foot for up to 5 seconds, dresses and undresses, draws a person with two to four body parts, and has better fine motor control (uses scissors and begins to copy some capital letters and square shapes).	Correctly names some colors, can count at least a few numbers, follows three-part commands, speaks in sentences of five to six words, has mastered some rules of grammar, recalls parts of a story, and works with others toward goals.	Plays and cooperates with other children, negotiates solutions to conflict, often cannot tell the difference between fantasy and reality, and imagines monsters from unfamiliar images.	Engages in pretend play; play is more independent and exploratory; plays house and other work and home roles; focuses on expression; peers and teachers begin to have influence.
5 years	Increases range of movements (hopping, somersaults, swinging, climbing, galloping); can copy triangle and other shapes, draw recognizable pictures, print some letters, and use silverware (fork and spoon); can take care of own toilet needs.	Speaks using sentences of more than five words; can count 10 or more objects; has better understanding of time; uses future tense; knows about common objects in the home (food, appliances, and so on); can recite name and address; can distinguish reality from fantasy.	Aware of gender; wants to please friends; shows more independence and can visit a nearby friend by him- or herself; can share or give and take in a group situation; peers, teachers, and the media are increasingly influential.	Play continues to mirror adult world; increasingly uses symbols and language in play; engages in expressive play that includes singing, dancing, and acting; wants to play with peers.
6–11 years	Strength increases; upper-limb coordination and dexterity improve.	Can distinguish right from left; can count in multiples of 2, 5, and 10; follows rules; later can complete tasks.	Begins forming cliques (identifying outsiders) and showing alliance to identified friends.	Enjoys collecting things, magic tricks, puzzles, and trading with others; engages in cooperative group play; starts competitive play; increase of cognitive abilities is reflected in increasing complexity of board and table games.
PRETEEN				
11–12 years	Rapid growth and changes in body start to occur; must relearn or adapt coordination and gross motor skills.	Thinks ahead to make plans and set goals, uses abstract thinking, can consider several options, and has ability to take the role of others.	Becomes concerned with social image (clothes, activities, and so on); close friends are important; peers are more important than family; preteens try out roles to discover who they are; budding of sexual identity occurs; most are aware of sexual intercourse.	School is still a major focus of activity; prefers same-sex groups and team games; prefers being in groups to being alone.

TABLE 9.2 CONTINUED

TABLE 9.2 CONTINUED

Development	Physical	Cognitive	Socio-emotional	Leisure focus
TEENAGERS				
Early adolescence, 13–15 years	Rapid increase in height and weight occurs; muscle mass continues to grow; refinement of skills continues; secondary sex characteristics develop because of change in hormone levels; experiences clumsiness because of bodily changes.	Begins to set goals for the future, to use abstract reasoning, and to look at choosing among different ideas.	Focuses on identity; develops heightened self-consciousness.	Enjoys group activities with both genders; segregates into athletic and nonathletic groups; spends 40% of waking time in leisure; socializes informally with friends, watches TV, listens to music; begins to develop sports and hobbies; develops sexual identity; team sports become exclusive; activities are expressive and immediate; leisure is a space for peers.
Late adolescence, 16–18 years	Body and brain continue to develop; needs to sleep longer.	Can conceptualize possibilities; can plan and try out ideas; abstract reasoning continues to develop.	Focus is self and intimacy with others; begins to distinguish self from group (autonomy).	Informal and activity-specific groups provide a context for identity development; leisure provides a context for bonding, opportunities for support, and a way to demonstrate competence and meaningful activity.
YOUNG ADULT				
19–29 years	Hormonal and body-mass growth slows.	Continues to develop values and abstract reasoning.	Establishes self in context of work and family; social network often changes many times during this period because of dating, marriage, having children, divorce, change in work or school environment; continues to develop self and discover who one is in a changing social context.	Adapts leisure from previous interests and is influenced by the available resources, associations, time available, and family and work obligations.
MIDDLE-AGE ADULT				
30–44 years	Growth slows.	Development continues.	Social role provided by work, family, and need for identify from what one accomplishes; needs to balance work, family, and leisure.	Leisure often focuses on the nurturing and development of children; reevaluates relationships and priorities; has more resources; leisure provides stability; divorce, death, and job changes can disrupt stability.

Development	Physical	Cognitive	Socio-emotional	Leisure focus
LATE MIDDLE-AGE ADULT				
45–65 years	Flexibility, strength, and muscle mass begin to decline.	Growth continues.	Focuses on dignity versus control.	Men shift values toward intimacy; women shift toward accomplishment and growth; renews activity involvement as children age.
RETIREMENT TO DISABILITY				
65 years and older	Gradual compounding of lifestyle behavior occurs; physical health varies greatly depending on whether health-promoting behaviors such as good nutrition and exercise were engaged in during early adulthood or whether health-risk behaviors such as smoking, heavy drinking, and inactivity were the norm.	Growth continues; long-term memory increases and short-term memory becomes less acute.	Reflects on accomplishments and reviews contributions made through life journey; needs to feel that one has lived a good life and contributed to the greater whole through children, life work, or other means (generativity).	Leisure becomes an integrating experience; quality of life is important; increases leisure involvement.
DISABILITY TO DEATH				
This phase is optional; if disability occurs these are some possible repercussions.	Flexibility, range of motion, and muscle strength and tone decline.	Short-term memory (ability to retain new information) gradually declines.	Deals with accepting death.	With loss of physical and cognitive abilities and loss of social network members, leisure provides a context for expressing loss, continuing interests, and adapting to changes. Leisure also provides a way to pass on one's history and gifts to the community and to the next generation.

Data from DeBord 1996, Kelly and Godbey 1992; Schaie and Willis 2002; Steinberg 2002.

impairment or spina bifida still has the need for intimacy, autonomy, and generativity.

Practice Settings

Because the term *developmental disability* represents a broad range of functional domains and abilities, nature and location of therapeutic recreation services for this population are equally broad. One major realm for therapeutic recreation programs is the public and municipal park and recreation setting. These agencies provide a variety of poten-

tial programs, including year-round recreation programs, summer camps, and after-school enrichment programs. In some cases, these programs may cater specifically to persons with developmental disabilities, although the Americans with Disabilities Act (1990) requires that services in such programs be provided in the least restrictive manner. As such, many city and county recreation agencies employ therapeutic recreation personnel to oversee inclusive recreation services. These professionals apply the therapeutic recreation process to community settings in a manner that maximizes involvement in general programs offered by the agency.

Another major provider of therapeutic recreation services to persons with developmental disabilities is in the private realm (both for profit and nonprofit). Many of the programs are community based, meaning that participants live at home and come to the agency to participate in programs. These organizations provide services such as work training and support, socialization opportunities, and various other support services. Services are similar to those offered in municipal programs. These agencies may plan camps, structured recreation, and special events, but they also may provide higher levels of support, such as day programs that provide a variety of educational and therapy experiences (including therapeutic recreation).

Also in the private realm are long-term residential agencies that assist adults in living independently and semi-independently (some such agencies also operate as state or local government entities). The general focus of such therapeutic recreation programs is to supplement and expand the main developmental needs of people with DD through recreation involvement, leisure education, and facilitation of **self-advocacy.**

Note that these categories represent general trends and do not reflect the fact that many private and nonprofit agencies receive funds from governments. In reality, various funding sources may support agencies that provide comprehensive services. Regardless, the role of the therapeutic recreation specialist within a particular agency will be based on the clients served.

Intellectual Impairment

Intellectual impairment is the largest subclass of DD. In the United States 1% to 3% of the population has some degree of intellectual impairment (Steinmetz, 2006). Intellectual impairment is characterized by (a) significantly lower intellectual functioning (IQ of 70 or below), (b) concurrent limitation in at least two adaptive skill areas, and (c) onset before age 18 (American Psychiatric Association, 2005a). **Adaptive skills** include communication, self-care, home living, social and interpersonal skills, use of community resources, self-direction, functional academic skills, work, leisure, and health and safety.

The diagnosis of intellectual impairment is used to determine eligibility for programs covered by **Individuals with Disabilities Education Act**

(IDEA, Public Law 101-478), Medicaid, and vocational rehabilitation (Schroeder et al., 2002). Intellectual impairment is often dually diagnosed with another DD such as Down syndrome, autism, or spina bifida. A related category of diagnoses is developmental delay (Schroeder et al.). A developmental delay has been used mainly in the educational system to indicate cognitive performance below the standard developmental level. This term has been applied to allow remedial or extra services to help the child develop the skills needed to function at a higher level. A developmental delay can be an early indicator of having intellectual impairment, or it may indicate only a need for extra services. The determining factor is the duration of assistance needed.

Similarly, a child can be diagnosed with a **learning disability,** the general term given to a child who is having significant problems with language or mathematical calculations, not related to intellectual impairment or emotional or psychological problems. The term includes the diagnoses of dyslexia, brain injury, and developmental aphasia (loss of ability to speak). A learning disability can be covered by services constituted by IDEA. A learning disability is not as severe as intellectual impairment, and a child with a learning disability

©Vegas Adaptive Recreation

One common goal when working with clients with intellectual disabilities is to ensure that they have access to a broad array of leisure possibilities.

JULIE VAN FOEKEN

Background Information

Education
Double major in Therapeutic Recreation and Spanish from Northwest Missouri State University

Credentials
CTRS

Special Affiliations
*KCATRA *NTRS *Douglas County Special Olympics *Covenant Cedars Bible Camp

Special Awards
Outstanding Employee Nomination

Career Information

Position
Recreation coordinator for Community Living Opportunities

Organization Information
Community Living Opportunities is a nonprofit organization formed in 1977 by a group of parents in Johnson County, Kansas, whose children have severe and multiple disabilities. The concept behind Community Living Opportunities is groundbreaking, compassionate, and extremely functional. The agency was created as an alternative to state institutions and became one of the pioneers in providing community-based services to people with developmental disabilities. The parent group organized, incorporated, and recruited a board of directors, advisors, and consultants that included professionals dedicated to progressive academic research and socially inclusive programming (including James Sherman, PhD, and Jan Sheldon, PhD, from the Department of Human Development and Family Life at the University of Kansas).

Organization Mission
Community Living Opportunities' mission is to help adults and children with severe developmental disabilities achieve personally satisfying and fulfilling lifestyles.

Job Description
Develop, support, evaluate, and refine recreational, educational, and therapeutic classes, special events, and other activities offered by Day Services within the center and also community-based settings. Develop class plans that outline the purpose/objective of the class, the needed supplies, and the teaching procedures for maximizing participant involvement. Ensure the class leaders are familiar with the class plans and that they are accessible to others and that all necessary class supplies/equipment are available for classes. Work within the budget and network/fund-raise with community businesses, civic organizations, and other resources to obtain monetary or in-kind donations for needed supplies/equipment. Design and distribute a Community Living Opportunities Communiversity Catalog that effectively markets the classes being offered and Community Living Opportunities in general, as well as serves as an option for enrolling in classes quarterly. Assist the Day Services Co. with hiring, training, supporting and evaluating the recreation leaders, recreation counselors and any Day Services teachers. Recruit, train, and supervise contractual class leaders from the community and within Community Living Opportunities (who have other primary positions). Develop and recruit practicum students and internships from within related fields at nearby colleges. Cover a class if a class leader is unavailable. Develop and lead at least one special event per site per month. Monitor and ensure high-quality recreation services by establishing, measuring and reporting data related to the critical outcomes and processes of the department and correct less than satisfying scores. Assess and compute data for all external clients.

Career Path
I started at Community Living Opportunities upon graduation from Northwest Missouri State University. I worked as a team leader and then director of Community Living in our residential program before moving to our Day Service department as the recreation coordinator.

Likes and Dislikes About the Job
I enjoy the creativity and problem solving, as well as enhancing the quality of life for those I serve.

Advice to Undergraduate Students
Be innovative and don't be afraid to try something new. Flexibility is key. The chance to enhance an individual's quality of life through recreational opportunities is amazing. A smile is an immeasurable reward.

can often learn adaptations to overcome its effects (Lokerson, 1992).

Causes of Intellectual Impairment

Causes of intellectual impairment range from genetic conditions to events occurring during pregnancy, birth, or childhood. Down syndrome, fragile X syndrome, and phenylketonuria (PKU) are all examples of intellectual impairment with genetic roots. Environmental causes can include drug and alcohol abuse during pregnancy, illnesses such as rubella during pregnancy, or deprivation of oxygen during birth. Some common causes of intellectual impairment during childhood include diseases such as meningitis and the measles, abuse or injury such as head injury or neglect from lack of proper nutrition, and exposure to toxic environmental elements such as lead or mercury (CDC, 2004a).

DOWN SYNDROME

Down syndrome is the most common chromosomal developmental disability and a form of intellectual impairment (NICHCY, 2004a). A **syndrome** is a group of symptoms or abnormalities that indicate a particular trait or disease. Down syndrome results from the production of an extra chromosome during cell development. Common symptoms include poor muscle tone, hyperflexibility, lowered resistance to infection, visual problems, slower physical and mental development, and premature aging as an adult (NICHCY, 2004a). The underlying genetic component predisposes people with Down syndrome to a variety of health problems including weakness of the spine, dementia, and heart problems (see chapter 13 for precautions for physical activity). Early interventions and enriched environments aid in lessening or preventing the development of poor health.

FRAGILE X SYNDROME

The most common inherited form of intellectual impairment is fragile X syndrome. Because the trait is carried on the X gene, the disability occurs more often and has more severe effects in males. Recent population estimates indicated that 1 in 3,847 people have the fragile X mutation (Beckett, Yu, & Long, 2005). The mutation of the gene causes the body to produce insufficient protein for development. This in turn produces varying degrees of intellectual impairment, sensitivity to sensation, behavioral problems, and certain physical characteristics including larger ears, jaw, and

Obesity, hyperflexible joints, accelerated aging, and early-onset Alzheimer's are common challenges for people with Down syndrome.

forehead; smaller stature; and extremely flexible joints. Other possible related physical conditions include weak connective tissue, heart murmur, and hand tremors. People with fragile X can have behaviors similar to those with autism because of their heightened sensitivity to sensations like loud noises and textures. This similarity extends to social behaviors and the ability to communicate in a socially appropriate manner (Child Development Institute, 2000).

PHENYLKETONURIA (PKU)

Phenylketonuria (PKU) is an inherited metabolic disorder that if not treated can lead to brain damage that causes intellectual impairment or cerebral palsy. Because of a genetic mutation, the body is unable to break down the protein phenylalanine. Treatment consists of changing the diet to limit the intake of phenylalanine, which is found in foods high in protein such as meats, fish, eggs, beans, nuts, milk and dairy products, and foods containing NutraSweet. Since 1961, when prenatal screening began, careful diet has prevented most cases of intellectual impairment. PKU is rare, occurring in 1 out of every 14,000 births (National Institutes of Health Consensus Development Statement, 2000; The ARC, 1997). Because a careful diet can usually prevent brain damage, the need for therapeutic recreation is limited. But people with PKU demonstrate the importance of being aware of the medical history of the client in all settings. In offering services the therapeutic recreation specialist must understand the dietary needs of clients as well as their physical needs. No specific program exists for people with PKU, but when dealing with a person who has cerebral palsy or intellectual impairment, service providers should be aware of potential contraindications such as the dietary restrictions indicated earlier.

Therapeutic Recreation Programs for People With Intellectual Impairment

During childhood, therapeutic recreation is used to supplement and extend educational services and provide opportunities for socialization. Common settings are after-school and summer camp programs offered by local and state parks and recreation departments, local agencies for serving people with disabilities, and organizations such as Easter Seals. The goal of the programming is to promote development of cognitive and social skills. Therapeutic recreation is specifically listed as related services to supplement education under the Individuals with Disabilities Education Act (IDEA). When a child is determined eligible for services, an interdisciplinary team develops an **individualized educational program (IEP).** Many programs, whether school affiliated or not, use the IEP to help address the specific needs of the child or teenager. As the person with intellectual impairment ages, therapeutic recreation can be used to address vocational or social skills, continue cognitive development, or address transitions such as a move or grief because of the death of a friend or close relative.

Most therapeutic recreation services for people with intellectual impairments could be identified under the general modality known as leisure education. Leisure education has been conceptualized as a major component of therapeutic recreation, as illustrated in the leisure ability model. In addition, several scholars and practitioners have worked to develop leisure education curricula that focus on people with intellectual impairment. Finally, specific programs or groups for this population are commonly in line with the elements of leisure education models and frameworks. Simply put, leisure education frameworks, curricula, and programs have been built on concepts that are consistent with the developmental or therapeutic goals commonly associated with people with intellectual impairment. Social skill development, leisure awareness, appropriate use of leisure resources, and activity skill development are all potential focal points when working with such people.

Autism and Other Pervasive Developmental Disorders (PDDs)

Autism is the most common form of **pervasive developmental disorder (PDD),** which refers to neurological disorders that affect a person's ability to communicate, understand language, play, and relate to others. Autism and PDD occur in approximately 1 in every 150 children and are four times more common in boys than in girls (CDC, 2007). Autism is related to several other developmental disorders, and three out of four people with autism are diagnosed with intellectual impairment. About half of those with autism and intellectual impairment have moderate to severe intellectual impairment, and 25% to 33% of people with autism have epileptic seizures (NICHCY, 2006).

A diagnosis of autism is given when the person exhibits 6 or more of 12 symptoms listed across three major areas: social interaction, communication, and behavior (NICHCY, 2006). Specific characteristics include lack of social or emotional reciprocity, stereotyped or repetitive motions, and lack of varied or spontaneous make-believe play. When children display similar behaviors but to a lesser extent, they are given the diagnosis of a nonspecific PDD.

Autism is one of the disabilities specifically defined in the Individuals with Disabilities Education Act of 1990 (IDEA), which defines the disorder as a developmental disability that significantly affects verbal and nonverbal communication and social interaction, usually evident before age 3, and adversely affects a child's educational performance (Public Law 101-476).

Characteristics listed under IDEA include inability to develop normal social relationships, delay in speech development, stereotypical play, lack of imagination, and insistence on sameness. Some or all of the following characteristics may be observed in mild to severe forms:

- Communication problems (e.g., using and understanding language)
- Difficulty relating to people, objects, and events
- Unusual play with toys and other objects
- Difficulty with changes in routine or familiar surroundings
- Repetitive body movements or behavior patterns

People with autism exhibit a broad range of cognitive abilities and behavior; some have little to no language skills, and others are highly intelligent. Unusual responses to sensory information such as loud noises, lights, and certain textures of food or fabrics are also common.

Therapeutic Recreation Programs for People with Autism

Interventions for people with autism or PDD focus on improving communication, social, academic, behavioral, and daily living skills. Use of a variety of sensory inputs such as visual and auditory cues is often effective in helping the person with autism or PDD learn better. Interaction with peers who do not have disabilities is important for providing models of appropriate language, social, and behavioral skills. To overcome frequent problems in generalizing skills from one setting to another, goals, experiences, and approaches should be done in a variety of settings including, home, school, and the community. As with intellectual impairment, therapeutic recreation specialists may encounter people with autism in a variety of settings ranging from structured therapy or education programs to municipal recreation programs. Because autism varies widely in severity and symptomology, the therapeutic recreation specialist must adequately identify client needs and abilities through assessment and adjust the program accordingly.

As with other developmental disabilities, developing a comprehensive understanding of the client is critical to the success of intervention. Because autism usually involves restricted interests, as well as substantial fixation on the interests that do exist, one major goal is to expand the client's repertoire of leisure behavior. Children who spend all their time reading the same book or playing with the same toy, often in a manner unrelated to the purpose of the toy, have limited ability to develop through typical play patterns. Stereotypic behaviors such as rocking or bouncing (forms of self-stimulation) often reduce the possibility of broadening play interests. But by understanding the interests of a child with autism, the professional can implement effective interventions. Pairing the preferred form of play with other play behaviors can gradually lead to a more diverse play pattern, which is fuel for learning and development. This process involves hands-on work. The therapeutic recreation specialist plays with the child, integrating the preferred form of play into various activities and encouraging the child to take part. The preferred form of play can also be used to reinforce desirable behavior. In severe cases, preferred forms of play may be limited to sensory stimulation such as use of a mirror or a vibrating toy. After the child begins to understand and enjoy using various toys in their intended manner, he or she is better able to socialize with other children. Early intervention is important in all cases.

Another commonly used technique is the relaxation room. Because children with autism often experience sensory overload when subjected to certain stimuli and to overwhelming environments in general, they often need opportunities to recuperate. Relaxation rooms are areas that contain a variety of soothing stimuli, such as beanbags, pillows, soft colored lights, soothing music, and even bubbles. This resource can help the child recuperate from overwhelming environments at school, therapy, home, or play.

Finally, community-based recreation programs for people with autism should be a regular part of the parks and recreation services provided in today's society and, when appropiate, inclusive.

Cerebral Palsy

Cerebral palsy (CP) refers to a group of disorders characterized by an inability to control muscular and postural movements. CP results from damage to the brain before age 12 (NICHCY, 2004b). The most common causes of CP are genetic conditions, infections (such as meningitis), child abuse, stroke, and head injury. CP can range from mild to severe. In the United States about 9,500 infants and children are diagnosed with CP each year. There are four main types of CP:

- Spastic CP is a result of tightness of the muscles, resulting in stiff movements of the arms or legs and immediate contraction of stretched muscles. People with this form of CP often "move their legs awkwardly, turning in or scissoring their legs as they try to walk" (NICHCY, 2004b, p. 2). Spastic CP can manifest in three forms: diplegia, in which only the legs are affected; hemiplegia, in which half of the body (such as the left arm and leg) is affected; and quadriplegia, in which both the arms and the legs are affected, sometimes including the facial muscles and torso. Spastic CP is the most common form of CP, affecting 70% to 80% of people with CP.
- Athetoid CP (also called dyskinetic CP) is a result of low muscle tone and manifests itself in slow, uncontrollable movements of the entire body. This disability makes it hard for the person to sit straight and walk.
- Ataxic CP results in a poor sense of balance in walking and standing. The person has trouble controlling muscle length or position and may overshoot objects when reaching for them.
- Mixed CP is a combination of types. A person with mixed CP exhibits both rigid and involuntary movements.

CP can range from mild, in which the person has only mild stiffness in walking, to severe, in which many bodily functions are impeded. The main areas affected are locomotion (walking and other forms of movement), gross and fine motor coordination, and communication skills because of limitations in controlling muscle movement. People with CP have a higher incidence of seizure activity and may have sensation, vision, or speech problems when they overexert themselves. Lack of movement and physical activity also results in a higher probability of being overweight (NICHCY, 2004b).

Therapeutic Recreation Programs for People With Cerebral Palsy

People with CP experience a variety of symptoms that can make recreation activities, and ADLs in general, difficult. For example, **pathological reflexes** often accompany CP. Reflexes are usually integrated into typical motor patterns as we progress through the developmental stages, but brain injury associated with CP can cause these reflexes to persist indefinitely. These pathological reflexes disrupt normal body movements with uncontrollable movement. For example, the asymmetrical tonic reflex (ATNR) is triggered when the head is tilted or turned (Sherrill, 2004). Simply turning the head to track a moving ball will cause the chin-side arm to extend out and the other arm to flex. This movement is uncontrollable. Therapeutic recreation specialists can, in some cases, work to inhibit these pathological reflexes through activities that work to develop motor skills. For example, ATNR reflex intervention might include having the person creep backward and forward with the head turned to one side (creeping works to integrate the ATNR reflex triggered by turning the head; see Sherrill, 2004, for additional techniques related to integrating pathological reflexes).

CP also involves imbalances in the inhibition or engagement of flexor and extensor muscle groups, which lead to spasticity (muscle stiffness). Spasticity causes limited flexibility and range of motion and can cause permanent joint contractures if untreated. Massage, stretching, and trunk rotations can be used to reduce such imbalances and maximize leisure skills. Aquatic programs are especially useful because buoyancy in the water makes movement and manipulation much easier, and warm-water pools (90 to 98 °F, or 32.2 to 36.7 °C) help relieve contractures.

Two increasingly popular modalities are therapeutic horseback riding and hippotherapy. Therapeutic horseback riding can help address disturbances in postural reactions (the ability to hold the body upright) and other physical abilities and can also be used to address social and emotional issues. Hippotherapy uses the movement of the horse to relieve spasticity and hypotonia (low muscle tone). These horse-based therapies require certification and collaboration with trained professionals.

Spina Bifida

Spina bifida is a condition in which the spinal column does not close during gestation. In fact, 40% of Americans have a form of spina bifida, but most do not experience any symptoms. Three forms of spina bifida present problems. Spina bifida occulta, the mildest form, is a result of one or more openings of the vertebrae with no discernible damage to the spinal cord. The second form occurs when the sac that protects the spinal cord, the meningocele, is pushed through an opening in the vertebrae. This form can easily be repaired and does not result in injury to the spinal cord. In the third type, myelomeningocele, the spinal cord protrudes through the person's back. This is the form commonly referred to as spina bifida. This condition results in muscle weakness or paralysis below the exposed area in the spine, loss of bladder and bowel control, and frequently (in 70% to 90% of the cases) causes accumulation of fluid in the brain (hydrocephalus) (NICHCY, 2004c). The treatment requires several operations throughout childhood and, if accompanied by hydrocephalus, placing a shunt in the child's brain to drain excess fluid. Buildup of fluid on the brain can cause further damage, resulting in blindness, seizures, or brain damage. Slightly less than 1 child in 1,000 has this third form of spina bifida (NICHCY, 2004c).

With proper medical care and supplementary services, 90% of all children born with spinal bifida live a normal life-span reference. Spina bifida is often classified as an orthopedic or neurological disability, but because of the early onset and possible cognitive impairments, some classify spina bifida as a developmental disability. Like other orthopedic disabilities, many people with spina bifida use assistive devices such as walkers, braces, wheelchairs, splints, or crutches. As with spinal cord

injury, possible loss of bowel and bladder control may require the use of a catheter (Kolaski, 2006; NICHCY, 2004c). Because of continued physical growth during childhood and adolescence, repeated operations are often needed. These procedures can result in loss of strength and low self-esteem.

Therapeutic Recreation Programs for People With Spina Bifida

Therapeutic recreation interventions focus on increasing muscle strength and flexibility, learning how to adapt activities, and increasing a sense of self and empowerment through leisure activities. Frequent operations during childhood create a need for continual strengthening of the muscles. The same adaptations and activities used with other people who have difficulty with mobility can be used with a person who has spina bifida. Possible precautions relate to complications due to hydrocephalia and the spinal cord lesion, which include possible seizures, cognitive impairment, apnea, swallowing difficulties, neck pain, and increased susceptibility to bladder and bowel dysfunctions and infections (for details see Kolaski, 2006; NICHCY, 2004c). Goals such as increasing upper-body strength to assist in ADLs and building self-esteem are common.

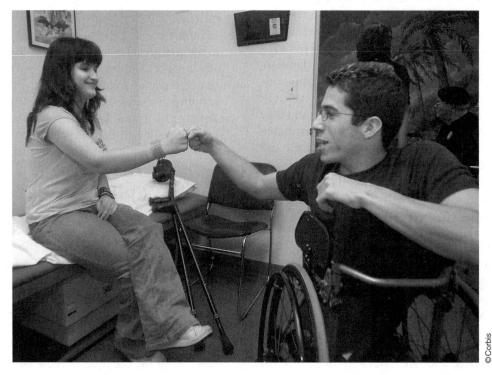

©Corbis

Spina bifida can result in various levels of impairment, often requiring crutches or a wheelchair for ambulation.

Duchenne Muscular Dystrophy

Muscular dystrophy (MD) is a group of chronic genetic diseases characterized by the progressive degeneration and weakness of voluntary muscles. MD results from a hereditary or mutated gene on the X chromosome that causes generalized weakness and deterioration of the muscles. The onset of four forms of MD occurs during childhood: Duchenne, Becker, congenital, and Emery-Dreifuss. Two other forms, facioscapulohumeral MD and limb-girdle MD, occur in late childhood to adolescence.

Duchenne MD, also called pseudohypertropic, is the most common type and most aggressive form of childhood MD. It accounts for over half of all forms of MD and occurs in 1 of 3,500 births. The genetic defect caused by Duchenne MD results in

the absence of the protein dystrophin, which helps keep the muscle walls intact. Signs of weakness, loss of reflexes, difficulty sitting up, and impaired breathing first occur when the child begins to walk (around age 2). As the disease progresses, the muscles become weaker and breathing becomes difficult. "Children with Duchenne MD are typically wheelchair-bound by age 12 and usually die in their late teens or early 20s from progressive weakness of the heart muscle, respiratory complications or infections" (NINDS, 2006, p. 3).

The other forms of MD cause varying degrees of muscle weakness that affect the ability to walk as well as the health of the heart and respiratory systems. Treatment focuses on helping the person with MD be as independent and comfortable as possible. Activities that improve movement and flexibility are recommended (NINDS, 2006).

Best Practices

In all stages of education and training of those with disabilities, a balance should be struck between traditional educational goals, such as learning the alphabet and learning how to read, and functional skills, such as learning how to cross the street safely or how to use the bus system. The former goals focus on skills fundamental to learning higher cognitive or physical competencies, whereas the latter goals focus on the ability to perform daily activity skills. The focus should ultimately be on the skills that the person needs to be as independent as possible or to live in the least restrictive environment.

Some additional practices to promote individual choice and independence include using adaptive equipment, offering opportunities for community integration, providing leisure education, utilizing activity and task analysis, and providing opportunities for practice and repetition. As technology continues to expand, so does the availability of new options for enhancing clients' skills.

One critical consideration to remember is that a person's cognitive level is not the same as a life-stage level. The therapeutic recreation specialist must offer and use age-appropriate activities and equipment. Although a person may have the cognitive abilities of a 5-year-old, that person should not be given only toys and activities that a 5-year-old would use. Rather than thinking of the diagnosis (such as having an IQ of 50 or not having the use of the lower extremity), the specialist should think of the person, his or her chronological age, and the

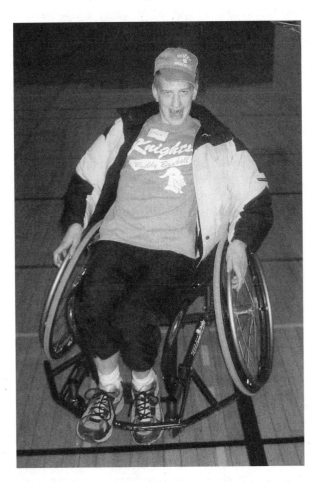

Severity of motor disturbances caused by cerebral palsy varies, with some individuals requiring the use of adaptive equipment. This young man can stand and walk but has difficulty with balance during complex activities.

person's interests. Focus should be on adapting age-appropriate activities that are of interest to the client and his or her cohort. Many opportunities should be provided to practice these activities, including opportunities within the larger community (i.e., community integration). For instance, a client who is in her mid-50s and has Down syndrome should not be given elementary-aged toys to work on goals. Rather, the therapeutic recreation specialist can use the client's interests in gardening, her cat, and her love of country music to achieve therapy objectives. The goal of increasing social integration could be achieved by helping the client enroll in a community garden club, having her volunteer to garden at a community garden plot, or aiding her in registering to show flowers at the county fair. These activities can be accompanied by engaging her in role-playing situations before the actual events (the client portrait for "Mary" on page 143 further explains this scenario).

Another technique often used to facilitate learning new skills is behavior modification. **Behavioral modification,** the process of changing behavior through a combination of rewards and punishments, is frequently used with clients who have developmental disabilities. Behavioral modification can be used not only to teach and reinforce a positive behavior, such as remaining focused on a task or learning a new skill, but also to reduce or stop a negative behavior, such as hitting or interrupting others. For additional information, review the comprehensive overview of behavior modification principles in chapter 10.

Another important practice is using multiple modes of communication or instructional prompts. Information can be presented verbally, visually, or even with other senses such as smell and touch. By using multiple prompts, the likelihood that the client will remember the information is increased. Leisure activities are ideally suited for using multiple senses. For instance, in using swimming to improve a client's physical fitness and endurance, the therapeutic recreation specialist can use verbal cuing (reminders) to swim, assisted movement (a physical prompt) to develop the position of the swimming stroke, and colored markers to reinforce distance traveled. Similarly, a repeated instruction can help the client focus on the task and process information. As with any learning, the more opportunities there are for practice and repetition, the more likely it is that the client will learn the behavior or task.

As described in chapter 6, activity analysis is the process of breaking down an activity into the skills and requirements (equipment, setting, and so on) necessary for successfully doing the activity. Similarly, task analysis was described as breaking an activity into its basic behavioral steps. Both of these procedures are especially important when working with persons who have a DD. As the therapeutic recreation specialist seeks avenues for utilizing client strengths and implementing necessary adaptations, these procedures provide a structured mechanism for finding age appropriate activities that meet the developmental capabilities and needs of the client. In regard to intellectual impairment, task analysis can be especially useful for identifying appropriate increments or steps of learning when using techniques such as chaining or shaping to teach complex behaviors.

The opportunity for community integration is important for all people with developmental disabilities. The concept developed from efforts to change the status quo of 30 years ago when the norm was to institutionalize people with developmental disabilities. The basic premise is to give opportunities to participate in a full life. Parallel to the concept of community integration is the concept of least restrictive environment. As the term indicates, every person should have the opportunity to participate in activities as he or she is able. The range of suitable opportunities will vary according to ability. Least restrictive environment often means that the person participates in community activities with some assistance. For instance, an adult with cerebral palsy might be able to snow ski after training in the use of adaptive equipment and being provided transportation to a nearby ski resort.

Leisure education is part of many of the therapeutic interventions with people with developmental disabilities. Leisure education focuses on goal areas such as expanding the range of recreation awareness and opportunities, exploring possible adaptations of activities, improving recreation-related social skills, and mastering activity skills. Modification of activities should continue in accordance with the developmental skills and limitations of the client. As mentioned earlier, modification can be accomplished through training in the use of various forms of adaptive equipment and by adapting the nature of the activity to client needs. Again, task analysis and activity analysis are important tools in identifying and developing necessary adaptations.

MARY

Mary is a woman in her mid-50s who has Down syndrome. Her interests include gardening, her cat, and country music. She has lived all her life in her family home, which now houses only herself and her 95-year-old mother, who thinks that she may need to move into assisted living. Mary says that she would love to meet other people but does not know anyone. During a recent visit from social services, it was determined that Mary would benefit from therapeutic recreation services. Goals would be increasing social integration and learning about community resources.

Objective

During the initial assessment interview, the therapeutic recreation specialist discovered that Mary had helped her father and some of her siblings take care of their large garden and many pets, including three horses. The animals were sold when her father died 11 years ago, so Mary now takes care of only two cats and a small flower garden. Mary spoke many times during the interview about how much she enjoyed working in the garden and caring for the horses. At the end of the meeting, three objectives were established for the general goal of social integration:

1. Mary will attend four different activities related to gardening within the community in the next month.
2. Mary will volunteer once a week for an hour at the local stables, where she will help groom the horses in exchange for a 15-minute horse ride.
3. Mary will talk to at least one other person (besides the therapist) for at least 3 minutes while at the stables and at the gardening activities.

Activity Analysis

Before Mary attends the meetings or volunteers, she and the therapeutic recreation specialist can role-play the gardening activities and what is expected in the volunteer job. Because Mary has both gardened and helped with horses in the past, extensive activity analysis will probably not be needed with these tasks. Even so, activity analysis can be useful in teaching the social skills needed for having a conversation. By breaking down the activity of introducing oneself (such as making eye contact, taking the right hand to shake when offered, saying hello, and waiting for a response), the therapeutic recreation specialist can determine what skills need further practice and role playing.

Behavior Modification

Positive reinforcers during role playing and both during and after participation in the community settings can be used to help achieve the goal of increasing social integration. During role playing, simple words of encouragement for correct actions, such as "You are a natural at this," accompanied by a smile are quite powerful. In the community, many natural reinforcers of social interaction will be present, such as getting to ride a horse and meeting people who are enthusiastic about the same activity. After being in the community, the therapeutic recreation specialist should be sure to emphasize the actions that are leading to achieving the objectives. For example, the specialist could say, "Mary you are becoming quite the social butterfly. I noticed that you introduced yourself to almost everyone at the plant exchange and talked to three people today." Open-ended questions are an effective way to prompt Mary to give herself praise ("So what did you do at the plant exchange? What did you talk about?").

Communicating With Mary About Community Integration

The therapeutic recreation specialist can further enhance the outcome of the interventions by using multiple sensory inputs. In working with someone with a cognitive impairment, use of pictures, music, simple verbal cues, and role playing (enacting the scenario) can help with retention of the lesson. The closer these cues come to simulating the community setting, the more likely it is that the behavior will be replicated. For example, to help Mary prepare for a plant sale sponsored by a local gardening club, a role play could be conducted using the same items that would be present at the plant sale (potted plants, pamphlets about the plants, money, and so on). Although the objective could be to meet people by passing out flyers at the local plant sale, the props can help Mary remember the role play. The therapeutic recreation specialist can also take advantage of many of the elements that naturally occur in the community setting to enhance the therapeutic results, such as using Mary's comfort in being around horses or plants to help her interact with others.

Other Developmental Disabilities

Many other developmental disabilities combine physical, cognitive, and socio-emotional delays. Diagnoses not covered include visual impairments, hearing impairments, and attention-deficit/hyperactivity disorder (ADHD). In all cases, the developmental needs of the person and his or her family should be considered along with the person's leisure preferences and talents. Leisure skills development should be transferable to the client's living environment.

Ever-Changing Terminology

Because of the power for negative connotation that comes with labels, the terminology used to refer to a person with intellectual impairment has changed over the years. Terms such as *mongoloid* and *idiot* were once commonly used but now are viewed as derogatory. In fact, even the term *mental retardation* is criticized by many as carrying negative connotations, and some are making an effort not to use this terminology as a formal label. During the summer of 2006 the American Association on Mental Retardation voted to change its name to the American Association on Intellectual and Developmental Disabilities. The new name is more consistent with commonly used international language and represents another step in acknowledging the person in a positive light rather than the limitation in a negative light.

Summary

Development is a lifelong process. Although a person is diagnosed with a DD during childhood, the delay or consequences of the disability extend throughout the person's life. This chapter has presented information about how to implement the goals required to improve the health of a person with a developmental disability. Whether or not the therapeutic recreation specialist works directly with someone with intellectual impairment or someone with another form of developmental disability, a fundamental understanding of how a person's life context can be enhanced by taking an integrative approach to therapy is the greatest insight that can be gained.

Therapeutic recreation can play a significant role in optimizing lifelong growth in people with developmental disabilities. Although developmental disabilities affect a wide range of abilities, the ability to adapt activities based on needs and interests of an individual is a trademark of the therapeutic recreation specialist. By expanding this skill to include the social environment in which the person lives and works, professionals can further facilitate opportunities for enjoyment, growth, and self-advocacy. By using expertise on how leisure evolves throughout life and across development, therapeutic recreation specialists are ideally suited to create an environment to support growth, social integration, and safety in dealing with and working through life transitions.

DISCUSSION QUESTIONS

1. Describe the commonalities and differences of the diagnoses of developmental disability, intellectual impairment, learning disability, pervasive developmental disorder, autism, cerebral palsy, Down syndrome, and spina bifida.

2. What are the main knowledge areas that a therapeutic recreation specialist should understand to work with a person with a developmental disability?

3. Explain the importance of age-appropriate interventions and give at least two examples.

4. Explain why taking the life-span approach is important when working with people with DD.

5. Explain what precautions need to be taken for the contraindications for each of the presented types of DD.

6. Identify potential goal areas for each of the presented types of DD.

Therapeutic Recreation and Mental Health

Terry Long, PhD

Northwest Missouri State University

Many therapeutic recreation professionals work with clients whose therapeutic goals are oriented toward psychological well-being. In fact, mental health centers often employ an entire department of therapeutic recreation specialists who work with clients who are receiving psychiatric care. These clients may be facing a variety of challenges including depression, anxiety, eating disorders, drug-related issues, schizophrenia, or personality disorders. Because leisure is a major domain of functioning that can both affect and be affected by such conditions, the therapeutic recreation specialist can play a significant role in psychiatric treatment programs. Therapeutic recreation programs designed to target psychological well-being are not limited to traditional mental health treatment facilities. Community-based support groups, after-school or summer programs, wilderness-based programs, and challenge-course programs all can be designed to address issues such as self-concept, sobriety, self-confidence, resilience, values, attitudes, and behavior.

Every therapeutic recreation specialist should have a basic understanding of psychological functioning and associated mental health concepts, regardless of the setting or clientele associated with his or her work. As pointed out in chapter 1, psychological well-being should be a consideration for all clients, even those with physical injuries or conditions. This chapter will first discuss the role of therapeutic recreation in the treatment of psychiatric disorders and its application to several diagnostic groups. Second, it will identify various psychological concepts that are relevant to all people, regardless of disability presence and type. Finally, specific therapeutic recreation interventions that have relevance to mental health outcomes will be presented. Regardless of where a therapeutic recreation specialist works, this chapter is important to his or her success as a professional.

Components of a Healthy Mind

What does it mean to be mentally healthy? Therapeutic recreation specialists should understand that mental health is one component of the more complex concept referred to as psychosocial health. This concept views a healthy mind as having four components: mental health, emotional health, social health, and spiritual health. A psychosocially healthy person has a positive self-image, gets along well with other people, is able to deal with the stress of everyday life, responds appropriately when experiencing negative emotions, and has a positive outlook on life. Additionally, psychosocially healthy people value all people and have a sense of how they fit into the world. Achieving psychosocial health is a lifelong process. Many factors influence a person's psychosocial health including heredity, the environment, family life, personality, patterns of daily life, self-efficacy, self-esteem, and level of optimism. Various factors can cause a person's psychosocial health to deteriorate. Physical problems, extreme stress, or environmental factors can result in problems that affect a person's ability to function in everyday life. In extreme cases, mental illness or a mental disorder may occur.

What Is a Mental Disorder?

Mental disorders are described in the *Diagnostic and Statistical Manual of Mental Disorders, 4th Edition, Text Revision (DSM-IV-TR)* (American Psychiatric Association, 2000) as "a clinically significant behavioral or psychological syndrome or pattern that occurs in an individual and that is associated with present distress or disability or with a significantly increased risk of suffering death, pain, disability or an important loss of freedom" (p. xxxi). The *DSM-IV-TR* is used by psychologists, psychiatrists, and other qualified mental health professionals to assess, diagnose, and classify mental health disorders based on diagnostic categories. By providing a diagnosis for a client's symptoms, mental health professionals are able to determine appropriate treatment. The *DSM-IV-TR* lists over 250 specific diagnoses and another 40 or so conditions that may be the focus of clinical attention. This chapter covers some of the more common diagnoses seen in therapeutic recreation clients who are receiving mental health services, as well as potential techniques, or modalities, for providing services to them.

Multiaxial System

Diagnostic information that results from a psychological assessment is often presented in a multiaxial format, meaning that multiple domains of functioning are considered. This system allows a comprehensive understanding of the client's current level of functioning and the ways in which psychosocial and environmental problems affect that functioning.

Five specific axes are typically addressed in a psychological assessment report. Each axis represents a specific place where particular information can be reported (and later located by professionals). Axes I and II are for reporting all the various disorders or conditions listed in the *DSM-IV-TR*. Most of these are to be listed under axis I, with intellectual impairment and personality disorders specifically reserved for axis II. Sometimes, patients have more than one disorder listed under axis I or II. In such cases, the principal condition (reason for the visit) should be listed first (American Psychiatric Association, 2000). When listing a particular disorder, the professional lists the disorder name and an associated diagnostic number (e.g., 317—mild mental retardation). The listed diagnostic number corresponds with the International Statistical Classification of Diseases and Related Health Problems, 10th Revision (ICD-10) (WHO, 1992), a comprehensive system for classifying health disorders developed by the World Health Organization (see chapter 15 for more information on the WHO classification system).

Axis III is used to indicate relevant medical conditions that the client is currently experiencing. ICD numerical codes are also reported on axis III, along with any corresponding physical condition that the client may have (codes listed in the *DSM-IV* regarding *physical conditions* correspond with the ninth revision of the ICD). Use of these international codes allows communication and comparison of health-related information and statistics across various regions of the world.

Axis IV provides information associated with existing psychosocial and environmental problems. Nine specific categories of psychosocial or environmental problems are listed in the *DSM-IV-TR*. For example, "Problems with primary support group" is the first category, and specific examples include issues such as physical or sexual abuse, inadequate discipline, divorce, and removal from the home. Other examples of the nine categories include educational problems, housing problems, economic problems, and problems related to the social environment (see American Psychiatric Association, 2000, p. 31 for a complete listing).

Axis V is designated for the reporting of the client's **global assessment of functioning** (GAF). This GAF score is based on a clinician's judgment of the client's overall level of functioning. GAF scores range from 0 to 100, with higher numbers indicating higher levels of functioning. Therapeutic recreation specialists do not determine GAF scores, but they can use the score to understand the client's overall level of functioning and track changes in function that may occur over time. The therapeutic recreation specialist who understands this system can quickly obtain information related to the client by reviewing the five axes and can discuss the client's situation in a common language with other treatment team professionals.

The following list is an example of a *DSM-IV-TR* multiaxial evaluation report based on a client with Down syndrome and dementia.

- Axis I—294.43 Dementia of the Alzheimer's type, early onset with depressed mood
- Axis II—317 Mild mental retardation
- Axis III—331.0 Alzheimer's disease, early onset; 758.0 Down syndrome
- Axis IV—Poverty, inadequate health insurance, death of family member (father)
- Axis V—GAF = 45 (current); 60 (highest level past year)

Note: If there is no diagnosis for axis I or II, the entry would be V71.09 no diagnosis. *DSM* still uses the term "mental retardation" to refer to "intellectual impairment."

Role of Therapeutic Recreation in Treating Mental Disorders

Therapeutic recreation specialists typically work as part of a cross-disciplinary team to address the general treatment goals of the client. In mental health settings, this team might consist of psychiatrists, psychologists, psychiatric nurses, art therapists, case managers, teachers, vocational rehabilitation professionals, and various other specialized service providers and support staff members. These people work together to identify and address the needs and strengths of clients under their care. One of the primary roles of the therapeutic recreation specialist is to communicate with this group by sharing information that might help others work with the client and by gathering information relevant to ongoing therapeutic recreation services. This sharing takes place through formal **progress notes** (charting), daily or weekly staffings (team meetings), and direct communication.

Another major responsibility is to provide services that follow the therapeutic recreation process (assess, plan, implement, evaluate; see chapter 6) to clients. To understand the context in which this process takes place, consider the general manner in which clients enter into mental health care.

Clients entering a mental health treatment program typically take part in a general intake assessment immediately after being admitted. A psychiatrist, psychologist, or master's-level therapist or social worker conducts this assessment. The intake assessment is designed to identify the client's current level of functioning (based on the multiaxial system described earlier) and establish general treatment goals. Results of assessment are typically accompanied by a general treatment plan that is implemented by the cross-disciplinary team of professionals.

The therapeutic recreation specialist uses this information when implementing the therapeutic recreation process. Therapeutic recreation assessment in mental health settings typically starts with a review of results from the intake assessment, including a summary of the five diagnostic axes. This document, as well as any other historical sources of client information (e.g., client portfolio, chart), provides a basic description of the client's **presenting problem,** which can then be used to develop therapeutic recreation assessment strategies. In most cases, therapeutic recreation assessments in mental health settings involve some form of client interview. The interview usually focuses on leisure interests, attitudes, barriers, and functioning (past and present behavior), although nonleisure information may be gathered when relevant to aspects of the client's presenting problem that can be addressed through therapeutic recreation. Other sources of information include observation and standardized assessments such as the leisure diagnostic battery or the comprehensive evaluation of recreation therapy. (See chapter 6 for a more detailed description of specific assessment instruments.)

After assessment results have been summarized in a therapeutic recreation assessment report and used to develop an **individualized program plan** (IPP), or therapeutic recreation treatment plan, the client is placed in therapeutic recreation groups or programs that will address the identified goals. At the same time, the therapeutic recreation specialist works to evaluate the progress of other clients already participating in these programs. Essentially, all four elements of the therapeutic recreation process are performed at once. Furthermore, an

Clients should be matched with appropriate groups or programs based on their individual needs and abilities.

individual client may cycle back through the process. For example, if ongoing evaluation indicates that a client is not responding as expected to a particular therapeutic recreation group, additional assessment and planning may lead to a change in how therapeutic recreation goals and objectives are addressed.

The nature and content of the groups, or programs, that clients might be placed into depend on the needs and abilities of the clientele served by the agency. Specific therapeutic recreation programs should be developed based on client needs and skills, and placement into programs should follow the same logic. Later sections of this chapter will elaborate on various therapeutic recreation modalities commonly used in mental health settings.

Levels of Care in Mental Health

Mental health organizations exist in a variety of forms in both private and public settings. Because therapeutic recreation professionals may work in any of these facilities, a description of several specific levels of care that can be provided will be useful. Clients may move through this continuum of services, or they may receive services at only one level. The most supportive level of care would be **crisis care,** in which clients receive supervision 24 hours a day for a short time, typically for 30 days or less. This level of care is appropriate for people who are at high risk of harming themselves or others. Clients who are more stabilized but still in need of extensive therapy services may seek **residential care.** Although extended stays are less common because of the deinstitutionalization movement and funding limitations, residential facilities can provide services for several months, or even years in some cases. Those who require less support may attend **day treatment** programs, in which clients spend part or all of the day in therapy and then return home. In some cases, day treatment and residential programs may coexist in the same facility, and clients can move from the residential program to the day program when appropriate. The most independent level of care that exists within this continuum is **outpatient care.** Clients who receive outpatient care come in up to several times a week to participate in therapy groups.

In some cases, mental health facilities are designated as **forensic,** meaning that the facility houses people who are under the care of the judicial system. A forensic unit may serve convicted criminals or people who have been declared incompetent to stand trial as a result of mental status. The exact nature of a forensic unit or facility and the clients served will vary from facility to facility. Because mental illness often coexists with substance abuse, drug and alcohol rehabilitation programs are often part of the mental health care system. Some facilities are primarily geared toward treating substance disorders, whereas other agencies provide drug and alcohol rehabilitation as part of a broader range of mental health services. As with mental health service providers, drug and alcohol treatment programs vary in intensity from outpatient care to residential programs.

Diagnostic Categories

The following sections present several of the more common diagnostic classes and some specific diagnoses and symptoms related to each class. A brief description of how therapeutic recreation relates to each diagnostic class is also provided.

Schizophrenia and Other Psychotic Disorders

The term *psychotic* is one of the most misunderstood concepts associated with mental health. Society often associates any bizarre or dangerous behavior with the term. This tendency not only mislabels behaviors that may be associated with other conditions but also reinforces stereotypes of people with schizophrenia. The most common misperception is that schizophrenia always indicates some sort of risk to society. The truth is that you have likely sat in a college classroom with one or more people with schizophrenia. Although some people who have schizophrenia can at times be dangerous to themselves or others, this is by no means a defining characteristic of a psychotic disorder.

Definitions of the word *psychotic* vary, and a variety of other conditions or disorders (such as drug use) may cause the same symptoms used to diagnose psychotic disorders. The *DSM-IV-TR* (American Psychiatric Association, 2000) describes psychotic disorders as a group of conditions characterized by some or all of a particular group of symptoms. Some of these symptoms include delusions, hallucinations, disorganized speech, catatonic behavior, and flattening of affect. **Delusions** are false beliefs related to the perceptions or experiences of the client, whereas **hallucinations** are perceived sensory experiences that do not really exist. Auditory hallucination, such as hearing voices, is the most common type, but hallucinations can occur in any sensory modality (American Psychiatric Association, 2000). Disorganized thinking is often reflected in the inability to maintain purposeful conversation. The speaker may jump from topic to topic, answer questions with unrelated responses, or speak in completely nonsensical phrases. Catatonic behavior can take many forms (rigid and unusual postures, purposeless movements) but typically represents some type of disturbance in reactivity to the environment (American Psychiatric Association, 2000).

Various psychotic disorders are listed in the *DSM-IV-TR*, including schizophrenia, schizophreniform disorder, schizoaffective disorder, and delusional disorder, but all involve some variation in the type, severity, and duration of the described psychotic symptoms. The first line of treatment for psychotic disorders is typically medication, but counseling and ancillary services such as therapeutic recreation can address functional deficits after more severely incapacitating symptoms are partially or fully managed.

For example, people with schizophrenia may have difficulty adjusting socially or partaking in purposeful activities even after they have ceased to experience hallucinations, delusions, or thought disturbances. To put it simply, jumping into daily life can be difficult when you have spent a significant portion of your life hearing voices, seeing people that do not exist, or struggling to communicate with the outside world. Paranoid delusions can make it difficult to trust even the ones you love the most.

Persons with schizophrenia vary widely in their level of functioning; therefore, services appropriate for this group vary widely. Still, several specific programmatic implications should be mentioned, most of which fall under the realm of leisure education. For people who are not yet ready to function in highly social situations, expressive and creative programs (such as painting or model building) can help develop leisure skills that serve as expressive mediums and coping strategies but do not require immediate socialization. Programs that develop social skills are also common and can range widely in complexity. Goals may range from being able to maintain appropriate eye contact to integrating into crowded social settings that produce high levels of anxiety. As such, social skill programs can involve both functional intervention and leisure education.

Exploring leisure awareness, identifying leisure resources, and developing activity skills are also relevant to therapeutic recreation programs for people with schizophrenia, specifically under the realm of leisure education. Besides determining appropriate levels of socialization during programming, the therapeutic recreation specialist must consider the client's ability to organize thoughts and participate in complex behaviors. These factors will determine the appropriate content for a particular therapeutic recreation program.

Mood Disorders

The most common mood disorders are major depressive disorder (MDD), dysthymia, and bipolar disorder. Each is characterized by a marked disturbance in mood that persists for a significant amount of time (American Psychiatric Association, 2000). MDD involves a cycle of significant depressive episodes, whereas dysthymia is a more persistent, but less intense, state of depression. Bipolar disorder involves cycling between depression and **manic** states.

As with psychotic disorders, medications can play a critical role in treatment of mood disorders. Medications can be especially necessary for bipolar disorder, which can involve extreme cases of mood disturbance. During manic episodes, clients may experience racing thoughts and be extremely distractible and impulsive. Because severe mania reduces the effectiveness of traditional counseling and education techniques, stabilization of mood through medications is the first step. Various counseling interventions, including therapeutic recreation, can then be used more effectively.

One major therapeutic recreation intervention for people with mood disorders is a healthy fitness routine. Exercise helps stabilize mood and can release endorphins that naturally enhance mood state. Coping skills can also be addressed through therapeutic recreation. The focus should be placed on issues such as decision making, problem solving, assertiveness training, and self-concept issues (self-esteem, self-efficacy, learned helplessness, and so on). These issues can be addressed through leisure education, experiential activities such as challenge courses, and appropriately facilitated recreation experiences in both clinical and community environments. Stress management is another potential therapeutic recreation intervention for people with depression or anxiety disorders.

Anxiety Disorders

Anxiety disorders are often characterized by one of two general symptoms. The first, agoraphobia, occurs when a person develops anxiety about, and often avoids, places that he or she may not be able to escape when panic symptoms occur (American Psychiatric Association, 2000). The second is the presence of panic attacks. A panic attack is defined as "a discrete period in which there is the sudden onset of intense apprehension, fearfulness, or terror, associated with feeling of impending doom" (American Psychiatric Association, 2000, p. 429). This psychological reaction is accompanied by physiological symptoms including shortness of breath, palpitations, chest pain, smothering sensations, and various other anxiety-related reactions. These conditions may coexist with specific phobias toward objects or situations (riding in elevators, taking the car on a long trip). Essentially, people with anxiety disorders may have limited recreation and leisure lives. Panic attacks, or the fear of having one, can lead to isolation and avoidance.

Specific anxiety disorders included in the *DSM-IV* include panic disorder, social phobia, obsessive-compulsive disorder, and post-traumatic stress disorder. As stated earlier, stress management can be a critical part of treatment, as can be teaching specific techniques for relaxing in anxiety-provoking situations. Panic attacks (a primary symptom of panic disorder) typically involve physiological reactions such as accelerated or pounding heart, chest pain, shortness of breath, and dizziness (American Psychiatric Association, 2000). These physiological reactions often escalate into extreme levels of anxiety and psychological distress. Teaching clients relaxation techniques that focus on physically counteracting the early signs of a panic attack is a common intervention.

Therapeutic recreation interventions for anxiety disorders may also be built around behaviorist-driven strategies such as **systematic desensitization.** Such techniques are intended to allow the broadening of potential leisure behaviors into social environments that might otherwise provoke excessive anxiety. Systematic desensitization can be especially useful in clients who are experiencing agoraphobia. Agoraphobia involves anxiety related to the fear of having a panic attack in a place where escape or help would be impossible. Persons with agoraphobia often avoid leaving the safety of their homes. They use extreme measures to ensure their safety when they do leave home (for example, by locating all police stations along the travel route). Gradually traveling farther from home, for longer periods, in increasingly crowded public places would be an example of how to apply systematic desensitization to agoraphobia.

Sheldon and Mendenhall (1995) presented another example as a case study in *Therapeutic Recreation Journal.* This case involved a young summer camp participant who demonstrated obsessive-compulsive tendencies during camp activities. **Obsessions** refer to "persistent thoughts, ideas, impulses or images that are experienced as intrusive and inappropriate and that cause marked anxiety or distress," whereas **compulsions** are repetitive behaviors or mental acts performed "to prevent or reduce anxiety or distress" (American Psychiatric Association, 2000, p. 457). Compulsions often occur as a means of relieving distress from a related obsession.

The child in the case study demonstrated compulsive behaviors related to cleanliness. He avoided participation in any activity that was "messy," persistently cleaned surfaces in his personal space, and avoided touching messy foods when eating. To address this issue, the CTRS made several initial activity adaptations that closed the gap between required behavior and client capabilities. These adaptations included offering all campers a washcloth during activities and providing alternative methods for painting during finger-painting activities. These adaptations were faded out as the client became more comfortable with the presented activities. For example, the washcloth was moved from the client's immediate possession at all times to a nearby area where it was available on request. This strategy demonstrated the use of systematic desensitization because the child gradually moved toward an anxiety-provoking activity. Also demonstrated is the concept of fading temporary adaptations, here accomplished by gradually removing the washcloth and offering alternative painting techniques. Fading is a technique regularly used to limit dependence on various types of prompts (reminders). Finally, the CTRS was careful to make adaptations for the child available to all campers, which minimized public attention toward his difficulty with "messiness."

Eating Disorders

The two most common eating disorders are anorexia nervosa and bulimia nervosa. The public usually associates bulimia with bingeing and purging, and associates anorexia with refusal to eat and overexercising. These features, however, are not the characteristics used to distinguish these disorders from one another. Bulimia and anorexia may or may not involve bingeing, self-induced vomiting, and other inappropriate behaviors intended to prevent weight gain. What separates the two is that people with bulimia do not experience significant weight loss, whereas anorexia involves significant weight loss which, in some cases, is life-threatening.

Some believe that societal norms and images in the media encourage eating disorders, whereas others believe that a psychological need for personal control is the cause. In all likelihood, both factors, as well as various other environmental and personal factors, contribute to the development of eating disorders. In selecting the treatment modalities to put in place, the therapeutic recreation professional should consider the underlying nature of a person's condition and the theoretical principles that drive treatment. This is accomplished by consulting with the treatment team.

Regardless of these factors, certain types of activity should be avoided when working with this population. Namely, aerobic forms of exercise are counterproductive to the goals of treatment. In addition, professionals must be conscious of other inappropriate behaviors that clients may exhibit. Eating disorders are hidden disorders, and those who have them are good at hiding their behaviors. Community outings or other free-time activities are times when these behaviors may occur. Professionals must be aware of client tendencies and monitor appropriately.

Specific therapeutic recreation interventions for eating disorders generally work to provide choice and empowerment through appropriate leisure activities. Enhancing the client's sense of control and self-concept are goals that will generally be in line with overall treatment goals. Interventions might include participation in self-esteem groups and leisure education programs geared toward developing a leisure lifestyle that enhances coping skills and encourages the client to exercise choice and experience control through healthy means.

Adjustment Disorders

Adjustment disorders are psychological responses to significant stressors in a person's life. People who react normally to traumatizing events can be diagnosed with an adjustment disorder if their symptoms significantly impair their functioning. Other cases of adjustment disorders involve a severe reaction that, based on the nature of the stressor, is not warranted (American Psychiatric Association, 2000). Adjustment disorders can involve anxiety, depression, and changes in behavior that cause significant impairment in function.

Working with people with adjustment disorders in the therapeutic recreation setting can involve techniques aimed at improving coping skills, enhancing self-concept, and exercising personal control. Various therapy approaches can be used to help the client improve his or her means of reacting to difficult situations. One approach is to encourage the client to examine his or her cognitive interpretations of the situation (cognitive-based approach). Another approach is to foster awareness, expression, and resolution of feelings toward the self and others (client-centered approach). These approaches refer to broad counseling paradigms, but the philosophy driving them is relevant to some therapeutic recreation environments, depending on the theoretical approach that a particular facility or treatment program adheres to.

For example, Northwest Missouri Psychiatric Center in Saint Joseph, Missouri, uses a cognitive-based therapy approach in treating all clientele. The four therapeutic recreation specialists who work with these clients implement problem-solving and decision-making groups that are built around these concepts. When these professionals utilize their challenge course, briefing and debriefing of the experiences might focus on concepts associated with how clients think through problems and experiences, how their thought processes affect emotions, and how thinking in absolute terms limits options.

If agencies do not promote a particular counseling paradigm, there may still be opportunities to integrate particular counseling frameworks into programs. Note, however, that counseling or talk therapy is not the purpose or the primary method of therapeutic recreation programs. Any such scenario would likely exceed the professional capabilities of the typical therapeutic recreation specialist (unless he or she also had adequate training in a counseling profession). Still, using counseling skills and concepts from a particular framework can be useful, and is sometimes required, in therapeutic recreation practice. Therapeutic recreation specialists must stay within the bounds of their training and seek professional development if their assigned job tasks begin to exceed their professional capabilities.

Theoretical Considerations

When providing therapeutic recreation services, daily work with clients should be aligned with theoretical models designed to provide guidance in the therapy process. A theory is like a lighthouse. The professional uses a theory to direct therapy efforts in a certain direction. To provide consistent and competent intervention, therapeutic recreation specialists can use the following theoretical concepts. As noted earlier, some agencies or settings may adhere to specific theoretical frameworks. Those entering the therapeutic recreation profession should be familiar with all the presented concepts and keep in mind that they will need a comprehensive understanding of one or more of these theories in the future.

Person-Centered Approach

Person-centered therapy, initially developed by Carl Rogers, is a basic theoretical guideline for therapy environments. Rogers identified three critical elements to a successful therapy relationship. The first element is **unconditional positive regard** (UPR). UPR refers to the philosophy that all people are inherently good and that only behavior is bad. Consequently, judgment is directed toward behaviors, not individual character. The therapist must have UPR toward the client, and the client must perceive the therapist as accepting him or her as a person, unconditionally. The second element of person-centered therapy is congruence, or, simply put, genuineness. The client must believe that the therapist is genuine in his or her concern and projects his or her true self. Last, the therapist must work to develop accurate, empathetic understanding of the client's situation.

According to Rogers, these three elements are necessary for a productive therapy relationship. Although some would argue that more is necessary, most would support the idea that Rogers' concepts are a critical element of therapy relationships. Of course, simply caring about people is not enough. A

OUTSTANDING PROFESSIONAL

GAYLE L. RESH

Background Information

Education
    *BS in Education with an emphasis in Health, Education, and Recreation from the University of Nebraska at Lincoln *MA with an emphasis in Therapeutic Recreation from the University of Nebraska at Omaha

Credentials
    *CTRS *CPRP

Special Affiliations
    *Nebraska Therapeutic Recreation Association *Nebraska Recreation and Park Association *American Therapeutic Recreation Association *YMCA

Special Awards
    *Outstanding Therapeutic Recreation Professional (1993–1994) *Fellow Award, Nebraska Recreation and Park Association (2002) *Distinguished Service Award, Nebraska Recreation and Park Association (2005)

Career Information

Position
Activity supervisor, Lincoln Regional Center-State of Nebraska Psychiatric Hospital

See? You have the most fun when you don't expect it!

Dennis the Menace

Job Description
Responsible for the assessment, planning, implementing, documentation, and evaluation of therapeutic recreation services for acute inpatient and secure residential patients. Implement Leisure Education Content Model: Leisure Awareness, Social Interaction Skills, Leisure Activity Skills, and Leisure Resources. Serve as part of a multidisciplinary treatment team serving mentally ill adults.

Career Path
I volunteered at Lincoln Regional Center as part of an undergraduate therapeutic recreation class thinking that I'd like to work in forensics. When a supervisory position opened, I was able to promote into it.

Likes and Dislikes About the Job
I like being able to help people make sense of their lives, aiding to develop a plan that really makes a worthwhile life, not just going through the motions. I dislike having to explain to the uninformed that I'm not a PE teacher and that I don't do bingo.

Advice to Undergraduate Students
Be flexible, be varied, and always be willing to learn.

critical part of this approach is the development of basic communication skills such as active listening, paraphrasing, summarizing, and confronting (see table 10.1). By fostering expressive communication from the client, the therapist facilitates the therapy process. For the therapeutic recreation specialist, these concepts are invaluable. They allow the development of trust and provide a basic framework for communicating with clients within the therapeutic recreation specialist's scope of practice.

Behaviorism

Behaviorism, a comprehensive and well-established theory, represents a cluster of therapy modalities. These modalities, or techniques, are based on B.F. Skinner's concept of operant conditioning (Hall, 1975). Operant conditioning consists of three elements. First, a triggering event occurs. Second, a behavior takes place in response to the trigger-ing event. Third, a consequence of the response occurs and is judged as desirable or undesirable. This consequence can be rewarding or punishing. Rewarding events reinforce the likelihood that a person's response will occur again, and punishing consequences discourage repetition of the behavior.

As a practical example, think of a time when you ran out of money. That circumstance would be a triggering event. One potential response to that event would be to ask a parent for some cash. The consequence of your response would be your parent's reaction to your request. If a parent gave you money, that action would reinforce your begging, and you would likely make the same request the next time you ran out of money. If the parent said no, that would be an undesirable consequence, and over time you would stop asking (this result is called extinction).

Table 10.1 Active Listening and Related Communication Skills

Active listening	1. Receive—focus attention, make eye contact, face the client squarely, and have arms open. Use verbal and nonverbal feedback to let the client know that you are listening.
	2. Process—think about the message and ponder its meaning. Consider biases and blind spots that may cause you to miss meaning.
	3. Send a message, either verbal or nonverbal—use paraphrasing, reflecting, clarifying, summarizing, and other communication and counseling skills.
Paraphrasing	Rephrase the content of the client's statement as you've heard it.
	"So, since you married your husband, you have taken on the house and child care responsibilities and given up your free time with friends" (look to client for confirmation).
Reflecting	Rephrase the affective part of the client's statement.
	"It sounds as if you are frustrated by your husband's lack of concern for how busy you are and by his unwillingness to help."
Clarifying	Ask a question by pairing it with a restatement of the client's statement.
	Client: "Yeah, he's as useful as a bike with no pedals."
	Therapist: "Are you saying that he could help if he wanted to or that you don't think he is capable of doing it right? What do you mean when you say, 'A bike with no pedals'?"
Summarizing	Condense two or more paraphrases or reflections into a clear and precise summary of the client's overall message.
	"So, since your husband has stopped contributing to responsibilities such as housework, caring for the kids, and working, you have really started to feel frustrated and, as you described it, trapped."
Common mistakes	1. Parroting—simply repeating information with no productive clarification or understanding.
	2. Giving inadequate attention to emotion.
	3. Sending verbal and nonverbal messages that don't match.
	4. Talking too much rather than listening.
	5. Giving advice or making suggestions too quickly.

In mental health settings, level systems based on these concepts are often used to encourage positive behaviors. As clients earn points for positive behaviors, they are advanced in the level system and have more freedoms. Likewise, undesirable behaviors, such as running away, can be grounds for lessening privileges or freedoms. In addition, more advanced systems of reinforcement known as token economies are commonly used to encourage positive behaviors. For a description of token economies and various other techniques for behavior modification, refer to table 10.2.

Table 10.2 Behavior Modification Techniques*

Technique	Description	Considerations
Positive practice (Azrin & Besalel, 1999)	When error occurs, stop and practice correction successfully several times.	• Avoid scolding and punishment. • Interrupt misbehavior immediately. • Positive behavior becomes habit.
Response cost (Thibadeau, 1998)	Simply put, consequences are applied for undesirable behaviors. Examples: • Losing recess for talking • Requiring payment of a fee for a late bill • Losing points or tokens for off-task behavior	• Technique is relatively mild compared with aversive forms of punishment. • Allows immediate feedback. • Does not disrupt environment. • When possible, consequences should be logically related to the causal behavior.
Shaping (Hall, 1975)	Teach complex behavior by rewarding successful progression through increasingly complex levels of the target behavior.	• Analyze tasks to determine levels. • Ensure that progressions are attainable. • Examples: hitting a baseball and riding a bike.
Chaining (Hall, 1975)	Teach complex behavior by sequentially introducing and rewarding parts of the behavior.	• Analyze tasks to determine steps or parts. • Ensure that progressions are attainable. • Can work backward or forward. • Example: In dance, teach step 1, then step 2, and finally step 3. • Each step builds on the previous one.
Fading (Esveldt-Dawson & Kazdin, 1998)	Gradually remove external reinforcers.	• Fading helps ensure that behavior is not indefinitely contingent on reward and helps shift the focus toward natural, intrinsic rewards.
Extinction (Hall & Hall, 1998a)	Ignore negative behaviors through techniques such as refusing to speak to or answer the person, looking away, turning the back toward the person, or removing self from environment.	• Pinpoint behavior to change. • Measure behavior and set goal. • Practice ignoring behavior. • Targeted behavior may first increase. • Reinforce appropriate behaviors. • Other people and staff must also ignore negative behaviors.
Modeling (Streifel, 1998)	Use prearranged models, or planned models, as a mechanism for learning through imitation.	• Make sure that the learner pays attention. • Ensure that the learner is physically and cognitively capable of behavior. • Model clearly and consistently. • Provide feedback and rewards.

TABLE 10.2 CONTINUED

TABLE 10.2 CONTINUED

Technique	Description	Considerations
Token economies (Ayllon, 1999)	Provide concrete reinforcers for appropriate behavior. Later, use a backup reinforcer.	• Tokens must be easy to administer. • Administer tokens immediately. • Tokens must be hard to counterfeit. • Establish and always follow rules for exchanging tokens for rewards. • Goal should be to fade out system.
Time-out (Hall & Hall, 1998b)	Decrease behavior by removing a person from the opportunity to receive attention or rewards for undesired behavior.	• Clearly explain undesired behavior and the specific consequence. • Typically works best with 2- to 12-year-olds. • Time-out area should be safe and free of reward. • Time-out areas should be easily monitored. • Time-outs should last 2 to 5 minutes and no longer than 1 minute for each year of age. • Add minutes for refusing to go or misbehaving in time-out, up to a maximum of 30 minutes. • Time-outs may not be appropriate for kids with a history of self-stimulation.

*Additional information regarding the methods presented in this table can be found in the "How to Manage Behavior" series edited by Vance and Marilyn Hall and published by PRO-ED.

Attribution Theory

Attribution theory explains how people perceive their successes and failures in life and the consequences of these perceptions. To illustrate this idea, consider a recent article in a midwestern newspaper that described how the local minor league football team won their league championship because the other team failed to show up for the game. Interestingly, the champions had lost to the other team twice earlier in the season. After the season ended, the coach of the championship team announced that he would return just for another chance to prove that he and his players were true champions. Attribution theory says that the factors we attribute our successes to will affect our beliefs about ourselves. How do you think the circumstances of the championship affected the coach's perceptions of himself and his team?

To illustrate the relevance of attribution theory to mental health, consider the explanation of depression presented by Abrahmson, Seligman, and Teasdale in their landmark 1978 publication concerning attribution theory and the concept of learned helplessness. In this work, the authors pointed out the relationship between the causal attributions that people make, the resulting development of learned helplessness, and the risk of depression.

Causal attributions are the beliefs that we hold about the causes of the events that occur in our lives. A causal attribution is our explanation as to why we succeed, fail, experience hardship, or find happiness. When we are fired from a job, we attribute it to factors such as our boss, our workmates, the fact that we didn't like the job, lack of effort, or, most concerning, our lack of ability. Repeatedly attributing failures to our own inadequacies will eventually lead to learned helplessness. If a person believes that he or she is helpless and can do nothing about it, the person is more likely to become depressed.

One approach to helping people break this negative thinking pattern is to focus on the attributions that they are making. In many cases, they may be ignoring outside influences and taking blame for all their misfortune. Statements like "If I could have made my wife happy, we would still be married" ignore the fact that other factors may have led to the event. This example is an internal attribution, as opposed to an external one. The statement "I always screw up relationships, I just don't have what it takes to make it work" is not only internal but also stable, as opposed to unstable. This type of attribution means that things are viewed as unlikely to change. Finally, a comment like "I just can't have cordial relationships with women at all, even at work or with family" represents a global attribution, as opposed to a specific one. Global attributions represent a generalization of the basic belief to other settings or situations. Ultimately, internal, stable, global attributions about our failures will lead to learned helplessness and depression. The therapist's job is to point out this type of negative thinking and encourage the client to think about alternative explanations for failures. The therapist must also watch out for external, unstable, specific attributions when a person succeeds. This pattern is equally dangerous to the depressed person and may be reflected in comments like "I never would have won if Joe had been trying harder." For the therapeutic recreation specialist, recognizing attribution patterns is critical in understanding leisure motives and experiences. Furthermore, leisure time can serve as a laboratory for building accurate and healthy attribution patterns.

Self-Efficacy Theory

Related to attribution theory is self-efficacy theory. **Self-efficacy,** in simple terms, refers to the extent to which a person believes that he or she is capable of successfully performing a specific task (Bandura, 1986). As you might have guessed, self-efficacy theory can also be applied to depression.

This theory states that four factors can influence self-efficacy. The first, and most powerful, is past performance. We obviously can't change the past, but what we do in the present and future will one day become the past. Based on this logic, creating successful experiences should be a primary objective when working with clients with low self-efficacy. The second technique is vicarious experience, which can come in two forms. The therapeutic recreation specialist can model behaviors for clients (show them how to do it) or ask them to mentally rehearse success (visualize success). Doing so will bolster clients' beliefs that they can succeed at the relevant task. The third technique is to create an optimal level of arousal for the client. This may mean psyching them up as a coach does a team, or it may mean helping them relax when they are overwhelmed by the task at hand. Finally, verbal persuasion can be used to increase self-efficacy. Again, you might guess that focusing on internal, stable, global reasons for successes and external, unstable, specific factors contributing to failure is the best approach.

The most important point to remember about attribution and self-efficacy theory is that these theories and the corresponding techniques require action on the therapeutic recreation specialist's part during therapy sessions or activities. Simply planning a day of activity and watching it take its course is not appropriate. The therapeutic recreation specialist is in the trenches interacting with clients and manipulating environments in ways that foster success. At the same time, success must be genuine, not the result of providing too much help or deceiving the client. Appropriate sequencing of activities and facilitation of experiences are critical in the process of creating real success, as is planning and anticipating situations during which these theoretical concepts can be used.

Psychoanalytic Theory

Several useful theoretical concepts come from psychoanalytic theory. One of the most significant is the acknowledgment that the unconscious mind can influence behavior. These unconscious behaviors (meaning that we are unaware of their presence and influence) often occur in the form of **defense mechanisms.** The unconscious aspect of the mind uses these mechanisms to protect our psychological well-being (Corey, 2004). In Freudian terms, a defense mechanism is a tool that the id (unconscious) uses to protect the ego (conscious awareness) from anxiety-provoking thoughts, beliefs, or situations. These mechanisms can be healthy or unhealthy, depending on the circumstances and consequences of using them. For example, denial of a serious illness may lead to further health problems, but using sport to redirect aggression related to work difficulties may be an acceptable alternative to assaulting the boss (this concept is called sublimation). Whether defense mechanisms are truly unconscious or just behavior tendencies that become engrained into daily routine is somewhat irrelevant. What is important is that clients become aware of such tendencies and realize how they might be affected by them. Some of the more common defense mechanisms are listed in table 10.3.

The psychoanalytic concepts of transference and countertransference are also relevant to the modern therapy environment. **Transference** refers to a circumstance in which the patient begins to associate the therapist with a person or situation from his or her past. This process is said to foster a productive therapy relationship. Transference may also manifest in negative ways if the client develops inappropriate expectations or feelings regarding the

Table 10.3　Common Defense Mechanisms

Defense mechanism	Description	Example
Denial	Insisting that a source of anxiety doesn't exist	Denying that you have been diagnosed with a serious illness
Displacement	Taking out impulses on a less-threatening target	Yelling at your children after a day of abuse from the boss
Intellectualization	Avoiding unacceptable emotions by focusing on intellectual aspects	Focusing on funeral arrangements to avoid facing the loss of a loved one
Projection	Attributing unacceptable aspects of yourself to another	Criticizing the work of others when you fail to complete an assigned project
Rationalization	Using faulty logical reasoning to ignore reality	Focusing on the choices that the coaches made even though you missed the winning touchdown pass in the end zone
Reaction formation	Believing or acting in a manner opposite your true feelings	Laughing hysterically and joking with friends when your girlfriend breaks up with you
Regression	Returning to a previous developmental stage	Throwing a temper tantrum in the grocery store line
Repression	Pulling information into the unconscious	Forcing yourself to forget the witnessing of a relative's suicide
Sublimation	Expressing unacceptable impulses through acceptable behavior	Using rigorous exercise as a way to express your frustration with work

Data from P. Fonagy and M. Target 2003; G. Corey 2004.

therapist. More relevant to this discussion is countertransference. **Countertransference** refers to a situation in which the therapist begins to associate the client with a significant person or issue from his or her own life. This is not a good situation, but its occurrence is a real possibility. Therapeutic recreation specialists must be aware of how the client's personal situation "touches home" with them. Consider the situation of a recent therapeutic recreation intern who was also recovering from anorexia. One day a client with anorexia was admitted to the mental health center where the intern worked, and the intern was immediately motivated to help. After a few weeks, it became apparent that the intern was so affected by the successes and setbacks of the client that her work in general, as well as her personal life, was negatively affected.

Thus, all mental health professionals should stay aware of such dynamics. Beginning psychotherapists are often encouraged to participate in counseling as a way of understanding the client's perspective and developing insight into their own psychological tendencies. For the therapeutic rec-

reation specialist, this exercise may not be feasible, but he or she can take steps to understand how his or her personal life interacts with and influences professional performance. For the intern described earlier, the first step was establishing open communication with the site supervisor. Interns should be encouraged to acknowledge their internal reactions to clients and discuss these reactions with seasoned professionals. Communication between professional colleagues can be equally beneficial, and professional counseling should never be dismissed as an option. Negley (1994) described how termination of a particular long-term therapeutic relationship with a client was especially challenging for her and how working through the issue with a staff psychologist was beneficial. Because therapeutic recreation services often reflect true-to-life social situations (such as community outings with friends), therapeutic recreation professionals should be especially conscious of the potential for boundaries between personal and professional relationships to fade away in the context of leisure activities. Openly discussing the nature of this relationship with clients can help remind both parties of such boundaries.

Social Contracts

Establishing social contracts, or agreed-upon norms, is a widely used concept in both therapeutic recreation programs and mental health in general. Programs that operate under this philosophy encourage clients to be accountable to one another. Issues and confrontations are brought to the group, and ownership is placed with the group to determine how to deal with such situations. Typically, a set of community principles or values is identified and used as a compass for guiding group decisions. The most practical application of this approach in therapeutic recreation is the use of value contracts in groups. These contracts are most effective when the group identifies the values by which the group will be governed, although in many cases the values have long been established as new group members come and go. Thus value contracts or social norms may need to be reestablished periodically. Value contracts ultimately empower clients to take responsibility and control of their own treatment program.

Mental Health and Secondary Disabilities

When treating someone with a disabling condition, regardless of type, understanding the psychological challenges that the client faces is a critical step in providing comprehensive treatment. Take a moment to read the following scenarios.

Scenario 1 depicts a woman whose presenting problem is Alzheimer's disease, which is a disorder listed in the *DSM-IV-TR*. Still, she does not fit the stereotypical profile of mental illness. Most of her primary symptoms are oriented toward dementia (e.g., orientation) and motor functions (e.g., gait). Still, the client's mental health is a secondary concern that is threatened by the primary problem (Alzheimer's). Specifically, depression is a treatable component of dementia, as are anxiety disorders. Interventions may have limited potential to restore

Healthy social relationships represent a common goal area for clients receiving mental health services.

SCENARIO 1: HELEN

Helen is a 92-year-old woman who resides at a long-term care facility for people with Alzheimer's disease. The primary focus of Helen's therapy regime is to maintain cognitive and motor abilities as long as possible. Daily interventions include ongoing reality orientation, sensory training, pet therapy, small reminiscence groups, and various forms of physical activity (see chapters 12 and 13 for a detailed description of these modalities).

SCENARIO 2: SUSAN

Susan is a 16-year-old girl who has been admitted to a secured residential treatment facility specializing in the treatment of substance abuse. Susan appears well adjusted in her daily life and is involved in a variety of extracurricular activities. Her parents admitted her after finding methamphetamines in her bedroom for the third time. Some of the therapeutic recreation interventions that Susan participates in are values clarification and a leisure education group.

SCENARIO 3: MIKE

Mike is a 45-year-old man who has been diagnosed with terminal cancer. He is receiving care in a rehabilitation hospital after having a large tumor removed from his spinal cord. The surgery left him paralyzed from the chest down. Doctors were not able to remove the entire tumor, and they expect it to affect vital functions within 6 months. Treatment at the rehabilitation center focuses primarily on activities of daily living and self-care.

---

cognitive functions, but therapeutic recreation modalities can be used to treat secondary mental disorders and significantly improve quality of life for a person with Alzheimer's disease. Review the modalities mentioned in scenario 1. Which do you believe would be useful in reducing depression or anxiety? Do any of these have the potential to be contraindicated?

Scenario 2 is similar to scenario 1 in that the public often does not associate the presence of substance abuse with a mental disorder (again substance abuse and dependence are included in the *DSM-IV-TR*). In truth, drug and alcohol disorders frequently coexist with depression, anxiety, and other mental disorders. Addressing these mental health concerns is critical to treatment, especially in cases in which such substances are being used to cope (self-medicate).

The presenting problem in scenario 3 is not a mental disorder, but it does represent a situation in which the therapeutic recreation specialist and the rest of the treatment team should consider mental health. The immediate physical changes that the client is facing, as well as the stressors associated with the terminal nature of his condition, will no doubt affect mental health. A therapeutic recreation specialist who works with people with physical disabilities should be knowledgeable in the area of mental health and specifically with the concepts presented in this chapter.

Common Therapeutic Recreation Modalities for Mental Health

The remainder of this chapter focuses on therapeutic recreation modalities that are commonly used in the mental health setting. Some of these modalities are also used with other client populations, but remember that any particular modality is appropriate only when it is consistent with the goals and objectives of the client. Therefore, the therapeutic recreation specialist should ensure that the content or focus of the utilized modality meets this requirement.

Leisure Education

Mental illness often has a direct effect on the same areas that leisure education is equipped to address. For example, virtually every mental illness has the potential to impair social skills both inside and outside the leisure realm. Likewise, long-term mental illness disrupts or discourages access to leisure resources that, ironically, can assist in the prevention of mental illness. Although leisure education is a broad concept in general, program content that is specific to the needs of clients with mental illness can be delivered within the framework of existing leisure education models (see chapter 5).

Values Clarification

Values clarification is a technique that can help clients examine their personal behavior, identify the values that are driving this behavior, determine whether these values are in line with their core personal values, and shift behavior to be congruent with personal core values. The values clarification process was conceptualized by Simon and Olds (1977) as consisting of three progressive categories of clarification processes (as presented in Austin, 2004). The first category involves choosing the core values by which we desire to live our lives. The second category focuses on cherishing these values. For example, this stage might involve sharing with others a decision to stop associating with known drug users. Acting is the final category, which involves behaving in a manner that is consistent with the chosen values. The power behind this technique is in the early work. As clients explore their values and how they have deviated away from what is truly important, they find it easier to share this personal desire with others and live by it.

Stress Management

Stress is a physiological reaction to the surrounding world. Our hearts pound, our muscles tighten, and our ability to function diminishes. Unfortunately, stress can have significant effect on our mental health. Thus, helping clients relax through various means is a common aspect of therapeutic recreation services in mental health settings. Specifically, various formal techniques for relaxation are implemented, as are recreation activities that directly affect stress levels, such as yoga, tai chi, aerobics, and other fitness-based activities.

Group Initiatives

One common technique is to use group initiatives or challenge activities as opportunities to practice and master various psychosocial functions. Examples of such functions include trust, problem solving, conflict resolution, communication skills, and the enhancement of self-perceptions. This strategy, grounded in **constructivism** (Fosnot, 1996; Piaget, 1970), is analogous to the concept of experiential education. Metaphors are a major therapy tool when using this modality, as the therapeutic recreation specialist works toward generalizing the immediate experience to relevant real-world concepts.

© Human Kinetics

Clients can benefit from the stress-reducing effects of activities like yoga or tai chi. For example, yoga helps this retired ballerina cope with arthritis pain.

Skilled facilitation is a key element of a successful group initiative. The therapeutic recreation specialist must create an environment that elicits insight and learning as a result of the experience and the associated discussion (see chapter 6 for more information on facilitating groups). Likewise, group initiatives, facilitation strategies, and the intended outcomes must be appropriate for the client's level of functioning. A skilled facilitator is able to create a situation that allows clients to step across the "gap" between where they are and where they are capable of going. If the gap is too small, no change will occur; if the gap is too large, clients will fail and potentially regress. This gap can be physical (a climbing wall, an elevated rope bridge), cognitive (a metaphor, riddle, problem), social (cooperation, conflict resolution, competition), or psychological (fear, anxiety, frustration). The therapeutic recreation specialist is aware of and manipulates such factors to empower clients to cross the gap on their own or with the group.

Self-Esteem Programs

Self-esteem programs are a common therapeutic recreation modality. In some cases, these programs are activity-based, focusing on building successes and a sense of accomplishment in those who participate. Other programs are more reflective, focusing on written work or journals to bolster the esteem of clients. In many cases, some combination of the two is used. A specific example of a journal-based tool for self-esteem programs is Sandra Negley's (1997) *Crossing the Bridge: A Journey in Self-Esteem, Relationships, and Life Balance*. This resource walks clients through a progression of self-reflective activities. The focus is on how people internalize messages that they receive from others and the process of challenging these messages. This workbook, as well as other worksheet-based resources, can be used with other activity-based methods, including initiatives, creative and expressive arts, and appropriately facilitated sports and games, to create a comprehensive self-esteem program.

Expressive Therapies

Expressive therapies are used regularly in therapeutic recreation programs, especially those located in mental health settings. Using drawing, painting, ceramics, clay work, writing, and a variety of other mediums for the expression of emotion can be a powerful therapy tool. In some cases, therapeutic recreation professionals work with art therapists to facilitate such groups. Final products that are long lasting serve as reminders and metaphors for clients even after finishing therapy.

Summary

Therapeutic recreation professionals can play a significant role in enhancing the psychological well-being of their clients. This result can occur as part of a structured treatment program for mental disorders; as a secondary goal in physical rehabilitation environments; as part of structured outreach

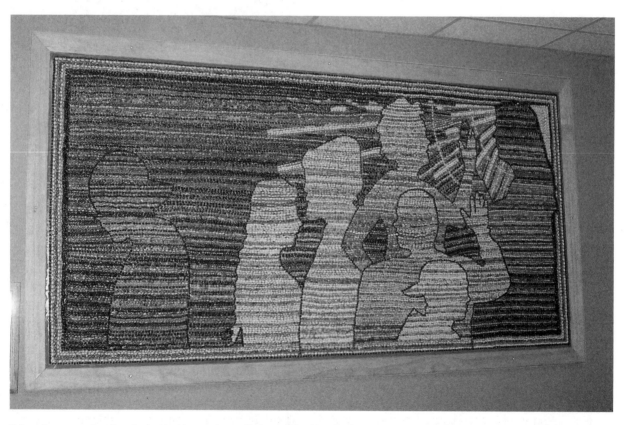

This collage made of various dried beans is on display at the Lincoln Regional Center in Lincoln, Nebraska. The collage is meant to show a silhouette of clients moving from deep depression to a celebration of life with arms raised and chins high. This moving work was the result of a therapeutic recreation intern's efforts to collaborate with the local arts council and many hours of work by clients who volunteered to take part in the project.

programs for at-risk populations such as the homeless, underprivileged, and elderly; or in general community-based programs designed to enhance the well-being of people with disabilities through both inclusive and segregated recreation programs. Ultimately, every therapeutic recreation specialist must be prepared to deal with and address issues associated with psychological functioning.

DISCUSSION QUESTIONS

1. Discuss the relationship between leisure, recreation, and mental illness. Do you agree or disagree with the author's assertion that leisure may be the most influential realm of functioning when it comes to mental well-being? Defend your answer.

2. Besides the mental disorders profiled in this chapter, what other disorders do you know of (if you don't know of any, look one up)? What are the basic characteristics of these disorders, and how could you address these characteristics through therapeutic recreation?

3. Interviewing is a major tool in assessment of clients with mental disorders. Discuss what content, issues, or questions would be important to cover in such an interview. Also discuss other nonverbal indicators. What nonverbal behaviors may be associated with depression, mania, anxiety, and schizophrenia?

4. Review Carl Rogers' concept of unconditional positive regard. Can you imagine a situation in which accepting a client as a good person might be difficult? How would you deal with such a situation? Ask your instructor his or her opinion on this issue.

5. Review the modalities presented in this chapter as being especially useful in mental health. To what other client groups might these methods be useful? Specifically, give examples of how the behavior modification techniques listed in table 10.2 might be useful for patients with orthopedic injuries, intellectual disabilities, or cognitive deficits (such as from a traumatic brain injury).

Youth Development and Therapeutic Recreation

Sydney L. Sklar, PhD, CTRS
University of St. Francis

Cari E. Autry, PhD, CTRS
Arizona State University

LEARNING OUTCOMES

After completing this chapter, learners will be able to demonstrate the following competencies:

- Identify and describe the stages of the continuum of risk in youth development
- Understand and describe influences of the environment and ecological systems on youth development
- Describe and apply the concept of positive youth development
- Identify and describe the purpose of therapeutic recreation in positive youth development
- Identify and describe theories related to youth development and therapeutic recreation practice with at-risk youth
- Describe the scope of therapeutic recreation youth development services including prevention, intervention, and community development
- Identify and describe various settings and opportunities for therapeutic recreation youth development programming
- Identify and describe specific needs of youth clientele, including those with a background of maltreatment, learning disorders, and behavioral disorders
- Describe current issues and trends in youth development services

The well-being of our society depends on the ability of communities to prepare well-adjusted, responsible, well-educated young people to step forward as the older generation passes. Yet many of today's youth are falling by the wayside (McWhirter, McWhirter, McWhirter & McWhirter, 2004). Rising rates of teen pregnancy, risky sexual behavior, youth gang involvement, poverty, crime, drug use, social isolation, physical violence, poor access to health care, physical inactivity, obesity, and depression are among the multitude of challenges that young people must overcome to achieve healthy physical and psychosocial development.

Since the earliest days of organized recreation, community programs have aimed to build healthier youth and address social problems that affect young people. With the Individuals with Disabilities Education Act of 1997 and its reauthorization in 2004, recent years have seen significant efforts in the education system to provide adequate support and services to help young people with challenges achieve their fullest potential. Among these efforts is the increased attention given to transition services, a planning and support mechanism for helping students successfully make the transition to the community after graduation. Recreation has been included within the spectrum of services that students may receive in preparing for a positive transition to adulthood.

Within the recreation professions, interest has grown in prevention and intervention programs that engage youth interests and energies in prosocial activities geared toward positive development. Therapeutic recreation has played a special role in addressing the problems of youth who present the most challenging behaviors.

The purpose of this chapter is to describe how therapeutic recreation principles and practices are employed to meet the developmental needs of contemporary youth. To achieve this purpose, we will (1) present terms and definitions related to youth development, (2) discuss the purpose of therapeutic recreation practice as it relates to both prevention and intervention, (3) present theoretical frameworks to guide professional practice, (4) outline the scope of therapeutic recreation practice in youth development services, and (5) describe a sample of settings and opportunities for providing therapeutic recreation youth development programs. Additionally, we will discuss emerging issues and trends in the recreation field pertaining to youth development services.

At-Risk Youth

According to the U.S. Census Bureau, the national youth population in 2000 was 71.7 million, and up to 50% of them were considered **at risk** (Lugalia, 2003; Sprouse, Klitzing & Parr, 2005). Over the past two decades, the term *at-risk youth* has been widely used—in education, psychology, medicine, social work, economics, as well as in state legislation and reports produced by the federal government—to describe a segment of the youth population that faces significant developmental challenges (McWhirter et al., 2004). Use of the term *at-risk youth* has been somewhat controversial, and both the professional and academic communities have lacked consensus on its meaning. One argument against using this label is that all youth are at some degree of risk, so using this term to describe particular groups of youth is misleading. We agree that real ambiguities surround this classification, but when clearly defined, the term *at-risk youth* provides a useful context for understanding youth needs. Therefore, our working definition is as follows:

> *At risk* denotes a set of presumed cause-effect dynamics that place an individual child or adolescent in danger of future negative outcomes. *At risk* designates a situation that is not necessarily current but that can be anticipated in the absence of intervention. (McWhirter et al., 2004, p. 6)

This definition of at-risk youth is best understood as a series of steps along a continuum of risk rather than as a single diagnostic condition (see figure 11.1). In a comprehensive text on at-risk youth, McWhirter et al. (2004) detailed a model for understanding the range of risk factors. On this continuum, youth are considered to be at relative degrees of risk depending on where they fall with respect to a variety of risk factors. Youth who face few psychosocial and environmental stressors; experience favorable demographics (such as higher socioeconomic status); and have positive, caring family, school, and social interactions are generally at minimal risk for future trouble. A young person's risk factors rise, however, as stressors compound, environmental conditions degrade, and interactions with support systems are increasingly negative.

Within the next category of remote risk, a young person's demographics are less favorable; social, family, and school interactions are less positive; and more stressors exist. The child at this point

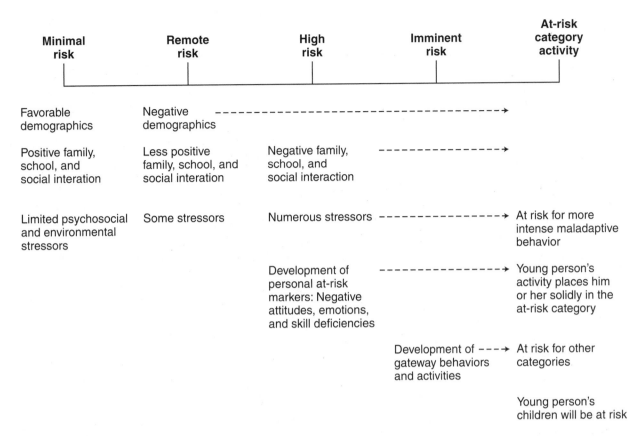

Figure 11.1 At-risk continuum.

in the continuum experiences certain markers of future problems that may include risky activities and behaviors more likely to appear than with a child at minimal risk. For example, although being a member of an ethnic minority does not necessarily predict future problems, minority membership is often associated with experiences of marginalization, oppression, racism, and psychosocial stressors that suggest the possibility of future problems.

Within the category of high risk, stressors are numerous and compounded to the point where negative attitudes and emotions may be characterized by signs such as aggression, anxiety, conduct problems, mental illness, or hopelessness. Deficits in social skills and coping skills may further emerge from and contribute to the person's environment. The high-risk youth experiences a number of personal characteristics that set the stage for gateway activities and behaviors.

Imminent risk implies that youth who are participating in gateway activities (e.g., mildly to moderately distressing activities that are often self-destructive) are generally on the brink of adopting deviant behaviors such as aggression toward other

children and authority. These behaviors can in turn lead to juvenile delinquency.

Beyond imminent risk, at-risk category activity describes youth who are participating in activities that define the at-risk categories. In other words, at this final step on the continuum, the young person's activity places him or her solidly at risk for more intense problems and maladaptive behaviors. For example, the child who is regularly truant from school is also at risk of academic failure and may ultimately lack skills for advancing in life. Additionally, the children of those who have reached this extreme will most likely be at risk as well.

Internalized and Externalized Maladaptive Behaviors

Youth in the high and imminent risk categories commonly exhibit a continuum of behavioral characteristics that includes externalized maladaptive behaviors (acting out, aggression, and anger) and internalized maladaptive behaviors (withdrawal, avoidance of social contact, depression, and anxiety) (Kentucky Department of Education, 2005).

Typically, we are more aware of and give more attention to the first set of behaviors, but internalized behaviors make a child at risk just as much as externalized behaviors do.

The social and peer domain is the most significant area affected in the lives of children and youth with externalized and internalized maladaptive behaviors. Characteristics surrounding this domain may include a lack of positive social behaviors with peers in comparison with typical peers; an inability to exhibit positive behaviors that peers can reinforce; an inability to interact with peers appropriately; a poor rating in the social status of students with behavior problems (as assessed by sociometric and teacher and parent ratings); susceptibility to the long-term effects of such poor skills, which include delinquency, discharge from the military, and use of substances; a classification that is based solely on the display of poor social skills; and inability to be mainstreamed into regular education classes and recreation programs.

At-Risk Youth and the Environment

Previous sections have defined at-risk youth within a continuum and identified behaviors. But one more layer needs to be added when we are referring to youth and the definition of risk. In providing a definition Gordon and Yowell (1994, p. 53) explain at-risk youth as "a category of persons whose personal characteristics, conditions of life, situational circumstances, and interactions with each other make it likely that their development and/or education will be less than optimal."

This definition emphasizes the person–environmental interaction, or system. To prevent failure for those who fall within the risk continuum, all parts of this system must be included within intervention and preventative measures (Kronick, 1997). This interaction is referred to as the **ecological system.** Therapeutic recreation specialists need to think of the ecology of the youth with whom they are working.

Ecological Systems

In a broad sense, ecology is the science of relationships between an organism and its environment. In relation to humans, the ecological perspective adopts a holistic view in seeing the person and his or her environment as a unit. In the context of working with at-risk youth, this view targets the youth (char-acteristics, behaviors, physiological factors) as well as the youth's relations with his or her environment. This environment encompasses the immediate settings and people (home, classroom, neighborhood, family, teacher, counselor, peer groups) surrounding the youth as well as larger contexts in which these settings and people are embedded (cultural, political, educational, community institutions) (Bronfenbrenner, 1989; Farmer, 1997; Germain, 1991). This relationship and interaction between the youth and environment is reciprocal and cyclical (Perkins & Caldwell, 2005). That is, the risk factors from the environment affect the youth and the factors that make the youth at risk affect the environment (people and settings) in which he or she exists.

Positive Youth Development

While clarifying the meaning of at-risk youth is helpful in creating a context for understanding youth problems, the term *at risk* remains problematic. Although we need such a context to understand the effect of risk factors, a philosophy that focuses on youth potential, not youth problems, provides an optimistic context for providing therapeutic recreation services. In recent years, the term *positive youth development* has emerged from a growing body of research concerned with the promise of youth potential. **Positive youth development** refers to a service approach that focuses on children's unique talents, strengths, interests, and potential (Damon, 2004). Partly in reaction to media and social distortions of youth, this new approach to youth development connotes a more affirming and welcoming vision of young people, viewing them as resources rather than as problems for society. "The positive youth development perspective emphasizes the manifest potentialities rather than the supposed incapacities of young people—including those from the most disadvantaged backgrounds and those with the most troubled histories" (Damon, 2004, p. 15).

The approach recognizes the existence of hardships and developmental challenges that affect children in various ways but resists conceptualizing the developmental process as an effort to overcome risk and deficits. Rather, it begins with "a vision of a fully able child eager to explore the world, gain competence, and acquire the capacity to contribute importantly to the world" (Damon, 2004, p. 15). This philosophy of practice aims to understand, educate, and engage children in productive activities rather than correct, cure, or treat them for maladaptive tendencies.

One model emphasizing youth potential has gained substantial notoriety within the youth-serving disciplines. The Developmental Assets model (Search Institute, 2007) provides a powerful alternative to deficit-based models for guiding youth work. According to research findings of the Search Institute, there are 40 assets (20 internal and 20 external) deemed necessary for youth to successfully navigate the journey to adulthood.

Studies by the Search Institute suggest there is a relationship between the number of assets present in a young person's life and the existence of positive attitudes and behaviors. For example, the more assets a young girl has in her life, the more likely she is to exhibit thriving behaviors such as exhibiting leadership and succeeding in school. The same girl would be less likely to exhibit negative behaviors such as problem alcohol use and risky sexual activity (Witt & Caldwell, 2005) than her peers with a fewer number of assets.

CLIENT PORTRAIT

EDUARDO

Eduardo is a 15-year-old Latino boy who is proud of his Mexican heritage. He lives in a low-income public housing development with his mother and younger brother. Eduardo's mother is single and supports her two children by working as a night auditor at a 24-hour grocery store. Because of her work schedule, Mom is out of the home overnight and sleeps most of the day. Eduardo's father is serving prison time for a drug conviction.

Eduardo's neighborhood consists of multiple blocks of poorly maintained low-rise apartment buildings and a poorly maintained park with outdated playground equipment. Drug deals often take place on street corners. Although Eduardo is not involved in drug activity, he feels pressure from his neighborhood friends to experiment. His free time is unstructured, and he spends most of it out of the home with friends.

Academically, Eduardo is a low performer. His teachers are concerned with his disruptive classroom behavior and poor attendance. During a session with the school social worker, Eduardo said that he thought schoolwork was pointless, that he was angry about his father's imprisonment, and that he had nothing to do after school. Eduardo was referred to a CTRS working with the local recreation department.

CTRS Plan

The CTRS conducted an assessment with Eduardo and discovered that he enjoyed sports, being outdoors, working with his hands, and helping others. Additionally, she learned that Eduardo's lack of structured activity was putting him at risk of experimenting with drugs with his neighborhood peers.

The CTRS helped Eduardo enroll in the Latino Teen Corps, which engaged members in hands-on service projects within the greater community (e.g., a peer mentoring program in which Eduardo could help teach younger children about their Latino heritage and various sport activities). Additionally, Eduardo was introduced to the after-school teen center sponsored by the recreation department, where he could receive adult assistance with homework and participate in open-gym activities. Here Eduardo enrolled in the center's Environmental Ambassador (EA) program, in which he and other participants volunteered with agencies related to environmental conservation and preservation. The EA participants also present information and educate city officials and the community about strategies to protect the environment.

Eduardo's Achievements

The structured peer and community recreation activities helped Eduardo achieve a sense of accomplishment and belonging while being engaged in activities of his interest and background and while maintaining distance from his drug-using acquaintances. With the homework assistance, Eduardo's grades stabilized and began to trend upward. The CTRS met with Eduardo and his mother to discuss common leisure interests and the importance of family-oriented leisure and to brainstorm strategies for making time for one another. Eduardo's mother was receptive and made an oral commitment to plan at least two family-oriented leisure activities per month. Finally, Eduardo was referred to the Mentoring Children of Prisoners program where he gained an adult male mentor with whom he met once weekly. With his mentor, Eduardo engaged in active recreation activities, developed a trusting relationship, and began to share his feelings of anger toward his father.

The 40 Developmental Assets from the Search Institute are divided into the following categories:

- Support
- Empowerment
- Boundaries and expectations
- Constructive use of time
- Commitment to learning
- Positive values
- Social competencies
- Positive identity

Positive youth development works best when multiple resources, service providers, and institutions organize around young people. Effective youth programs put youth at the center and involve parents, school personnel, local government officials, social workers, juvenile justice personnel, youth workers, and recreation personnel. In other words, when a range of resources comes together in the interest of youth development, youth stand to reap greater benefits.

Purpose of Therapeutic Recreation in Positive Youth Development

Considering the profession's history in disability-related treatment, education, and recreation, therapeutic recreation has been slow to take up the cause of positive youth development in community-based settings. Rather, the broader recreation profession has championed the cause of youth development, and the last decade has seen laudable progress in this arena. Yet with the unique skills that therapeutic recreation specialists offer, we need to see ourselves as partners in positive youth development efforts. Grounded in the philosophical principles of the universal right to leisure, self-determination, and quality of life (National Therapeutic Recreation Society, 1996) and offering expertise in leisure-related assessment, planning, implementation, and evaluation, therapeutic recreation practitioners are well prepared to serve key roles in positive youth development initiatives. Special recreation associations (SRAs) have been leading the profession in youth development through both independently delivered youth programs and collaborative efforts with parks and recreation departments and public

mental health agencies (Brown & Sevcik, 1999; Shulewitz & Zuniga, 1999; Sprouse et al., 2005).

Theories That Guide Therapeutic Recreation Practice

As we have defined how youth exist within a continuum of risk, how risk factors exist as a consequence of and as an effect on the youth's environment, and how positive youth development focuses on developmental needs of youth rather than on deficit-based problems, several theories play additional and vital roles in helping us understand the relationship between therapeutic recreation and youth development. These theories tie in the social and psychological aspects of the youth who exist on the risk continuum. We begin this discussion by further exploring the ecological perspective and its implications for therapeutic recreation. We will also address another more social-based theory of social capital and then tie in more of the psychological-based theories of anomie, hope, optimism, and flow to inform more completely the practice of therapeutic recreation when working in youth development.

Ecological Perspective

What is the role of the therapeutic recreation profession in addressing the needs and strengths of youth who exist within the risk continuum? When taking on the ecological perspective described earlier in the chapter, our duty is to evaluate circumstances and environments surrounding the individual youth in addition to individual characteristics and behaviors. As we assess and target the physical, cognitive, social, emotional, and leisure needs and strengths of our clients, we have to realize that family, peers, school, law enforcement, church, and other societal factors influence their behaviors and thoughts. These people and settings can be negatively or positively influential in the strengths and needs of the youth and in the collaborative outcomes necessary within our intervention and prevention programs. Within the therapeutic process, our profession must look at the person *with* his or her environment throughout the assessment, planning, implementation, and evaluation (APIE) process. Four concepts expressed through positive person–environmental interaction include human relatedness, competence,

A therapeutic recreation specialist must look at a youth's environment completely, taking into consideration both the physical surroundings as well as the people in the environment.

self-direction, and increased self-esteem (Germain, 1991). In therapeutic recreation, the primary goal of intervention and prevention programs is to help our youth clients attain these concepts. Ultimately, we want to help them help themselves to maximize their own quality of life (Howe-Murphy & Charboneau, 1987).

In summary, the ecological approach when working with at-risk youth provides the practitioner a guide to facilitate "a much broader range of contextual understanding" of this population (Rappaport, 1987, p. 34). A person interacts with and affects a unique combination of subsystems in his or her environment. In return, this environment (in addition to physiological and personality factors) ultimately affects the development of behaviors and beliefs of that person. Within the ecological system one person does not "own" a disturbance, disability, or condition, and no one is blamed for it (Paul & Epanchin, 1991). Taking on this perspective helps us realize as professionals that *at risk* is not just about the youth; it is a function of, responsibility of, and most of all, a target of intervention and prevention for the youth and the people, settings, and societal influences that surround him or her. We can help decrease the cause–effect dynamics that place a child or adolescent in danger of future negative outcomes (McWhirter et al., 2004). We in therapeutic recreation can play a vital role in positive youth development by understanding and working within this perspective and the environment in which youth live, learn, and play.

Social Capital

A second theory that we are increasingly becoming aware of in therapeutic recreation and using when working in youth development is **social capital.** Essentially, social capital is the notion that human beings fair better in life when bonded together (Putnam, 2000). Social capital exists when social networks have value and facilitate cooperation for a common benefit. Social capital also exists when two important ingredients are present within this network: reciprocity and trust (Cullen & Wright, 1997; Hagan & McCarthy, 1997; Putnam, 2000). Reciprocity is achieved when everyone, including the youth, plays a role in giving and receiving within the relationships in the network and when all contributions are respected. Trust is necessary and achieved only when members forgo a "what can you do for me attitude" and when respect and role expectations from all within the network are clear and achievable. When boundaries of roles are less clear, dissonance and ultimately a lack of trust can occur within the relationships. This inability to trust causes greater role segmentation and isolation (Seligman, 1997).

The presence of social capital facilitates positive reinforcements for youth and offers them access to positive role models; recreational, educational, and vocational support; and mentors (Putnam, 2000). Communities that are high in social capital have the capability to realize common values, maintain higher-trusting networks, and sustain social control so that youth can become empowered members of the group (Cullen & Wright, 1997; Hagan & McCarthy, 1997; Putnam, 2000; Sampson, 2001). For example, neighborhoods that are high in social capital exhibit less crime because they have set up networks of trust, reciprocity, and cohesion within their neighborhood watch (Putnam, 2000). Neighborhoods that are low in social capital are characterized as socially disorganized communities and include residential instability, anonymous neighbors, and few local organizations. Resident youth are prone to creating their own "social capital" through gang membership. According to Putnam, "in areas where social capital is lacking, the effects of poverty, adult unemployment, and family breakdown are magnified, making life that much worse for children and adults alike" (p. 317).

According to Hagan and McCarthy (1997), social capital, in general, refers to a variety of resources that originate in an ecological perspective in which social relationships connect youth to groups of other people in neighborhoods, churches, schools, recreation, and law enforcement.

Social capital can connect the youth to these social relationships by connections with the youths' families (traditional or nontraditional). That is, the social network of the family is important. Just as important are networks within other social groups that connect the parent–child relation to other parents, children, neighbors, teachers, police, recreation personnel, human service personnel, and church members (Hagan & McCarthy, 1997). Making such connections can only help in the transference and generalization of outcomes from the therapeutic recreation services into the youths' community and family life. If we do not work within these support networks in the community and family, the opportunities and benefits of the services that we provide could be lost after the youth goes home for the day or when the youth finishes our programs.

Anomie Theory and Hopelessness

Before we provide a discussion on the theory of hope and optimism, the theory of **anomie** and its relationship to hopelessness will be addressed to guide the reader to the importance of hope for youth who exist on a risk continuum. One of the risk factors and challenges that youth face, particularly those in the high and imminent risk categories, is that of hopelessness or low hope. In general, people who are less skilled in developing attainable and realistic goals have low hope. Low hope is also exhibited when an intense negative emotional response occurs when a person's goals are blocked or when he or she encounters barriers. All these reactions can create a cycle of hopelessness for the person (see figure 11.2). Furthermore, those with low hope are less likely to be able to negotiate alternative goals when faced with barriers or a blocked original goal and are less likely to view themselves as being able to adapt successfully to such situations. They are caught in a cycle of hopelessness (Rodriguez-Hanley & Snyder, 2000). In summary, people who have less success in establishing positively directed goals or in planning an appropriate means to meet goals can be plagued with low hope as a result (Snyder, 2000).

What happens when a person remains within this low-hope cycle? According to Snyder (2000), the person can follow a path to apathy through a variety of stages. Apathy is what leads a person into a state of anomie, or a state of mind in which there is a "breakdown of the individual's sense of attachment to society" (Passas, 1997, p. 80). In relation to youth, this is what we would refer to as a state of delinquency. According to Orrù (1987), anomie is a conflict of belief systems and causes conditions of alienation in which a person progresses into a dysfunctional ability to integrate within normative situations in his or her social world. Because of this alienation, people perceive themselves to be and will appear to be alienated from the economic, cultural, political, and primary socialization group systems (Orrù, 1987).

We can see that external or social factors can influence a person to become even more at risk of failure or in danger of future negative outcomes (McWhirter et al., 2004), especially if he or she does not have the internal tools to engage in goal setting or to negotiate blocked goals. Goals facilitate hope in the person's future. Again, we see the dynamic relationship between the social world

Figure 11.2 Anomie theory says that messages like these can throw an individual into a state of low hope and alienation.

(environment) of the youth and its cause and effects on the psychological world of the youth. Therefore, the theory of hope plays a vital role in working with youth in therapeutic recreation settings. Facilitating and promoting hope and optimism for their futures are crucial within intervention and prevention programs.

Hope and Optimism

As many as 20% of youth may experience clinical depression by the time they graduate from high school (Lewinsohn, Hops, Roberts, & Seeley, 1993). Similar rates of youth anxiety and suicide rates have been reported (Centers for Disease Control and Prevention, 2004b; Twenge, 2000). Such marked indicators of mental illness suggest a widespread deficit in youth optimism and the need to foster hope among youth.

As a protective factor against such harms, optimism is largely an attitudinal strength. Tiger (1979) proposed a useful definition for optimism: "a mood or attitude associated with an expectation about the social or material future—one which the evaluator regards as socially desirable, to his [or her] advantage, or for his [or her] pleasure." Peterson (2000) suggested that optimistic attitudes are linked to "positive mood and good morale; to perseverance and effective problem solving; to academic, athletic, military, occupational, and political success;

to popularity; to good health; and even to long life and freedom from trauma" (p. 44). Pessimism, on the other hand, tends to indicate passivity, failure, social estrangement, morbidity, and mortality.

Youth optimism can be fostered through structured, meaningful engagement in recreational activity. Involving young people in continual opportunities to challenge themselves, build competence and confidence, experience flow, enact self-determined choices, and take active roles in decision-making processes encourages future expectations for engagement and success.

Flow

Among the many problems confronting contemporary youth is the challenge of structuring time in positive developmental pursuits. Nearly 40% of adolescent waking hours is discretionary time (Bartko & Eccles, 2003), and youth seem to make the poorest activity choices when they are out of school (Pawelko & Magafas, 1997). Studies have shown that large portions of adolescent daily life are experienced as boredom (Csikszentmihalyi & Larson, 1984; Larson, Csikszentmihalyi & Freeman, 1992; Larson & Richards, 1991), even among teens considered least at risk for future problems.

Developing skills for the constructive management of discretionary time is paramount to youth development (Witt & Crompton, 1996). Yet for all youth, finding constructive and interesting ways to occupy time and avoid boredom can be challenging (Witt & Crompton, 2002b). The excitement of illicit activities and the action and entertainment of video games and popular media compete with youth motivation for interesting, challenging, developmentally positive pursuits (Witt & Crompton, 2002b).

Research on enjoyment and optimal experience has produced the concept of flow, a term used to describe intensely absorbing, self-rewarding experiences (in which challenges match a person's skills and in which the person tends to lose track of time and self-awareness). Flow has been described as the experience of "concentration, absorption, deep involvement, joy, and sense of accomplishment . . . what people describe as the best moments in their lives" (Csikszentmihalyi, 1993, p. 176).

It has been suggested that the ability to engage in flow promotes overall psychosocial development of youth (Csikszentmihalyi & Larson, 1984). Young people who regularly engage in complex flow-producing activities may be less prone to boredom

and anxiety, and may have developmental advantages over those who do not have such experiences.

Prevention

A major challenge that a youth-serving agency must address is targeting risk factors that may not have happened yet or that come from an environmental history. Most risk factors are known to be cumulative and synergistic. That is, they exist within a cycle and can be passed across generations (Simeonsson, 1994). The best way to target such risk factors is through prevention services because intervention and treatment services will become overwhelmed by addressing such problems alone (Simeonsson, 1994). With the growing numbers of youth and families with identified problems, human services including therapeutic recreation must understand and be involved with youth, families, and their communities and be able to implement prevention-based programs.

In general, prevention is defined as stopping something before it happens. But we must be aware that just as risk exists on a continuum, prevention also moves along various degrees of addressing the needs of the youth who exist on this risk continuum. The following section will discuss three areas of the prevention continuum: primary, secondary, and tertiary.

Primary prevention focuses on reducing the number of new cases of identified problems or conditions occurring within a population. Primary prevention can be defined as the primary promotion of health and development (Simeonsson, 1994). It is also seen as a logical and needed strategy to reduce physical, social, and psychological problems. Programs using such a strategy should target youth who are at increased risk based on group characteristics rather than on individual characteristics (Simeonsson, 1994). According to McWhirter et al. (2004), primary prevention would target the general population and youth who exist within the minimal and remote risk levels. Chamberlin (1994) describes prevention using an analogy of a river and a drowning child. He explains that children upstream, or those youth who would benefit from primary prevention, are not being taught to swim and are not being kept from falling in the river. They are still on the ground but are at risk for "jumping or falling into the river because of some family and community dysfunction" (Chamberlin, 1994, p. 37). Examples that may relate to the involvement of therapeutic recreation include isolated and depressed single mothers who are having a difficult time dealing with stress, children who are neglected in overcrowded and unsafe child care environments, and adolescents who are hanging around on the street corner.

Secondary prevention can be equated with early intervention or recognition (Chamberlin, 1994; McWhirter et al., 2004) and focuses on "reducing the number of existing cases and lowering the prevalence of the manifested problems or conditions in the population" (Simeonsson, 1994, p. 7). Chamberlin's river analogy explains that what occurs in this stage is evaluation of whether the children and youth who have fallen or have jumped are at risk for drowning. These youth may exist on the high-risk continuum and need selective intervention to help reduce the problems that already exist (McWhirter et al., 2004; Simeonsson, 1994). Groups targeted with secondary prevention may be youth who are exposed to specific environmental stressors such as coming from families who have low incomes, have experienced divorce, have mental health problems, or have substance abuse problems.

Tertiary prevention focuses on the reduction of harmful effects and complications that occur within an existing disorder and identified condition (Simeonsson, 1994). According to Chamberlin (1994), the child is already downstream and the human service provider has already assessed that the child needs to be rescued from drowning from such harmful effects and complications. Tertiary prevention can also be seen as treatment and rehabilitation. The youth who need such services are within the imminent and in-crisis categories of risk (Chamberlin, 1994; McWhirter et al., 2004).

Intervention

Prevention and intervention can be difficult to distinguish from one another because the two concepts overlap. Prevention programs can often be seen as intervention, and vice versa. Adam, for example, had been having trouble developing positive peer relationships in middle school and was exhibiting signs of aggression. He was referred to a wilderness therapy intervention for youth who were expected to have a difficult transition to high school. Through the program, Adam developed new friendships with peers and adult mentors and began to see himself as likeable. Adam's boosted self-esteem and his developing support network in turn helped protect him from future problems associated with social isolation.

A framework (figure 11.3) presented by McWhirter et al. (2004) reconciles this ambiguity

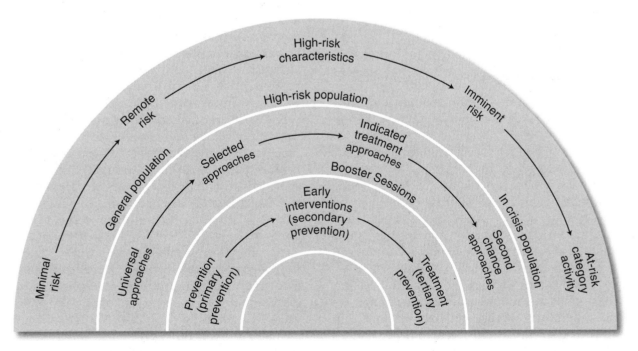

Figure 11.3 Risk, approaches, and prevention continuum.

From At-Risk Youth: A Comprehensive Response, For Counselors, Teachers, Psychologists, and Human Services Professionals 3rd edition by MCWHIRTER/MCWHIRTER/MCWHIRTER/MCWHIRTER. © 2004. Reprinted with permission of Wadsworth, a division of Thomson Learning: www.thomsonrights.com. Fax 800 730-2215.

by integrating intervention approaches with the at-risk continuum presented earlier in this chapter. Universal approaches to intervention are appropriate for all young people, not just those considered at risk. For example, all children in a low-income neighborhood are provided a program, although some are at only minimal risk. Selected approaches, such as Head Start programs offered to lower-income families (who are more likely to experience additional stressful circumstances), serve children who have increased risk of developing future problems. Booster sessions further enhance the effectiveness of interventions by adding a longer-term element. To sustain outcomes, intervention approaches must be of sufficient duration (Kirby, 2001). One-time efforts are less effective because program effects are not sustained over time (McWhirter et al., 2004). Indicated approaches target young people who are at imminent risk for problem behavior or who have already adopted risk-oriented behaviors. Such approaches are developed for youth whose underlying problems, characteristics, and behaviors are directly related to an at-risk activity. For example, an anger management program may be indicated for young people who have exhibited aggressive behaviors and as prevention for future problems such as violence or juvenile detention. Finally, second-chance interventions are needed for young people who are already engaged in at-risk behaviors such as substance abuse or violence, or have dropped out of school or become pregnant.

Attaining Outcomes

Just as prevention and intervention frequently overlap in purpose and practice, likewise do outcomes. Research in the area of recreational youth program outcomes has demonstrated a multitude of benefits to youth. Evaluation of a youth recreation after-school program, for example, found that participants benefited from engagement in goal-oriented activity (which they had previously lacked), experienced feelings of acceptance among adults, and gained skills in conflict resolution and peer collaboration (Scott, Witt & Foss, 1996).

Another study of Boys and Girls Club leaders suggested that youth who participated in the recreation prevention program developed leadership skills that increased self-esteem and perceptions of competence. The club, described by the youth members as a second home, fostered feelings of safety, belonging, and adult nurturance. The importance of supportive adult relationship and sustained program duration cannot be overemphasized because other studies have shown that outcomes are not as likely to endure post program if these elements are lacking (Autry, 2001; Boccaro & Outley, 2005; Sklar, 2005).

Community Development

In her review of the role of recreation and leisure in community processes, Pedlar (1996) noted that the widening gap between the advantaged and disadvantaged indicates that recreation and leisure professions should seek to foster **community development** and citizenship. According to Rubin and Rubin (2001), "community development occurs when people strengthen the bonds within their neighborhoods, build social networks, and form their own organizations to provide a long-term capacity for problem-solving" (p. 3). In addition, community development can be defined as a process for empowerment and transformation that focuses on identifying and resolving problems of a physical, social, and political nature and is embedded within the community members' abilities to change conditions (Reid & van Druenen, 1996).

Pedlar noted that community-based recreation has historically concentrated more on service management and programming to foster change in people and groups. She advocated for a movement that is more process based and less outcome oriented. She did not negate the value of a planned and prescriptive approach by the therapist or programmer or the need for accountability through outcomes. Her argument was for the process-based trend of facilitating a closer connection between practitioners and other citizens so that recreation is more praxis than product. This process would include reciprocity and colearning between these groups. In summary, Pedlar (1996) contended that, if the social reality of a community is recognized and validated and a community is more invested in the service, the members of this group would become more empowered. Empowerment comes from within the collective group, and a community of citizens who are included as genuine partners may in turn play an important and active role in establishing recreation and leisure as a public good. As a result, a process that allows community members to take control of their lives will also facilitate a realization of their ability to determine their own outcomes.

Many disciplines (community psychology, health education, health promotion, education, anthropology, and sociology) have incorporated such systems for societal environmental change. "Bringing about community change through grass-roots activity, neighborhood revitalization, and the creation of coalitions is an integral part of the fields of . . . community organizing" (Maton, 2000, p. 26). But other allied disciplines, including the field of therapeutic recreation, must align with such a viewpoint (Maton, 2000; Pedlar, 1996). Because we need to address services for youth within the ecological perspective, adopting the process of using recreation as a tool for community development parallels a philosophy that runs deep within our profession: that recreation can serve as a means to provide individualized and contextualized benefits for our clients. Using recreation to help develop communities at a grass-roots level can have long-term benefits for youth by having empowered people working together to improve the quality of life for the youth, family, and ultimately the community.

Within the context of after-school programs, Witt (2001) emphasized the need for those in the field of recreation and therapeutic recreation to find a balance between the voices of service providers and the voices of other stakeholders within the community (the youth, parents, teachers, and public at large concerned with prevention of risk behaviors) to provide differing views of what programs should entail. O'Sullivan (2001) concurred within her statements on repositioning and advocacy of parks and recreation as essential to well-being. She suggested that issues should be taken to the public to gather values surrounding recreation of the residents and youth of local neighborhoods. She also advocated that professionals in the field of recreation create ecological links and connections to citizens.

Community development related to recreation for youth who exist on a continuum of risk may be a process that exceeds the traditional boundaries of therapeutic recreation. But as Sylvester, Voelkl, and Ellis (2001) professed for our profession, this issue points to the need for systematic change in how professionals do their business.

> Empowerment is not simply teaching a social skill or a new leisure activity. It literally means *power to the people*, which implies that people with disabilities [including at-risk youth] must be supported in assuming more control over their lives, not just in terms of biopsychosocial functioning, but socially, culturally, and politically as well. This will require new thinking, models, and practices of therapeutic recreation. (p. 241)

Settings and Opportunities for Therapeutic Recreation

Youth services professionals, including traditional parks and recreation practitioners, face numerous challenges in providing adequate developmental programs because of the complex problems and behaviors that youth often present (Sprouse et al., 2005; Witt & Crompton, 1996). Interdisciplinary collaborative approaches that include a variety of social service personnel from the community provide more powerful programs with broader influence than do single-focus attempts. Under the partnership approach to service delivery, therapeutic recreation personnel can be a strong source of support for positive youth development services (Sprouse et al., 2005), and practitioners may be found working across a range of youth development settings. Among these settings are public parks and recreation departments, public therapeutic recreation programs, youth mental health services, therapeutic wilderness and adventure programs, and services within the juvenile justice system.

Public Parks and Recreation Departments

Nationwide, parks and recreation departments have sought innovative ways of serving youth in their respective communities, and many of these programs represent opportunities for therapeutic recreation specialists to make significant contributions of skills and expertise. In a series of case studies on youth public recreation programs, Witt and Crompton (2002a) brought to light a number of best practices examples throughout the United States. One exemplary case covered the accomplishments of the Phoenix Parks and Recreation Department (PPRD), which has organized for youth on multiple levels. The department's Youth Development Division (formerly the At-Risk Youth Division), formed in 1993, has offered a number of programs that range in focus from providing alternatives to juvenile court to promoting youth leadership and civic engagement.

Witt and Crompton (2002a) described selected programs offered by the Youth Development

Division that targeted the city's youth. Among the more than 20 youth programs offered by PPRD are Project BRAVE, the Young First Offender Program, and the Phoenix Activity City (PAC).

- At the request of the Phoenix police department, Project BRAVE was developed to provide domestic violence workshops for youth aged 6 to 19 years who might be subject to abuse in their homes. The program was created to assist in prevention efforts to counteract the cycle of family violence. The Youth Development Division collaborates with multiple departmental and community organizations in delivering this program.

- The Young First Offender Program represents a partnership with the Maricopa County Juvenile Court and the city's Human Services Department. The program was designed for offenders under the age of 13 who commit a first misdemeanor offense. The objective of the program is to deter delinquent behavior before it progresses to offenses that are more serious or incarceration. Children are required to do 3 hours of supervised community service and 3 hours of supervised recreation, which exposes them to positive recreational activities. Shoplifting offenses have accounted for the majority of referrals to this program (City of Phoenix, 2004).

- The PAC program reaches out to area schools by offering free after-school and summer programming and helps in providing specialized prevention services to the sites. The program components are life skills, educational support, healthy living, social and peer interaction, physical activity, cultural awareness, fine arts, crime prevention, and fun.

Community-Based Special Recreation

Therapeutic recreation programs based in the community have taken strides to address the growing need for community-based services for vulnerable and troubled youth. An enduring example of a public therapeutic recreation agency that targets the needs of young people is in the mental health programs of the Northern Illinois Special Recreation Association (NISRA). NISRA collaborates with the McHenry County Mental Health Board and McHenry County Court Services to provide programs for youth with a range of mental health concerns. Among those served are children with severe behavioral and emotional disorders and youth who are involved in the courts, are disadvantaged economically, or are at risk for placement out of home or school (Northern Illinois Special Recreation Association, 2005). These programs are designed to emphasize challenge and cooperation activities while incorporating a leisure education component. Through its youth mental health programming, NISRA focuses on both leisure education and recreational activities to provide participants with personal skill development including self-esteem, peer interactions, positive socialization, conflict resolution, and leisure awareness (Shulewitz & Zuniga, 1999).

Among the programs NISRA has offered is Monday Night Adventures, which serves court-involved teens. Participants are referred to NISRA by their probation officers and are required to complete the weekly recreation program. During the summer, participants are offered the opportunity to go on a high-adventure trip called Therapeutic Adventures of a Lifetime. Additionally, NISRA provides a Saturday recreation program to clients involved with the McHenry County Mental Health Board's Screening, Assessment, and Support Services (SASS) program. Participants range in age from 6 to 13 years and include children with mental illness, behavioral disorders, emotional disorders, and youth who are considered at risk of out-of-home placement.

Adventure Therapy

Adventure therapy is an intervention approach widely used with young people in which outdoor experiential activities are employed to accomplish treatment-related goals (Datillo, 2000). Adventure experiences, characterized by perceptions of risk and challenge, equip the therapeutic recreation specialist with useful techniques to facilitate behavioral and attitudinal change within their clients (Datillo). Through purposive facilitation, adventure therapy can provide empowering outcomes for youth who experience low self-perceptions and engage in self-destructive behaviors (Autry, 2001).

Adventure therapy occurs in wilderness settings or within a variety of facility-based settings including psychiatric, educational, and correctional settings. Programs in which therapeutic recreation specialists use adventure therapy are typically treatment settings for people who have been diagnosed with mental health problems (e.g., chemical dependency or depression) or alternative programs for young offenders referred by the courts (Autry,

©Getty Image

Adventure therapy is an active approach to helping clients build a sense of accomplishment and self-confidence.

2001; Davis-Berman & Berman, 1999). A common approach to adventure therapy is to offer it as an ancillary treatment to traditional therapies in the psychiatric setting. This approach might involve the use of low-level teams course elements or a high-ropes course. Adventure therapy may also be delivered as a sole treatment modality (Davis-Berman & Berman, 1999) in a multiday wilderness intervention program. Whatever the delivery mode, program efficacy is well documented in the short term, but research has also demonstrated the need to conduct long-term follow-up with participants to ensure sustainable outcomes (Autry, 2001; Russell, 2002; Sklar, 2005).

Specialized training is necessary to deliver adventure therapy programming safely and appropriately. Training opportunities are available through college curricula, professional workshops, or certification programs available through individual programs and facilities (Carter et al., 2003). Therapeutic recreation specialists who deliver adventure therapy may work in a number of settings including clinical mental health facilities, community-based diversional programs, backcountry wilderness programs, and residential wilderness camps for juvenile offenders.

Juvenile Justice System

People under age 18 who engage in patterns of behavior that deviate from cultural norms and threaten the welfare of others are labeled as delinquent (Carter et al., 2003) by the juvenile justice system. In the United States the juvenile justice system includes approximately 4,000 juvenile courts that specialize in the problems of youth. Most operate with a philosophy that even the worst delinquent is not a criminal but instead an erring, vulnerable child who needs help. Police arrest about 2.8 million young people for crimes annually, but the courts process only about 1.8 million as delinquents (O'Connor, 2004).

Therapeutic recreation work with young offenders occurs in both residential settings and community-based programs. Residential programs include juvenile prisons, youth detention centers, and youth camps. The therapeutic recreation specialist in the residential program functions as a member of a treatment team that serves incarcerated youth who may also be substance abusers, have intellectual impairments, or have psychological disorders. Therapeutic recreation specialists in these settings lead skill development classes; supervise recreation areas like the library, exercise, and game rooms (Carter et al., 2003); and conduct leisure education classes including leisure awareness and social skill development. Community-based services involve day treatment services, diversionary programs, and public parks and recreation department programs (Carter et al.).

In community settings, therapeutic recreation specialists collaborate with law enforcement, education, and nonprofit and government agencies to provide direct services to youth considered at risk of involvement with the courts (Carter et al., 2003). A primary focus within the community is prevention of future problems (Shultz, Crompton & Witt, 1995). Therapeutic recreation plays a valuable role in preventing youth from engaging

MARK A. WIDMER

Background Information

Education

PhD of Leisure Studies/Therapeutic Recreation from University of Utah

Credentials

*TRS *WFR (NOLS) *PSIA ski instructor

Career Information

Position

Professor in the Department of Recreation Management and Youth Leadership at Brigham Young University

Organization Information

Brigham Young University is a private university located in Provo, Utah, with 30,000 undergraduate students and 7,000 graduate students. Its Therapeutic Recreation department consists of 125 students, 5 faculty, and 10 graduate students who also serve as teaching assistants.

Organization's Mission

Brigham Young University prides itself on educating the best practitioners in the world and conducting cutting-edge research.

Job Description

Teach a therapeutic recreation class on assessment and theory-based programming at the undergraduate level. Teach a graduate class on youth and family recreation. Teach mountain biking and a ski instructor course. Consult on theory-based programming and outcome research with a number of therapeutic wilderness companies. Research the role of adventure/therapeutic wilderness programming for at-risk youth and their families. Direct the WILD Project/ Camp WILD, an adventure program in Idaho on the Salmon River that provides therapeutic recreation students with hands-on experience in developing and researching programs and staffing a camp.

Career Path

I worked as a white water raft guide for years, got my BA in philosophy, taught outdoor courses, completed an MA in Recreation Administration, ran a group home for men with developmental disabilities, received my PhD in therapeutic recreation, taught outdoor courses, and finally

got a job as a professor. Now that I am a full professor, my goals are to continue to research, make my classes even better, work with students, run study abroad programs in New Zealand, and continue training and consulting in wilderness therapy programs.

Likes and Dislikes About the Job

I like teaching therapeutic recreation and research, as well as my colleagues and the students. I particularly like reading literature and writing about issues related to quality of life, motivation, and so on. I don't like administrative issues.

Advice to Undergraduate Students

Therapeutic recreation is a great field to become involved in. Think about creative opportunities—it is a wonderful way to serve people and promote quality of life. Consider becoming a professor—we need happy, motivated, bright people to teach, particularly in therapeutic recreation. Working as a scholar and educator in therapeutic recreation is an incredible opportunity. Therapeutic recreation students are warm and engaging, my colleagues are wonderful and interesting people, and engaging in ongoing learning is invigorating. Doing what you love is a much wiser choice in life than seeking wealth. Look for opportunities and take advantage of them.

> It is what you learn after you know it all that counts.
>
> John Wooden

in risky behaviors like substance abuse that contribute to criminal acts (Witt & Crompton, 1996). Resiliency factors (skills and attitudes needed to adapt and cope with everyday life) (Carter et al.) become the focus of many community programs that emphasize tolerance, a sense of acceptance, resource awareness, and collaborative relationships and services that address both nonrecreative needs and positive leisure experiences (Allen, Paisley, Stevens & Harwell, 1998).

Special Concerns

Young people bring a diversity of needs and backgrounds to recreation programs. Yet within the spectrum of providing youth services, the therapeutic recreation specialist may encounter young people with specific needs. Among them are youth with histories of maltreatment and those who have learning or behavioral disorders.

Child Maltreatment

Of concern to therapeutic recreation specialists working with children are those with histories of abuse or neglect. Reports of child maltreatment have risen over the years as the resources of child protective agencies have decreased (Carter et al., 2003; Jewel, 1999). Therapeutic recreation has much to offer in addressing the needs of maltreated children. Therapeutic recreation specialists may address child abuse and neglect in a variety of settings including summer camps, schools, psychiatric settings, residential placements away from the family, and within the juvenile justice system.

The scope of therapeutic recreation services for children who have been maltreated includes assessment, education, prevention, and the promotion of well-being (Carter et al., 2003). Assessment of developmental needs can occur through observation of children in natural play environments. Leisure education can enhance motor and self-concept development and develop skills in relationship building, self-expression, coping, and resource awareness (Carter et al.). Family education and skills training (e.g., time management and stress management training) may be offered to mitigate the likelihood of future maltreatment. To apply a prevention approach, the specialist should act as a positive role model, helping youth establish trusting relationships with reliable adults (Jewel, 1999).

Learning and Behavioral Disorders

Therapeutic recreation services are frequently used to address childhood problems associated with learning and behavioral disorders. Although these disorders commonly manifest during the developmental years, they may result in significant difficulties in employment or social adjustment during adulthood. Thus interventions in the developmental years should attempt to minimize or reduce the extension of problem behaviors into adulthood. In the *DSM-IV-TR*, the American Psychiatric Association (2000) identified a number of disorders of child development including learning, motor skills, communication, and attention-deficit/hyperactivity disorder.

Intervention approaches are intended (1) to prevent and remediate maladaptive behaviors and inappropriate interaction; (2) to assess and promote the acquisition of skills that support academic, motor, and socio-emotional functioning, community involvement, and inclusion; and (3) to facilitate confidence and enhance self-esteem (Carter et al., 2003). The therapeutic recreation specialist may address self-confidence and physical well-being through a variety of activities such as aquatics, relaxation, cooperative games and sports, leisure awareness, and expressive therapies. Cognitive experiences such as playing board games, keeping score, and reading directions can reinforce academic skill development (Carter et al.). Adventure and challenge experiences further encourage sensory integration to support cognitive functioning while also supporting development of self-confidence, self-esteem, and cooperation skills.

Issues and Trends in Youth Development and Therapeutic Recreation

Within the parks and recreation field, interest has grown in developing a clear definition of youth development as it pertains to recreation services. Of particular note are the efforts of the National Recreation and Park Association (NRPA) to establish youth development as an area of emphasis for the public parks and recreation profession. In August 2005 NRPA convened the Youth Development Summit to form a strategy for building a national youth development agenda. The summit defined several key areas for the profession to target: (1)

training, workforce development, and professional preparation; (2) best practices research and evaluation; (3) a common language and a youth development framework; (4) public visibility for the youth development movement; and (5) best practices guidelines including youth-driven programming and intentional outcomes (Spangler, 2005).

In October 2005 a meeting of 33 interested members of the recreation and leisure studies academic community was held during the NRPA national congress to advance efforts to develop a youth development research network (Spangler, 2005). Reflecting this growing academic interest and the overall need for youth professionals, a number of higher education programs in recreation and leisure studies have created degree programs and specialization areas in youth development at both the undergraduate and graduate levels.

In November 2005 the NRPA adopted a consensus definition of youth development to guide the organization's work in this area and provide a common language for the field. According to this new definition, youth development involves helping youth acquire basic needs and competencies necessary for successful teenage and adult life. The youth development framework considers youth problems as interrelated and stemming from the ecological systems in which they live, and the framework suggests that these problems can be addressed through strategies that engage youth in positive ways. Overall, youth development processes are designed to encourage and support youth in actively shaping their own development. These processes are structured to enable youth to gain skills for employment, social relations, self-nurturing, civic engagement, and participating in cultural activities (P.A. Witt, personal communication, November 18, 2005).

These recent events within the parks and recreation field reflect the rapid growth of interest in youth development as well as the expanding commitment of professionals to elevate the quality of practice in youth services. The expansion of higher education programs in recreation and youth development further suggests the growing need for recreation professionals who are properly trained to provide youth services.

Summary

The therapeutic recreation profession has an opportunity to play a central role in the expanding youth development conversation and agenda setting. As a profession, therapeutic recreation is well established in designing outcomes-based programming with the most vulnerable populations. The therapeutic recreation process of assessment, planning, implementation, and evaluation (APIE) can be readily applied to youth development service settings. Whether youth development goals lie in prevention, diversion, or primary treatment, therapeutic recreation offers a universal process, established service models, and standards of practice to the broad field of youth development.

DISCUSSION QUESTIONS

1. Review the characteristics of the five levels of risk on the at-risk continuum. Create mock clients for each risk level and describe the risk factors and behaviors of each client.

2. How can therapeutic recreation address the needs of troubled youth? How does the therapeutic recreation profession fit within the framework of positive youth development?

3. Describe the importance of taking an ecological perspective when working in therapeutic recreation with at-risk youth. What are some factors within the youth's environment that a therapeutic recreation specialist would need to consider when providing intervention services? When providing prevention services?

4. Briefly describe the theories that guide the therapeutic recreation profession when working with at-risk youth. Provide examples of therapeutic recreation programs that would put each theory into practice for a youth such as Eduardo (case on page 169).

5. Compare and contrast the concepts of prevention and intervention in youth development services.

6. Briefly describe community development and its importance in therapeutic recreation services for at-risk youth.

Aging and the Life Span

Judith E. Voelkl, PhD, CTRS

Clemson University

Begum Aybar-Damali, MS

Clemson University

LEARNING OUTCOMES

After completing this chapter, learners will be able to demonstrate the following competencies:

- Describe the characteristics of the older adult population in the United States
- Identify the key theories of successful aging
- Describe the basic tenets of each theory and explain how they differ from one another
- Describe the characteristics of older adults who (a) receive services in an adult day center, (b) reside in assisted-living facilities, and (c) reside in nursing homes
- Describe the typical activity offerings in each type of setting
- Describe the innovative programming that therapeutic recreation specialists are currently providing to older adults

Consider the older adults who are present in your life. Perhaps they are your grandparents, relatives, neighbors, or members of your community. How would they describe their later years? How are their participation patterns in recreation influenced by factors typically associated with aging, such as retirement, relocation, loss of a spouse, or decline in functional abilities? Some of the older adults whom you know might say that they have experienced a sense of freedom as they age, enjoying recreation pursuits as frequently as they would like, given the relinquishing of their work-related obligations. Other older adults whom you know may experience their later years as a time of physical, social, and cognitive decline. In actuality, many older adults enter their later years enjoying increased freedom from the constraints of employment, and over time they may experience some of the functional decline frequently associated with age.

What does this picture of aging mean for future therapeutic recreation specialists? To consider how best to serve older adults through the provision of therapeutic recreation services, we must ask several questions. For instance, how can recreation activities affect the life satisfaction of older adults? What role can a therapeutic recreation specialist have in programming recreation activities to enhance the day-to-day experiences of older adults? In what settings might a therapeutic recreation specialist work if he or she would like to provide therapeutic recreation services to older adults?

This chapter is designed to answer the preceding questions. We will explore the characteristics of the older population in the United States and the theories of successful aging that help us understand the predictors of positive aging in later life. In addition, we will examine the typical service settings in which therapeutic recreation specialists are employed, including adult day programs, assisted-living facilities, and nursing homes. Finally, we will discuss several innovative programs currently being offered in service settings.

Whom Do We Work With?

American society is growing older. The number of older adults, worldwide, is growing because of increased access to health care and a decrease in women's mortality because of childbirth. Like other industrialized countries, the United States has never had as many older adults as it has today, and the senior population is expected to explode as baby boomers (those born between 1946 and 1964) hit 65. Think back to the last time that you walked in the downtown area of your hometown. What percentage of citizens were 65 years of age or older? Today, there are approximately 36 million older people in the United States. They account for 12% of the overall population, or approximately 1 in every 8 citizens. The size of the senior population is expected to grow to almost 87 million by 2050. The oldest old (those age 85 and older) will grow faster than the young old (65 to 74 years of age) or old (75 to 84 years of age) segments of the older population (Administration on Aging, 2004).

The profile of older adults is ethnically diverse. According to 2003 Census reports, non-Hispanic white people make up the majority (approximately 83%) of the older population, followed by African Americans (8%), Hispanics (of any race, 6%), and Asians (3%) (Administration on Aging, 2004). The older population, age 65 and older, will grow more diverse. Therefore, recreation programs and ser-

Active engagement of two older adults in a nursing home.

vices for older people will require greater flexibility to meet the needs of a more diverse population.

Today's older Americans are living longer. In the United States, females have a life expectancy nearly 7 years longer than that of males; therefore, women outnumber men in the older population. Women live, on average, 15 years as widows, and they are less likely to remarry than men are; therefore, a large number of women live alone. Among older adults in the United States in 2001, 41% of women and 73% of men were married. Among the same group, 46% of women and only 14% of men were widowed. In 2002, 41% of women and only 18% of men lived alone (Administration on Aging, 2004).

Decline in personal resources becomes an important issue in later life. Older adults' household income depends mainly on social security benefits (90%). Census data show that 10% of older adults, mostly women living alone, were below the poverty level in 2002. Older Hispanic women who lived alone experienced the highest poverty rate (47%) (Gist & Hetzel, 2004). Still, today's older Americans are enjoying greater prosperity than any previous generation, and fewer older Americans are living below the poverty threshold.

Older adults are not alike. All adults enter their later years with unique characteristics depending on the particular environmental, cultural, and personal aspects of their lives. The majority of the older population report that at least one disability affects their activities of daily life. Limitations in activities because of health conditions are more likely to occur in advanced years. Twenty-eight percent of the population between age 65 and 74 and 50% of the population age 75 and older experience limitations in activities because of chronic health conditions (Gist & Hetzel, 2004). Approximately one in every five persons age 65 and older does not drive because of disability-related functional limitations.

In 2000, 28% of the population age 65 and older lived alone in a household, 6% lived in group homes such as assisted-living facilities or nursing homes, and 66% lived with others in a household. Note that the majority of older adults age 50 and older choose to remain in their current homes as long as possible (American Association of Retired Persons, 2005). Health reasons, quality of their current home or apartment, and affordability of their current housing are the main reasons that people choose to or need to move to a new residence. Among the movers, the majority of those age 65 and older (59%) stay in the same county, and those 85 and older are more likely to move compared with those who are younger.

Theories of Successful Aging

Paul's neighbor, Alice, is a 93-year-old woman who worked hard as a teacher for her whole life. When Alice was a young woman, she illustrated many children's books and wrote many stories for children. Although she does not publish books any more, she likes to read her books to children every chance she gets. Alice reminds Paul of his grandmother, who recently died at age 75 from Parkinson's disease. Paul still remembers the stories that his grandmother told him when he was a kid and thinks that she was the happiest older person he knew. Paul wonders whether people age differently.

As we saw in the previous section, many more people are living to an older age compared with the time of your great-great-grandparents. This exciting and important change has the potential to affect the practice of therapeutic recreation. Over the past 50 years many theories of successful aging have been proposed. This section explores four of the major theories that explain successful aging, including activity theory, continuity theory, socio-emotional selectivity theory, and selective optimization with compensation theory. An understanding of these theories can be helpful in planning therapeutic recreation programs for older adults.

As you read the following theories, think about the life of an older person whom you know well. Where does he or she live? What does he or she like to do during his or her free time? How does his or her use of time, activity involvement, and living environment influence his or her level of day-to-day happiness or general life satisfaction?

Activity Theory (Versus Disengagement Theory)

Almost half a century ago, it was proposed that a mutual withdrawal between society and older adults is an effective way of coping with the changes that come with age (Cumming & Henry, 1961). This understanding underlined the disengagement theory, which states that by decreasing emotional ties with others and with the society as a whole and by becoming more self-occupied, people could experience enhanced life satisfaction in later years. This theory has been found to be of limited value, because a significant proportion of older people are interested in being active members of society (Lemon, Bengston & Peterson, 1972; Schroots, 1996).

Another influential perspective, activity theory, states that when older people are active, engaged with life, and energetic, they age more successfully and experience higher levels of satisfaction (Lemon, Bengston & Peterson, 1972). Activity theory has been the theory of successful aging most commonly used as a guide for therapeutic recreation service providers, because research has shown that involvement in leisure activities provides many benefits for the well-being of older adults. For therapeutic recreation specialists who work with older adults, discovering what is meaningful for people and providing them with choices and opportunities for engagement in meaningful roles in life are important aspects of programming. For example, Paul's neighbor volunteered at the elementary school nearby to read stories to children. She told him that volunteering gave her a sense of being needed and helped her deal with the void in life caused by the loss of her husband.

Continuity Theory

Continuity theory states that people develop habits, attitudes, preferences, and relationships while growing old (Neugarten, Havighurst & Tobin, 1968; Atchley, 1989). This aspect of life-span development becomes an important part of one's personality, and older adults seek to maintain meaningful habits, preferences, and relationships. According to continuity theory, people develop their own adjustment styles over the life span, and prior behaviors and attitudes become the predictors of their adaptation to aging. Therefore, activities and the relationships maintained over a long time are related to well-being.

Unlike disengagement and activity theories, continuity theory emphasizes individual differences. For example, think about an older person whom you know well. Think about an activity that he or she likes to do in his or her free time and ask yourself how this person would react if this preferred activity were constrained. Would he or she become depressed, cease participation, or replace the activity with something else? According to continuity theory, people adapt to aging in various ways. Therefore, understanding personal lifestyles, attitudes, and preferences developed in the process of becoming an adult is important in planning therapeutic recreation programs.

Selective Optimization With Compensation Theory

The selective optimization with compensation theory (SOC) was proposed by Paul Baltes and his colleagues (Baltes & Baltes, 1990). The theory defines successful aging as an adaptation process of the minimization of loss and the maximization of gains. The strategies of selection (S), optimization (O), and compensation (C) are the major mechanisms that form successful adaptation of people to aging (figure 12.1).

The selection process addresses the choice of goals or life domains, and optimization and compensation address the means to maintain chosen goals. Through selection, people experience restriction in their involvement in one or more domains of life. Selection can occur in two major dimensions: elective and loss based. If restrictions occur because of responsibilities of new demands and tasks in one's life, selection is elective. If restrictions occur because of one's expectation of losses in personal or environmental resources, selection is loss-based.

The second component of the theory, optimization, is about adequacy of the person's behavioral

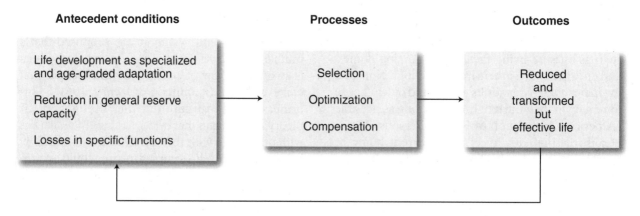

Figure 12.1 Selective optimization with compensation.

Reprinted from P.B. Baltes and M.M. Baltes, 1990, *Successful aging: Perspectives from the behavioral sciences* (Cambridge, MA: Cambridge University Press).

capacities and skills in achieving the selected goals. This component denotes the enhancement and modification of available resources such as building new skills, practicing previously acquired skills more often, or allocating time and energy for achieving an optimal level of functioning in a selected range of actions. The third component of the theory, compensation, is about adaptation of the person's limitations such as accepting support from others or using assistive technology to accomplish targeted goals. Baltes and Baltes (1990) give the example of concert pianist Arthur Rubinstein to illustrate the use of these mechanisms to adapt to aging-related changes:

> For instance, the pianist Rubinstein remarked in a television interview that he conquers weaknesses of aging in his piano playing in the following manner: First, he reduced his repertoire and plays a smaller number of pieces (selection); second, he practices them more often (optimization); and third, he slows down his speed of playing prior to fast movements, thereby producing a contrast that enhances the impression of speed in the fast movement (compensation). (p. 26)

Losses related to personal or social changes in one's life are often considered prominent in later years. But people experience them in wide variation by adopting these selection, optimization, and compensation strategies in various forms. Previous life experiences, current values and interests, skills, and personal and social resources determine how well and in which forms people use those strategies. Studies show that use of SOC may be difficult in advanced years because people experience limitations in resources such as skills (Lang, Rieckmann, & Baltes, 2002). Therefore, helping people negotiate aging-related limitations would be important in interventions. For example, an older person who loves cooking and has cooked all her life might continue cooking following physical decline. A therapeutic recreation specialist may help by encouraging her to narrow her selection to a few favorite recipes, organizing her kitchen in a way that makes it more accessible, and providing assistive kitchen devices such as electronic mixers to compensate declines in her physical strength.

Socio-Emotional Selectivity Theory

Socio-emotional selectivity theory was developed by Carstensen (1991, 1995). According to the theory, people are motivated to have social contact by a variety of goals, but several of these (i.e., emotional regulation, development and maintenance of self-concept, and information seeking) are present throughout the life span. According to the theory, older adults are selective about their social network by withdrawing from social contacts that are peripheral to their lives and by staying in contact with close friends and relatives with whom they have meaningful relationships.

Older people have fewer associates than do younger adults, but they all have the same number of close emotional relationships (Lang & Carstensen, 1994). This process is a social selection that reflects motivational choices, not a social withdrawal from social relationships determined by biological or physical changes or declines (Carstensen, 1995).

Close friendships are important to the well-being of older adults (Myers & Diener, 1995). A study has found that lower levels of depression among people in retirement housing were related to social support received from old friends residing outside the retirement community, not new friends within the community; old friends are more meaningful and psychologically beneficial to older adults than their new friends are (Potts, 1997). Aspects of socio-emotional selectivity theory may be used to guide therapeutic recreation program planning because leisure activities typically occur in social contexts. Activities can maintain and strengthen relationships in smaller but meaningful social circles and ultimately enhance emotional well-being. Therapeutic recreation specialists may incorporate family and close friends in programs to enhance an older adult's social ties with old and familiar friends and family members.

Where Might We Work?

As discussed earlier in this chapter, a growing number of older adults are living healthier and longer than ever before. Many older adults are independent and may participate in recreation services provided by community or commercial agencies (e.g., public recreation departments, fitness centers, community parks). Traditionally, therapeutic recreation specialists provide services for older adults who are in need of long-term care. Long-term care settings, including **adult day programs, assisted-living facilities,** and **nursing homes,** provide "assistance . . . over a sustained period of time to people who are experiencing long-term inabilities or difficulties in functioning because of a disability" (Kane, Kane & Ladd, 1998, p. 4). In this section we will address the three long-term care settings in which therapeutic recreation specialists are most frequently employed, including (a) adult day programs, (b) assisted-living facilities, and (c) nursing homes.

Adult Day Programs

Adult day programs provide community-based services, including health and social services, for older adults with physical, cognitive, and social impairments. Such programs allow older adults to remain living in the community and provide respite for family caregivers, including adult children or spouses. Services are typically provided from 7 a.m. to 6 p.m., thereby covering the hours when family members may be at work. Services provided include the monitoring of health conditions and medications, therapy services (e.g., physical therapy, occupational therapy, speech therapy), salon and bathing services, and social or recreation services.

Cox reported that in 2003 there were 3,407 adult day centers in the United States (Wake Forest University Baptist Medical Center, 2003). Over 5,000 new adult day centers are needed nationwide to meet the needs of our aging population and their family members. Although data on the specific conditions of attendees of adult day centers are not available, research has suggested that 43% of individuals enrolled in adult day centers need help with toileting, 37% with walking, and 24% with eating (Wake Forest University Baptist Medical Center, 2003).

A general characteristic of adult day centers is the provision of a full day of engaging activities (Henry, Cox, Reifler & Asbury, 2000). Programs may be designed to support participants' involvement in meaningful, lifelong pursuits, thereby enhancing life satisfaction as described by activity theory and continuity theory. The reports from several adult day centers speak to the important role of activity programming (Henry, Cox, Reifler & Asbury, 2000):

- The Sunshine Terrace Adult Day Center (Logan, Utah) created a music therapy program that enabled people with dementia who had not played a musical instrument in years to rediscover their talent. The program also awakened musical interest in those who had never shown it before.

- The Kona Adult Day Center (Kona, Hawaii) used art therapy to help participants express their feelings and achieve a sense of accom-

plishment. Participants learned how to make silk paper greeting cards, and the center began selling these to raise money. The center operates a program of parallel activities, or track programming, to provide options that fit participants' interests and abilities. Three or four activities, such as art, gardening, cooking, and exercise, may be going on simultaneously.

- The Center for Active Generations (Sioux Falls, South Dakota) offers an hour-long, warm-water exercise program using the facilities at the local YWCA. Because the YWCA facility is not far from the center, staff and participants walk there, engaging in two activities in one outing.

The Southwest Florida Interdisciplinary Center for Positive Aging at Florida Gulf Coast University provides an innovative example of an adult day center. The center provides year-round programming for community-dwelling older adults who have some level of cognitive decline. The director, Dr. Linda Buettner, is a CTRS. Full-time staff include a geriatric nurse practitioner and two CTRSs. As is evident in table 12.1, most of the programming consists of recreation programs designed to maintain and enhance the physical, social, cognitive, and emotional functioning of participants. Older adults choose to participate in activities based on their current or past leisure interests as well as the social relationships that are honored and developed through participation. Programming provides family members with 4 to 5 hours of respite care Monday through Friday.

Assisted-Living Facilities

Assisted living is a relatively new option in the long-term care services that provides an alternative to living in a nursing home. Typically, the older adults who reside in assisted-living facilities need less medical care than nursing home residents do. Older adults moving into an assisted-living facility may select either a studio or a one-bedroom apartment. In many cases, residents may choose to furnish the living space with cherished belongings from their lifelong home. Residents may have a private bathroom or, in some facilities, a shared bathroom. Just less than half of assisted-living facilities offer kitchens within private living space (National Council for Assisted Living, 2001).

According to the National Academy for State Health Policy, in the year 2000 there were 32,886

Table 12.1   Schedule of Therapeutic Programs in an Adult Day Center

Day of the week	Therapeutic programs
Monday	Brain fitness, lunch in the community cafe, therapeutic dancing
Tuesday	Exercise or chair volleyball, brain training, therapeutic cooking, psychosocial groups (based on leisure interests), relaxation
Wednesday	Physical fitness for care partners and persons with memory loss, health promotion class, lunch in the community cafe, memory class, creativity-based projects for self-expression
Thursday	Exercise or chair volleyball, brain training, therapeutic cooking, psychosocial groups (based on leisure interests), relaxation
Friday	Exercise or chair volleyball, brain training, therapeutic cooking, psychosocial groups (based on leisure interests), relaxation

Personal communication from L. Buettner 2005.

licensed assisted-living facilities in the United States with 795,391 beds (National Council for Assisted Living, 2001). Several characteristics are common to all facilities that fall under the umbrella of assisted living. For instance, according to the National Council for Assisted Living (2001), assisted-living facilities are

> congregate residential settings that provide or coordinate personal services, 24-hour supervision and assistance, activities, and health-related services; designed to minimize the need to move; designed to accommodate individual residents' changing needs and preferences; designed to maximize residents' dignity, autonomy, privacy, independence, choice and safety; and designed to encourage family and community involvement.

According to the National Council for Assisted Living (2001), the typical resident of an assisted-living facility is a woman (69% are females) who is 80 years of age. Eighty-one percent of residents need assistance with one or more activities of daily living (i.e., bathing, dressing, transferring, toileting, eating). Most residents receive assistance with housework (93%) and daily medications (86%).

At present no systematic standards require assisted-living facilities to offer activity programming, but most facilities make some programs available on a daily basis. The breadth of activity offerings in assisted-living facilities is evident in the activity calendar of Tiffany Court (2005) (see figure 12.2). Typically, programs are available to all residents, who can freely choose to participate in activities that match their lifelong interests (continuity theory) and foster meaningful social engagement (socio-emotional selectivity theory). The role of the therapeutic recreation specialist involves assessing participants' activity interests and social relationships as well as their needs for activity modification to ensure that they are able to maintain participation in meaningful recreation activities.

Nursing Homes

According to the National Nursing Home Survey of 1999 (Jones, 2002), there are 18,000 nursing homes with 1,879,600 beds in the United States. Most older adults who live in nursing homes in

Sunday	Monday	Tuesday	Wednesday	Thursday	Friday	Saturday
10:00 Church service 2:00 Family ice cream social	9:30 Painting 11:00 Walking club 3:00 Gardening group	9:30 Trivial Pursuit 11:00 Stretch and tone 1:30 Visiting pets	9:30 Reminiscence 11:00 Stretch and tone 3:00 Bingo	10:00 Men's club 11:00 Walking club 6:00 Movie night	10:00 Music group 11:00 Stretch and tone 3:00 Cards and games	10:00 Current events 11:00 Stretch and tone 2:00 Out trip: Botanical Gardens

Figure 12.2   Activity calendar in an assisted-living facility.

LINDA L. BUETTNER

Background Information

Education

*BS in Adapted Physical Education from State University of New York at Cortland *MEd from Bowling Green State *PhD from Penn State

Credentials

*CTRS *F-GSA *F-AGHE *Delta Society Instructor and Team Evaluator *Licensed Dementia Trainer FL Levels I and II

Special Affiliations

*Delta Society Animal-Assisted Therapy International *Gerontological Society of America *ATRA

Special Awards

*Fellow of Gerontological Society of America *Fellow of the Association of Gerontology *Senior Faculty Scholarship Award at Florida Gulf Coast University *ATRA Scholarship Award *Geraldine Dowling Gerontological Nursing Award

Career Information

Position

Recreation therapist, Center for Positive Aging

Organization Information

The Center for Positive Aging (CFPA) serves as a model of evidence-based health care for people with memory loss in a community setting. It currently serves 100 families in Southwest Florida managing a loved one with Alzheimer's disease or a related disorder. Dementia is a public health epidemic that will continue to grow, and community-based solutions need to be tested. We study and find sensitive, cost-efficient recreational therapy care models for Florida and for the nation and beyond. In our model, programs and services are not just for those diagnosed with Alzheimer's disease or a related disorder; nor are they only for those who

are considered senior citizens. It is a continuum of care and active engagement in life in the community across the life span. The way we are able to make this innovative model work is that we have a preventative component, as well as many services that are appealing to people with and without cognitive impairments. We have created a mix, which seems to fit and serve the older adult community well. It is designed to maintain our older members in their homes and with the people they love.

For those without memory problems, we provide peace of mind and opportunities to actively engage in the prevention of memory loss. For the older adults and their families, friends, and community who are challenged with problems related to memory disorders, we offer education, therapies, and psychosocial assistance for the entire family. Coping methods are a priority for all.

> Imagine all the people living life in peace. You may say I'm a dreamer, but I'm not the only one. I hope someday you'll join us, and the (RT) world will live as one.
>
> John Lennon

Job Description

Provide hands-on interventions to individuals with dementia while implementing applied research.

Career Path

I worked as a CTRS at Willard Psychiatric Center in Gero-Psychiatry until this hospital closed. My first position after obtaining my PhD from Penn State was director of the Casella Alzheimer's Center at Binghamton University. I then moved to Florida and became the director of the Center for Positive Aging and served as a faculty recreational therapist.

Likes and Dislikes About the Job

I love the mix of research and service in my community plus the opportunity to shape student learning through my clinical practice.

Advice to Undergraduate Students

Listen to the clients you serve. Their needs drive our programs and services and lead us to successful interventions.

the United States are female, age 75 or older, and in need of assistance in more than three activities of daily living (e.g., dressing, bathing, toileting) (Jones, 2002). More specifically, as we consider the characteristics of the 1,628,300 older adults who live in nursing homes, we find that 16.4% of residents are between the ages of 65 and 74 (i.e., young old), 35.1% are between the ages of 75 and 84 (i.e., old), and 36.8% are 85 years of age and older (i.e., oldest old). Females make up 62% of residents. Most residents need assistance with bathing (93.8%), dressing (86.5%), and toileting (56%). Residents' impairments are also evident in their need for eyeglasses (62%) and wheelchairs (62%).

Older adults who reside in nursing homes typically live in a small bedroom that they share with a roommate. Meals are served in a common dining area. The day typically begins with morning wakeup at 6 a.m. and staff assistance with dressing and toileting. Breakfast follows in the dining room. Morning hours consist of bathing, current events, and exercise groups. Afternoon hours usually include group activities at 2 or 3 p.m. Dinner is served at approximately 5 p.m. Most residents go to bed between 7 and 9 p.m.

Researchers have described the characteristics of residents in relation to their participation levels in group activities (e.g., Shore, Lerman, Smith, Iwata & DeLeon, 1995; Voelkl, Fries & Galecki, 1995). In a study based on the activity participation of 3,008 residents, Voelkl et al. reported that residents' mean time in activities was less than 4 hours per week (mean time of 217 minutes per week). More specifically, residents with moderately severe or severe cognitive impairments had high levels of time in activities, whereas residents with very severe cognitive impairments had the lowest average time in activities. Residents who were not depressed and those with a high sense of involvement in the facility had high levels of activities in comparison with residents who were depressed and those with a low sense of involvement. Residents with a preference for the day area also had high levels of time in activities in comparison with residents with a preference for their own rooms or no preference. Lastly, women spent more time in activities than men did.

Understanding the relationship between residents' characteristics and activity participation levels, as reported in the previous paragraph, can be useful in targeting the actions of therapeutic recreation specialists. For instance, therapeutic recreation specialists need to monitor and support the recreation involvement of residents with low levels of activity participation, including those who receive high levels of nursing care, those who are depressed, and those with very severe cognitive impairments. Therapeutic recreation specialists also need to consider how to design inviting and comfortable activity spaces for residents who typically prefer staying in their own rooms. Such actions are essential in supporting residents' quality of life (remember the basic tenets of activity theory and continuity theory). Furthermore, therapeutic recreation specialists skilled in activity modification will be able to assist residents in remaining active in meaningful pursuits even as they experience functional decline. Such skill supports residents' selective optimization with compensation.

Long-Term Care Strategies

For several decades **gerontologists,** older adults, and family members have criticized the provision of long-term care in the United States (e.g., Vladeck, 1980). Over the past two decades we have seen many positive changes in the provision of services. For instance, the variety of service settings has expanded from nursing homes to include the alternative options of adult day programs and assisted-living facilities. Concurrently, we are seeing new directions in programmatic offerings in long-term care designed to foster positive experiences and provide residents with choice, control, and a sense of comfort within their "home" environment. In this section we will briefly review two innovative program strategies, including treatment protocols and culture change. Readers may also find it helpful to review the modalities, in particular sensory stimulation, validation therapy, animal-assisted therapy, and intergenerational programs, presented in chapter 5. Many of these modalities are effective with older adults, depending on their unique needs.

Treatment Protocols: Focus on Dementia Care

Dementia is characterized by loss of intellectual functioning, memory loss, loss of functional skills, and behavioral symptoms such as agitation and passivity. One out of every 10 Americans age 65 or older has some type of dementia (Alzheimer's Association, 2005). Furthermore, half of all nursing home residents have Alzheimer's disease or a related disorder. These statistics speak to the need for therapeutic recreation professionals who work in long-term care to understand the symptoms and functional decline associated with dementia.

Buettner and Fitzsimmons (2003) stated that the role of the therapeutic recreation professional is to provide therapeutic programs that will affect the "bio-psycho-social well-being of the client" (p. 1). Older adults with dementia have been observed to display a range of disruptive behaviors, ranging from apathy, depression, physical aggression (e.g., kicking, hitting), wandering, repetitive vocalizations, and yelling, to name a few. These disruptive behaviors are viewed as representing unmet needs on the part of the older adult with dementia. Such unmet needs may include the need for companionship, communication of one's needs, happiness, or hunger. The health care provider has the task of understanding and identifying the needs expressed through the disruptive behaviors and meeting such needs.

Buettner and Fitzsimmons (2003) have developed 82 evidence-based protocols designed to address the disruptive behaviors of older adults with dementia. The protocols range from life stories to postcard collectors, airmat therapy, animal-assisted therapy, wheelchair biking, social dance club, music and motion, sensory cooking, newsletter, dominoes, photo therapy, gardens alive, sensory bird club, hooked on golf club, and sensory travel club. Evidence suggests that the protocols are effective. A common feature of these protocols pertains to the structure of the intervention. Each protocol is conducted in small groups of six or fewer residents, contains challenging tasks that match the skills of the residents, is conducted in a restraint-free environment, and contains tasks that are meaningful and promote functional abilities.

The treatment protocols for dementia care provide therapeutic recreation specialists with one approach to maintaining or enhancing residents' functional abilities. When using protocols to enhance the functioning of older adults with dementia, the therapeutic recreation specialist may work with the older adult and his or her family members to select activities that optimize his or her functioning while compensating for cognitive loss, as outlined in the selective optimization with compensation model (Baltes & Baltes, 1990).

Culture Change

Over the past decade there has been movement in nursing home care to change how care is provided, shifting from a medical model to a community or homelike model. Nursing homes typically have a physical design similar to that of a hospital, with long corridors, prominent nursing stations, and institutional-scale dining rooms. Many facilities are working to transform "traditional institutions and practices into communities in which each person's capacities and individuality are affirmed and developed" (Pioneer Network, 2005). Inherent in this transformation is the redesign of the physical environment to include dining and living rooms that are similar to those in a typical home environment, kitchens that are accessible 24 hours a day, and bedrooms that reflect the personality of the resident.

A national movement called the **Eden Alternative** is an example of culture change in long-term care. Many nursing homes are becoming Eden

A critical factor in successful aging is maintaining a connection to the things we love and care about. Eden Alternative strives to maintain this "human habitat."

JIM

Jim is an 83-year-old man with Alzheimer's type dementia who, up until now, spent all of his time under the care of his wife. Difficulty with remembering where he is, what he is doing, who others are, and what year it is has made life very frustrating for Jim. Recently, his difficulty with memory and orientation has become dangerous. Jim recently wandered from his home underdressed in very cold weather. A family friend found him shivering at a bus stop a block from the house. He also has fallen several times because of the shuffling gait caused by his Alzheimer's. Jim often becomes frustrated by the seemingly inconsistent and unusual circumstances of his life. For example, he recently accused his wife of hiding his cowboy boots, even though he had not owned a pair of boots for 20 years. Most recently, his wife came home from the grocery store to find the water kettle whistling on the stove while Jim was sitting in the living room with no awareness that he had left the kettle on the stove. Unable to ensure Jim's safety and still tend to her responsibilities, his wife has decided to enroll him in an adult day care program during the week.

Jim's Therapeutic Recreation

The therapeutic recreation specialists who work with Jim at the adult day care program focus on two general goals. The first is to provide him with satisfying activities that allow him the opportunity to exercise as much as possible both his strengths and the skills that his condition impacts. One area that Jim has always excelled in is woodworking. As such, therapeutic recreation specialists provide him with woodworking projects that fit his capabilities and interests. He also participates in painting classes, a men's dinner club, and choir. A second major goal is to help reduce the anxiety and frustration Jim experiences as a result of his disorientation. For example, he participates in various reminiscence-based programs that focus on keeping Jim oriented to his past life, current identity, and understanding of the outside world. These activities reinforce the contributions that Jim has made to his family and society in general. In addition, all staff members implement reality orientation strategies such as regular reminding and environmental prompts to facilitate Jim's understanding of the surrounding world. Finally, the therapeutic recreation program houses a variety of pets (fish, birds, dogs) and maintains a community garden to create a home-like environment that provides various opportunities for mental and physical engagement.

Alternative nursing homes. The founder of Eden Alternative, Dr. William Thomas (1996), defines the movement as "the creation of a human habitat where people thrive, grow and flourish, rather than wither, decay and die." Eden Alternative facilities are as homelike as possible. Animals—cats, dogs, birds, and rabbits—coexist with residents in Eden Alternative facilities. The intent of creating this environment is to reduce the use of medication while increasing the residents' contact with the outside world (Barba, Tesh & Courts, 2002).

Eden Alternative facilities support activity programming that promotes residents' engagement in meaningful pursuits that reflect their lifelong interests. This aspect speaks to the important role of the therapeutic recreation specialist in Eden Alternative facilities. Responsibilities may include assessment of residents' lifelong interests and the planning and implementation of activities that include residents, staff, and family members.

Summary

We began this chapter by considering the older adults in our own lives and the many factors that influence their recreation participation and life satisfaction. Facilitating meaningful engagement in recreation, regardless of the older adult's functional decline or the living environment in which he or she resides, fosters quality of life. Therapeutic recreation specialists possess the unique skills necessary for understanding older adults' lifelong interests and ensuring that they can maintain participation. Such skills are essential to providing quality care in day care programs, assisted-living facilities, and nursing homes.

1. Which of the theories of successful aging would be most useful to a therapeutic recreation specialist who is designing programs in an adult day center? In an assisted-living facility? In a nursing home? Explain.

2. Discuss the challenges facing older adults within each of the three settings reviewed. What actions may a therapeutic recreation specialist engage in to assist residents in overcoming such challenges?

3. Review the modalities presented in chapter 5. Which of these do you believe would be most useful when working with an elder with dementia? Which would be useful in working with a nursing-home resident with no sign of dementia but with multiple physical limitations?

4. Interview an older adult regarding his or her current lifestyle, focusing on the role of recreation participation. Consider which theory of successful aging best fits the person's life experiences.

5. Visit a traditional nursing home and an Eden Alternative nursing home. Describe how the two facilities are different and similar.

6. Observe a therapeutic recreation specialist implementing a dementia practice guideline protocol. How well does the implementation of the protocol support the tenets of the theories of successful aging? Explain.

7. Which of the five theories can help you best as a therapeutic recreation specialist? Explain.

PART

Trends in Therapeutic Recreation

Wellness Through Physical Activity

Sheila Swann-Guerrero, CTRS

National Center on Physical Activity and Disability, Department of Disability and Human Development, University of Illinois at Chicago

Chris Mackey, BS

Recreation and Physical Activity Coordinator, FPG Child Development Institute, University of North Carolina at Chapel Hill

LEARNING OUTCOMES

After completing this chapter, learners will be able to demonstrate the following competencies:

- Understand the importance of physical activity for people with disabilities
- Know how inactivity affects people with disabilities
- Identify the role of therapeutic recreation in health promotion programs
- Know the considerations for using physical activity in therapeutic recreation
- Understand the basics of exercise and disability
- Describe the components of an exercise program
- Realize the importance of accessibility
- Recognize how environmental access affects how people with disabilities participate in physical activity
- Know the exercise considerations for specific disabilities in relation to fitness

In 1979 the United States surgeon general released *Healthy People,* a report that laid out goals and objectives designed to promote healthy living and disease prevention among Americans. The most recent version of this document, *Healthy People 2010,* continues to guide health initiatives in the United States as we have moved into the 21st century. One of the component goals of *Healthy People 2010* is to "promote the health of people with disabilities, prevent **secondary conditions,** and eliminate disparities between people with and without disabilities in the United States population" (Centers for Disease Control and Prevention and the National Institute on Disability and Rehabilitation, n.d.). Therapeutic recreation should be, and often is, directly involved in efforts to achieve this goal. As such, the inclusion of fitness in therapeutic recreation programs and treatment plans is essential to the success of the client and our overall health initiatives. Ultimately, the therapeutic recreation specialist can motivate, educate, and empower people with disabilities to be physically active to the best of their abilities. This chapter focuses on techniques and considerations related to integrating fitness-related goals into the therapeutic recreation process. Such integration can better prepare clients to reach their full potential to live healthy lives.

Whom Do We Work With?

Nearly 60 million people in the United States have a disability. When disability does occur (and it affects everyone at some point in life), the risk of experiencing various threats to health and wellness often increases. For example, arthritis can present an entire array of secondary health conditions. The pain, weakness, and limited mobility associated with arthritis can lead to an increased risk of obesity and diabetes. At the same time, we should recognize that disability and wellness can coexist. As therapeutic recreation specialists, we are often in a position to educate and assist people with disabilities in developing a healthy lifestyle that includes **physical activity** and promotes overall wellness. This element should be part of every therapeutic recreation program, because wellness is an important aspect of every person's life.

Where Are Such Programs Provided?

Earlier chapters of this text discussed common delivery sites for services associated with specific client groups (i.e., orthopedic, mental health, geriatric). This chapter is different in that it focuses on the idea that all recipients of therapeutic recreation services, regardless of disability, have the need for physical activity. As such, therapeutic recreation services that include exercise and physical activity can exist in virtually any setting from physical rehabilitation to home-based services. In addition, such programs should be part of every domain of functioning. For example, people receiving psychiatric care can benefit substantially from physical activity, as can persons with cognitive impairments.

Traditionally, fitness activities are thought of as taking place in designated exercise facilities that provide equipment and space for clients to work out. Therefore, much of the discussion in this chapter refers to the use of exercise equipment that would be located in this type of facility. But remember that physical activity does not require a fitness center, and by no means is it limited to lifting weights or using a treadmill. Walking around the local city park, pushing a wheelchair around the neighborhood, or conducting stretching exercises in one's own living room can all add significantly to a person's level of activity. The point here is that therapeutic recreation specialists must be familiar with general fitness concepts and specific issues associated with disability when implementing programs involving physical activity.

Defining Physical Activity

Health-related activities are likely to incorporate physical activity. The definition of physical activity includes all forms of bodily movement produced by the contractions of skeletal muscles that substantially increase energy expenditure (Caspersen, Powell & Christensen, 1985). The subcategories of physical activity are leisure-time physical activity, planned and structured exercise, household activity, and occupational activity. Although this chapter focuses primarily on the first two subcategories, the presented concepts can be applied to any of the four.

Why Is Physical Activity Important?

Physical activity is an essential component of wellness and a healthy lifestyle, and it is critical to the development of **physical fitness.** The definition of physical fitness is the ability to perform daily activities with vigor and to be at low risk of premature development of the hypokinetic diseases or conditions associated with sedentary behavior (Caspersen, Powell & Christensen, 1985).

People should engage in regular physical activity at a level appropriate to their capacities, needs, and interests for 30 minutes at moderate intensity on most, and preferably all, days of the week (NIH, 1995). Regular physical activity need not be of vigorous intensity for improved health. Health and exercise professionals agree that health benefits are proportional to the amount of activity. Consequently, every increase in activity can have a positive effect on health. This focus on the amount of activity rather than the intensity offers increased options to incorporate physical activity in the daily lives of people with disabilities, who may need the most flexibility (Centers for Disease Control and Prevention, 1996).

Of course, people can obtain greater health benefits by engaging in physical activity of more vigorous intensity or of longer duration, but the U.S. surgeon general hopes that by encouraging people to engage in moderate amounts of activity and to choose activities that they enjoy and are suited to their abilities, more people will include physical activity in their daily lives.

Disability and Inactivity

According to *Healthy People 2010* (U.S. Department of Health and Human Services, 2000), people with disabilities have increased health concerns, including increased risk of developing secondary conditions. Secondary conditions are medical, social, emotional, family, or community problems that a person with a primary disabling condition likely experiences. The likelihood of experiencing these conditions is the reason that physical activity is especially important for persons with disabilities. Secondary conditions vary across disabilities but often include heart disease, hypertension, diabetes, obesity, depression, joint disorders, high cholesterol,

The benefits of getting clients up and moving go beyond the physical—they can be emotional, cognitive, and social as well.

pain, fatigue, and an overall decrease in the ability to conduct activities of daily living (ADLs).

Considerations for Using Physical Activity in Therapeutic Recreation

When introducing people with disabilities to fitness or physical activity, some general rules can be followed to ensure that the participant's experience will be beneficial. People with disabilities should be treated the same as those without disabilities. Avoiding overprotective behavior and allowing people to make their own decisions about what they can and cannot do are critical. This approach will help people develop leisure skills that they can use after participating in a rehabilitation process.

In some cases, particularly in community-based settings, a person with a disability may be accompanied by an assistant, companion, or interpreter. The therapeutic recreation specialist should focus on the person with the disability, not the assistant he or she may have. Whenever possible, speak directly to the person with a disability, even if he or she has an interpreter.

Mobility Disabilities

As with any person who wants to be involved in physical activity, the therapeutic recreation specialist should assess and be aware of the person's ability level. Some people with mobility limitations have difficulties with issues such as balance, muscle **contractures,** and spasticity. A person may take medication or undergo some other treatment to alleviate these symptoms. For example, someone with a spinal cord injury who experiences spasticity may take medication, and a person with cerebral palsy may have muscle contractures that require stretching before exercise begins. In other cases, the therapeutic recreation specialist may have to make adaptations to equipment or the activity. For example, someone with spinal cord injury may need extra padding to use a strength-training machine to prevent skin breakdown or need assistance with transferring onto the machine. In many cases, a person with a disability may experience several or all the aforementioned conditions; therefore, it is important to gather as much information as possible about the person and his or her condition. Obtaining input from and cooperating with other professionals such as exercise physiologists, physical therapists, physicians, or personal trainers will help ensure development of a safe and beneficial physical activity program (North Carolina Office on Disability and Health, 2001).

Cognitive Impairments

Cognitive disabilities occur in many forms, including varying levels of intellectual impairment or learning disabilities. Cognitive disabilities are often not easily noticeable. Usually, conditions in this category affect a person's ability to process information. He or she may also have difficulty with memory or explaining his or her needs. The manner in which the therapeutic recreation specialist works with a person with a cognitive disability is therefore extremely important. Repeating instructions for an activity several times may be necessary if a person has problems with memory. It can also be helpful to model activities or exercises whenever possible and be sure that the client imitates (repeats) the behavior within 30 seconds of the observation (Sherrill, 2004). This method helps reinforce learning and verifies that the client comprehends the directions. Corrections can also be made if clients incorrectly perform the skill.

As with other kinds of disabilities, a person with a cognitive disability may need extra time to complete a task. Instructions should be given only one or two steps at a time, and each step should be specific. When gathering information from someone with a cognitive disability, it may be necessary to ask questions that require brief answers, such as yes or no. Clients should be allowed at least 10 seconds to respond to a question or carry out a requested action before prompting (Sherrill, 2004). This approach helps those who need a bit more time to process information and allows the client maximum opportunity to succeed independently.

Presenting activities in **alternate formats** that are easier for a person with a cognitive disability to understand may be necessary. For instance, rather than telling someone how to stretch properly after warming up, the therapeutic recreation specialist could, as noted earlier, demonstrate the stretches or create flash cards that the person can reference. Always engage the person with a cognitive difficulty in activities that are age appropriate (North Carolina Office on Disability and Health, 2001) and avoid speaking to an adult client as if he or she were a child.

Many people with cognitive disabilities often want to please those around them. In some cases, clients may indicate that they understand a task when they really have not grasped the presented information. With any physical activity, ensuring that the client understands how to perform the task safely is vital to safe and effective participation. Again, understanding a person's disability and seeking outside help if necessary will help create effective and enjoyable physical activities (North Carolina Office on Disability and Health, 2001).

Visual Disabilities

Visual disabilities vary greatly in severity. Such impairments can range from blurred vision (resulting from conditions such as cataracts), to partial sight (some people can detect different levels of light or may be light sensitive), to total blindness. When working with a client with a visual disability, orientation to the environment is essential. If possible, try to keep the layout of the area and the location of equipment consistent. When introducing someone to a new environment or activity, ask the person how he or she would like to be oriented to the environment. The person may want to be led physically around the room or may prefer an oral description of the environment. When describing the environment, use exact directions, such as "You need to walk 100 feet to your right." An alternative is the use of clock cues. For example, an object directly in front of someone is at 12 o'clock, whereas an object directly behind the person is 6 o'clock. To gain a client's attention, say his or her name and do not approach or leave the person without indicating that you are doing so. Finally, many people have service animals that assist them in maneuvering through the environment. When asked to take control of a service animal, ask how to do so and take the dog by the leash rather than the harness that is usually attached. This method indicates to the animal that its owner is not controlling it (North Carolina Office on Disability and Health, 2001).

Hearing Loss or Deafness

As with other conditions, levels of hearing loss will vary. Always ascertain how the person prefers to communicate. Not everyone with hearing loss can read lips. Only about 30% of spoken language is actually visible on the lips, so even those who can read lips may not be receiving all necessary information. Although many deaf people use what is known as American sign language, there are several other forms of communication. Some people may use cued speech or simply prefer a pencil and paper. If an interpreter is present, he or she may stand behind the hearing person or between the hearing person and the deaf person. Always address the client, not the client's interpreter. When speaking with a deaf client, gain their full attention and never cover the mouth, chew gum, or speak while writing a message. Some people may have limited ability to speak. When unable to understand what the person is saying, politely ask the person to say it again (North Carolina Office on Disability and Health, 2001).

Speech Disabilities

In working with people with speech difficulties, patience is important. Such people may need extra time to communicate. Give the client your undivided attention and tell the client if you cannot understand what the client is saying. It may be necessary to ask questions that require brief answers or a gesture such as a head nod. As with persons who are deaf, paper and pencil can facilitate communication with someone with a speech disability. Do not automatically assume that a person with a speech impairment also has a cognitive impairment. Persons with only speech disabilities are cognitively high functioning.

Basics of Exercise and Disability

Persons with disabilities should always have their fitness or ability level for the chosen activity assessed. In many case, therapeutic recreation specialists work with an exercise specialist who may use a battery of tools to set a starting point for the client's program. In any physical activity setting, the typically recommended stages of exercise (warm-up, stretching, activity, and cooldown) apply to persons with disabilities just as they do to persons without disabilities. The same safety considerations also apply. Clients must wear appropriate clothing, be properly hydrated, and refrain from participating if they are sick (if they have a urinary tract infection, for example). If the client experiences any abnormal symptoms such as dizziness, nausea, clammy hands, or shortness of breath, it is important to stop any activity immediately and seek medical assistance. The following factors are important to consider when designing exercise or physical activity programs for persons with disabilities.

- Consult a physician or medical care professional for **precautions** and **contraindications** of medical conditions, medications, and exercise.

- Know the person's medical history and current health status.

- Check the person's **blood pressure**—supine, resting, seated, and standing.

- Determine the client's range of motion and the effects of conditions such as arthritis, spasticity, contractures, **hypotonia,** and **hypertonia.**

- Find out if the client is taking medications that can affect exercise, such as beta-blockers or **seizure** medications.

- Remember that emotional and behavioral status can affect participation.

- Get opinions and recommendations from the client's health care professionals.

- Keep in mind that ability may determine the level of activity or participation.

- Use, when appropriate, a **rating of perceived exertion (RPE)**—a subjective rating by the person exercising (people with cognitive conditions may not be able to use this scale).

Components of Exercise

The three most commonly targeted components of exercise are cardiovascular exercise, strength training, and flexibility. **Cardiovascular exercise** is essential to maintaining a healthy heart and having endurance to perform activities of daily living. **Strength training** maintains or improves skeletal muscle strength and endurance. **Flexibility** helps maintain or improve range of motion and avoid spasticity and contractures. The following sections present guidelines relevant to each exercise component.

Cardiovascular

For activities involving cardiovascular exercise, clients should exercise at a pace that feels good but still provides some cardiovascular benefit. The conversation rule can be used to determine whether a client is overexerting himself or herself. If the person exercising cannot carry on a normal conversation during the workout, the person should rest. The client should use slow, deep breathing when exercising. Persuading someone with a disability to become involved in cardiovascular exercise will often require the therapeutic recreation specialist to be creative and open to alternative methods of exercising. Activities such as walking, cycling, using an ergometer, pushing a wheelchair, or swimming can be beneficial. Activity should also be incorporated into the client's average day. Using time such as coffee or lunch breaks, or even during TV commercials, for cardio activity can be beneficial if done properly (Rimmer, 2005a).

Strength

As with cardiovascular exercise, proper breathing is important when performing strength exercises. Clients should not hold their breath while train-

Aerobic activity is very beneficial to the overall health of the client.

ing because doing so can cause lightheadedness or dizziness and can stress the heart. They should exhale while moving against resistance and inhale while letting the weight down. Maintaining good posture is also essential (they should think tall). Each movement should be performed through a complete range of motion (Rimmer, 2005b).

Keep in mind that strength training can focus on muscular endurance or strength. To improve endurance, the client can use a lighter weight and perform at least 8 to 12 repetitions. For improving strength, the client can use a heavier weight and do fewer, perhaps 5 to 8, repetitions. Again, creativity is often necessary when working on strength training for persons with disabilities. Weight machines with swing-away or removable seats, free weights such as dumbbells or barbells, **elastic tubing,** or medicine balls are all effective strength-training tools. Whatever the situation, always consider alternatives. What works for one client may not work for another (Rimmer, 2005b).

Flexibility

Flexibility training, designed to improve a person's range of motion, balance, and coordination, should be incorporated before and after the workout routine. Any muscle group used during a workout should be stretched before and after the workout. A good rule is to hold stretches for at least 10 seconds and progress slowly. Stretching should never be painful for anyone. Certain activities, such as yoga, Pilates, and tai chi, can also improve a person's flexibility (Rimmer, 2005b). Always be cautious with people who have hypotonia, or low muscle tone, because flexibility exercises can lead to further loosening of the joints and cause injury.

Accessibility

Regardless of the setting, environmental access is important when people with disabilities participate in physical activity. When the client's goal involves use of a typical fitness gym, specific accessibility factors should be considered. Ensuring that usable equipment is available is a vital step. Some weight machines have a swing-away or removable seat that allows a person in a wheelchair to use them. Wider seats are easier to use for someone with limited balance, and simple Velcro straps can provide additional support. Different kinds of gloves or mitts can be used to assist in gripping handles. With machines that use cables, Velcro cuffs can serve as an alternative to traditional grips or handles. It is important that the client matches the piece of equipment that he or she would like to use. It may be necessary to hold limbs that are not being used in place and ensure that any pedals or footrests can be reached or secured to the client's feet. Finally, a good way to assess whether a machine is potentially beneficial for the client is to determine whether he or she can perform one repetition of the exercise and still receive benefit (North Carolina Office on Disability and Health, 2001).

In many environments, weight machines are not readily available, so alternatives are essential. Different kinds of elastic bands offer an inexpensive and portable way to engage in strength training. In addition, low-weight free weights or small weights that can be wrapped around the wrists are useful. When addressing cardiovascular fitness in a typical fitness gym, machines called ergometers are a viable option for almost anyone. These machines are basically stationary bikes for the arms or both the arms and legs (North Carolina Office on Disability and Health, 2001).

Alternative types of activities can improve the fitness level of a person with a disability, and they are more readily available in many cases. Besides offering excellent cardiovascular benefits, aquatic activities provide greater freedom of movement than land exercise does. Clients can benefit from simply walking or wheeling around their neighborhoods regularly. Activities such as gardening or using a seated aerobics video are excellent choices for those who choose to remain at home. Seated or standing yoga, tai chi, and martial arts are becoming more popular and help improve flexibility and reduce stress (North Carolina Office on Disability and Health, 2001).

Disability-Specific Recommendations

Regular physical activity helps improve fitness, functional independence, and quality of life, yet when developing a safe and effective exercise plan for clients or participants who have a disability, therapeutic recreation specialists must be knowledgeable about the specific considerations for the disability.

Each disability has conditions that are affected by exercise. Some conditions associated with

BARB SACCO

Background Information

Education

BS in Recreation Leadership from the Department of Health, Physical Education, and Recreation at University of Wisconsin-La Crosse

Credentials

CTRS

Special Affiliations

*Therapeutic Recreation Association of Greater St. Louis *American Therapeutic Recreation Association

Career Information

Position

Director of Recreational Therapy and Child Life at Shriners Hospital for Children in St. Louis, Missouri

Organization Information

Twenty-two Shriners Hospitals for Children in North America provide care, at no cost, to children from newborn to 18 years of age with orthopedic conditions and burn and spinal cord injuries.

Organization's Mission

The Shriners Hospitals work to provide the highest-quality care, without cost, to children within a compassionate, family-centered, and collaborative care environment; to provide for the education of physicians and other health care professionals; and to conduct research to discover new knowledge that improves the quality of care and life for our children and families.

Job Description

Organize, direct, and assist with the delivery of medically directed therapeutic recreation/child life programs for inpatients and outpatients. Interview, hire, supervise, and evaluate all recreational therapists, child life specialists, and hospital teachers. Develop and manage budgets for the Patient Education and RT/Child Life departments. Work as a member/chairman of Performance Improvement teams to continuously improve services. Write and update policies and procedures that ensure compliance with JCAHO and Health Department standards. Oversee the hospital school program as well as specialty camps and retreats for our patients that are designed to foster independence, improve social skills, and transition to adulthood.

Career Path

I worked four summers during college for the Beaver Dam, Wisconsin, Park and Recreation Department planning and implementing programs on the city's playgrounds. Then I supervised the Manitowoc, Wisconsin, Parks and Recreation summer playground programs for a year before working as the Manitowoc-Two Rivers YMCA program director and summer camp coordinator for two years. In 1975, I moved to Missouri to begin working as director of Recreational Therapy at Shriners Hospitals for Children.

Likes and Dislikes About the Job

I enjoy helping make a difference in the quality of life of the children we serve. I like the way our child life specialists and recreational therapists work together to meet the social and emotional needs of our hospitalized children. I dislike the increasing amount of paperwork required.

Advice to Undergraduate Students

Get as much experience as you can by working or volunteering with various populations and leisure agencies. You never know which setting will ignite your passion. It may surprise you! Though you may not get rich, the rewards are endless! Working in therapeutic recreation was the best decision I ever made.

> One hundred years from now it will not matter what my bank account was, the sort of house I lived in, or the kind of car I drove...but the world may be different because I was important in the life of a child.

disability require monitoring of blood pressure, whereas others require awareness of impaired **thermoregulation,** reduced exercise intensity, or behavioral strategies. Being aware of the client's disability-related conditions is a primary responsibility when integrating physical activity into the therapeutic recreation process. The following considerations relate to specific disabilities and are general guidelines for developing fitness plans for clients.

Spinal Cord Injury

Spinal cord injury is a partial or complete impairment of the spinal cord that results in a loss of sensation and motor function. The loss of function is at the point of injury to the spinal cord and below. The injury can be a complete separation or an incomplete or partial separation. Depending on the location of the injury to the spinal cord, the injury is classified into one of two categories: paraplegia, which occurs at the T2 (thoracic) and below and affects the trunk and lower extremities, or quadriplegia, also known as tetraplegia, which occurs at the T1 (thoracic) level or above and affects the upper and lower body, including all four extremities. The National Spinal Cord Injury Association (NSCIA) reports that 47% of spinal cord injuries are paraplegia and 53% are quadriplegia or tetraplegia.

CONSIDERATIONS DURING EXERCISE: SPINAL CORD INJURY

Spinal cord injury can affect both maximum heart rate and advisable levels of training intensity. The maximum heart rate for people with quadriplegia does not exceed 130 and typically falls within a range of 110 to 130 (Durstine & Moore, 2003b). Training intensity should be between 50% and 70% of maximum heart rate (MHR). The heart rate is typically regular for a person with a T7 injury and below, but consulting a physician on this matter is advisable before initiating a physical activity program.

Spasticity is an involuntary increase in muscle tone that shortens and weakens muscle groups. This condition may develop in people with SCI and usually occurs in the muscles below the level of injury. Spasticity can be exacerbated by physical exercise, cold conditions, and urinary tract infection. To reduce pain, injury, and contractures, a person with spasticity should stretch spastic muscle groups and incorporate flexibility exercises.

Autonomic dysreflexia (AD) is a condition of extreme hypertension caused by an exaggerated autonomic nervous system response to a noxious stimulus. AD is experienced by 60% to 80% of people with an SCI of T6 or higher, can be life threatening, and requires immediate medical attention. To prevent AD, the bladder should be emptied before exercise. Other precautions include checking for regularity of bowel movement, periodically checking blood pressure, and checking for skin trauma during transfers. Inducing AD to improve exercise performance, known as boosting, can be fatal. For example, athletes have used methods such as sitting on a thumbtack to induce AD.

Orthostatic hypotension is a decrease or drop in blood pressure because of the pooling of blood in the lower extremities and abdominal area. Paralyzed leg muscles are unable to pump blood back to the heart, resulting in decreased blood flow to the brain. Discouraging quick movements, providing sufficient time for people to move from supine to upright positions, encouraging hydration, and having people use compression stockings and an abdominal binder can help prevent orthostatic hypotension. Blood pressure should be monitored during exercise if participants are at risk of experiencing this condition.

Impaired thermoregulation, or regulation of body temperature, is another common challenge among individuals with SCIs. Therapeutic recreation specialists should be sure to monitor external temperature, provide fans and water in warm environments, and ensure that clients wear extra clothing in cool areas.

Loss of bladder and bowel function occurs in people with lesions above the S2 (sacral) level. They should empty their bladders or urinary bags before exercise.

Pressure ulcers that cause damage to the skin and possible underlying tissues may result from prolonged pressure on bony weight-bearing areas of the body, such as the sacrum, coccyx, hips, and ankles, or excessive sweating or pressure on an area of the body during a fall. Relieving pressure and regularly checking skin to avoid skin breakdown are essential, especially when participation in physical activity can increase pressure. Prevention of pressure ulcers is especially important because of the slow healing that accompanies poor circulation and the additional risk of infection.

Spina Bifida

Spina bifida, the most common neural tube defect in the United States, is the second-leading cause of orthopedic impairments in children. The condition results from incomplete development of the brain, spinal cord, or meninges, which is the protective covering around the brain and spinal cord. This defect occurs during the first month of gestation development when closure of the spinal column is incomplete, resulting in spinal cord damage. The level and exposure of the spinal cord will determine the severity of injury. The nerves below the injury will be affected.

There are three types of spina bifida: occulta, meningocele, and myelomeningocele. Occulta, the mildest and most common type of SB, seldom results in a disability. Meningocele occurs when the meninges protrude from the spinal opening. Myelomeningocele, the most severe, occurs when the spinal cord is exposed, resulting in partial or complete **paralysis** below the spinal exposure. Low-level paralysis or paraplegia may occur, affecting mobility. **Hydrocephalus,** an accumulation of cerebral spinal fluid, is common in myelomeningocele. A **shunt** is usually used to drain the fluid. People with myelomeningocele and hydrocephalus may have learning disabilities, partial paralysis, bowel and bladder dysfunction, latex allergy, and emotional and sexual concerns, such as precocious puberty (or early onset of puberty), depression, and decreased bone length growth (Winnick, 2005a).

CONSIDERATIONS FOR EXERCISE: SPINA BIFIDA

Considerations during exercise for people with spina bifida are similar to those for people with a spinal cord injury, with the additional consideration that a surgically implanted device, referred to as a shunt, may be used to drain cerebral spinal fluid. The client must be careful to avoid trauma to the shunt, and the therapeutic recreation specialist must be sure that the client's physician has approved any plan for physical activity. Also, **scoliosis,** or curving of the spine, is common among those with spina bifida. Therapeutic recreation specialists should determine the physical limitations associated with this condition. Recent surgeries or the placement of rods in the spinal area may limit activity and, in general, trauma to the back should be avoided. Finally, latex allergies commonly coexist with spina bifida. Therefore, elastic exercise bands and other equipment should be latex free.

Amputation

Amputation is the removal or absence of an extremity because of diabetes, vascular disease, trauma, cancer, infection, or other cause. Malformation and congenital absence of limbs are referred to as limb differences. The three major categories of amputation are above-the-knee amputations, below-the-knee amputations, and other amputations. People of all ages have amputations, yet there is an increased prevalence of amputations among people over 65 years of age.

Phantom pain, or the feeling that the amputated limb is still present, is experienced in the amputated limb shortly after the amputation and is usually temporary. A prosthesis, or artificial limb designed by a **prosthetist** is fitted to the amputated extremities when healing is complete. Proper care of the amputation site and sock is extremely important in preventing infection and the occurrence of additional problems (National Center on Physical Activity and Disability [NCPAD], 2005a).

CONSIDERATIONS DURING EXERCISE: AMPUTATION

Amputation can affect both movement and balance. Modern technology has provided a great variety of prosthetic devices designed specifically for physical activities. In general, the prosthesis needs to be comfortable and appropriate to the activity of choice. After an appropriate device has been acquired, the therapeutic recreation program can address stabilization and maintenance.

As with spinal cord injuries, pressure sores and skin care are a primary concern. This issue can be in reference to the use of a prosthetic device or a wheelchair. Some people with lower-limb amputations may use a wheelchair as their primary means of ambulation.

Stroke

The National Center for Health Statistics reports that stroke is the third-leading cause of death in the United States. Also called the cerebrovascular accident (CVA), or "brain attack," stroke is a sudden disruption of blood supply to the brain by a blood clot or hemorrhage. The location and severity of the stroke determine what functions are affected and to what degree they are impaired. Impairments can include diminished motor and sensory function in one extremity (monoparesis) or both extremities on one side (hemiparesis or hemiplegia), communication, swallowing, vision, emotion, and cognition (including memory loss and judgment).

CONSIDERATIONS DURING EXERCISE: STROKE

A medical examination by a physician is highly recommended to ensure that the heart is capable of exertion. The physician should approve the client's exercise program before it is implemented. **Hypertension** (high blood pressure) is a major risk factor for stroke and an important consideration when working with those who have had strokes in the past. Blood pressure should be monitored periodically throughout exercise. If blood pressure is above 200/110 mmHg, the client should stop exercising. Checking blood pressure also allows the professional to evaluate for orthostatic hypotension (NCPAD, 2005b).

Effects on movement can include a **paresis** or paralysis of two or all four extremities depending on the location and severity of injury. Impairments in motor control, coordination, and range of motion may also be present. Balance can also be affected for both sitting and standing positions.

Speech and language can be affected depending on the location of injury in the brain. Aphasia, or the inability to speak, comprehend, read, or write, and expressive **apraxia**, the inability to perform common expressive gestures on request, may occur. As such, alternative forms of communication may be necessary during activity.

Acquired Brain Injury

Each year, 1.9 million Americans acquire a brain injury. Acquired brain injury is damage to the brain after birth. The brain injury can be either a closed head injury or an open head injury that impairs normal brain function. Brain injury may result from a variety of causes, including strokes, brain tumors, loss of oxygen, neurological diseases, vehicular accidents, falls, violence, and shaken baby syndrome. Brain injury can range from mild to severe depending on location and severity. Impairments can affect cognition with decreased attention span; memory loss; processing and judgment problems; perceptual impairments with vision, hearing, and balance; irritable behavior; heightened or flattened emotional states; aggression and decreased tolerance; and physical impairments including headache, fatigue, spasticity, seizure, photosensitivity, sleep problems, motor planning difficulties, paresis, paralysis, and speech impairment (Winnick, 2005b).

CONSIDERATIONS DURING EXERCISE: ACQUIRED BRAIN INJURY

Considerations associated with acquired brain injury are similar to those for people who have had a stroke. Both conditions can affect virtually every aspect of functioning, but the consequences of an acquired brain injury are less predictable because of the uniqueness of each injury. One important consideration is the risk of seizure following an acquired brain injury. Appropriate adaptations should be made for people who experience seizures, including head protection when participating in physical activities and life vests when swimming. Knowledge of what stimuli tend to trigger seizures for a particular client is also valuable information for the therapeutic recreation professional.

Brain injuries can result in mood swings, depression, anxiety, apathy, or difficulty controlling emotional status. Outbursts of anger, periods of uncontrollable crying, or sexual dysfunction may occur (NCPAD, 2005c). Medications prescribed for seizure control or mood altering may have side effects that affect exercising.

Multiple Sclerosis

Approximately 400,000 Americans have multiple sclerosis (MS), and most of them are women. According to the National Multiple Sclerosis Association, MS is an autoimmune disease that affects the central nervous system (CNS), which includes the brain, spinal cord, and optic nerve. MS is a **demyelinating disease** that affects the myelin sheath of nerves. This sheath insulates the neural pathways and allows them to conduct impulses or signals to and from the brain. Multiple sclerosis is usually diagnosed between the ages of 20 and 50, yet may be diagnosed at younger ages (National Multiple Sclerosis Society, 2005).

There are four types of MS. Relapsing-remitting MS is characterized by **exacerbations** followed by partial or complete recovery. This type makes up 85% of cases of MS. Primary progressive MS, characterized by continuous worsening of the disease, makes up 10% of cases. Secondary progressive MS is characterized by an initial period of relapsing-remitting MS and a steady worsening of the disease that may or may not have flare-ups or remissions. Progressive relapsing MS includes a steady worsening of the disease from the onset with or without recovery between relapses. Progressive relapsing MS accounts for about 5% of MS cases.

CONSIDERATIONS DURING EXERCISE: MULTIPLE SCLEROSIS

Cardiovascular dysautonomia is a dysfunction of the autonomic nervous system (ANS) that causes blunted heart rate and reduced blood pressure. Blood pressure and heart rate may need to be monitored, and intensity may need to be reduced during exercise.

Profound fatigue and motor fatigue may also result from continual or intense physical activity for those with MS. Also common is a decrease in heat tolerance, which may result in further fatigue. Medications can further exacerbate fatigue and strength limitations (NCPAD, 2005d).

Movement can be affected by tight muscle groups, especially hip flexors, hamstrings, calf, and chest. Ambulation may be impaired, affecting mobility. Muscle weakness begins in the lower extremities and moves upward. This condition can include paresis and paralysis. Problems with balance and coordination increase the risk of falls. Optic neuritis can occur with painful blurring or loss of vision. Related conditions include systagnus, which is rapid movement of the eyeballs, and strabismus, a condition in which the eyes are not properly aligned with each other. Abnormal sensations of numbness, tingling, and pain, which may be asymmetrical or symmetrical, may be present.

Muscular Dystrophy

Muscular dystrophy (MD) is a group of hereditary diseases characterized by progressive degeneration of the skeletal or voluntary muscles. Muscular dystrophy affects males at a higher rate than it does females; 8 out of 10 people affected are males. The most common characteristic is progressive loss of strength, which leads to decreased functioning. The development of this disorder depends on the type of muscular dystrophy involved. Earlier symptoms generally lead to more rapid progression. The nine forms of muscular dystrophy are Duchenne, Becker, Emery-Dreifuss, limb-girdle, facioscapulohumeral, myotonic, oculopharyngeal distal, and congenital (Muscular Dystrophy Association, 2005). Duchenne, facioscapulohumeral, and limb-girdle types are the three most common forms of muscular dystrophies (Paulsen-Hughes & Sherrill, 2004). Each of these progresses differently, but all involve progressive muscle weakness resulting from changes to the muscle fibers.

CONSIDERATIONS DURING EXERCISE: MUSCULAR DYSTROPHY

A variety of symptoms associated with MD can affect the client's ability to participate in physical activity. These symptoms include muscle tightness (spasticity), involuntary movements, ambulation impairments, and balance and coordination impairment. Exercise in general can help slow the progression of the incapacitating aspects of MD and can play an important role in maintaining quality of life (Paulsen-Hughes & Sherrill, 2004). For example, stretching can significantly reduce contractures of the Achilles tendon among children with Duchenne MD (the most common and severe type). Limiting contractures is especially important with this condition, which eventually leads to spending more time in a wheelchair or a bed. Distortions of the chest wall, kyphoscoliosis, and respiratory problems commonly develop after the child becomes a wheelchair user (Paulsen-Hughes & Sherrill). As such, breathing exercises and stretching become extremely important.

Cerebral Palsy

Cerebral palsy, a nonprogressive group of conditions that affect muscle control and coordination, is caused by damage to the brain in the area that controls motor function. Cerebral palsy can occur before or during birth (90% of cases) or after birth up to 3 years of age (10% of cases) (Sherrill, 2004). Type and degree of cerebral palsy depend on the location and extent of the injury. Impairments include muscle spasticity, mobility problems, involuntary movements, reflex development, speech impairments, vision impairments, hearing seizures, bowel and bladder problems, and cognition impairments.

The four types of cerebral palsy are spastic with a high degree of muscle tone (70% to 80% of cases), athetoid with uncontrolled flailing movements (10% to 20%), ataxia with balance and coordination impairments (10%), and mixed with a combination of types.

CONSIDERATIONS DURING EXERCISE: CEREBRAL PALSY

Depending on the type and severity of cerebral palsy (CP), movement and motor conditions may include monoplegia, hemiplegia, diplegia, paraplegia, quadriplegia, and primitive reflexes and coordination of movements (NCPAD, 2005e). Delayed motor development may cause muscle tightness (spasticity), involuntary movements, ambulation balance impairments, and coordination impairments. CP is manifested differently from person to person. Therefore, considerations and adaptations for participation in physical activity are numerous and diverse in nature. Because CP is the result of a brain injury at or around the time of birth, virtually any aspect of function can be affected.

Exercise is important to optimal development and maintenance of balance and motor skills, specifically for people who have ataxic cerebral palsy (NCPAD, 2005e). Stretching tight (spastic) muscle groups and incorporating flexibility exercises are helpful in reducing pain, injury, and contractures. If scoliosis is present, the person may have problems with breathing (NCPAD). People with CP may range from normal intelligence to intellectual disability, but therapeutic recreation professionals must not confuse speech difficulty with intellectual impairment. Seizures are common among people with cerebral palsy. As such, previously mentioned precautions should be taken to avoid dangerous falls and further injury during activity. Common preventative measures include use of helmets, soft exercise surfaces, and special precautions during water activities. Temperature extremes such as cold pool water, stress, and flashing lights are common seizure triggers that might be present during physical activities. Being aware of the client's seizure history and the environmental factors that might exacerbate seizures is important. Sherrill (2004) notes that cerebral palsy is estimated to coexist with intellectual impairment between 30% and 70% of the time. These estimates vary widely, but they suggest that the following section on intellectual disability may be relevant to those who work with persons with cerebral palsy.

Intellectual Disability

Intellectual disabilities (ID) are the most common developmental disability in the United States. Intellectual disabilities occur before age 18 and include a significant limitation in intellectual functioning (IQ below 70) and adaptive behavior (AAMR, 1992). The causes of intellectual disabilities are varied and include chromosomal abnormality, alcohol or drug use during pregnancy, prematurity, malnutrition, childhood diseases that affect the brain, environ-

mental factors, and others. Down syndrome, fetal alcohol syndrome, and fragile X syndrome are the three major known causes.

CONSIDERATIONS DURING EXERCISE: INTELLECTUAL DISABILITIES

Impairments in memory, learning, and processing information are common among people with intellectual disabilities. The therapeutic recreation specialist must therefore adapt the information presented and the method of teaching to meet the intellectual needs of the client. Repetition, modeling, reward systems (without food), and appropriate pace of speech are useful tools. **Shaping** and **chaining** are also useful strategies for maximizing independence in physical activities. These techniques teach small parts or simplified versions of a behavior with each lesson building on (chaining) or slightly modifying (shaping) the previously taught information. For example, chaining could be used to teach the client to move independently through a series of machine exercises. The therapeutic recreation specialist may teach the proper use of a new machine each week, allowing the workout to become progressively more complex. For additional information on shaping and chaining as well as other behavior modification techniques, refer to chapter 10 of this text and chapter 7 of Sherrill (2004).

Besides the expected intellectual limitations, several physical considerations are important. Congenital heart conditions commonly coexist with Down syndrome (in up to 40% of people), and the **maximal heart rate** for people with intellectual disability is 8% to 20% lower than expected (Durstine & Moore, 2003a). A health care provider should be consulted to determine appropriate levels of activity for such individuals.

Hypotonia, or low muscle tone; hypermobility of the joints; and poor muscle strength may also occur (Durstine & Moore, 2003a). Flexibility exercises can lead to further loosening of the joints and cause injury among those with hypotonia. Likewise, **atlantoaxial instability,** or a loose ligament between cervical vertebrae C1 and C2, is present in 17% of Down syndrome cases. This condition can lead to slippage of cervical alignment during certain physical activities or movements, resulting in spinal cord injury (Durstine & Moore). If this condition is present, the therapeutic recreation specialist should avoid design programs that include diving, butterfly swim stroke, squat lifting, high jump, contact sports, horseback riding, gymnastics, and alpine skiing. In fact, a medical care provider should clear participants with Down syndrome before they participate in any activity program that presents the possibility of stress and injury to the C1–C2 region.

Autism

Autism is a spectrum of conditions of neurobiological origin with no known cause. It appears to be inheritable (Bailey et al., 2005). Autism is the most common of the five pervasive developmental disorders (PDD). The other four are Rett's disorder, child disintegrative disorder, Asperger's disorder, and pervasive developmental disorder not otherwise specified (PDD NOS).

Difficulties are present in both verbal and nonverbal communication, limited or absent initiation or reciprocal interaction in social situations, restrictive range of play and interests, and repetitive behaviors. Impairments range from mild to severe, and one area of development can be mild while another area may be severely impaired. No two children are alike. Autism is generally evident by age 3 (American Psychiatric Association, 2000).

CONSIDERATIONS DURING EXERCISE: AUTISM

Autism presents a broad range of severity; therefore, a single set of guidelines is difficult to establish. We can safely say that people with autism typically have significant social impairment. As such, they commonly display behaviors of rigidness, solitary play, difficulty socializing with others, and self-stimulating behaviors such as repetitive spinning, rocking, and hand flapping (American Psychiatric Association, 2000). Communication ranges from verbal to nonverbal and may include difficulty expressing needs, impairments in initiating and maintaining conversations, and repetitive use of language (**echolalia**).

CLIENT PORTRAIT

ALLANAH

Allanah is an 18-year-old woman who has Down syndrome. Allanah is friendly and has a great sense of humor. She enjoys watching comedy shows, listening to music, and being with other people, yet she has significant trouble staying on task because of a reduced attention span. She is moderately overweight and has never been involved in athletics or a structured physical activity program. She likes walking and having fun in the water but does not initiate exercise and does not know how to set up a physical activity plan. Allanah's family is concerned that she does not participate in any regular physical activity, has limited motivation to exercise, and has gained weight. They would like Allanah to learn how to be physically active at home and in the community. Allanah registered for a local park district therapeutic recreation program.

Allanah's Therapeutic Recreation Program

The therapeutic recreation specialist assessed Allanah's needs, abilities, and interests. Together they developed a physical activity plan that incorporated what Allanah enjoys, what physical activities she needs to do to gain health benefits such as reducing her weight and increasing her strength, what activities she needs to avoid because of Down syndrome, what tools she can use to track her physical activity, what she can do to stay motivated, and what rules she needs to abide by as an adult member of a fitness center.

Before Allanah began the physical activity plan, her physician examined her. Because Down syndrome can present concerns such as hypotonia, hypermobility of the joints, atlantoaxial instability, reduced heart rate, and lower muscle strength, the physical was important. After reviewing results of the physical, the therapeutic recreation specialist learned that Allanah has hypotonia and hypermobility of her joints and atlantoaxial instability. Flexibility exercises were contraindicated. Before beginning the program with Allanah, the therapeutic recreation specialist reviewed the potential physical activity plan with an exercise physiologist in her department to be sure that the recommended exercises did not increase the risk of injury.

Allanah's Physical Activity Plan

Allanah's plan is presented in table 13.1. Note the use of relevant supports, as well as avoidance of activities that may exacerbate the hypermobility of joints (avoiding the use of unstable balance equipment).

Table 13.1 Sample Physical Activity Plan (see client portrait)

Exercise type	Activities	Tools	Frequency
Cardiovascular	• Walking in neighborhood, on a treadmill, or on a track • Water walking or aquatic exercise	• Pedometer to track steps each day • Simple tracking log to record steps each day • Exercise buddy • Music to listen to while exercising	• 20- to 60-minute session • 5–7 days per week
Strength	• Weight machines in fitness center	• Picture flash cards that show the before, middle, and completion of exercise positions • Staff to teach how to adjust weight and height of machines • Supervision and monitoring	• Three sets of 8–12 repetitions (with supervision) • 2–3 days per week
Flexibility	• None recommended		
Balance	• Standing on one foot using a chair or stationary object for support if needed	• Balance equipment, such as inflatable domes, pods, or cushions, not recommended	• Consult National Center on Physical Activity and Disability staff or fact sheet • 2–3 days per week
Collateral skills	• Proper hydration during exercise • Following rules of fitness center (wiping down machines and so on) • Transportation to and from fitness center	• CTRS to teach skills initially • Assistance from exercise buddy as needed	• To be determined

Therapeutic recreation specialists who conduct activities with this population should be aware of several factors. For example, response to auditory stimulus can be low despite adequate hearing. Difficulties with **sensory integration** (the process by which the brain organizes and interprets sensory information) are common. Hypoactive or hyperactive responses occur to the five basic senses—sound, touch, taste, vision, and smell—as well as to the proprioceptive and vestibular systems. Modification of the environment may be needed to limit distraction and stimuli that can cause sensory overload. The client may also experience seizures. Muscle tone may be low. Gross and fine motor skills may be impaired, although fine motor skills are more affected. Motor planning difficulties may be present. Because of communication impairments, sensory processing deficits, and difficulty understanding social interactions, people with autism may display difficult behaviors.

Working closely with the client's care providers is critical to success in providing activity programs to individuals with autism. Each client possesses unique tendencies and abilities, and each will react differently to certain stimuli.

A model physical activity or recreation plan (NCPAD, 2005f) for people with autism would include activities and exercises that

- are of interest and fun to the individual;
- work on core muscle strength;
- use the large-muscle groups and provide continuous motion, such as climbing, jumping, and running for children;
- include aquatics activities when appropriate, to provide sensory motor exercise, such as swimming, which can offer deep pressure for those who may need that type of sensory stimulation;
- build on the individual's strengths, such as martial arts, which offer the visual cues of the instructor's modeling of movement or forms;
- promote positive experiences that a person will want to repeat;
- develop lifelong leisure and physical activity skills; and
- are well organized because unstructured time and waiting are usually difficult.

These activities can be incorporated into the daily routine:

- Walking, jogging, bike riding, or other physical activity in the morning, when possible, allows for a good start to the day.
- Jumping, pushing, swinging, and stretching can be calming and assist with refocusing during the day.
- Yoga, used for calming and relaxing, can be incorporated as soothing activities before or after transition times when appropriate.
- Sports can provide excellent opportunities for incorporating physical and social activities.

Prader Willi Syndrome

Prader Willi syndrome is an uncommon genetic disorder of chromosome 15 that affects both males and females and all races. It is inherited in only 2% or less of cases. Prader Willi syndrome is difficult to diagnose in infants. Characteristics include specific facial features, hypotonia, lethargy, delayed development, incomplete genital development, and special feeding techniques. As development continues, short stature, small hands and feet, central nervous system dysfunction, and poor muscle strength become evident, as well as an insatiable drive for food, which begins before age 6. Impair-

ment in the hypothalamus may also occur (Prader Willi Syndrome Association, 2005).

CONSIDERATIONS DURING EXERCISE: PRADER WILLI SYNDROME

One of the unique characteristics of Prader Willi syndrome is an uncontrollable and persistent physiological urge to eat that results in food sneaking and stealing. Compulsive and obsessive eating begins between 2 and 4 years of age. Behaviors related to getting more food are common. Food supplies must be consistently monitored and secured, especially in long-stay or residential programs such as camps. Food sneaking and stealing are common among people with Prader Willi syndrome.

Controlling the urge to eat is complicated by the intellectual challenges associated with the syndrome. Because people with Prader Willi syndrome often exhibit a range of mild to moderate intellectual impairment, and those with average intelligence often have learning disabilities, adaptations pertaining to attention span, short-term auditory memory, and capacity for abstract thinking may be necessary. In addition, the typical considerations for working with a person with intellectual disabilities should be addressed (such as hypotonia). Difficult behaviors of rigidity, opposition, manipulation, and stubbornness develop with age and continue through adolescence. Depression is extremely common.

Cardiovascular activity for 30 minutes or more a day is useful in controlling weight, and the activity can decrease depression and improve behavior. Strategies for behavior management and food-related behaviors need to be developed based on the client's behavioral tendencies, and appropriate supervision is essential during all activity. For additional recommendations related to working with people with intellectual impairment, autism, Prader Willi syndrome, or other cognitive (intellectual) disabilities, refer back to the section in this chapter on cognitive impairments (page 202) and to chapter 9.

Summary

Therapeutic recreation specialists can have a positive effect on the health of people with disabilities by incorporating physical activity into their treatment plans, programs, and services. People with disabilities are at increased risk of developing secondary conditions that can compromise their functioning and independence. Therapeutic recreation specialists need to know how to provide safe, effective physical activity programs for people with disabilities to reduce their risk of developing secondary conditions and encourage them to live healthy leisure lifestyles.

Knowledge of disability is central to therapeutic recreation, yet therapeutic recreation specialists must also understand how to design a fitness program and how to develop and adapt exercise for individuals with disabilities. This chapter has discussed techniques and considerations related to integrating physical activity into the therapeutic recreation process. Therapeutic recreation specialists should always seek to collaborate with other health care professionals, such as physicians, exercise physiologists, or physical therapists, when developing a fitness plan for clients or participants.

DISCUSSION QUESTIONS

1. Discuss how the contents of this chapter relate to the health initiative in the United States.

2. How do therapeutic recreation specialists affect the wellness of people with disabilities?

3. Where does physical activity occur?

4. How can clients be physically active other than in a fitness center?

5. Based on this chapter, how would you define physical activity and physical fitness?

6. What is the recommended level of physical activity?

7. Define and give examples of secondary conditions.

8. List a few general rules to follow when introducing physical activity to a person with a mobility disability, a person with cognitive impairment, a person with a visual disability, a person with hearing loss or deafness, and a person with a speech disability.

9. Describe the recommended stages or components of exercise.

10. What are the safety considerations when designing exercise or physical activity programs for people with disabilities?

11. How does the environment affect participation in physical activity for people with disabilities?

12. What are some alternatives to exercise machines in a typical fitness center?

13. How is the maximum heart rate affected in people who have tetraplegia?

14. What precautions should be taken when a client has a shunt? Orthostatic hypotension? Autonomic dysreflexia?

15. What are two consequences associated with amputation?

16. What is a major risk factor for stroke that is important to address in any exercise program?

DISCUSSION QUESTIONS CONTINUED

17. What symptoms can result from intense physical activity in people who have multiple sclerosis?

18. Why is stretching important for people who have muscular dystrophy? Cerebral palsy?

19. List three considerations when working with people who have an intellectual disability.

20. What exercises need to be avoided if a person has atlantoaxial instability?

21. What three areas are affected for people who have autism?

22. How can sensory overload be avoided for people who have autism?

23. Why is it important to incorporate cardiovascular activity for people who have Prader Willi syndrome?

Demographics, Economics, Politics, and Legislation

John McGovern, JD

Executive Director, Northern
Suburban Special Recreation
Association, Northbrook, Illinois

LEARNING OUTCOMES

After completing this chapter, learners will be able to demonstrate the following competencies:

- Describe the basic demographics of Americans with disabilities
- Explain the components of the legislative process
- Identify specific strategies for engaging the political process
- Understand federal legislation affecting therapeutic recreation services
- Describe the potential effect of this legislation on the therapeutic recreation scope of practice
- Identify potential therapeutic recreation-related state and local legislative actions

This chapter will discuss the changing demographics of America with regard to disability. It will also define economic impact and the way in which **politics** is applied to the delivery of therapeutic recreation services. We will identify the components of the legislative process, whether at a city council meeting or the halls of Congress. Finally, throughout the chapter we will discuss the never-ending connection between therapeutic recreation and demographics, economics, politics, and legislation.

It's All About Relationships!

This section is about people. People we serve. People we work with. People to whom we provide information about what needs to be done right now and in the future. Even people who tell us what to do by passing laws and adopting regulations that govern our practice. Understanding all these groups is critical to successful delivery of therapeutic recreation services.

First, we must understand those we serve. Therapeutic recreation specialists work with a wide range of people with disabilities and their families.

According to the U.S. Census, in 2000 more than 72 million families were living in households in the United States, and more than 20 million of those families had a family member with a disability. When including extended families, it is likely that one of every two families (either by household or by relationship) is touched by disability today.

We need to consider not only the people whom therapeutic recreation specialists serve but also the array of people with whom they work to provide services. Chapter 7 listed just some of the professional disciplines that a therapeutic recreation professional might work with in his or her career. Consider the following list of potential collaborative partners.

- You might work with architects to make sure that a new parks and recreation facility being constructed is accessible to and usable by people with disabilities.

- You might work with parks and recreation professionals to provide support for interaction between people with and without disabilities in a parks and recreation program.

- You might be part of a team that is planning educational services for a child with a disabil-

Illinois State Senator Don Harmon (D, Oak Park), his son Don, and Illinois State Representative Julie Hamos (D, Evanston) enjoy a day as the guests of honor at a minor league baseball game in Schaumburg, Illinois. Harmon and Hamos sponsored legislation that frees up about $60 million annually for statewide community-based therapeutic recreation programs in Illinois, provided by regional agencies called special recreation associations.

Photo provided courtesy Ragen E. Sanner

As a therapeutic recreation specialist, one of your jobs might be making sure that your clients have access to the places they want to go, like public gardens, parks, and hiking trails.

ity, and in that process, work with teachers, therapists of all types, and the family of the student.

- You might be part of a rehabilitation team that includes counselors, occupational therapists, and physical therapists and is working to restore leisure functioning for injured soldiers returning from the Middle East.

These are the day-to-day contacts that make up our work. But other contacts, political in nature or related to legislation, have a significant effect on our workplace and the associated resources.

The therapeutic recreation professional of the 21st century must be a good service delivery professional and have strong communication skills. As therapeutic recreation specialists, we must also be advocates—knowledgeable about outcomes, aware of history, and able to help politicians understand what they can do to help us help others. The need for such advocacy and the associated knowledge base has become more important as our communication and daily interaction expand to include community parks and recreation professionals as opposed to medical model professionals. Legislative action directly affects this growth, and it is our job to understand, influence, and address current mandates and potential future legislative action.

Demographics of Disability

Based on the 2000 Census, the median income of a family with a child with a disability is $39,000, whereas the median income of a family without a child with a disability is $49,000. Experts debate the cause, but here is a commonsense view about why such a discrepancy exists. People who change jobs typically say that they did so because they are likely to earn a higher salary at the new job. People move from job to job for a variety of reasons, but earnings or earning potential is always a factor. As a result, the typical person actively seeks out, or at least considers, opportunities for increased earnings.

For families with a child who has a disability, the pattern is different. The 1990 and 2000 Harris polls commissioned by the National Organization on Disability both cite the lack of health insurance portability as a factor in a wage earner's reluctance to seek another job. As a result, some parents of children with disabilities stay at one company, concerned that their son or daughter will not have the same benefits if the wage earner takes a new job. In addition, the attitudes of employers regarding necessary time away from work for doctor visits, individual education program meetings, and other meetings directly related to the disability of a child cause many wage earners with children with disabilities to stay in the job that they have. Their **income growth** remains relatively flat in comparison with wage earners who do not have a child with a disability and are free to pursue other jobs whenever they choose.

At the same time, advances in medical technology have caused the number of people with disabilities to increase. Development of more effective treatment options and improvements in emergency care, diagnostic techniques, and prenatal and neonatal care have allowed more children and adults to survive health conditions and disorders, even trauma, and return to the community with disabilities. At the other end of the age spectrum, more children born with disabilities or health conditions survive longer, and they too remain in the community. The families of these adults and children expect a full array of programs and services in their communities, including therapeutic recreation.

The implications of demographics and health care advances with regard to disability are staggering. Generally, the incidence of disability among persons between the ages of 3 and 65 is 16%, but the incidence of disability for persons 65 or older is 31%. As you are reading this book, a large number of 50- to 70-year-old Americans, the baby boomers, are aging, and as they age, they are acquiring disabilities—strokes, head injuries, arthritis, respiratory disorders, Alzheimer's, diminished hearing, impaired vision, and other conditions. Because medical technology is saving more of this large group of baby boomers, therapeutic recreation specialists will have more opportunities in the next decade to work with older people than they will with other groups of people with disabilities.

Economics of Disability and Therapeutic Recreation

Providing recreation opportunities and therapeutic recreation services for people with disabilities is more costly than providing the same for people without disabilities. Several factors contribute to this reality, but the single greatest factor is the higher cost of personnel, whether in a health care setting or in a parks and recreation department.

Why is this true? For a parks and recreation agency, when a person with a disability chooses a

CASE STUDY

GREENACRE PARKS AND RECREATION DEPARTMENT

The City of Greenacre is a mature community of 120,000 people. The Greenacre Parks and Recreation Department has a proud 100-year history and offers high-quality recreation facilities and services to Greenacre residents.

In 1976 Greenacre started a community-based therapeutic recreation program. The therapeutic recreation program professional staff is made up of three certified therapeutic recreation specialists, one of whom serves as a manager. The professional staff hires and trains qualified and interested persons to work part-time and carry out programs. The program format has people with disabilities participating alongside each other rather than with people without disabilities. Using the therapeutic recreation process of assessment, planning, implementation, and evaluation, the staff plans programs and services.

The parks and recreation department offers programs that build self-esteem, physical health, communication skills, leisure skills, and social skills through recreation activities such as sports, art, summer camps, and more. The community believes this to be a successful program.

In the last year, however, more people have asked Greenacre Parks and Recreation to support inclusive participation, in which people with and without disabilities enjoy recreation together. While attending the National Recreation and Park Association Congress, the director of the parks and recreation department heard her peers talk about how to fund inclusion and how to support inclusive recreation participation. She conducted a survey of the families of people with disabilities and found that most, especially those with young children with disabilities, would prefer inclusive participation to separate participation.

Working with the city manager and the city council, she prepared a proposal to add two full-time professional staff to the department. The city council eventually approved a reduced version of the proposal, adding one certified therapeutic recreation specialist to the staff to coordinate inclusion and training.

recreation opportunity, more staff time will almost certainly be required. The added staff time will be used to register that person and to plan for his or her safe and enjoyable participation in the program. More staff will have to be hired and trained to carry out the program. And the greater the participants' physical or cognitive limitations, the greater the amount of staff time required.

Employees assigned to work with people with disabilities usually need more training than do staff assigned to work with people without disabilities. The typical ratio of staff to registrants without disabilities is 1 to 15. The typical ratio of a community-based therapeutic recreation program is 1 to 4 and may often be 1 to 1. This higher staff ratio is necessary to assure that the recreation program is safe and enjoyable. This discussion is illustrated in table 14.1.

As you can see, if a higher staff ratio, such as one staff for one registrant, is provided, the costs are even higher than what is shown in this example. A safe assumption for planning purposes is that the cost of providing an equivalent recreation program for a person with a disability will be at least three times greater than the cost of providing a program for a person without a disability.

In a clinical setting, safety and treatment protocols often require high staff-to-patient ratios. As a result, costs are typically higher. Although society has accepted higher health care costs as a part of its commitment to a healthier society, it has not yet, in all settings, agreed to provide funds or resources to continue that higher quality of service outside the clinic, hospital, or treatment center.

In the latter part of the 20th century, public parks and recreation agencies were under intense pressure. Demand for service was rising as the population increased and as Americans adopted a culture that valued leisure and recreation. Public parks and recreation agencies were also being asked to address social problems like poverty, unemployment, substance abuse, sexism, and racism.

At the same time, a growing conservatism affected politics in many parts of the country. State legislatures in California, Missouri, Illinois, and other states imposed restrictions on spending by states and local governments. These limits were driven by a desire to reduce the amounts paid by taxpayers to governments. Oddly enough, these conservative initiatives sometimes played on the fears of the same demographic group that was driving the increase in demand for service—people over the age of 50.

Public parks and recreation agencies are locally funded. As state legislatures and city councils across the country tried to reduce the amount of taxes paid by residents, parks and recreation agencies charged participants higher fees. The result of this trend is that the user of public parks and recreation, instead of the community in general, paid for a greater amount of the cost of the department. This change is significant.

Applying this model to therapeutic recreation programs is not difficult. The arithmetic remains the same, but a new element in the formula is the **Americans with Disabilities Act (ADA)**. The

Table 14.1 Staff and Cost Considerations for Providing Camps to People With Disabilities

Program—summer camp	Registrants without disabilities	Registrants with disabilities	Staff assigned for people without disabilities	Staff assigned for people with disabilities
Number of participants or staff	65 participants	12 participants	5 staff members (at 1:15 ratio)	3 staff members (at 1:4 ratio)
Cost to camp*			180 hours at $9 per hour for 6-week camp, $8,100	180 hours at $10 per hour for 6-week camp, $5,400
Cost per camper**	$124 for entire camp	$450 for entire camp		

*Does not include benefits, supplies, facility rental, or overhead, all of which drive up the cost for every registrant.

**Does not include the cost of training employees.

ADA specifically prevents local governments from charging a person with a disability more for a program or service than it charges a person without a disability. Consider a hypothetical summer camp that requires participant fees to be sufficient to meet all costs of the program. Our example in table 14.1 shows that a summer camp fee of $124 would cover such costs, but the necessary fee for a person with a disability, who requires more personnel cost, would be $450. The ADA requirements, however, make setting higher fees for a person with a disability a violation of that person's civil rights. The fee for a person with a disability must be $124, the same fee charged to people without disabilities. If

OUTSTANDING PROFESSIONAL

CINDY BURKHOUR

Background Information

Education
*BS in Therapeutic Recreation, Minor in Psychology from Grand Valley State College *MA in Recreation and Park Administration from Central Michigan University

Credentials
*CTRS *CPRP

Special Affiliations
*National Council for Therapeutic Recreation Certification *National Recreation and Park Association *Michigan Recreation and Park Association

Special Awards
*Recreation Provider of the Year, Associations for Retarded Citizens/Kent (1985) *Therapist of the Year, American Business Club Jenison Chapter (1988) *Program Leadership Award, Michigan Recreation and Park Association (1988) *Professional of the Year, ARC of Midland (1994) *Outstanding Achievement Award, Michigan Recreation and Park Association (2001) *President's Award, Michigan Disability Sports Alliance (2002) *Certificate of Appreciation, State of Michigan (2003)

Career Information

Position
Inclusive recreation consultant, Access Recreation Group, LLC

Organization Information
The Access Recreation Group is a collection of highly trained and experienced recreation and accessibility professionals. The Group offers a full range of consulting services to park and recreation providers and to the recreation industry. With the passage of the Americans with Disabilities Act, many recreation providers are in need of some assistance in making the transition to fully include individuals with disabilities in all recreation opportunities. The Access Recreation Group offers assistance in meeting the challenge of providing accessible facilities, programs, and services for implementing the Americans with Disabilities Act.

Job Description
Review site plans and evaluate existing programs, services, and facilities. Advise on the planning and development of fully accessible facilities; accessible, inclusive programs; sensitivity and awareness training for staff, boards, and commissions; marketing, program promotions, and funding; community and customer relations; policies, procedures, and process that welcome all people; accessible playground design and safety inspections; and long-range recreation Americans with Disabilities Act self-evaluations and transition planning.

Career Path
Before coming to work with the Access Recreation Group, LLC, I served as director of a community recreation department and coordinator of therapeutic recreation services for a community recreation program. I taught Therapeutic Recreation and Adapted Physical Education on the adjunct faculties of Grand Valley State University, Aquinas College, and Wayne State University and as a visiting professor at Eastern Michigan University. I also served on the U.S. Access Board's Recreation Accessibility Advisory Committee and the Regulatory Negotiation Committees on Access to Play Facilities and Access to Outdoor Developed Areas to establish the ADA compliance rules for recreation facilities.

fees are raised, they must be raised equally across all participants.

Another trend is the rise in **charitable solicitation** by public parks and recreation departments. As local tax dollars were restricted or became more difficult to obtain, many agencies formed nonprofit foundations. These foundations sought donations from companies, other nonprofits, and individuals. Although the Internal Revenue Code treats a gift to a local governments as a deductible gift, just as it does a gift to a nonprofit, many people prefer to give to nonprofits. As a result, these related foundations have had measurable success in many communities across the country.

Is charitable giving on the rise? It depends on the community and the time. Some of the catastrophes of the early 21st century, such as the September 11 incidents in New York and Washington, D.C., in 2001 and Hurricane Katrina in New Orleans and Mississippi in 2005, spurred charitable giving. Many giving analysts reported that charitable donations by individuals rose, whereas those by companies dropped. Most agencies, because of the opportunity here, have made solicitation of charitable gifts part of their funding plans.

One caution about reliance on charitable giving to fund therapeutic recreation is that grants eventually go away. And grants, when used properly, create greater demand for therapeutic recreation. An agency that relies on grants must build a plan to replace grant revenue with more reliable sources of funding, such as property taxes and fees. Acquiring such funding often requires political engagement.

Politics and Therapeutic Recreation

What is politics? WordNet at Princeton University defines it as "social relations involving authority or power." This simple definition can open doors to an important discussion regarding politics and therapeutic recreation.

Success in politics for therapeutic recreation professionals hinges on the development of good relationships with local elected officials, state legislators, and members of Congress. The relationship is the funnel through which you, as a therapeutic recreation professional, feed facts and observations to a legislator. Without a relationship, placing favorable information in the hands of the legislator is difficult. The facts are necessary and must be in your favor, but many times the facts are not enough. The legislator listening to you as a therapeutic recreation professional must know you, trust you, and believe that you are motivated to do the right thing.

To get to that point, your legislator must recognize you as a person, and you must recognize your legislator as a person too. If you call your legislator only when you need a law passed or a proposed law stopped, you will not succeed. Inviting city council members, state legislators, and members of Congress to events with families of therapeutic recreation participants is critical. Let them see your work and your participants, and just as important, let your participants see the legislators.

Most state parks and recreation associations, state and regional therapeutic recreation associations, and national therapeutic recreation associations are involved in the political process. Therapeutic recreation professionals across the country monitor proposed legislation, seek legislators who will introduce favorable laws, and play an active role in drafting and reviewing state and federal administrative regulations. As a therapeutic recreation specialist, you have a personal responsibility to carry out this role and develop such relationships. It is through this process that resources and favorable legislation exist for therapeutic recreation.

It is tempting to classify people, as well as politicians. Liberals. Conservatives. Independents. Students. Professors. Republicans. Democrats. Which are you? Are you in one category all the time, or do you change as it suits your needs and the situation? Classifications are thought to represent what the people in that class believe. Instead, classifications represent what we *think* the people in the class believe. As such, classifications are inherently dangerous. The therapeutic recreation specialist must develop relationships with all types of people in the political process. Being liberal or conservative in your personal political views will not, in most cases, affect your success or failure in therapeutic recreation political action. On issues of importance to therapeutic recreation, success is more likely to occur when a coalition of legislators of all types supports a position. Avoid making the assumption that liberals or conservatives, or Democrats or Republicans, will always take one position or another.

In this process of building relationships, keeping therapeutic recreation, in some way, on local political agendas is important. The best way to accomplish this goal may be to enlist the help of families who have a family member with a disability.

Encourage people with disabilities and their families to become involved in politics. They can build relationships with lawmakers and policy makers in personal ways.

Legislators at every level are people just like you, with interests, likes, and dislikes. They don't know everything about every subject. Instead they rely on you and other professionals for facts, information about how current or proposed laws affect what you do, and information about how people with disabilities are involved and included in the community. Your obligation is to give them that information.

Therapeutic recreation specialists must follow legislative developments and become advocates for the profession and for those served by the profession. You can start now by doing some of the things listed here. These are just a few of the many ways that you can become well informed and more active in legislative issues.

- Talk to students who are not studying therapeutic recreation about the benefits of therapeutic recreation for people with disabilities.

- Ask students who are not studying therapeutic recreation about how they view people with disabilities in the community and urge them to take on a more inclusive and accepting attitude.

- Go do something! Volunteer, not for class credit, in a center for independent living or some type of disability advocacy agency.

- Suggest that the therapeutic recreation student organization conduct a benefit that supports legislative advocacy regarding disability issues and therapeutic recreation.

- Bookmark legislative Web sites for the state in which you live or attend school. Visit the sites frequently to become better informed.

- Meet your local legislator at home or in the community in which you go to school. Suggest that the therapeutic recreation student organization invite legislators to an informal discussion about the legislative process and how you can become involved.

- Attend the National Recreation and Park Association annual legislative midyear meeting.

The Legislative Process and Therapeutic Recreation

Legislation starts with an idea, and the **legislative process** is all about how the idea makes its way through a complex set of rules. In each of the 50 states and in the U.S. Congress, the rules regarding legislation vary, but there are some consistencies. This section discusses typical legislative processes and highlights some actions that a therapeutic recreation specialist can take to make success more likely.

The legislative process is complex in some ways, but not in others. Legislation passes because of the relationships that you build before you ask a legislator to sponsor a **bill.** After the relationship is in place, things become much easier, but the actual legislative process is detailed and knowing the details is an important part of your job as a therapeutic recreation specialist. The following section outlines this process and the individual steps that occur. The first step, coming up with an idea, often starts with you.

Ideas   The idea comes first. The idea may be to increase funding for therapeutic recreation or to allow people with disabilities to spend state or federal funds on therapeutic recreation. Or it may be to create therapeutic recreation licensure or certification. The idea can come from you and your colleagues in therapeutic recreation, from your employers, or from those receiving therapeutic recreation services.

Finding a Sponsor   What comes after the idea? Finding a **legislator** who will introduce it and push it! This step is all about the relationship that you have, or your state or national therapeutic recreation association has, with a legislator. Who is the right legislator? Look for these traits:

- Knows you and believes in your issue
- Has a good record of passing legislation, even better if it is related to your idea
- Works well with other legislators on both sides of the aisle (Republican and Democrat)
- Is a good communicator

Other factors here include knowing which political party is in charge of the house in which your bill could be introduced. For example, if the Republicans are in charge of the house, ask a Republican as the lead sponsor and a Democrat as a co-sponsor. Always try to obtain sponsors from both parties.

Language   Don't fixate on finding the right words. Every state legislature and the U.S. Congress have expert technical writers. Spend your time refining the idea so that you can write it simply and briefly and say it simply and briefly. Lawyers are good at doing this. If your idea is complex, at some point consider hiring an attorney who is skilled in legislative drafting. But remember always to use the same words. If you call it a car one week, don't refer to it as a hybrid car next week, or an auto the week after, or a set of wheels the following week. A car is a car is a car. The expert drafted version of your idea is now ready for the spotlight.

Fact Sheets   Most legislators and legislative staffs want short, concise written statements about the value of the proposal, the cost to the state or to taxpayers, and the benefits to people with disabilities, service providers, and professionals. These **fact sheets** are used to encourage other legislators to become sponsors or to support the idea. These statements don't need to be technical in nature but should instead use common words to describe the idea and its outcomes.

In the process of introducing a bill, a sponsoring legislator may have to seek permission from the leadership in his or her legislative body. A sponsor will also try to find other legislators to join him or her as a co-sponsor. Now it is time to introduce the bill.

Committee   Most legislatures have some type of screening committee, often called a rules committee. Although the committee does establish rules for the process of reviewing a bill, its most important function is to decide which legislative committee to send the bill to for initial review.

In committee, which is made up of a representative mix of members of the two parties, you should brace for challenges to your idea. Most bills are stopped in committee. Committees hold some type of review or hearing, which is a good opportunity for a therapeutic recreation specialist to testify in front of legislators about the good that the bill will do (or about the harm that the bill might cause to the profession or those we serve).

Bills in committee are often amended. Some amendments improve a bill, but others make the bill so unlikely to pass that it dies in committee. The sponsor pays close attention to amendments. To

RELIEF FOR THE ILLINOIS SPECIAL RECREATION PROPERTY TAX LEVY IN 2003

In 1992 the Illinois legislature passed a bill that capped property tax increases, and the governor signed it. The legislation, called the tax cap, limited property tax increases to under 5%. This cap was important because Illinois, unlike most states, funds public parks and recreation with special property taxes dedicated to parks and recreation. One of those tax levies could be used only for recreation for people with disabilities, and it too was capped. Statewide, that property tax levy generated about $18 million for "special recreation" programs conducted by local governments or community-based therapeutic recreation agencies.

From 1990 to 2003 the number of people with disabilities rose dramatically in Illinois, and more people with disabilities demanded their ADA rights in recreation settings. But with taxes capped at under 5%, few public parks and recreation agencies could meet the demand. More people with disabilities were on waiting lists, user fees were steadily rising, and pressure for a solution was growing.

After 2 years of fact finding, Illinois parks and recreation professionals and therapeutic recreation professionals proposed a solution: uncap the so-called special recreation tax. A team was developed to answer questions, make calls, visit legislators, and move the idea forward. More than 500 people touched this effort in ways large and small, including parks and recreation professionals, therapeutic recreation professionals, persons with disabilities, lobbyists, disability rights groups, students, and others.

State Representative Julie Hamos of Evanston, a respected incumbent Democrat, was asked to be the key sponsor in the House of Representatives. She knew a lot about special recreation and was a recognized advocate for people with disabilities and public parks and recreation. Before the 2003 meeting at which she agreed to become the sponsor, she received recognition as legislator of the year by parks and recreation agencies in Illinois. Representative Hamos introduced a bill to remove the tax cap, and we prepared for hearings. At the same time, State Senator Don Harmon of Oak Park,

a newly-elected Democrat, introduced the same bill in the Senate. This tactic is called a companion bill and gives proponents two chances for passage.

At first, Senator Harmon's bill moved slowly while Representative Hamos' bill moved quickly. Then the tide turned, and the House froze all tax-cap bills for political reasons. All eyes turned to the Senate. Had Senator Harmon's bill not been introduced, our chances could have died in the House. Senator Harmon's bill was heard in committee. Our team testified, and the bill passed. It came to the floor and relied almost solely on Democrats for passage.

Next came the House, where Representative Hamos picked up Senator Harmon's bill. She aggressively sought more co-sponsors. Before the floor vote, the Republican leader of the House guaranteed and delivered 20 votes. The bill, having passed the Senate, now passed the House. On to the new governor!

Three days before the 90-day deadline for veto, when the bill would become law, the governor's staff told us that he would veto the bill because although he supported services for people with disabilities, he was concerned about raising property taxes. On the 88th day, the governor vetoed the bill.

But Senator Harmon and Representative Hamos were not done. Both sought and obtained permission from their respective party leadership to pursue a veto override, which required 60% affirmative votes.

Senator Harmon eloquently introduced the bill and stated why the veto should be defeated. The veto override passed the Senate with great momentum and went to the House. Representative Hamos worked the House, and the bill passed by a tremendous margin there too. On November 18, 2003, the bill became law. This piece of legislation has made up to $40 million more available every year to fund community-based therapeutic recreation programs in Illinois. In just 20 months after the bill became law, the number of communities providing special recreation programs increased by 10%. As you read this, swimming pool lifts, accessible golf carts, accessible playgrounds, and every type of therapeutic recreation program imaginable occur in Illinois. Hamos and Harmon never gave up, had good facts, had an inexpensive solution, and had bipartisan support. If only the legislative process could always be like this!

be passed out of committee, whether amended or not, a bill must make a compelling argument, have a good solution, and have bipartisan appeal.

But this is just the first discussion about your idea, the bill. The committee now sends it to the floor of the first legislative body (only one state, Nebraska, has only one legislative house; all others have a senate and a house).

Floor   After a bill is sent to the floor, all the members of that legislative body have the opportunity to review it and amend it, or vote in favor of it or against it. Most legislative bodies have a two- or three-tier floor process for review, or what is often called reading. If a bill gathers support, it makes it to second or third reading, where the legislative body will finally vote on it for adoption. Usually, only a simple majority is required for adoption.

Congratulations! Your idea, thanks to your legislator, just passed. Or you may have to come back and try again. Attempts to pass a bill may go on for 3, 4, or even 5 years before a bill hits the right time and passes, so don't be discouraged.

Next House   Once out of the first legislative body, the bill is sent to the next legislative body (except in Nebraska, which has only one legislative house). The original sponsor has already, with your help, identified a sponsor to pick up the bill in the second legislative body. The same rules apply: Find the right legislator.

As in the first house, a screening or rules committee will decide which legislative committee to send the bill to. Sometimes, bills from one body are treated more critically in the next legislative body. Your sponsor will be of great help here. As in the first legislative body, the committee is critical. Match your testimony to the members of the committee. If your coworker lives in a committee member's legislative district, let him or her testify instead of you. That tactic offers a better chance of a connection and shows that more people have an interest in the bill. Get that bill passed out of committee! The process that occurred in the first legislative body occurs again on the floor of the second legislative body. Every member of the second legislative body has an opportunity to change your bill, support it, or oppose it. The stakes are higher here, but the results can be the same as in the first legislative body. The bill passes or dies. Again, usually only a simple majority is required for passage.

Reconciliation or Agreement   Often a bill passes one legislative body but is amended and then passed in the second legislative body. When this happens, a select committee of members of both bodies meets and reconciles the different versions of the same idea. Some legislatures require the amended bill to be sent back through the first legislative body for approval. Again, everything can happen all over. A strong sponsor committed to the bill is critical.

A Bill Becomes a Law and Veto Options   After a bill passes both legislative bodies and has been reconciled, it goes to the governor for action. Although the rules vary from state to state, governors generally have 60 to 90 days to act. And in many states, because the legislature passed the bill, it becomes **law** if the governor does not act.

Governors can also **veto** a bill. Some vetoes kill a bill, but in some states an **amendatory veto** changes words or amounts. Most states require the governor to explain to the legislature why he or she vetoed the bill. Legislatures can, by getting more votes (usually 60%), override a veto by the governor. The bill then becomes law because the legislature passed it. These vetoes are addressed in what is usually called a veto session, a special but short period about 4 or 5 months after the legislature meets, when the legislators spend time on nothing but vetoes.

Implementing Regulations   Some complex bills require a detailed regulation that explains how the provisions of the new law are to be defined and implemented. For example, regulations are necessary for the Americans with Disabilities Act because of its broad scope. Furthermore, every state has an environmental law that requires some type of state regulation to explain the law.

Effective Date   Laws, once passed, are effective immediately unless a later effective date is part of the legislation.

Current Legislation and Therapeutic Recreation

Several important laws at the federal level address therapeutic recreation or recreation for people with disabilities.

- Americans with Disabilities Act (ADA)—The ADA became effective January 26, 1992. This federal civil rights law prohibits discrimination on the basis of disability by providers of recreation services, whether governmental agencies, privately owned, or nonprofit. Unlike other federal laws, it applies regardless of whether the agency has ever received federal funds. The ADA also requires that services be provided in the most integrated setting. The ADA has changed the way that public parks and recreation agencies serve people with disabilities. Many of these agencies employ professionals trained in therapeutic recreation to provide adapted and inclusive recreation programs.

- Individuals with Disabilities Education Act (IDEA)—When IDEA became law in 1974, it contained provisions for the employment of therapeutic recreation specialists by school districts. Few school districts do so, but related provisions within IDEA make it an important law regarding therapeutic recreation. Extended school year (ESY) in many states offers a connection between summer school and summer camps.

- Medicaid—States enter into agreements with the federal government regarding services for people with disabilities in the state. An important door for therapeutic recreation is the **Medicaid waiver** process. Waiver programs are created to assure people with disabilities that staying in the community is a good alternative to going to an institution. The person with a disability waives his or her right to receive service in an institution and instead receives it in the community in which he or she lives. In some states—New Jersey, New Mexico, and others—Medicaid waiver recipients can use **Medicaid** to pay for therapeutic recreation services. Other states, like Illinois, are pursuing this opportunity.

- Illinois special recreation legislation—Illinois uniquely funds community therapeutic recreation agencies, known as special recreation associations. These intergovernmental partnerships are formed only to provide therapeutic recreation. In early 2006, 28 such partnerships served more than 190 communities. In addition, the Chicago Park District, serving the entire City of Chicago, provides therapeutic recreation services.

The Illinois model is unique. Relatively small communities make up much of the state. This legislation recognizes that circumstance and allows local governments that join together to serve people with disabilities to levy a small property tax in support of that effort. The Illinois legislature recognized that sharing resources saves taxpayers money, offers more opportunities to people with disabilities, and eliminates duplication of service. The Illinois model works well in densely populated suburban and urban areas, and several states across the country have copied parts of it. In other states, local governments fund community-based therapeutic recreation as a component of public parks and recreation, which is a department within city or county government. This approach has the potential to develop efficient service delivery systems, but doing so will require legislative involvement on the part of professionals who work for such agencies.

Summary

As therapeutic recreation specialists, we must recognize that we don't exist in a vacuum. Federal laws and regulations affect us and our practice, as do state laws and regulations. Local governments, like park districts in Illinois, affect us. Other professions, such as parks and recreation professionals in the community and health care professionals in the health care system, are involved with us. Trends such as greater numbers of people with disabilities and the growing number of older people have direct implications regarding future service needs. Changing funding mechanisms and the increased cost of providing services bring new challenges as well. Our society is set up to support the needs of people, but for this to occur, advocates must engage and use the legislative process. Keeping a finger on the pulse of the political environment is vital to the success of therapeutic recreation specialists in meeting the challenges of today and tomorrow.

1. Who are your state and federal government representatives? What means do you have for meeting and communicating with them? Work with your classmates to identify and develop a strategy for establishing a relationship with these people.

2. If you were to explain the concept of therapeutic recreation to a politician or a non-therapeutic recreation professional, what would you say? What would you include in a fact sheet designed to communicate the importance of therapeutic recreation to such people?

3. Review the steps of the legislative process. Which part of this process seems most challenging? What strategies could you implement to overcome the challenges associated with this particular aspect of the process?

4. Discuss with classmates and your instructor what you know about the Americans with Disabilities Act. Create a fact sheet that outlines the implications for therapeutic recreation associated with this law. Be sure to address both facility access and program access, as well as who is covered under the law and to what extent. Work in small groups to research these issues online and in the literature and then compare your findings.

5. What does it mean to be liberal or conservative? Republican or Democrat? What stereotypes come to mind when you think of these categories? What political party or parties do your local representatives belong to? What positions, or platforms, are associated with these groups? What challenges do you see in working with government representatives who favor positions not in line with your personal political viewpoints, and how would you deal with these differences?

A Global Perspective of Therapeutic Recreation

David Howard, PhD, MSW, CTRS

Indiana State University

Rodney Dieser, PhD

University of Northern Iowa

Heewon Yang, PhD, CTRS

Southern Illinois University

Shane Pegg, PhD

Senior Lecturer, University of Queensland, Brisbane, Australia

Julie Lammel, PhD

Lock Haven University

LEARNING OUTCOMES

After completing this chapter, learners will be able to demonstrate the following competencies:

- Communicate the nature and purpose of the World Health Organization and the *International Classification of Functioning, Disability, and Health (ICF)*, and discuss their relevance to therapeutic recreation

- Recognize the barriers to, benefits of, and strategies for implementing the *ICF* into ongoing therapeutic recreation programs in the United States

- Describe similarities and differences between the historical development of therapeutic recreation in the United States and in other countries
- Identify political, socioeconomic, and cultural factors that might affect the nature of therapeutic recreation services in various regions of the world
- Describe current trends and issues in the therapeutic recreation profession as they exist in several different countries
- Discuss alternative possibilities regarding the conceptualization, development, and delivery of therapeutic recreation services in the United States, as well as other regions

This chapter is made up of several short narratives that describe various issues and examples of therapeutic recreation from a global perspective. The first section, written by David Howard, summarizes the World Health Organization's *ICF* paradigm for health care services and describes ways in which it is related to therapeutic recreation. The next three sections provide descriptions of therapeutic recreation as it exists in other countries. Rod Dieser starts things off with a discussion of Canada. Next, Heewon Yang describes how therapeutic recreation has developed in South Korea. Shane Pegg then describes things from an Australian perspective. The last section consists of a description of a therapeutic recreation program in Switzerland and mentions some of the cultural factors that influence services. Julie Lammel, an American certified therapeutic recreation specialist who spent four years working in the region, wrote the piece.

Through this discussion of an international paradigm for services and specific examples of therapeutic recreation movements in other countries, students can expand their understanding of possibilities while grasping the importance of global communication and standardization.

WHO, the *ICF*, and Implications for Therapeutic Recreation

The World Health Organization (WHO) was formed by the United Nations in 1948. That same year, the WHO established a definition for health that is still being used today. By defining **health**

as "a state of complete physical, mental and social well-being and not merely the absence of disease or infirmity," the WHO set in place the ideal of a **holistic** approach to health. In an effort to further describe this concept of holistic health and to make possible a worldwide system of standardized communication and collaboration in health care, the WHO published the *International Classification of Functioning, Disability and Health.* Commonly referred to as the *ICF,* this document was the result of 7 years of work and collaboration with health professionals in more than 60 countries (WHO, 2001).

The overall aim of the *ICF* is "to provide a unified and standardized language and framework for the description of health and health-related states" (WHO, 2001, p. 1). This aim manifests through four primary goals: (a) to provide a scientific basis for the consequences of health conditions; (b) to establish a common language to improve communications among health professionals; (c) to permit comparison of data across countries, health care disciplines, services, and time; and (d) to provide a systematic coding scheme for health information systems.

One key characteristic of the *ICF* is that it requires health care professionals to use an integrative approach rather than focus on a medical or social model. This method entails considering all factors that interact to influence a person's health, including the importance of recreation, leisure, and play. This approach is different from the traditional health care paradigms that focus solely on **etiological** causality and the linear progression of a person's disease or disability.

By offering a framework to consider the context in which people live instead of just the person (see figure 15.1), the *ICF* further empowers therapeutic recreation specialists to create and enhance communities that support positive free-time choices and experiences. The *ICF* is also intended for application across cultures as a universal model without reliance on Western concepts, encouraging our discipline to view and use the diversity within our clientele as a positive for all people. Finally, the *ICF* is designed to be operational and not exclusively theory driven, and it does not focus on any minority population or age group (WHO, 2001). Some work is being done, however, on a version of the *ICF* that focuses specifically on children and youth *(ICF-CY)*. Its aim is to create an integrated system to clarify constructs, improve communication, and enhance coordination of health services for children and youth (Lollar & Simeonsson, 2005). This document will provide unique opportunities for therapeutic recreation specialists who work with young people.

The *ICF* presents a unique and timely opportunity for the therapeutic recreation profession to promote and educate others about the importance and relevance of therapeutic recreation. The concepts of the *ICF* and its terminology are compatible

with therapeutic recreation practice. Therefore, therapeutic recreation practitioners, educators, and researchers can further their discipline by being attentive and willing to participate in efforts to align health care and the therapeutic recreation discipline with the *ICF* as a global conceptualization of health.

Recently, the board of directors of the American Therapeutic Recreation Association (ATRA, 2005) approved and published the following position statement regarding the *ICF:*

> The concepts and terminology of the *ICF* are compatible with recreational therapy practice. ATRA supports the use of *ICF* language and terminology in recreational therapy practice guidelines, standards of practice, curriculum development, public policy, international relations, and research. ATRA also acknowledges the significance of the use of the *ICF* classification and coding system as a vehicle to clarify and enhance practice and research in recreational therapy.

These professional efforts, and the resulting actions, demonstrate the need for therapeutic recreation specialists to understand the WHO perspective on health and the corresponding resources that are intended to guide practice. The *ICF* should

International Classification of Functioning, Disability, and Health (ICF)
World Health Organization (2001)

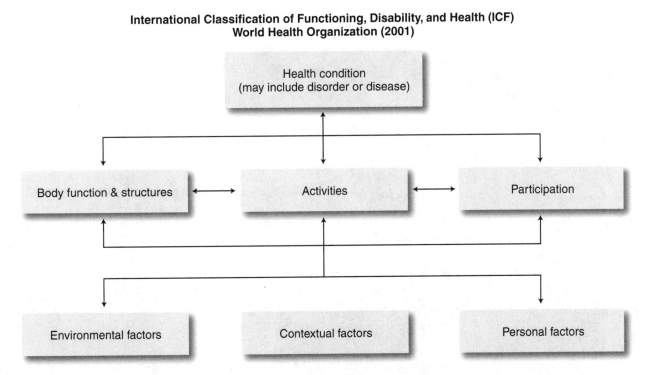

Figure 15.1 The *ICF* is an interactive model that illustrates the relationship between the concepts of a person's health condition, body structures and body functions, activities and participation, and environmental and personal factors (WHO, 2001).

be a critical piece of every therapeutic recreation specialist's professional training and skill set. The following sections describe basic concepts and mechanisms used in the *ICF*.

Health Condition

The use of the term **health condition** refers to the current health status of each person, regardless of whether a disease, disorder, or trauma exists. The *ICF* does not classify or code disorders or diseases, deferring to another of the WHO's family of classifications, the *International Classification of Diseases,* or *ICD*. The *ICD* has its origins in the 1850s and now exists in its 10th edition (WHO, 1989). A useful simplification is to view the *ICD* as a manual that codes the various ways in which people experience disease or disorder and die, and the *ICF* as a manual that describes and codes the way in which people live.

Body Structures and Functions

Body structures and functions are identified in eight sections: (1) the nervous system and mental functions; (2) related structures of the eyes, ears, and sensory functions (including pain); (3) structures involved in voice and speech and corresponding functions; (4) cardiovascular, immunological, and respiratory systems and related functions; (5) digestive, metabolic, and endocrine systems and corresponding functions; (6) genitourinary and reproductive systems and corresponding functions; (7) structures related to movement and neuromusculoskeletal functions; and (8) structures and function related to the skin. The term **impairment** is used when a significant deviation, loss, or problem in a body function or structure is present (WHO, 2001).

Activity and Participation

The features of the *ICF* that are of greatest salience to therapeutic recreation are probably the **activity** and **participation** sections. The *ICF* describes activity as being able to execute and complete tasks (e.g., reading, thinking, walking, dressing, voiding, solving problems, engaging in basic interpersonal interactions, making decisions). **Activity limitations** are difficulties experienced when attempting to perform tasks.

Participation is defined as involvement in meaningful life situations (e.g., going shopping, spending time on a hobby, dating, completing work tasks,

Rather than focusing solely on disease or disability, the *ICF* framework considers contextual factors of health, including recreation, leisure, and play.

©Vegas Adaptive Recreation

volunteering, attending a sporting event). Participation restrictions include any and all elements or situations that interfere with participating in meaningful life events. Within the *ICF* book, activities and participation make up nine chapters: (1) learning and applying knowledge; (2) general tasks and demands; (3) communication; (4) movement; (5) self-care; (6) domestic life areas; (7) interpersonal interactions; (8) major life areas; and (9) community, social, and civic life. This last chapter includes descriptions of recreation and leisure with separate definitions of play, sports, arts and culture, crafts, hobbies, and socializing (WHO, 2001).

Contextual Factors of the *ICF*

Within the *ICF* are two types of contextual factors—environmental and personal. Environmental factors are classified within five groups: (1) products and technology; (2) natural and human-caused changes to the environment; (3) services, systems, and policies; (4) support and relationships; and (5) attitudes. Personal factors include characteristics that have a role in health and disability such as gender, race, age, fitness, lifestyle, behavioral patterns or habits, upbringing, coping styles, social background, economic circumstance, education, profession, past and current experience, individual psychological and personality traits, and other such characteristics. Personal factors are not classified or given codes as are the other parts of the *ICF* because of the large social and cultural variations associated with them (WHO, 2001).

ICF's Schematic Coding Scheme

Within the *ICF* is a schematic coding scheme that allows body functions, activities and participation, and personal and environmental factors to be given a numeric code. A generic 5-point qualifying scale (from no problem, coded as 0, to complete problem, coded as 4) can be used with each code. Use of qualifiers allows further description of what a person is or is not able to do. For example, in coding activity and participation components, a **performance qualifier** (what a person does in his or her current environment) and a **capacity qualifier** (a person's highest probable level of functioning) can be indicated and differentiated depending on whether activity and participation are occurring with or without assistance. Body structures are coded based on (a) the extent or magnitude of impairment, (b) the nature of the

change to the body structure, and (c) the location of the impairment (e.g., left versus right, front or back, proximal or distal) (WHO, 2001).

How codes are created using the *ICF* coding scheme deserves a brief introduction. Codes always begin with a letter that designates part of the *ICF*—body structure (s), body function (b), activities and participation (d), and environment (e). The remaining digits of the code are numbers that refer to the level of classification. The first number corresponds to the *ICF* chapter. For example, b2 refers to a body function, more specifically sensory functions and pain, which is the second chapter of the body function section of the *ICF*. More precise levels of classification describe this portion of a person's health condition, such as seeing functions (b210), quality of vision (b2102), and contrast sensitivity (b21022). Case examples provided later will further illustrate how coding works.

Procedural Manual and Guide for a Standardized Application

One of the most significant developments related to the *ICF* is the creation of the *Procedural Manual and Guide for a Standardized Application of the ICF.* This document, expected to be published in 2007, is intended to help practitioners apply the *ICF* to practice settings. Directed by the American Psychological Association, this document has been drafted with the assistance of practitioners representing the National Association of Social Workers, the American Speech-Language-Hearing Association, the American Occupational Therapy Association, the American Physical Therapy Association, and the American Therapeutic Recreation Association. The involvement of ATRA in this project began soon after the publication of the *ICF*, under the leadership of John Jacobson, then chair of the ATRA Public Health–World Health Organization team. Since 2002, ATRA has sent representatives to the annual meetings of the North American Collaboration Center Conference on *ICF*. Attendance has included the delivery of professional presentations intended to signify the interest and ability of therapeutic recreation professionals to contribute to the furtherance of the *ICF* in health care and health promotion venues. These included presentations about community integration (McCormick, Lee & Jacobson, 2004) and the significance of environmental factors in the lives of men who had cancer (Howard, 2006).

Although the scope of this chapter does not permit additional extensive description of the *ICF* and its relevance to therapeutic recreation, the following case history illustrates several important concepts. The case shows how the *ICF* would be used to identify and code aspects of a client's involvement with a therapeutic recreation specialist.

Considering Therapeutic Recreation in Other Nations

The *ICF* has given health care professionals a system through which they can communicate and collaborate on an international scale to improve the services that they provide. Mastering this system is an important aspect of a therapeutic recreation specialist's responsibility to maintain an understanding of current best practices, and it is a job requirement because *ICF* terminology and coding are becoming more common in the workplace. Likewise, the therapeutic recreation specialist should gain an understanding of international developments related specifically to therapeutic recreation and health care in general. Therapeutic recreation takes a different path in various countries and regions. By studying these developments, the professional can gain a larger perspective on the possibilities of therapeutic recreation and learn about ways in which international collaboration concerning information, resources, and programs might be possible in the future. The following sections consist of information regarding therapeutic recreation in several countries. An author with personal knowledge and experience in the named country or region wrote each segment.

Therapeutic Recreation in Canada

As in the United States, intolerance for people with special needs was widespread in Canada throughout the 1800s. Most people with special needs were hidden in Canadian society through institutionalization. According to Hutchison and McGill (1998) it was not until the late 1920s that Canada moved away from following an institutional–custodial model of care to having people with special needs live in the community (see Hutchison & McGill for a listing of Canadian legislation and critical events related to deinstitutionalization). Before the 1980s most provinces and territories in Canada had informal therapeutic recreation programs usually associated with broader health and human service professional organizations, such as the Adapted Programs Committee of the Canadian

ICF CASE EXAMPLE

NINA

Nina is a 35-year-old female who sustained a closed head injury in an automobile accident. She was hospitalized for a week and then discharged to a rehabilitation unit. A comprehensive evaluation of functioning revealed complaints of headaches, forgetfulness, and irritability, although she was even tempered before the injury occurred. Nina had difficulty learning material at the first exposure but improved with repeated exposure. Staff noted that she had problems completing multistep tasks. She was an active chess player before the accident, but even with cues from the therapeutic recreation specialist, she did not improve enough to allow her to strategize sufficiently to complete a game.

ICF codes pertinent to Nina's therapeutic recreation specialist included the following: (a) body functions—regulation of emotion (b1521.2), moderate impairment—current performance qualifier; (b) body functions—cognitive flexibility (b1643.2), moderate impairment—current performance qualifier; (c) activities and participation—solving complex problems (d1751.1), mild impairment—current performance qualifier; and (d) activities and participation—play (d9200.332), severe impairment—current performance qualifier, severe impairment—capacity without assistance qualifier, moderate impairment—capacity with assistance qualifier. Nina's ability to play chess, with its attending features of being able to think and solve problems, can be identified using qualifiers to indicate the level of difficulty that she is experiencing, as well as progress that she may make during rehabilitation over time.

MOCK From G. Reed, and L. Bufka, 2005, *Implementing the ICF in health care delivery.* Paper presented at the American Therapeutic Recreation Association Mid-Year Professional Issues Forum, Arlington, VA.

Association for Health, Physical Education, and Recreation (Velde & Murphy, 1994). A brief overview of **Canadian federalism** (political ideology of Canada) will be useful in explaining therapeutic recreation in Canada because the issue of Canadian federalism is at the core of contemporary therapeutic recreation practice and professional development in Canada (Dieser, 2002b, in press; Ostiguy & Dieser, 2004).

Canada and Canadian Federalism

Canada is a bilingual country. Its two official languages are English and French. The country consists of 10 provinces (similar to states in the United States) and 3 large northern territories. Furthermore, the provinces and territories exhibit strong cultural differences. For example, Quebec has a large French culture, Alberta has a large English culture, and Nunavut has a large Inuit culture. Furthermore, within these broad provincial and territorial regions are within-group and between-group differences. For example, a small French-speaking population (4% to 6%) resides on Baffin Island in Nunavut, and among Canadian provinces Saskatchewan has a higher population of First Nation people (Canadian American Indians) than other provinces (Statistics Canada, 2004).

Multiculturalism (the political ideology of the mosaic) is at the core of Canadian federalism. Canadian federalism is a political system in which the constitutional authority to make laws and public policy is divided between a national government and regional governments (Brooks, 2000). The result is that throughout Canada, provinces and territories have a paramount role as guardians of regional and cultural identities and differences (Vipond, 1991). Canadian federalism is an "expression of both diversity and unity" (Gagnon, 1995, p. 23). As such, Canadian provinces and territories have jurisdiction over health and human services, such as programs to help people with disabilities (Cameron & Valentine, 2001). In short, this means that provinces and territories in Canada can have distinctive health and human services legislation, public policies, and human services programs (unlike, for example, in the United States, where the Americans with Disabilities Act allows the federal government to override the states on a variety of issues). For example, table 15.1, created from the *Canada Health Act Annual Report for 2002–2003* (Health Canada, 2004) and the 2001 Canadian Census (Statistics Canada, 2004), highlights how Alberta and Nunavut have vastly different health and wellness concerns, programs, population groups, and community characteristics. Hence, Canadian federalism, which allows diversity in provincial and territorial health and human services programs, is different from American federalism, which is based on homogeneity, standardization, and melting-pot cultural practices (Laselva, 1996).

Table 15.1 Different Health and Wellness Concerns and Programs in Alberta and Nunavut

Alberta	Nunavut
New health and wellness vision including the Health Professional Act (law regulating health care professions)	Incorporation of traditional Inuit values, known as Inuit Oaujimajatuqangit, into program policy and service delivery
The Provincial Nominee Program expedites the immigration process of foreign professionals to help them gain permanent resident status.	Upgrading and expansion of telehealth sites, which offer a broad range of services including health promotion and prevention activities
Tobacco reduction strategy including a youth prevention program	Three territorial regions are situated across three time zones: Qikiqtaaluk (formerly Baffin), Kivalliq, and Kitikmeot.
Large white English-speaking population	Eighty-five percent of residents are Inuit. A small French-speaking population (4–6%) resides on Baffin Island.
Aboriginal people make up approximately 5% of the population.	Aboriginal people make up approximately 85% of the population.
Median age is 35.	Median age is 22.

Adapted from Health Canada 2004; Statistics Canada 2004.

A Brief History of Therapeutic Recreation in Canada

Both knowingly and unknowingly, the political ideology of Canadian federalism has been at the root of professional therapeutic recreation development in Canada. Until recently, Canada has had no national therapeutic recreation professional organization, such as the National Therapeutic Recreation Society or the American Therapeutic Recreation Association in the United States. Instead, provincial and territorial therapeutic recreation organizations (e.g., British Columbia Therapeutic Recreation Association, Therapeutic Recreation Association of Quebec, or L'association de loisir thérapeutique du Québec) have had strong professional leadership roles in their respective provinces and territories.

The development of a national therapeutic recreation professional organization in Canada occurred during the mid-1990s. As Reddick (2000) noted, in 1993 during the third International Therapeutic Recreation Symposium (held in Ontario, Canada), a conference session by Velde and Murphy (1994) about the future of therapeutic recreation identified the need for a national association. The conversation that developed from the Velde and Murphy presentation eventually led to the development of a National Coordinating Committee (NCC) made up of therapeutic recreation representatives from across Canada (Reddick, 2000). Approximately 3 years later, in August 1996, the Canadian Therapeutic Recreation Association (CTRA) was born. Today, the mission of the CTRA (see www.canadian-tr.org and Mobily & Ostiguy, 2004) is to advocate and develop the profession of therapeutic recreation by

- promoting and facilitating communication between and among members in therapeutic recreation,

- developing and implementing a plan that will lead to national certification of therapeutic recreation practitioners,

- promoting and advancing public awareness and understanding of therapeutic recreation,

- developing and promoting the adoption and implementation of professional standards for the delivery of therapeutic recreation services, and

- supporting excellence and advancement in education and research in therapeutic recreation.

Canadian Federalism and the Development of Therapeutic Recreation in Canada

An intense debate is currently occurring in Canada about whether the CTRA should (a) adopt the Mosaic Certification Framework (MCF), (b) align with the United States National Council for Therapeutic Recreation Certification (NCTRC) certification model or (c) hold off on developing a credentialing certification framework for the short term (Diane Bowtell, personal communication, October 14, 2005). Again, Canadian federalism is at the core of this issue because the MCF is explicitly based on (1) maintaining Canadian multiculturalism and the mosaic political ideology (e.g., protecting regional and cultural differences) and (2) rejecting the NCTRC certification model in Canada because it is clearly, yet covertly, based on white American individualistic melting-pot political ideology (Dieser, 2002a, 2004b, 2005b, in press), which unknowingly assimilates people from different cultures and countries into white American individualistic values (Dieser, 2005a, in press).

According to Dieser (2002a, 2004a, 2005a, 2005b, in press), the MCF is based on three important axioms. The first axiom is to follow the political ideology of Canadian federalism, which would develop a national therapeutic recreation credentialing and certification framework in which the CTRA would work in partnership with the 10 therapeutic recreation provincial organizations and the 3 therapeutic recreation territorial professional organizations. This action would support Canadian federalism because it would allow provincial and territorial therapeutic recreation professional organizations to protect regional and cultural differences. Table 15.2, adapted from Dieser (2005b), underscores the relationship between Canadian federalism and the MCF.

The second axiom of the MCF is to follow collaboration and unity within a paradigm of diversity among the CTRA, provincial and territorial therapeutic recreation organizations, and universities and colleges. Unity can occur by having the CTRA identify the entry-level core competencies through genuine dialogue with university and college administrators and provincial and territorial therapeutic recreation organizations. For example, Dieser (in press) suggested four standardized courses oriented toward (a) foundational aspects of therapeutic recreation (e.g., history, concepts,

Table 15.2 Relationship Between Canadian Federalism and the Mosaic Certification Framework

Canadian federalism	Policies of the CTRA
Divides public policy between a national government and regional government organizations (provincial or territorial TR organizations), and universities and colleges	Divides TR policy (e.g., education) between a national organization (CTRA) and regional organizations
Recognizes the paramount role of provincial or territorial governments as guardians of regional identities and differences	Recognizes the paramount role of provincial and territorial TR organizations as guardians of regional identities and differences
Establishes practical and flexible institutional arrangements and relationships that allow intercommunity cooperation	Establishes practical and flexible TR institutional and provincial or territorial arrangements and relationships that allow intercommunity cooperation
Celebrates cross-cultural diversity in educational structure in different regions of Canada	Celebrates cross-cultural diversity in curriculum

Adapted from R.B. Dieser, 2005, Outlining a Canadian framework for therapeutic recreation professionalism: A mosaic certification framework part II (Planting seeds), *Tribune* pgs. 7-9.

theories, therapeutic recreation practice models, and professional organizations), (b) therapeutic recreation program design (e.g., assessment, planning, implementation, evaluation), (c) therapeutic recreation intervention and facilitation techniques (e.g., animal-assisted therapy, bibliotherapy, community integration), and (d) leisure theory (e.g., Neulinger's leisure paradigm, postmodern leisure, flow, serious leisure).

The third axiom of the MCF is to have a strong multicultural commitment. Provincial and territorial therapeutic recreation organizations and universities and colleges can collaborate to develop a list of specialty multicultural courses and fieldwork experiences that are relevant to their regions.

Table 15.3, adapted from Dieser (in press), underscores the similarities and differences of the MCF and the NCTRC. The result is that beyond taking the four standardized classes, students who graduate from one university in Canada would have competencies and skills different from students who graduate from another university. For example, the University of Regina (Saskatchewan) could require that all therapeutic recreation students take course work and a fieldwork experience related to First Nation culture, whereas the University of Waterloo (Ontario) could require students to take multiple course work in assessment and evaluative procedures. The MCF, like Canadian federalism, relies on the concept of tolerance, harmony, and unity within a paradigm of diversity.

Therapeutic Recreation in South Korea

The historical origin of therapeutic recreation in South Korea may be found in the leisure and recreation movement of the 1960s. O-Joong Kim, a pioneer in the field of leisure and recreation in South Korea, established the Leisure and Recreation Association in Korea (LRAK) in 1960 (Kim, 2000). South Korea was in an adverse economical, political, and societal situation in the 1960s because the country had gone through national tragedies such as the colonization by Japan (1910–1945) and the Korean War (1950–1953). Thus, during the 1960s, the primary purposes of recreation programs were to provide Korean people with pleasurable experiences and help increase economic productivity through enjoyable recreational activities (Noh & Lee, 2004).

In 1963 Ewha Women's University offered recreation as an academic course for the first time in South Korea, and in the late 1980s several universities created recreation-related majors in their graduate programs. These academic efforts introduced the concept of therapeutic recreation to South Korea (Noh & Lee, 2004).

It was not until the late 1980s that the public began to view recreation as an essential component of people's lives. People regarded recreation as simple games, and recreation leaders were considered game leaders. But since 1988, when South

Korea hosted the Seoul Paralympics, opportunities for sports and recreational services for people with disabilities and interest in recreation and therapeutic recreation have steadily increased in South Korea. The following sections address therapeutic recreation professional organizations, the therapeutic recreation certification system, therapeutic recreation education and training programs, and the challenges of growth faced by therapeutic recreation in South Korea.

Emergence of Therapeutic Recreation Professional Organizations in South Korea

In the 1990s people with social work backgrounds ignited the development of therapeutic recreation in South Korea. For instance, in 1990 Jun-Ahn Chae established the Center for Recreational Services for People with Disabilities, and in 1992 Chae started some experimental therapeutic recreation programs for people with mental disabilities. In the following year (1993), Chae established the Korean Therapeutic Recreation Association (KTRA), which can be regarded as the first therapeutic recreation professional organization in South Korea. KTRA contributed to the development of therapeutic recreation in South Korea in many ways. For instance, the organization introduced the concept of

therapeutic recreation to the Korean general public, initiated therapeutic recreation services in health care settings including hospitals and rehabilitation centers, established a clinical center, and started education and training programs for potential therapeutic recreation specialists.

Until recently, KTRA has been primarily working on three service areas: (a) development and provision of therapeutic recreation programs to clients in many areas, (b) research on the effectiveness of therapeutic recreation intervention programs, and (c) education and training programs for future therapeutic recreation specialists. Although the initial efforts, in both research and practice, have been directed primarily to older adult populations, KTRA has been trying to expand its target populations to include people with developmental disabilities, psychiatric disorders, and mental illnesses, as well as children and adolescents (KTRA, 2006).

Since 1995 several books about therapeutic recreation have been published, and academic publications such as theses and dissertations have been available. But during the 1990s most of the material and resources regarding therapeutic recreation introduced only the leisure ability model (Peterson & Gunn, 1984, Stumbo & Peterson, 2004), focusing on recreation participation and appropriate leisure lifestyles.

Table 15.3 Similarities and Differences Between the NCTRC and the MCF Credentialing Processes

Organization	Credentialing process
NCTRC academic path requirements	1. A baccalaureate degree or higher from an accredited college or university with a major in therapeutic recreation or a major in recreation or leisure with an option in therapeutic recreation.
	2. A minimum of 18 semester hours or 27 quarter hours of therapeutic recreation and general recreation content course work with no less than 12 semester hours or 18 quarter hours in therapeutic recreation content.
	3. Supportive courses to include a total of 18 semester hours or 27 quarter hours of support course work with a minimum of (a) 3 semester hours or 3 quarter hours course work in the content area of anatomy and physiology; (b) 3 semester hours or 3 quarter hours course work in the content area of abnormal psychology; and (c) 3 semester hours or 3 quarter hours course work in the content area of human growth and development across the life span. The remaining semester hours or quarter hours of course work must be fulfilled in the content area of human services as defined by NCTRC (e.g., adapted physical education, psychology).
	4. A field placement experience of at least 480 hours over 12 consecutive weeks in therapeutic recreation services that uses the therapeutic recreation process as defined by the current NCTRC Job Analysis Study under the supervision of an onsite field placement supervisor who is NCTRC CTRS certified.

Organization	Credentialing process

MCF academic path requirements	1. CTRA would develop a national credentialing structure in which (a) a therapeutic recreation technician holds a 1- or 2-year diploma from a college, (b) a therapeutic recreation specialist holds a bachelor's degree from a university, and (c) a recreational therapist holds a master's or doctorate degree from a university. The diploma or degree must be from a college or university with a major in recreation, leisure, or therapeutic recreation studies.
	
	2. For national consistency, CTRA maintains that the TR technician, TR specialist, or recreational therapist must have entry-level competencies in
	
	  a. leisure theory (e.g., serious leisure, flow, classic leisure, postmodern leisure, Neulinger's leisure paradigm);
	
	  b. foundational aspects of therapeutic recreation (e.g., history, concepts, theories, TR practice models, and professional organizations);
	
	  c. therapeutic recreation program design (e.g., assessment, planning, implementation, evaluation); and
	
	  d. therapeutic recreation intervention and facilitation techniques (e.g., animal-assisted therapy, bibliotherapy, community integration).
	
	3. Specialty courses and field placement developed by university and college departments in partnership with provincial or territorial therapeutic recreation professional organizations will be different in different provinces or territories and universities or colleges.
	
	  a. Examples: critical thinking, community development, clinical TR practice, community TR practice, women in politics, leisure education, medical terminology, leadership, qualitative evaluation, marketing and promotion, tourism, disabling conditions, recreation programming, issues and trends in health care, ethics in human services, counseling psychology, health promotion, human anatomy, park design, film studies, adapted physical education, outdoor education, computer technology, research and evaluation, abnormal psychology, sociology of mental disorders, history of human services, environmental philosophy, family ecology, statistics, theories of sex and gender, management and administration, disaster relief, crime and public policy, sign language.
	
	4. Specialty course and field placement focused on multiculturalism will be different in different provinces or territories and universities or colleges.
	
	  a. Examples: cross-cultural therapeutic recreation, cross-cultural counseling, cross-cultural communication, cross-cultural perspectives on mental health, critical pedagogy in indigenous education, First Nation perspectives on nature, fieldwork placement into a diverse culture, Indigenous feminism, cross-cultural policy reform, French language, classic Chinese poetry, Korean art, Spanish language, Japanese music, history of Ukrainian Canadians, Hungarian dance, foods from East Asia, international relations, history of Canadian multicultural policy, Francophone culture, ritual and symbolism, cultural museum studies, cross-cultural conflict resolution, cross-cultural substance dependency, gender in cross-cultural perspective, cross-cultural gerontology, social inequality, world religions, cultural perspective of death and dying, cross-cultural leisure theory.

Adapted from R.B. Dieser, 2005, Outlining a Canadian framework for therapeutic recreation professionalism: A mosaic certification framework.

Several professional organizations and institutes were established after the emergence of KTRA. For example, Daehan Therapeutic Recreation Association (DTRA) was founded by Jaesub Yoon in 1995. Yoon and his colleagues decided that therapeutic recreation needed a more focused organizational advocate. That is, they were more concerned with the clinical practice of therapeutic recreation and viewed therapeutic recreation as a specific tool of treatment or rehabilitation effective in combating difficulties associated with primary disabilities. Examples of their primary practice and research areas include (a) natural and ecological therapeutic recreation programs for people with mental illness and psychiatric disorders, (b) therapeutic recreation intervention programs for sexually abused adolescents and victims, and (c) therapeutic recreation intervention programs for older adults with dementia. During the last decade, DTRA published 8 books and 11 academic journal articles, and hosted more than 200 sessions of educational seminars and workshops.

In 2001 Yongkoo Noh started the Korean Therapeutic Recreation Research Center (KTRRC). The focus of KTRRC is to provide for the growth of clinical practice through aggressive research and scholarly activities and by providing education opportunities for both the public and future therapeutic recreation specialists. Currently, KTRRC has been providing a good number of academic seminars, workshops, professional conferences, and educational and training sessions.

As a result of a collaborative effort between DTRA and KTRRC, the Korean Therapeutic Recreation Academic Society (KTRAS) emerged in 2002. During that same year, KTRAS published the *Korean Therapeutic Recreation Journal (KTRJ)*, the first scholarly journal in therapeutic recreation in South Korea. The academic and scholarly activities initiated by these entities are likely to serve as a springboard for sound development of therapeutic recreation in South Korea.

Therapeutic Recreation Certification in South Korea

The Korean Council for Therapeutic Recreation Certification (KCTRC), established in 2001, administers the certification exam. KCTRC is an independent nonprofit credentialing body for the profession. Although KCTRC was initiated primarily by leaders from KTRA, leaders from other entities have recently joined. Collaboration among members maintains the power balance among organizations.

KCTRC has an organizational system similar to that of the National Council for Therapeutic Recreation Certification (NCTRC) in the United States. For instance, KCTRC has three specific committees: the Standards Review Committee (SRC), Standards Hearing Committee (SHC), and Exam Management Committee (EMC). Since 2002, the organization has offered the certification exam twice a year. By 2005 over 500 people had become certified therapeutic recreation specialists.

To determine the eligibility of applicants for the certification exam, KCTRC considers three items: (a) a minimum of a high school diploma or equivalent educational background, (b) a minimum of 140 hours of academic course work (80 hours of educational courses from designated education and training agencies or colleges and 60 hours of field experiences), and (c) a minimum of 6 credit hours in the human services area (KTRA, 2006).

Education and Training Programs for Therapeutic Recreation Specialists

Because therapeutic recreation is still in its infancy, no academic institutions offer degrees in the field. But more than 30 universities and colleges in South Korea offer courses related to therapeutic recreation, and several universities may create therapeutic recreation departments. Most of the instructors who teach therapeutic recreation courses have academic backgrounds in social work, physical education, special education, or rehabilitation (KTRA, 2006).

Besides universities and colleges, several education and training institutes, such as the Korean Digital Therapeutic Recreation Association (KDTRA), the Daehan Therapeutic Recreation Association (DTRA), and the Korean Therapeutic Recreation Research Center (KTRRC), offer instruction. These organizations offer unique education programs and training processes for potential therapeutic recreation specialists.

Challenges for the Growth of Therapeutic Recreation in South Korea

The growth of therapeutic recreation in South Korea for the last 15 years has been remarkable. In particular, the development of professional organizations and research centers, publication of an academic journal, and development of an autonomous credentialing body are incredible achievements in such a short period.

But the rapid growth of therapeutic recreation in South Korea raises some important questions. One concern is whether the eligibility criteria (education and experience) of the current certification system will produce professionals who can provide quality clinical practices in current Korean health care settings. Producing certified therapeutic recreation specialists who are not fully equipped with the necessary academic background and practical skills in the field may possibly cause harm to clients. This question raises a serious concern about establishing a healthy identity and sound image of therapeutic recreation in South Korea. Without a

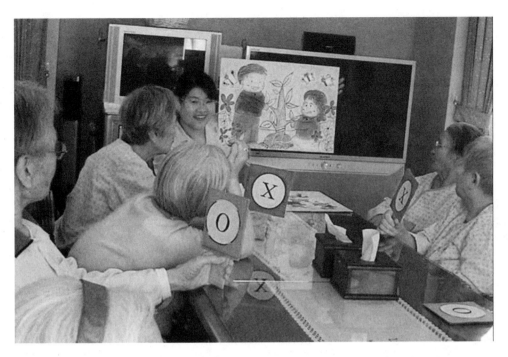

Great strides have been made in South Korea to develop therapeutic recreation.

scientific, reliable, outcome-oriented knowledge base, and without a cadre of qualified professionals, the long-term success of a new profession is problematic. The development of appropriate education and training systems, such as academic programs at colleges and universities that produce quality therapeutic recreation specialists, may be required for therapeutic recreation in Korea to confirm its identity as a profession.

In addition, having professional organizations with different philosophical approaches in South Korea provides both opportunities and problems in growth, as it does in the United States (with NTRS and ATRA). Open communication, flexible thinking, and collaboration among the organizational leaders and staff will help establish a firm sense of identity. Lastly, advocating therapeutic recreation to third parties and the public with evidence-based practice would promote the future success of the profession. Currently, most of the certified therapeutic recreation specialists in South Korea are not hired as full-time staff, in either clinical or community settings. Again, this reflects the somewhat hasty introduction of certification without first determining the needs of the job market and establishing scientific basis.

In sum, although both the quality and the quantity of education and training programs are still below the standards of those in the United States, therapeutic recreation in South Korea is rapidly growing in the number of professional organizations, publications, and people certified. Now is the time for therapeutic recreation professionals in South Korea to communicate with each other and work on the challenging tasks that lie ahead.

Therapeutic Recreation in Australia

Although therapeutic recreation has been firmly embraced in many developed countries as a useful form of intervention in helping people live a more healthy and satisfying life, in Australia the concept (and indeed the practice) is yet to be fully accepted in the health care setting. The historical development of therapeutic recreation and leisure services, and even the terminology used in this country (i.e., diversional therapy instead of therapeutic recreation) has led to a fractured notion of what the term means today and what that service entails in many parts of Australia. Such services in this context are being referred to as those that help people develop, make choices about, and participate in a leisure lifestyle that may ultimately lead to a higher quality of life through increased physical health, emotional well-being, and social connections (Stumbo & Peterson, 2004).

Indeed, the range of therapeutic recreation staff titles used across the country is diverse, to say the least. The more commonly used titles are leisure therapist, recreation therapist, diversional therapist, activities officer, and activity therapist. Although the title for staff engaged in therapeutic recreation provision may vary significantly based on locality, the industrial award under which the person is employed, and whether the person is in the public or private health care system, the day-to-day tasks and core service values are generally consistent with those espoused as appropriate by the primary professional body in this country for therapeutic recreation staff, the Diversional Therapy Association of Australia (DTAA). The association, with a current membership of approximately 2,300 spread across the full gamut of operations in the health and aged care sectors, including rehabilitation and hospital units, community centers, residential aged care, palliative care units, and mental health services (DTAA, 2005), has a philosophy and vision similar to that outlined by similar overseas organizations such as the U.S.-based National Council for Therapeutic Recreation Certification (2004). For instance, the Diversional Therapy Association of Australia (2005, p. 1) considers diversional therapy to be "the facilitation and coordination of recreation and leisure services for individuals who experience barriers to choosing, deciding and participation in activities with the aim of good work practice to ensure that the barriers created by disability, ageing and social stigma are minimized."

Historical Development of Therapeutic Recreation Services in Australia

Although most researchers acknowledge that therapeutic recreation had its formal origins in the health care industry in Australia in the early 1940s, its history can be traced back to the First World War, when nursing staff used forms of recreation to assist in the rehabilitation of injured servicemen who had returned home after fighting in the European sector. Such services were also geared to assisting those with permanent disabilities to assimilate back into community life. After the Second World War, and in recognition of gaps in the range of health services on offer to those seeking assistance, the Australian Red Cross initiated training courses in basic crafts and the like to health care staff. Although the 3-month-long courses were offered to the public until 1976, they were significantly modified from their original form in the late 1960s to accommo-

date the growing recognition that the diversional activities required in the health care sector were far broader than just handcrafts alone, and that staff therefore needed to be suitably skilled to adapt a range of services to suit the needs of their clientele (DTAA, 2005). Concurrent with this shift, the commencement of the deinstitutionalization process in Australia in the late 1960s and early 1970s, perhaps best exemplified by significant reforms in the psychiatric and disability sectors, saw therapeutic recreation become a formally accepted area of study and a vocational outcome in the late 1970s. This was achieved by the progressive establishment of recreation courses at colleges of advanced education throughout Australia from 1976 onward. The Diversional Therapy Association of Australia was formed at this time as an outcome of a meeting of seven graduates of the Red Cross course who had a common interest in improving service to their primary older adult clientele (DTAA, 2003).

These early and somewhat limited training offerings, usually offered at the undergraduate associate diploma or diploma level, have evolved to the point that universities throughout Australia now offer programs with a specific therapeutic recreation focus, primarily at the undergraduate bachelor's degree and postgraduate master's levels. Consistent with the early development of these programs, empirical research in the Australian setting began to emerge in the early 1980s about the benefits of therapeutic recreation. The focus was to evaluate the principles and practices that guide interventions with consumers of therapeutic services (Trowbridge, 1988). Such effort has, however, not been widely engaged by many of those working in the field as therapeutic recreation practitioners, despite the general shift in the Australian health care sector over the last decade toward a greater expectation that service be driven by evidence-based outcomes and that workplace preparation be grounded in an appropriate range of training and education opportunities.

Ongoing Australian National Reform

The provision of therapeutic recreation services in Australia over the last decade has been greatly influenced by a sweeping array of reforms, most of it at the federal level, with respect to the health and community services sectors. Three reforms are worthy of particular mention at this juncture. First are the nationwide reforms to community-based public health services, particularly those services targeted toward people with mental illness and older adults. Each of these reform agendas has brought forth greater consideration of quality of life issues and has recognized for perhaps the first time that legislation, policies, and funding at the national and state levels must be properly aligned to achieve successful implementation of the proposed reforms across the nation. For example, the National Health Strategy, a key nationwide initiative announced by the Commonwealth government in 1994, noted for the first time at the federal level that health services need to be holistic. Since then, government policies and community actions have increasingly reflected the relationship between leisure and health. For instance, efforts made in recent years with respect to the Active Australia and Get Activated campaigns within the health care field have focused on the importance of community-based living and the need for physical activity to be incorporated into a more holistic and healthy lifestyle (Australian Institute of Health and Welfare, 2000; Australian Sports Commission, 2005).

Similarly, the National Mental Health Plan, first released in 1992 and updated in 1998, has focused on promotion, prevention, and early intervention; development of partnerships in service reform; and the quality and effectiveness of service delivery. These core reforms were reinforced further in 2006 with the tabling of the Parliament of Australia Senate (2006) report titled *A National Approach to Mental Health—From Crisis to Community,* which has recommended, among other things, that greater attention (and resources) be given to the issues of social reintegration of consumers and the level and quality of rehabilitation services, inclusive of therapeutic recreation-based programs, available to them.

In terms of aged care, the Home and Community Care Act 1985 and the Aged Care Act 1997 have become the reform platform used to "support healthy ageing for older Australians and the provision of quality, cost effective care for frail older people as well as their careers" (Department of Health and Ageing, 2003, p. 3). Such support has included what are considered other therapies. Under this banner, therapeutic recreation and other leisure-based services have been funded in residential aged care facilities across Australia.

Although all these reforms have been initiated at the national level, each has been affected at the state and regional level by the ideology and policies of the state or territory government in power, and even more at the local level by the service provider and health care practitioner overseeing program delivery. In terms of therapeutic recreation services in Australia, such practitioners have been either occupational therapists or diversional therapists, each of whom offered service that reflected his or her professional philosophy of service provision. Occupational therapists, for example, continue to align quite strongly with the medical model of health service provision. They are key members of case management teams in which they are being required to undertake large caseloads encompassing largely the evaluation of client competencies and the associated administration of services. Case management in Australia today is an integral component of the overall services offered by health service providers. With its implementation has come the progressive withdrawal of many occupational therapists from the face-to-face delivery of programs.

As a consequence, the shift in duties for OTs has been a boon for many therapeutic recreation-based staff because they have been required to step in to fill the void. As such, diversional therapists have remained very much hands-on because their services are now more in demand than ever. That stated, they too have been asked in recent times to be more accountable for what they offer and how they do it. A significant number of diversional therapists have expressed the view through their professional association that they are uncomfortable with the notion of being required to undertake any form of critical evaluation to demonstrate client outcomes, or even to justify service offerings. This is an unfortunate stance because greater accountability for health care expenditure in the Australian setting is already a reality. Their position, if it remains unchanged, will surely bring them into conflict with the relevant authorities in the immediate future.

Therapeutic recreation professionals in Australia, through their everyday interactions with consumers, play a major role in supporting people with a wide variety of care and health needs by facilitating improved leisure functioning, resulting in a better quality of life. Despite this fact, many professionals and paraprofessionals in the health and community care field continue to dismiss therapeutic recreation services in the Australian setting as little more than time fillers and diversionary activities.

Although issues of professional training and accreditation, social change, national health care

Options for therapeutic recreation are endless in Australia, where even some zoo creatures can help provide a little "pet therapy."

and the services that they offer will continue to sail on troubled waters.

Working as a CTRS in Switzerland

The opportunity to work in Switzerland as a CTRS allowed for a great deal of professional and personal development. Switzerland, a small, centrally located European country, is well known for the Alps, chocolate, cheese, and quality time pieces. What few people realize is that Switzerland has four official languages: German, Italian, French, and Romansh. The country is surrounded by Italy, Germany, France, Liechtenstein, and Austria. The central location of Switzerland in the midst of Europe allows easy access to other countries, so one can readily experience a distinct change in culture. The Swiss culture, infused as it is with many other cultural influences, provided the backdrop for tremendous learning opportunities. The challenges were immense yet manageable. The cultural and lingual differences were noteworthy but ultimately not as significant as the similarities.

Evolution of the Therapeutic Recreation Program in Valens

Klinik Valens is an acute care rehabilitation facility located on the eastern side of Switzerland. The Klinik primarily serves persons with neurological and orthopedic disorders on both an inpatient and an outpatient basis. The therapeutic recreation program at Klinik Valens originated in 1977 under the solitary efforts and direction of Carol Bishop. Ms. Bishop's initiative in finding a clinical setting that would allow her to pioneer a therapeutic recreation program in Europe provided the profession an opportunity to expand services in cross-cultural settings (Lammel & Emmerichs, 1992).

The original program was led by one CTRS and consisted primarily of group therapies and evening activities. In 1987 a work permit for a second CTRS was granted, and with that the program developed into a four-track treatment program that included community integration, individual therapy, group therapy, and leisure education in addition to the evening programming. The program remained under the direction of a CTRS until 1997. At this time, the Klinik administration hired a Swiss-trained

reform, and the level of government funding at both the federal and state levels have all affected how therapeutic recreation is perceived and used in Australia, the harsh reality is that it remains generally a concept (and service) not well understood by the Australian public. Moreover, therapeutic recreation remains a form of service that appears to be under constant threat.

Although recent action by the DTAA to establish minimum standards for the professional preparation and in-service education of therapeutic recreation practitioners is a purposeful step in the right direction, numerous issues remain to be addressed. As noted by Stumbo, Martin, and Ogborne (2004), until therapeutic recreation professionals in Australia take action to articulate and document a clear purpose to service provision, develop more standardized services to clients, demonstrate an ability to target and achieve valued client outcomes, improve the credibility of service provision and service providers to other providers and payers, and achieve greater equity with other health care and human services professionals, such employees

THOMAS "ANDY" FERNANDEZ

Background Information

Education
MA in Recreation from University of Northern Colorado

Credentials
*CTRS *CPRP *Certified Ropes Course Instructor, Clark County, Nevada. *Mandt, Behavior Management Certification

Special Affiliations
*Oregon UCEDD/OHSU *Nevada Advisory Council on Children With Special Health Care Needs *U.S. Senator John Ensign's (R-NV) Disability Task Force *Lakeside Chapter of Disabled Sports USA *National Recreation and Parks Association Congress *Nevada Recreation and Park Society *National Therapeutic Recreation Society *National Institute on Recreation Inclusion *University of Northern Colorado Recreation Program Advisory Board *Colorado Therapeutic Recreation Society

Special Awards
*Employee of the Month, City of Las Vegas (1996) *Nevada Recreation and Park Society Program Excellence Award—Project D.I.R.T. (1996) *Nevada Recreation and Park Society Program Excellence Award—F.L.O.A.T. (1997) *NRPA PacSW Region Program Excellence Certificate Award—F.L.O.A.T. (1997) *New Professional of the Year Award, National Therapeutic Recreation Society (1999) *Presidential Citation, National Therapeutic Recreation Society (2000, 2002)

Career Information

Position
Adaptive recreation manager, City of Eugene, Library, Recreation, and Cultural Services Department/Adaptive Recreation Services

Organization Information
As the primary public provider of community recreation services for people with disabilities in Eugene, Oregon, direct services include recreation programs adapted to serve people with disabilities, individualized and group skills training, assistance to make activities accessible, adapted equipment, and referral or information assistance. Adaptive Recreation Services maintains partnerships among community support groups, nonprofit agencies, and public commissions representing the concerns and needs of people with disabilities. Staff provides training, consultation, and adapted equipment to city departments and community groups to facilitate the inclusion of people with disabilities in their programs, including compliance with the Americans with Disabilities Act. Adaptive Recreation Services also provides students and volunteers with crucial hands-on experience and training while working with a variety of disabilities and populations.

Organization's Mission
Adaptive Recreation Services provides a diverse choice of recreation activities to empower Eugene's citizens with disabilities to develop active, healthy, and playful lifestyles.

Job Description
Manage operations of the Adaptive Recreation Services section of the Library, Recreation, and Cultural Services Department. Responsible for supervision of all staff and facilities, partner and rental programs, section budget, and the development of policy and procedure.

> If it's not fun, why do it?
> *Jerry of Ben and Jerry's*

Career Path
I specifically chose positions with premier agencies that would give me the opportunity to gain valuable experience in community TR. I have worked with the University of Arizona Adapted Athletics, the Breckenridge Outdoor Education Center, the City of Boulder EXPAND Program, the City of Las Vegas Adaptive Recreation, and as the creator and supervisor of the City of Reno Inclusion Services.

Likes and Dislikes About the Job
I like the ability to create and directly impact community services for people with disabilities. I dislike the bureaucracy, but sometimes that is the nature of the game.

Advice to Undergraduate Students
Always apply for a position you are interested in, even if to just test if you qualify or not. Get involved professionally on projects, committees, and programs. Experience is the number one resume builder and what separates the job candidates from the job applicants.

activity therapist and a sport therapist. Currently, the Klinik continues to offer "Rekreationstherapie" and places primary emphasis on groups that include creative work, painting, games, cooking, singing, drumming, and pain reduction. Large festivals and evening events remain under the direction of the recreation program. Sport therapy offers cross-country skiing, snow shoeing, mountain biking, traditional sport activities for fun, and swimming.

The goals of the recreation and sport programs resemble the earlier goals instituted by the American CTRS. They include social opportunity, increased life satisfaction, community involvement after discharge from the facility, continued involvement in recreation activities following discharge, and a general appreciation for leisure (www.klinik-valens.ch).

Language and Therapeutic Recreation Services

The ability to communicate with clients has a significant role in establishing a healthy client–therapist relationship. The language factor in Valens was a complex issue. The primary language used in the Klinik was German, but it was not unusual to hear people speaking fluent French, Italian, Yugoslavian, or Portuguese.

On average, a CTRS worked with the clinic for approximately 2 years and spent the first full year developing a working knowledge of German and Swiss German languages as well as a bit of French and Italian languages. As a result, when a new CTRS with a minimal background in the German language replaced a CTRS who had been at Klinik Valens for at least 2 years, the continuity in the program was temporarily interrupted. This disruption hindered not only the effectiveness of the therapy but also the ability of the CTRS to participate fully as a member of the treatment team (Lammel & Emmerichs, 1992). At the same time, many of the patients spoke German as a second or third language. In many ways this circumstance produced a bonding opportunity as both the therapist and the client learned to communicate effectively in a secondary language. Replacing words as the primary means of communication were creative interactions that were at times frustrating and at other times humorous. The challenge of language also created empathy and deeper understanding for clients who have difficulty with communication because of injury or disease.

Even with some fluency in the language, an obstacle remained in creating an understanding of recreation and leisure. In the German language, *leisure* can be directly translated into *Muße*, but that word is seldom used and not well understood. No direct translation exists for the word *recreation*. Words used as a substitute for *recreation* in the German language include *Freizeit*, which means "free time"; *Beschäftigung*, which has an emphasis on doing and not on enjoyment; and *Aktivierung*, which means "to make people active."

Unfortunately, none of these translations truly captures the meaning of recreation as defined by American culture. Granted, one cannot easily grasp the meaning of the word *recreation* by reading a definition out of the dictionary. Recreation is experiential. But when recreation is interpreted as free time or as a means of keeping oneself busy, most people develop an immediate partial perception or false perception that affects their attitude toward recreation participation (Lammel & Emmerichs, 1992). This idea is supported by the Whorfian hypothesis (Whorf, 1956), which suggests that languages are not only a means of transmitting thoughts but also, and more importantly, a part of culture that shapes how people think and perceive. Our language, directly or indirectly, molds our recreational attitudes, which directly shape our lifestyle.

Culture and the Influence on Therapeutic Recreation Treatment and Services

One of the biggest challenges of working in a foreign country revolved around understanding a culture and lifestyle different from what was familiar. In regard to providing therapeutic recreation services, culture was important for several reasons. One of the most difficult aspects of promoting recreation and leisure as essential to a healthy lifestyle was the cultural attitude toward recreation. Although the Swiss value vacation time, they seem to compartmentalize work and leisure, and both tend to be production-oriented or goal-oriented in nature. Swiss culture places high priority on perfectionism, social status, and conformity. These values are clearly seen in their work ethic and work efforts, as well as in their recreation and leisure pursuits. Work was unquestionably more than just a job or a means of earning a living. Professional pursuits were the means by which many Swiss created their identity and their sense of purpose. Recreational pursuits were often a way to fill time.

Understanding and working with the Swiss and their attitudes toward recreation pursuits were definitely a challenge for the CTRSs, yet they quickly understood that working with a client is not necessarily about making the client believe as the therapist does. A mutual negotiation process resulted, which allowed the CTRSs to recognize and appreciate the Swiss cultural attitudes toward recreation. The CTRSs were then able to facilitate opportunities for clients to continue recreation pursuits after discharge from the rehabilitation hospital.

Working in Europe as a CTRS offered immense challenges, not only with the obvious exposure to different languages and cultures, which in itself was demanding and rigorous, but also in the professional realm. CTRSs working with the Klinik Valens program had to make significant adaptations to apply knowledge of therapeutic recreation in a clinical setting in which therapeutic recreation philosophy and practice were little understood. Yet those daunting challenges also offered the CTRS the opportunity to be creative and grow personally and professionally. Working as a CTRS in a foreign country requires learning new languages—the languages of culture, of understanding, and of recreation. One realizes quickly that although words are important, the more important means of communication come from understanding and accepting differences in people. Communication and cultural understanding are highly pronounced in recreation and leisure pursuits. Working in Valens provided the opportunity to embrace cultural differences and to explore the meaning of leisure and recreation.

Summary

These descriptions of therapeutic recreation from various international perspectives make it apparent that the challenges that professionals in these countries face are often similar to current challenges experienced by therapeutic recreation professionals in America. At the same time, each particular cultural, political, and economical scenario creates unique challenges and opportunities. These commonalities and differences further highlight the potential benefits of an international health care paradigm such as the one presented by the WHO. Through such a mechanism, seemingly isolated therapeutic recreation and health care systems can benefit from the opportunity for improved communication and collaboration.

Students have much to learn from these international descriptions. For example, the scenarios illustrate the importance of multicultural competence and the potential dangers of applying models and methods from one culture to another. The WHO acknowledges these risks and has worked to develop the *ICF* in a manner that accounts for environmental and cultural differences. Another important lesson embedded in these scenarios is that therapeutic recreation is indeed an international profession and that opportunities for growth and collaboration exist at this level. To explore these and other issues related to this chapter, students should review the discussion questions and share their thoughts with classmates. These questions are designed specifically to help students recognize the limitations and opportunities associated with each of the described systems. Furthermore, exploring the value of alternative perspectives and approaches to therapeutic recreation can be a useful tool in envisioning future possibilities at both the national and international levels.

DISCUSSION QUESTIONS

1. Discuss the potential benefits of implementing the *ICF* across American and international health care systems.

2. How might such a change enhance awareness and acceptance of therapeutic recreation among other health care professionals, both nationally and internationally?

DISCUSSION **QUESTIONS** CONTINUED

3. Interview two or three current health care practitioners. Were they aware of the *ICF*? If yes, did it affect their daily work? What possible implications does their level of awareness have for the potential use of the *ICF*? Compare your results to those of other class members. Were certain professional areas of practice more or less familiar with this system?

4. Based on these interviews, your reading, and your own opinion, what challenges will come with aligning therapeutic recreation standards of practice with the *ICF*?

5. What similarities and differences exist between the American history and perspective of therapeutic recreation and those of other countries?

6. Recreation and leisure are an inherent part of culture. What implications does this present in regard to the purpose and nature of therapeutic recreation? Is it possible that the American perspective is irrelevant or unhealthy in other cultures?

7. What steps can you take to ensure that you are competent in your work with people from other cultures?

Paradoxes in Leisure Services and Therapeutic Recreation

Jesse Dixon, PhD
San Diego State University

LEARNING OUTCOMES

After completing this chapter, learners will be able to demonstrate the following competencies:

- Recognize paradoxes that confuse or conflict people about the meaning of leisure, recreation, and therapeutic recreation
- Recognize characteristics of leisure, recreation, or play behavior
- Recognize a critical force that influences the degree of experience in leisure, recreation, and therapeutic recreation
- Understand why leisure, recreation, and therapeutic recreation have value for people with differing abilities, education, and opportunities
- Understand the contribution of leisure, recreation, and therapeutic recreation across the life span
- Recognize different orientations to motivation for therapeutic recreation intervention

- Recognize different values used to support leisure, recreation, and therapeutic recreation beyond concerns for a cost outcome
- Understand the value of choice and authentic behavior in therapeutic recreation treatment
- Understand the value of therapeutic recreation in preventing illness and maintaining health

This chapter is intended to identify some of the paradoxes that occur in the context of leisure and therapeutic recreation services. A **paradox** is a situation or perspective that links contradictory ideas or feelings to provide an explanation. Recognizing paradoxes in the context of work or the classroom may be useful for professionals or students who want to consider new perspectives for services or address questions concerning services. Because paradoxes typically lead to questions, I will use what I call common questions to introduce discussion of the paradoxes. The questions may be easier to relate to work and classroom settings than are the titles of the paradoxes. As part of the learning process, readers should try to answer the common question for each paradox to consider their own knowledge and belief boundaries before reading my response. I will address the questions to provide a position for the reader with respect to leisure services and therapeutic recreation services.

In reviewing the topic headings for this chapter, the reader can note two characteristics. First, the topics distinguish the subject of leisure or recreation services from other categories of services. In the last 30 years, the significance of leisure and recreation services has been repeatedly challenged in the context of budgeting for social service settings. Clearly, distinguishing leisure and recreation services from other types of helping services will only clarify the unique and positive opportunities that are possible for patients and clients. Second, all the paradoxes that apply to leisure services apply to therapeutic recreation services. During the last 30 years, society has moved from mainstreaming and normalization issues to the philosophy of inclusion. Through service efforts that incorporate accessibility and communication, therapeutic recreation services can benefit from the same advocacy and education efforts used for leisure or recreation services.

The Paradox of Confusing Leisure or Recreation With Achievement Behavior

Common question: How can people assert, "My work is my play," or "My play is my work"?

I make a distinction between the context of leisure or recreation and the context of achievement or work (Dixon, 1995). Leisure experiences define people through the characteristics of choice and authentic affect in behavior. **Leisure behaviors** are appropriate when people are seeking a continuation of behavior (Ellis, 1971). **Achievement behaviors** are appropriate when people want to change what they have to do or when they want to solve a problem (Mitroff, 1998; Nachmanovitch, 1990). Because of organization, schedules, and deadlines, achievement experiences are oriented to a termination of behavior. Both contexts of behavior offer people opportunities for satisfaction.

Distinguishing Leisure and Recreation From Achievement or Work

Leisure and recreation originate with choice, whereas behavior in the context of work and achievement originates with obligation (Cordes & Ibrahim, 2003; Ellis, 1973). The separate origins lead to different characteristics of behaviors in achievement and leisure while permitting both categories of behavior to change by **degree.** For example, achievement behavior can be changed to appear more or less like work, and leisure can be changed to be more or less playful. This degree of change can cause a person to think that entertaining work is the same as play or that play with extreme limits is the same as work. This paradox or confusion can occur if the origin of the behavior is overlooked.

The context of leisure or recreation is different from the context of achievement or work. The origin of the behavior in leisure emphasizes choice. When people initiate behavior based on choice, the experience is a stronger concern than the outcome (Ellis, 1971). The positive affect that people experience in leisure is authentic compared with the conjured affect used to motivate people in the context of work or achievement. People in leisure can be less linear, develop their own rituals, orient the activity to themselves, and be less conscious of time. The participant chooses the process, orients it to his or her preferences, and places more significance on it than on the outcome (Dixon, 1995).

In the context of achievement, people are usually obligated to respond to a problem or react to a demand (Mitroff, 1998; Nachmanovitch, 1990). Achievement behavior can readily change without responding to the preference of an individual. Problem solving frequently includes a focus on an outcome and may include feelings of discomfort and change. For example, workers frequently change or eliminate their work behavior if they are told that the behavior has no value. This change is reasonable because they may not be paid or may not be appreciated. In short, people in the context of work perceive some obligation, quantify their time, orient their work to the needs of an external source, use standardization as a ritual, and are rewarded for following a linear path of experience (Dixon, 1995). The phrase *Time is money* and the term *merit pay* represent concepts common in the context of work or achievement and reflect concerns for efficiency and outcome.

Figures 16.1 and 16.2 illustrate the two sets of characteristics that occur within each experience. The figures suggest that the two types of experiences are different and dynamic. Each experience can be altered by changing one or more of the five characteristics. In addition, each experience can be changed by degree to reflect more or less of these characteristics. The degree feature permits leisure to become more like work and work to become more like leisure. Such changes could explain why people might mistake their work for leisure or their leisure for work. The key distinction is to observe that the behaviors originate differently. In leisure and recreation, people consider a continuation of behavior. In work and achievement, people consider a termination of behavior.

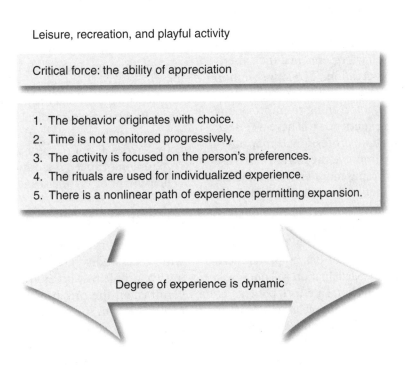

Leisure, recreation, and playful activity

Critical force: the ability of appreciation

1. The behavior originates with choice.
2. Time is not monitored progressively.
3. The activity is focused on the person's preferences.
4. The rituals are used for individualized experience.
5. There is a nonlinear path of experience permitting expansion.

Degree of experience is dynamic

Figure 16.1 Distinguishing characteristics of leisure, recreation, and playful activity.

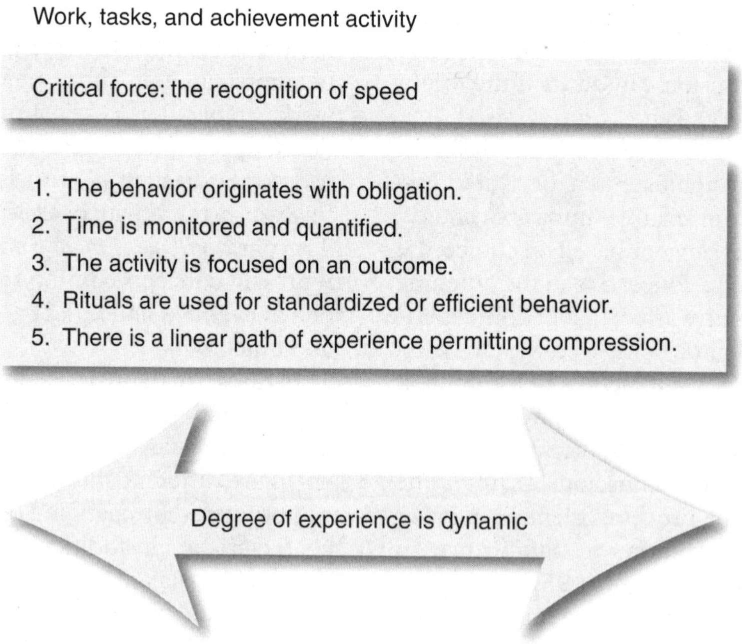

Work, tasks, and achievement activity

Critical force: the recognition of speed

1. The behavior originates with obligation.
2. Time is monitored and quantified.
3. The activity is focused on an outcome.
4. Rituals are used for standardized or efficient behavior.
5. There is a linear path of experience permitting compression.

Degree of experience is dynamic

Figure 16.2 Distinguishing characteristics of work, tasks, and achievement activity.

Different Critical Forces for Leisure and Achievement

Schwartz (1996) suggests that the understanding of experiences includes consideration of critical forces or influences. A **critical force** is a factor that can significantly change an experience. A person's ability to appreciate the characteristics of the behavior can diminish or enhance the experience of leisure or recreation. The appreciation of leisure or recreation is a critical force because without this capacity, intervening to improve any characteristics of the experience will have no effect. In therapeutic recreation, professionals may intervene with patients to improve the degree of leisure or recreation by providing more choices, allotting more time for participation, or including additional personal preferences in designing participation (see figure 16.1). But if a patient does not appreciate the difference between different activities, does not want to invest the time, or has no preferences regarding participation, participation will not result in a continuation of behavior. In effect, patients or consumers have to be able to appreciate what makes leisure or recreation a different context of behavior for improving their quality of life.

In achievement behavior, the recognition of speed is a critical force for a successful outcome (Grulke, 2000). The variables that characterize achievement in figure 16.2 will not be relevant if people cannot conclude tasks within prescribed time limits (termination of behavior). For example, knowing information after an exam will not change the grade on a test. Paying a bill after the due date results in a penalty. An idea submitted to the patent office after someone else has already done so does not qualify as an original idea. In treatment settings with therapeutic recreation, the failure of a patient to take a medication at the prescribed time will not result in the desired medical benefit. Professionals who impose safety precautions after an activity is completed will not prevent an injury. In sum, the recognition of speed is a critical force in validating achievement or work tasks.

Application to Therapeutic Recreation

Providing services to people who have issues with accessibility and differences in skills may involve problems with motivation and attributions. Contrasting the origin of behavior for leisure or recreation with the origin of behavior for work or achievement can clarify the value of professional intervention. Therapeutic recreation is an alternative intervention approach that uses the medium of recreation activities to facilitate positive changes in a person's treatment needs. The positive changes include the patient or client's awareness of his or her preferences for motivation in a context that reflects personal choices, discoveries, and a desire for future participation. The perspective for a playful continuation of behavior is different from the termination of behavior that is emphasized as an outcome of work or achievement. The patient or client is permitted to use a positive authentic affect, which provides therapists with an accurate individual perspective beyond standardized medical interventions. In other words, patients or clients can experience a better understanding of who they are. Characteristics of leisure and achievement occur in marriage, parenting, management, and leadership. All these situations benefit from authentic, sincere relationships with people. The process or experience in therapeutic recreation can help patients or clients be themselves for personal satisfaction and successful relationships.

Professionals may also want to consider this paradox when distinguishing therapeutic recreation from another form of intervention in which a therapist might use a game as a medium to teach vocational skills or academic skills. Achievement games use outcome to determine the success of the intervention, which explains why patients or clients may experience negative affect when they lose or experience difficulty. In effect, the outcome rather than the process may determine the nature of the affect or satisfaction. Planning treatment strategies for chronic illness or disease based on patient-determined choices or motivation is more likely to result in a continuation of behavior compared with achievement behavior oriented to outcome.

The Paradox of Applying Terms Like *Leisure* and *Recreation* With People Who Demonstrate an Inequity

Common question: How can we use terms like *leisure* and *recreation* to label experiences with people who demonstrate wide ranges of ability, education, and awareness levels?

John Kenneth Galbraith is a world-renowned expert on economic beliefs. He suggests that there is a paradox in applying the concepts of work and lei-

sure to people who have distinctively different levels of success in careers. Galbraith (2004) proposed that labeling experiences as work (or leisure) for people who are successful in careers and for people who have less opportunity is a type of **fraud.** For example, Galbraith argued that people with less opportunity live nothing like people with prestige and money. Applying this perspective of fraud to leisure services, Galbraith may be suggesting that people with less financial resources would also have less quality in leisure. I disagree with Galbraith's perspective of fraud.

Financial Wealth and Narrow Values

Financial wealth is typically based on achievement behavior, which originates differently than leisure behavior does (see figures 16.1 and 16.2). Leisure and recreation behaviors originate with making a choice rather than solving a problem. As a result, participation satisfaction will be influenced by a person's skill and knowledge in addressing personal preferences, not a profit outcome. The distinction between achievement behavior (centered on wealth) and leisure behavior (centered on experience) may explain why it is possible to be wealthy and "successful" without being happy. A single outcome of achievement behavior is inadequate to serve as a quality of life indicator because, as an outcome, it does not address the five characteristics of a leisure or recreation experience.

Degree as a Factor in the Quality of Life

Galbraith (2004) appeared to ignore the potential effect of changing experience by degree and the use of value to change the experience of participation. If leisure or recreation activities were a static product, the possibilities for inequity would apply. A certain percentage of poor-quality and high-quality leisure products would be available in the market place. People would have to be able to absorb the losses (disappointments) with part of their leisure and use the power of wealth to buy the higher-quality leisure products. For example, buying a low-quality CD or a dinner that is poorly prepared could result in dissatisfaction. But people could also use information in choosing entertainment. Reading reviews, previewing samples, and taking advantage of discounts could make the experiences have more value and certainty. Regardless of one's income, a person can make experiences (not products) more

Leisure and recreation center around activities and behaviors that are chosen, not required.

playful (see figure 16.1). People can recognize more choices, expand rather than contract time, orient the activity to individual needs, create unique rituals, and follow a less linear path of behavior. The previously mentioned strategies suggest a proactive approach to leisure or recreation participation and permit participation to change by degree when using these alternatives. The possibility of modifying the characteristics of a leisure experience is a significant issue for participants who want more out of participation.

Application to Therapeutic Recreation

The public may have difficulty perceiving people who are coping with disabilities as happy and motivated people. The temptation to focus on the disability of a person could result in the failure to consider leisure or recreation as a relevant experience for that person. For example, people with a serious illness could find that other people think of them as victims (Cohen, 2004). In effect, the passive role of a victim may not suggest the image of a person who is developing hobbies and leisure interests based on joy and passion. I suggest that there is no fraud in facilitating a positive quality of life for people who function with impairments.

Cohen (2004) argued that people should be supported to live and function well under all circumstances including illness. Programmed use of recreational activities can result in a positive quality of life for all people who are coping with physical, psychological, or mental limitations.

The Paradox of Playful Assimilation Behavior and Adult Accommodation Behavior

Common question: How does the nature and function of playful behavior for children differ from the playful behavior of adults?

The playful behavior of infants and young children is often characterized as egocentric because they tend to be limited to their own perspective (Cordes & Ibrahim, 2003). The limited abilities and awareness of a young child often result in relationships centered on his or her interests. In contrast, adult leisure behavior is far more subject to the competing demands of obligations to careers, government,

OUTSTANDING PROFESSIONAL

MARLA KNOX

Background Information

Education

Graduate of Recreation Therapy program, San Diego State University

Special Awards

*Ray Butler Award, California Park and Recreation Society, Division XII (1992) *Directors Award, City of San Diego Park and Recreation Department (1994, 1998, 2000, 2001) *Part-Time Professional Award, California Park and Recreation Society (1996) *Merit Award for Jr. Wheelchair Sports Camp, California Park and Recreation Society (1999) *Full-Time Professional Award, California Park and Recreation Society, District XII (2001)

*Crusberg Award, Pacific Women's Sports Foundation (2002) *BlazeSports Fund Development Achievement Award (2005, 2006) *Jack LaLanne Fitness Award presented to JAWS (2005)

Career Information

Position

Founder and executive director of the San Diego Adaptive Sports Foundation

Career Path

Since my graduation, I have worked as a supervising recreation specialist with the City of San Diego Therapeutic Recreation Service, a recreation therapist for Sharp Healthcare Rehabilitation Services, and the director of the San Diego Junior Wheelchair Sports Camp and Junior Athletes in Wheelchair Sports (JAWS program).

---

and family life. Consequently, changes in playful behavior occur as humans grow and develop awareness and abilities.

Playful Behavior Developed Across the Life Span

Playful behavior is observed in children and adults. Preferences for behavior are noted very early in life and are typically managed throughout the life span. For example, children can laugh before they ever have language, independence, or mobility. Children choose to laugh or be playful because they have the capacity and can distinguish an interaction or a stimulus from contexts in which they are obligated to behave differently. For example, many children can tell when a parent or an adult is kidding and will laugh accordingly. Most parents in child rearing learn what information entertains their child and what information their child initially resists or dismisses. As children age and mature, they are asked to conform, be responsible, and be successful. Piaget referred to this process as a transition from **assimilation** to **accommodation** (Cordes & Ibrahim, 2003).

Assimilation and Accommodation

As a psychologist, Piaget concluded that children do not think as adults do. He suggested that chil-

dren have their own logic and order for processing information (Papert, 1999). Because children do not have the same degree of skill and knowledge that adults do, they use thinking or logic so that reality matches their own thoughts (Cordes & Ibrahim, 2003). This egocentric behavior is characterized as assimilation and provides adults with opportunities to learn about the unique preferences and abilities of children. As children age and experience school and structured social situations, they are expected to alter their thoughts and behaviors to fit the demands of reality (Cordes & Ibrahim). In adulthood, people are expected to be motivated, to find happiness, and to follow the rules of society. In effect, successful adults can accommodate the demands or expectations of society and still find happiness in adult forms of playful behavior.

The Three Helpful Stages of Piaget

Using numerous observations and interactions, Piaget suggested that children move through three **stages of playful behavior:** (1) sensorimotor, (2) symbolic, and (3) cooperative. Infants and very young children can be observed touching, tasting, seeing, and listening to their world. The sensorimotor abilities of children permit them to interact with their environment and process information before they have language. They typically learn to distinguish pleasure and pain, rough and smooth, loud and soft, large and small, shapes, color, and textures. Note that besides playing an important role in infancy and early childhood, sensorimotor abilities are used throughout the life span in the contexts of leisure and achievement.

As children mature physically and mentally, Piaget observed that they engage in fantasy or symbolic play. In brief, children learn to use their imagination to create or relate to symbols and scenarios for playing. For example, many children's television shows create talking characters and circumstances for children to see as a representation (symbol). Children also create games in which they take on an adult role, imaginary role, or superhuman character to have desired experiences. The use of fantasy or imagination is an important ability for children to have if they are going to be successful in future leisure or achievement situations in which they have to be creative or solve problems (e.g., art, music, science, construction, business) (Fritz, 1991; Mitroff, 1998). Like sensorimotor playful behavior, creative symbolic playful behavior can continue across the entire life span. Many adults enjoy reading books, watching films, or planning vacations that involve fantasies.

As they develop motor skills and social skills, children typically evolve from playful behavior that is solitary, to play that is parallel with others, and finally to cooperative play with others. Cooperative playful behavior is a significant ability in games with rules. Children are clearly moving from assimilation to accommodation when they have to defer to the presence or roles of other children and the structure of a game. Children learn to consider information beyond their own preferences as a necessary process to enjoying participation and interactions. Like sensorimotor playful behavior and symbolic playful behavior, cooperative playful behavior can occur across the entire life span. Many adults play team sports, group card games, or cooperate in large groups to enjoy a concert or sporting event. The failure of adults to develop abilities in any one of the three types of playful behavior could result in limited or diminished leisure or achievement experiences. Many daily life activities involve the ability to process information accurately (sensorimotor), to relate to the purpose of participation (symbolic), and to benefit from interactions with other people (cooperative). Most people use skills from all three types of playful behavior throughout the life span to improve their quality of life through leisure and to be successful in the context of achievement.

Application to Therapeutic Recreation

People who demonstrate some type of impairment or are coping with an illness can benefit from a positive quality of life. People can improve their level of fitness and experience physical pleasure through playful behavior that is oriented to sensorimotor experiences. Associating playful behavior with cognitive concepts by using imagination and fantasy can provide pleasurable experiences for both children and adults. Watching theater, listening to music, creating art, and seeking adventure can be enjoyable experiences for all people regardless of impairment if they have appropriate appreciation of affect and a level of sensory capacity. Finally, therapeutic recreation specialists typically organize group recreation opportunities for people who have impairments (Wheel Chair Athletics, Special Olympics, Senior Olympics). Therapeutic recreation events provide opportunities for people who are coping with impairments to demonstrate their motivated abilities and their capacity for experience. Therapeutic recreation programs can be valuable references for insights into treatment and the determination of the true (accurate) ability levels of people who are coping with impairments or illness.

The Paradox of Similar Motivations in the Context of Leisure and the Context of Achievement

Common question: **Can similar orientations to motivation serve the context of leisure and the context of achievement if the contexts originate differently?**

Different origins of behavior result in different experiences for leisure behavior and achievement behavior (see figures 16.1 and 16.2). Leisure behaviors are unique to the person participating, so leisure or recreation can appear nonlinear and is often extended or expanded. In contrast, the use of monitored time and standardization in work results in a concern for time or economy, and work is often compressed and linear. This distinction could explain why so many people comment about wishing the weekend could have lasted longer or about looking forward to the end of the workweek.

Therapeutic recreation specialists provide clients with the opportunity to have sensorimotor experiences such as watching theatre, listening to music, creating art, or seeking adventure.

Despite the differences in the experiences, both leisure and achievement involve consumers and can be improved with considerations for economics and service.

Different Experiences with Similar Orientations to Motivation

Dixon (1984) identified four **orientations to motivation** used in advertising leisure products and services to communicate quality and value to consumers. The four motivations were acquisition, prevention, maintenance, and serendipity. Wolf (1999), Jacobs (2000), and Lewis and Bridger (2000) discussed these orientations to motivation as strategies in the context of business and leisure activities. Wolf (1999) and Lewis and Bridger (2000) suggested that people use these orientations to improve their quality of life whether they are in the context of achievement or the context of leisure.

For example, acquisition is described as gaining something by one's own efforts (Guralnik, 1975). Efforts to acquire something material (e.g., buying comfortable shoes), to develop specific skills (e.g., taking classes), or to have types of experiences (e.g.,

seeking challenges) can serve the person in both the context of leisure and the context of achievement. Likewise, prevention is described as action to avoid a negative consequence (Guralnik, 1975). For many years, authors have identified the use of leisure and recreation activities to avoid dysfunction or illness resulting from stress (Avedon, 1974; Shivers & Fait, 1985). Efforts to prevent negative consequences can make the leisure experience more enjoyable and the work experience more productive. This logic has led to a movement toward corporate-sponsored fitness and recreation programs.

Maintenance is described as a continuation of experience as well as a satisfying process or outcome (Ellis, 1971; Kelly, 1982). The concept of maintenance could explain why people repeatedly plan leisure activities or patronize commercial forms of leisure or recreation. In the context of achievement, many businesses recognize that products and services must please the consumer if they are to have future business success. Ongoing satisfaction is a valuable basis for evaluation and future planning in the contexts of leisure and achievement.

Serendipity can be described as a discovery or awareness of desirable things not sought (Isaac &

Michael, 1971). People who participate in leisure or recreation activities without long-term goals or preconceived notions allow the elements of surprise or spontaneity to influence the experience (Chubb & Chubb, 1981; Nachmanovitch, 1990). In the context of achievement, Wolf (1999) and Jacobs (2000) suggest that discovery will play a strong role in developing and preparing all ages of people for living in the world of the future.

Applications for Therapeutic Recreation

The field of therapeutic recreation uses the orientations to acquisition, prevention, maintenance, and serendipity. For example, rehabilitation involves the *acquisition* of relevant skills for patients or clients. The advocacy of healthy choices and leisure activities is intended to help people *prevent* illness, injury, or addiction. Planning and programming regular opportunities for leisure or recreation are proactive ways to *maintain* or preserve health and abilities within a lifestyle. Finally, many leisure experiences such as reading books or watching movies involve *serendipitous* participation. Recreation professionals may find that people who are bored or uncooperative can be surprised and entertained through participation (Carter, Van Andel & Robb, 2003).

The value of recognizing these orientations for therapeutic recreation service is that they represent alternative orientations that can be used when other strategies fail. For example, if a person with a spinal cord injury is not interested in acquiring athletic skills, he or she may be interested in being active to maintain muscle tone and the efficiency of body processes. Similarly, if a youth offender is not receptive to the authority structure in sports, he or she may find the serendipity of a camping adventure more motivating and participate with more enthusiasm.

The therapeutic recreation specialist operates within the context of achievement when he or she is trying to reach goals and objectives for a patient or client. But the participant in therapeutic recreation programs can demonstrate accurate levels of ability and authentic preferences for motivation as a result of choices and experiences in leisure or recreation activities. The four orientations for motivation presented here have relevance for both categories of behavior.

The Paradox of Promoting the Quality of Leisure and Serving the Bottom Line of a Budget

Common question: How can the value of service articulated by professionals in leisure or recreation services coexist with the emphasis placed on costs by administrators?

People use different values to make decisions (Cordes & Ibrahim, 2003). Distinguishing between different types of values permits people to solve problems and reduce conflicts as individuals or within a group. Values specific to a situation can be called **instrumental values** and permit a person to negotiate for specific preferences through increased analysis. Values that represent broad concepts are called **terminal values** and tend to result in affiliation.

Instrumental Values

Instrumental values are typically oriented to objective characteristics that permit measurement and analysis with reduced affect (subjectivity). For example, reducing the number of staff positions and maintaining the same services will result in a specific saving in the budget. Similarly, providing services within a fixed amount of money can be planned to avoid a budget increase. Both of these examples conform to specific planned objectives (save money, "the bottom line"), but they fail to address broader terminal values.

Terminal Values

Values with generalization are called terminal values and permit people to affiliate with their choices with less analysis (Cordes & Ibrahim, 2003). For example, administrators, political leaders, or managers may have an overall mission to be "lean and mean" or to "do more with less." Such terminal value phrases often communicate an affect, or subjective feeling. Because of differences in values, recreation professionals may think that there is a paradox when emphasizing a terminal value of serving people while limiting services with an instrumental value like cost. In effect, the terminal value of helping people is countered by the instrumental value of limiting spending to the fixed amount of money in a budget. Unfortunately, a rise in costs has been a recurring problem in the field of human services. Leisure and recreation professionals frequently encounter the rationale of cost as a reason for proposed cutbacks in services or staff.

Cost as the Dreaded Single Criterion

There is always a temptation to use cost as a criterion for making programmatic or budget decisions. Basing decisions on a cost outcome is typically using an instrumental value for planning. If professionals object to using cost as the only consideration, they could introduce additional criteria. Professionals have several alternatives for moving beyond a **cost-only condition.** First, they should recognize that cost is an appropriate criterion when inflation, poor value, or bad risk is present. If these conditions do not apply, leisure and recreation professionals can choose from the following:

1. Identify how a service directly affects the agency or patient. This approach moves the benefit close to the decision maker.

2. Present a competitive terminal value. For example, asking people to do the right thing or to balance services suggests a global standard instead of a local short-term solution.

3. Identify an economic benefit for the service. For example, affordable leisure or recreation services may reduce the need for police efforts and reduce community problems with youth at risk. The benefits of affordable physical activity for mature citizens may result in fewer health problems and less social isolation for families with aging relatives.

4. Position leisure or recreation services as a necessity for meeting a standard or quality of life. For example, property values for homes can be enhanced by the proximity of a beautiful park. Family-oriented activities can build a sense of community and reduce the need to budget for graffiti removal or damage to city infrastructure. In short, the intent of these strategies is to expand the equation "cost = value" to an equation that reads "cost + quality = value."

Application to Therapeutic Recreation

The common use of a bottom line or outcome approach in evaluating therapeutic recreation services may not recognize the terminal value of diverse treatment data. For example, an emphasis on the process of treatment could result in a long-term benefit that has value beyond the outcome within a period of treatment. Consider a patient in a mental health setting who is overweight and relies on prescriptive activity for weight loss. Orienting to achievement is satisfactory in the short term because the objective is measurable and recommended. But when the patient meets the objective, the directive for weight loss terminates. Long-term benefits could occur with recreation activity that the patient chooses based on interest or passion. People are more likely to continue a healthy lifestyle when the activity is authentic and based on individual preferences. In contrast, achievement activity typically focuses on outcomes, permits sacrifice, and depends on external directives (conjured experience). In effect, participants may focus on the termination of the experience when the process is not based on authentic preferences.

Similar to other interventions, therapeutic recreation service has a strong concern for achievement and therapy outcome with patients or clients. Permitting a behavioral skill outcome to define the total benefit to the patient or client as an instrumental value may ignore the process outcome typically noted by therapeutic recreation specialists. People who receive treatment in health service settings can benefit from having the terminal values of being proactive and positive. The motivated ability and the initiation (choices) demonstrated by patients or clients are necessary for making accurate (authentic) predictions for future successes in rehabilitation or treatment settings. Therapeutic recreation offers an alternative treatment approach and treatment information that will generalize to other life settings.

The Paradox of Choice for Leisure and Achievement

Common question: Can choice be viewed as a negative factor in leisure or recreation behaviors when it represents the origin of such behaviors?

DEMETRIO

Demetrio is a 48-year-old man who was severely injured in an industrial accident 10 years ago. His injuries caused disabilities severe enough to require significant assistance in his daily living activities. From 2000–2005, Demetrio participated in various Medicaid-funded programs that were provided by his local independent living center (ILC). These included 5 hours of weekly in-home personal assistance for tasks such as meal preparation and self-care. Without this assistance, Demetrio fears he would be unable to care for himself and that he would have to move away from his wife and into a nursing home.

Instrumental Values at Work

In 2006, the governor of Demetrio's home state reduced the eligibility guidelines for Medicaid assistance from 100% of poverty level to 78% of poverty level. This meant that anyone who made more than three quarters of the going poverty rate would be ineligible for health care services through Medicaid. Fortunately, those under the poverty level can pay a "spend-down," which is like a deductible for insurance. This means they have to spend a certain amount of money before Medicaid kicks in. This spend-down makes up the difference between your income and the current poverty level. When the governor made these changes, Demetrio found himself in poverty but ineligible for Medicaid because he received "too much" disability and social security income (about $9,000 a year). As a result,

Demetrio had to spend $240 on health care each month before his Medicaid would start helping. Ironically, the governor's effort to save money by cutting the bottom line was actually about to cost the state more. The only way Demetrio could pay his spend-down was to give up his apartment and spend his rent on spend-down. This would force him to move into a nursing home, which would increase the state's expense tenfold.

Terminal Values at Work

In response to the governor's rule change, the ILC that provided support to Demetrio developed a plan to actually pay the spend-down for those who had been unexpectedly dropped from the program. The staff proposal was reviewed by the board of directors and, after much debate, adopted for implementation. The board faced a dilemma of spending the agency's money to compensate for the governor's decision, but when considering their mission to maximize independence for as long as possible, the answer seemed clear. As a result, the ILC carries a small portion of their clients on a spend-down support program, which initially amounted to about $5,000 a month. This program pays an agreed-upon portion of the client's spend-down, which makes the client immediately eligible for all Medicaid services. Over time, the clients have adjusted to their situation, and the spend-down expense for the agency has decreased dramatically. More importantly, people like Demetrio were able to stay in their homes and maintain their health and independence.

Schwartz (2004) implied that too much choice diminishes life experience because the person has too many decisions to make. Schwartz asserts that people are changing jobs too frequently, have increasingly more responsibility to invest for their own retirement, spend too much time looking for bargain prices, face too many denominations of churches to consider for prayer, and face too many romantic circumstances in the media. Schwartz consistently pointed out the chore of having to make choices and implied that life would be simpler and easier with fewer choices (less pressure).

Selection Under Pressure Versus Choice as a Preference

Schwartz (2004) did not distinguish between the contexts of achievement and leisure. For example, his conclusion that people are shopping more

than they used to and enjoying it less could be a response to financial difficulties (pressures) and the need to buy more carefully by getting the best prices. Schwartz would not be alone if he were to wish for economic achievement to be easier (Campbell, 2002). Shopping to save money on obligated purchases like groceries, appliances, and clothing is an achievement behavior. But people who shop for clothing as a leisure activity (e.g., a gift for themselves) would be disappointed if choice was limited (Lewis & Bridger, 2000; Wolf, 1999). The role of choice in leisure activities helps clarify the authenticity of feelings that people have in the process of participation (Dixon, 1995).

Leisure and recreation are distinct from achievement and work behavior because activities originate with some level of choice (Dixon, 1995; Cordes & Ibrahim, 2003). Reducing choices in the context of achievement or work only increases the degree of obligation, standardization, and linear behavior. One management benefit of reducing choices in work or achievement may be increased predictability and consistency of behavior. In contrast I argue that reducing choices in leisure could reduce the analysis experienced by participants. Participants in leisure and recreation activities can use analysis to appreciate the details within a larger context of activity (Nachmanovitch, 1990). In other words, participants may have positive feelings for the total process by recognizing the details of the experience. A nonlinear path of experience can support the appreciation of details. When leisure activities have uncertainty, participants may distinguish and evaluate new information (Nachmanovitch). As a result, emphasizing choice in leisure and recreation can serve as a source of satisfaction rather than a source of distress (Wolf, 1999).

Application to Therapeutic Recreation

The **therapeutic recreator's dilemma** identified by Ellis (1973) emphasizes the importance of choice for therapeutic recreation professionals and participants. Ellis (1973) suggested that programmed therapeutic recreation activities should result in intrinsic motivation and exist in a concept of normalcy. Normalcy can become a constraint for those receiving therapeutic recreation services

in that clients are expected to behave or participate within the norms and rules of society. The dilemma described by Ellis comes from determining how to provide choice within the constraints of structured normalcy. These constraints might include therapy restrictions, daily schedules, or behavior expectations that are unfamiliar to the client.

The goal of therapeutic recreation specialists, therefore, is to assess patient or client preferences and program activities utilizing characteristics associated with leisure and recreation participation (see figures 16.1 and 16.2) to facilitate successful and satisfying participation within the limits of normalcy.

The Paradox of Leisure as a Zero-Order Behavior

Common question: Why doesn't leisure behavior receive the same reinforcement (support) as achievement behavior if both contexts of behavior are sources of satisfaction?

People typically receive congratulations and rewards for personal achievements. For example, students receive good grades and recognition for exemplary

Part of your job as a therapeutic recreation specialist is to provide boundaries for your clients.

academic work. Workers who attain targeted levels of productivity gain recognition and financial rewards. Professionals who manage a context of achievement are sensitive to positive and negative outcomes as they relate to human wants, needs, and problems. Outcomes that are not relevant to performance criteria or productivity may not receive the same reinforcement as positive outcomes do. In academic settings, probation and disqualification may be used to redirect students to achieve positive outcomes. In vocational settings, threats of probation, limited earnings, demotion, and termination of employment may be used to redirect workers and achieve positive productivity levels. The importance of outcome in achievement behaviors often results in strategic terminations of behavior to meet management-determined objectives. Overall, the focus on outcome within the context of achievement results in a sense of polarization for behaviors. Workers and students learn that behaviors that have a positive order (**positive-order behaviors**) are consensus outcomes and are reinforced accordingly (Nachmanovitch, 1990; Mitroff, 1998).

Zero-Order Behaviors and Leisure

Many behaviors in life do not have consensus-based outcomes. Examples include the amount of debt that people should have, the amount of time that should be spent with family, the number of holidays that should be celebrated, and the amount of money that should be spent on gifts. The lack of consensus for determining specific objectives results in large variances in these types of behaviors. In fact, attention to these behaviors may not occur without orienting to the problem of absence. When only the absence of behavior prompts external intervention, the behaviors may be considered to have zero status.

Zero-order behaviors are described as behaviors that receive attention for intervention only when they are absent (Gold, 1980). For example, in school or work settings, people do not typically receive thanks from others for using deodorant, brushing their teeth, fixing breakfast for their children, doing the laundry, paying their monthly bills, or staying monogamous in a marriage. These types of behaviors are expected to occur without additional reinforcement; thus, they have zero status. But if people do not perform these behaviors, there can be a request by other people to correct the behaviors.

Leisure or recreation behaviors may be treated like zero-order behaviors when compared with achievement behaviors. In school settings, activities like recess, band, athletics, and chorus are often labeled as extracurricular. Participation is determined by opportunities instead of mandate, and academic work is expected to take priority. Students receive comparatively little attention for these activities unless they have a negative experience in participation. Similarly, people in work settings receive little attention for their preferred diets, pet ownership, or choices about vacation. But poor fitness, charges of pet abuse, or illegal behavior during a vacation would bring the attention of a manager, animal control officer, or police officer. The zero-order label for behaviors indicates the absence of day-to-day reinforcement, but the importance of intervention when these behaviors are absent also indicates a maintenance value. Attempts to justify leisure and recreation behaviors in service settings could benefit by recognizing the value of potential zero-order behaviors that have maintenance value.

Considerations for Behaviors With Maintenance Value

The categories of zero-order and positive-order behaviors have value for people who are oriented to improving the quality of life and being productive. Leisure or recreation behaviors may be considered to have little value within the context of achievement as positive-order behaviors because the focus is not on outcome. Instead, identifying leisure and recreation activities as zero-order behaviors that have maintenance value and contribute to productivity could help managers of achievement behavior be more proactive in avoiding performance losses in academic or work settings.

By design, leisure and recreation behaviors reflect authentic motivation, personal skills, and knowledge (Cordes & Ibrahim, 2003). These three factors dramatically affect levels of physical and mental health. In the context of achievement, workers or students may not receive reinforcement for having positive social skills, getting enough sleep, participating in leisure activities, and living a healthy lifestyle. But a decline in physical health, reduced satisfaction with lifestyle, and negative social behaviors could significantly diminish outcomes in the context of achievement.

People are employed in contexts of achievement to be continuously productive. Managers schedule achievement and expect students and workers to be ready to learn and work. In addition, students and workers are expected to maintain their ready status on a daily or yearly basis so that optimal outcomes occur. If people in achievement settings become dysfunctional or impaired because of ongoing health problems or domestic conflicts, productivity could decline. Unfortunately, health care costs for the treatment of illness and dysfunction appear to be increasing and have to be reconciled with the loss of productivity in families, schools, and work settings (Carter, Van Andel, & Robb, 2003).

Applications to Therapeutic Recreation

Therapeutic recreation specialists serve many patients and clients who have experienced significant declines in physical and mental health (Carter, Van Andel, & Robb, 2003). Many of these cases are attributed to the effects of work and domestic stress. Addressing domestic problems, inappropriate leisure activity, and poor lifestyle choices only after people demonstrate impairments is reaction rather than proaction (prevention). Significant financial costs for health care, worker replacement, and corrective management might be avoided if behaviors with maintenance value were recognized and supported (Cordes & Ibrahim, 2003). Supporting zero-order behaviors such as leisure or recreation for the purpose of maintaining productivity in achievement settings could be a proactive strategy that would benefit families, schools, and work settings.

Summary

The paradoxes suggested in this chapter appear to occur when there is no distinction between leisure and achievement while people seek to improve their quality of life. As such, it is critical that therapeutic recreation specialists understand this distinction and the associated implications for practice.

Specifically, therapeutic recreation service settings provide a context of achievement for professionals and a context of leisure or recreation for patients and clients. Professionals assess people and evaluate service efforts within limited periods, so the time spent meeting goals or objectives is always an issue. The results are considered in a context of achievement to evaluate the cost of services and measure the benefits to patients or clients. Specific achievements can include patient initiative, accurate mobility skills, improved fitness levels, increased knowledge of resources, and the development of personal skills. Such achievements can positively affect the speed of treatment.

At the same time, the use of leisure or recreation activities is an alternative approach that uses positive individual choices based on authentic motivation (leisure or recreation context). Because of the cost of health care, the diverse nature of human problems, and the unique characteristics of individual patients, strategies that strongly involve a patient or client in the treatment process will be needed. Treatment issues such as occupational stress, eating disorders, substance abuse, physical injury, disease, illegal activities, and mental health problems often involve long-term attention and a need for sincere patient initiatives. Services for people who demonstrate impairments or dysfunction typically include helping to create awareness or appreciation of experiences that can lead to positive lifestyle changes. Enhancing the abilities of people to appreciate the importance of positive choices and the experience of positive activity can be a significant part of improving long-term health and function.

DISCUSSION QUESTIONS

1. How can a paradox exist for understanding leisure, recreation, or therapeutic recreation if the experience is distinctly different from achievement behavior?

2. What critical force can you identify for therapeutic recreation services?

3. Can you recognize the importance of skills from Piaget's three stages in the contexts of physical rehabilitation, psychiatric settings, and settings with seniors?

4. What would a therapeutic recreation activity look like if you eliminated choice and authentic behavior?

5. Discuss with your instructor how each of these paradoxes has been observed in real life professional issues in the past.

Envisioning the Future:

Therapeutic Recreation as a Profession

Terry Robertson, PhD
Northwest Missouri State University

LEARNING OUTCOMES

After completing this chapter, learners will be able to demonstrate the following competencies:

- Identify primary elements of the model of personal and professional development
- Apply the proposed model to develop a long-term plan for personal and professional development
- Identify at least three social, economic, or cultural trends that may affect the therapeutic recreation profession in the future
- Recognize and use six paradigms for understanding and addressing future trends, challenges, and opportunities in therapeutic recreation

No person knows the future, nor does any nation, professional organization, political party, or corporation. The future is yet to be determined. Events, political influences, and social needs shift from moment to moment, creating an ongoing, and often unpredictable, process of change. Everything from natural disasters and technological advancements to expectations of consumer groups has the potential to create change, and so do you! As we speak, cultures, practices, techniques, and opportunities are changing or disappearing, and new ones are being created. This change offers both opportunity and risk. If we are not careful stewards of our profession, we run the risk of losing our useful place within society. Cultural change agents are all around us, and the potential for rapid change is increasing as we move ahead in time. So the profession is open to you—the future leaders, providers, administrators, and educators. You have the responsibility to make the profession the best it can be for you and for society. Finally, you should note that you will be able to influence these changes during your career. If you can harness the opportunities while navigating the risks, you have a tremendous opportunity to lead the profession into the future.

Embracing Our History

I believe that the practice of our profession will be very different in 5 years, much less 10, 50, or even 100 years. The impending changes will represent a continuation of what has occurred in the past, as each decade has involved a significant metamorphosis toward our present status as a profession. The following milestones shed light on how this growth and change have occurred over time and how quickly the future can arrive.

Living Our Legacy

During 2006 at least three related modern-era national professional organizations celebrated significant anniversaries—the Alberta Therapeutic Recreation Association (ATRA), 20 years; the National Council on Therapeutic Recreation Certification (NCTRC), 25 years; and the National Therapeutic Recreation Society (NTRS), 40 years. In addition, the American Therapeutic Recreation Association (ATRA) entered its 22nd year of existence in 2006.

The year 2006 also marked the 35th anniversary of the Midwest Symposium on Therapeutic Recreation and the 30th anniversary of the Mid-East Symposium. Although these symposiums are not organizations, they are two of the best attended conferences on therapeutic recreation in the world, and the individuals participating in them have made significant contributions to our profession for many years. The year 2006 also marked the 30th consecutive year that the state of Utah maintained its therapeutic recreation licensure law. Utah was the first state to pass such a law (S. Post, personal communication, October 14, 2006). The law provided governmental permission for those properly prepared and duly qualified in our profession to practice within the state. The year 2006 was also the first year that a licensure law was in place for those working in New Hampshire and the second year for a licensure law in North Carolina. A final example of our profession's relatively short but effective and diverse professional contribution to modern society is that 2006 was the 34th year of community-based therapeutic recreation services for the city of Las Vegas and the 30th year for similar services for the city of Eugene, Oregon.

Utilizing Change

All these organizations, conferences, and municipalities have experienced changes during their existence—changes in leadership, focus, services, policies, membership, and effectiveness. Change should be expected and planned for. Change, however, is often viewed as a surprise and a threat. Sometimes, those who are trying to maintain or manage organizations, households, or personal situations view change as negative. Others view change as positive, as growth, or as movement to be current. The struggle is to achieve balance between the two perspectives. Consistency (absence of change) helps build or establish identity (thus recognition, brand identity, specialization, and strength), and change helps build relevance (new, expanding, or changing markets and needs).

So as you consider your future and the future of this profession, you should think about your comfort level with these concepts (consistency versus change), both personally and professionally (or academically). Then you need to think about the short term (the situation right now, your first internship, your first job) and finally the long term (your goals for 5 years from now, 10 years, 50 years). You

WHO'DA THUNK IT?

Let us look at a couple of general examples of how change has occurred in the practice of other professions and how they have been considered both good and bad for some in certain societies. They are familiar change agents to many of you. The younger you are, the less you may know about their history.

Take a minute and think about computers and how big (or small) they are and how you use them. Now, take a moment and think about phones and how big (or small) they are and how you use them. Believe it or not, these two things were at one time completely separate entities and provided completely separate experiences and opportunities for both the professionals involved in their development and use, as well as with their consumers and users. Originally, they were not directly related to each other, but they did share some common knowledge and some common technology. Now they are so intertwined that it would be difficult for most of you to think of them as separate or unconnected to each other.

The common knowledge base (electronics) combined with a common purpose (communication—verbally, numerically, or graphically) and an open and willing consumer base (real or perceived demand) created the right atmosphere for cultural change agents (belief systems, use patterns, expectations, and so on) to develop in both industries and allow them to grow. These changes were experienced individually at first and then together in ways beyond many providers' imaginations. In both cases, however, these changes were viewed skeptically by some, with fear by others, and by the actual loss of jobs for others, as well as the development of new jobs for still others.

If you are confused, let us slow down and approach this from a different perspective. To begin with, you need to think historically about each of these areas of technology (computers and telephones) and note that all of these changes have happened within the past 40 to 100 years, depending on where you lived.

First, examine the items in table 17.1. Then think about the development and changes in personal communication hardware options from the current technology back to past practices or services. Note that Blackberries and Bluetooth technology are essentially an integration of these technologies and think about what your grandparents would have thought if you told them as teenagers about this synergy.

Depending on when you first encountered either of these technologies and how and why you use them, you may view them as either helping people become more connected to each other or separating people as we struggle to keep up with change. For example, some senior citizens love e-mail because it allows them to do things like communicate with distant family and friends or shop online, when "getting out" might be difficult, but others are intimidated by the prospect of learning how to use computers or they may fear that online shopping is dangerous due to the risk of identity theft. The latter group would much rather use a telephone or an "in-person" experience, and when societal demands discourage this, they feel disconnected. Thus, differing levels of technological knowledge and use can both separate and connect us with family, friends, and society in general.

Ultimately, changes in familiar technologies such as these can be viewed as factors affecting cultures worldwide. How these changes affect us, whether they harm or hurt us, and how society should react, are all debatable points that should be considered.

Table 17.1 Evolution of Technology in Popular Culture

Time period	The telephone	The computer
Good ol' days	Smoke signals Pony Express Telegraph Party lines	Cave drawings (records) Abacus (calculations) Dictionary (information) Encyclopedia (information)
1960s	Rotary phones	Room-sized computers
1970s	Push-button phones	Desktops
1980s	Bag phones	Internet
1990s	Pocket cell phones	Laptops
2000s	Text messages	Palm Pilots
21st Century	Multiple technology devices such as Blackberries and Bluetooth	

Consider your comfort levels and desires when deciding if you want to pursue a career in therapeutic recreation.

©PhotoDisc

will have many choices as you move through your life, and the decision to make your career within this profession is but one.

The Emergence of a Global Society

Significant changes in culture and interdependent belief systems are happening all around us. These cultural changes are occurring worldwide, not just in the United States or North America. Furthermore, change is occurring faster than it did in the past, largely because of technology. We are becoming a more global, more mobile, and in some ways a more dissatisfied and segregated society—economically, socially, educationally, politically, ethnically, and in terms of health status, human rights, and quality of life (Putnam, 2000; Veblen, 1899). The eventuality of a one-world economy has been discussed and debated for years. The European Union, the World Bank, the United Nations, the World Health Organization, the expansion of **capitalism,** the growth of multinational organizations, the increase in **outsourcing,** the growth of collaborative relief and aid work, and the application of democracy and

free enterprise to other countries are all evidence of efforts to create or control economic and political systems worldwide. Embedded within these change agents are fundamental issues that also need to be addressed—race, religion, age, gender, language, terminology, cross-cultural concerns, immigration versus refugee status, and best or better practices in serving those affected by these changes.

So where and how do these situations, groups, organizations, efforts, or changes affect our profession and those whom we serve now and in the future? Are we connected to any one of these potential influencers? If not, could or should we be connected? If so, how and why should we be connected? Are we an influencer? If yes, at what level and how widespread is our influence? Are we a player or an influencer in our own country or state, within our community, or within our place of employment? You and your instructor should recognize these as rhetorical questions. Each question also contains a **problatunity**—a problem and an opportunity residing in the same space at the same time.

Acknowledging that our world is ever changing and will evolve with or without our involvement is critical. The challenge before you both as an individual and as a group of preprofessionals is to start thinking globally and then plan to act locally. It has been said that if you control the questions, then you also control the answers. So, what should be on the scoreboard (criteria) to determine how much, or even if, we contribute to global society? What must we do to influence policy, legislation, regulations, the practice of the profession, and day-to-day services so that ultimately we can meet the needs in our society?

For an example, consider an article in *USA Today* newspaper by Paul Leavitt (2006) based on wire service reports. The article indicated that the United Nations Development Program's **human development index** identified Norway as the best place to live in the world, followed by Iceland, Australia, Canada, Japan, and then the United States. According to the article, 2006 was the sixth consecutive year for Norway to be ranked first by the United Nations. Some of the indicators (criteria) used in support of this top ranking were that Norwegians earn 40 times more than those who live in the lowest-ranked countries (the lowest-scoring countries were Niger and Sierra Leone) and that they (the Norwegians) live almost twice as long and have a literacy rate that is nearly five times higher than those who live in the lower-scoring countries. Norway is also an oil-rich country. The report was not able to rank 17 countries, including Iraq, Afghanistan, and Somalia, because of insufficient or missing data. How many of these indicators are also tied to quality of life? How many of those living in these countries consider leisure or recreation an important or essential part of life? Which countries have viable therapeutic recreation professionals practicing or providing services in them now? Which ones would be open to our services and why? Which countries could benefit the most from our profession and why?

We have considered enough broad questions for the time being. Now we need to consider our future and help you decide on both the directions and the methodologies that we can use to get us where we (you, current practitioners, and current and future recipients of your service) want to be.

The Future of Therapeutic Recreation as a Profession

Rather than attempt to predict exactly what the future practice of this profession will be, this chapter presents two primary tools for you to use in creating the future of our profession. First, a model of **professional development** is presented. You can immediately start applying this model to your professional development as a student, and later on you can use it as a professional, which will ultimately further develop the profession. Second, six different **paradigms** for understanding the future of therapeutic recreation are presented. You should consider each paradigm individually and collectively, discuss the implications of these paradigms with each other and with your instructor, and brainstorm ways to apply them within your own practice (life, current situation, occupation, and future career). You can then use them to have a positive influence on the future of our profession through your professional decision making, your life choices, and your personal and professional affiliations and commitments (organizational alliances; memberships; donations of time, money, or intellectual thought; and your various networks).

Developing a Collective Wisdom

The collective knowledge base of a profession and the applicability of that knowledge base to practice will influence future directions of the profession. If the knowledge base and applicability of a profession do not grow or change to meet new expectations, or are not shared and used both internally and externally (settings, populations, situations, purposes, professions), opportunities for positive influence and the potential of our profession are limited. For that reason, besides considering the six organizational paradigms presented later in this chapter, you should already be considering your personal and professional development. Applying the following model to your personal and professional development will ultimately enhance the collective wisdom of therapeutic recreation.

A Model of Personal and Professional Development

The model of personal and professional development presented in figure 17.1 was created in the early 1990s. It was used in consulting practices with organizations and individuals and was presented at the Midwest Symposium on Therapeutic Recreation (Robertson, 1993) in a session titled "The Wheel of Fortune or the Wheel of Torture? A Conceptual Model for Professional and Personal Development."

The model uses the wheel of a bike as a metaphor. We begin by imagining our professional and personal body of knowledge (what we know about our profession and its applicability to help others and to manage ourselves and our practice) as the hub of a wheel on a multigeared bicycle. The spokes are the delivery mechanisms to put our body of knowledge to work. They are the link between theory (the hub), practice or application (the tire rim), and the consumer group (the tire itself). The spokes are also a mechanism to help build or increase our individual or corporate body of knowledge. The tire rim can also represent the organization or management structure, and the tire tread can represent face-to-face, day-to-day service delivery. The size of the tire may represent your sphere of influence, community size, or the size of your role in a given job. (Use the worksheet in figure 17.2 to assess yourself in relation to the four spokes provided as examples. Think about your potential motivation or source of energy to rotate the tire.) The four example spokes (reading, writing, speaking, and doing or practicing) are the minimum requirements for professionals who are trying to keep up with best practices and keep ahead of changes.

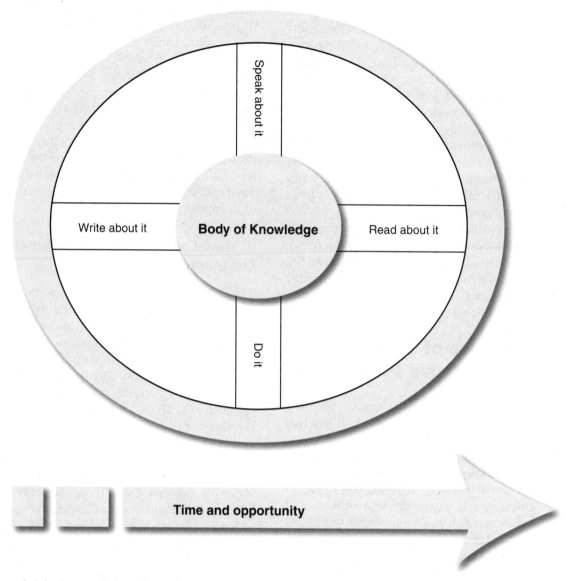

Speak about it

Write about it

Body of Knowledge

Read about it

Do it

Time and opportunity

Example of other spokes—Alternative credentials in addition to CTRS or licensure, work experience in new settings or working with folks with other types of disabilities, involvement with other aspects of your organization or agency, new knowledge or new technology, experimentation, research or evaluation of services, quality assurance, active involvement with a related or unrelated professional organization, and so on.

Example of other gears—More education, more or higher levels of responsibility, time in a given position or role, trying other disciplines or new body of knowledge to your practice, and so on.

Figure 17.1   A conceptual model of personal and professional development, previously presented as "The Wheel of Fortune or the Wheel of Torture?"

At first your body of knowledge may be small, but over time and given the many opportunities that you will find in this profession, the size and shape of your spokes may change. Long and thin spokes could represent specialization; thick and short spokes may represent lots of experience, but in one role, capacity, or comfort. As you seek to develop each spoke, you are adding to your knowledge base and possibly the knowledge base of the profession. If you focus on the development of a single spoke, the others will be shorter or smaller so you will need more effort to move your wheel or bike ahead (a lack of development). Of course, the four example spokes are just the beginning of

PROFESSIONAL DEVELOPMENT SELF-ASSESSMENT

Part I: Spokes

Rotate the following verbs—*read, write, speak,* and *do*—into each of the following questions. Please answer all using *read* first, then *speak,* then *write,* and finally *do, did,* or *done.*

1. What was the last thing that you _____ related to your profession?
2. How much have you _____ related to your profession in the past year?
3. What do you regularly _____ related to the profession? Not related?
4. How many people have _____ anything that you have _____?
5. On a scale from 0 to 7 (0 being nonexistent and 7 being the most important thing that you do), rate your enjoyment of _____ing.

Part II: Short Answers

Answer the following questions as best you can.

1. In your opinion, is what you do more like an art or a science?
2. How is what you do like and unlike what the director of a three-ring circus does (or an auto mechanic, medical doctor, archaeologist, or salesperson)?
3. If you could eliminate all but one role or job function of your job, what would you keep and why?
4. At the end of a day, how do you know how well your work has gone?
5. If you never had to go back to work again and could still be paid, what *thing* might cause you to return to work and why?

Figure 17.2 Worksheet for applying the conceptual model for personal and professional development.

our analogy. You could add any number of spokes to strengthen yourself and our profession and to improve intervention efficacy. Here are a few that you might add: alternative credentials, work experience in new settings or with folks with other types of disabilities, involvement with other aspects of your organization or agency, new knowledge or new technology, experimentation, research or evaluation of services, quality assurance, and active involvement with a related or unrelated professional organization. Of course, if you add gears, more education, more specialized knowledge or skills, more or higher levels of responsibility, or more time, you might move along quicker or more effectively.

GROWING PAINS

The model was initially called the wheel of fortune or the wheel of torture because it implies that you, yourself, are responsible for development. It also implies that if you are not active, you can become stuck in a rut, spend your time spinning your wheels, or lose a spoke and become wobbly, broken, and useless (or need a repair). You also run

the risk of overdoing things and burning yourself out. On the other hand, the model could be the mechanism that leads you to growth, a satisfying and rewarding career (you determine what you find important and satisfying for yourself), and thus your fortune. Note here that personal growth and professional development are processes, not events. They require work, focus, practice, time, and some level of competition and stress. Keep in mind the benefits and obligations of purposefully pursuing your personal and professional development. Using the model can help ensure that you experience such benefits and live up to your obligations.

REACHING OUT

We, as a profession, need to be preparing potential professionals like you to meet many roles. The first is to provide direct care services and then to manage or direct others to provide services. Next is to prepare you to research and track local, state, national, and international trends and best practices, and finally to be culturally competent. Likewise, we need to seek access to and become a positive

A PORTRAIT OF A FUTURE OUTSTANDING PROFESSIONAL

Up until now, every chapter has presented an "Outstanding Professional" as a way to help you understand what your future might entail as a therapeutic recreation specialist. For this chapter, we are asking you to consider what it will take for this portrait to some day be about you. Reflect back on chapter 1 where it was suggested that this profession, or any particular job opportunity it brings, may not be right for everyone. In part, this is a personal choice, either you do or do not have a desire for this profession. But also, it is a matter of competence, or being adequately trained and prepared to do the job. Don't let this latter part derail your career. You can be the "Outstanding Professional" of the future if you commit yourself to working hard and seeking answers. Below are some suggestions that can help ensure your professional competence and the associated success. You are encouraged to create a professional development plan that addresses each of these items.

- Don't be afraid to ask questions and seek answers from the following people as often as possible.
  - Current and former students at your school and other schools
  - Professors from your school and other schools
  - Professionals from a variety of different settings
  - Leaders of therapeutic recreation professional organizations
  - NCTRC or state licensure staff and representatives
- Investigate beyond what you learn in class
  - Read books, journals, and newsletters related to therapeutic recreation.
  - Join a list-serve, chat room, or blog related to therapeutic recreation.
  - Regularly visit NTRS, ATRA, NCTRC, and other professional Web sites.
  - Join professional organizations—get and stay involved, become a leader.
  - Attend professional trainings and conferences.
  - Visit therapeutic recreation programs and organizations.

- Complete as many hours of volunteer, service learning, or other hands-on experiences as you can.
  - Choose your internship(s) wisely—again visit many sites before choosing.
- Consider how additional schooling and training might enhance your abilities.
  - Master's degree or PhD
  - Child Life Certification
  - Training and certifications in other areas such as therapeutic riding, challenge course facilitation, wilderness first responder, and aquatics
- Be prepared to meet or exceed all credentialing requirements for the state or setting that you hope to work in. These could include national certification, state licensure, state registration, or any combination of the three.
- WORK HARD—your success is ultimately dependent on your willingness and dedication toward learning, and the ability to apply what you learn.
  - Remember the ABCs: Your Attitude affects your Behavior, which in turn affects both your Communication and your Committment, thus the Consequences of your choice and your performance. Possible outcomes include success, stagnation, or stinks
- Get D.I.R.T.Y: Developing an Interest in Risk Taking (in one or all of the five domains of living and learning: social, emotional, physical, intellectual, and spiritual), and the Y is for You.
- Be a role model for those you work with by enjoying the opportunities you are given, taking time for your own leisure and recreation.

Through this process, you will begin to develop a vision for your future, a professional philosophy, and a bond with the values of our profession. Take a second to try to imagine what your vision might look like. Where will you be and what will you have accomplished 30 years from now? Then spend a few minutes writing an "Outstanding Professional" description of yourself in 30 years. Share what you write with others as a way to reinforce this vision for your future.

influence on non-therapeutic-recreation-focused groups or organizations (i.e., the World Health Organization; the United Nations; state legislatures; specific advocacy groups such as Easter Seals, the ARC, AAMR, and the Autism Society; centers for independent living; and private for profits, private nonprofits, foundations, faith-based organizations, and charities). Individually, you need to feel comfortable and be willing to take our knowledge base and apply it in many different settings and service arenas. As a profession we need to find more ways to collaborate with like-minded organizations and professions so that we can influence both policy and practice. Think back to the earlier discussion of our global community and to the telecommunication and computer examples. As you read the following section, think about how this highly interconnected world might provide challenges and opportunities for our profession both inside and outside our traditional roles and realms.

Finding the Optimal Perspective

Here is where your new work begins. Introduced here are six potential **worldviews** (paradigms, perspectives, or conceptual models) that our profession might consider as we work to determine how to operate in the future. These are not new models or ideas; some are over 100 years old. They do, however, represent differing perspectives of how one might view the world (positively, negatively, or with uncertainty), how we live and interact within it, and make decisions. Ultimately, these viewpoints have the potential to affect the profession and how we practice therapeutic recreation now and in the future. In the latest *Megatrends* book, Aburdene (2005) suggests that future generations should seek to work at places that are congruent with their own personal paradigm.

Social and Civic Engagement Paradigm

The social and civic engagement perspective asserts that everything is framed and dealt with through the art and science of citizenship, politics, and democracy to identify and deal with issues such as social capital, social equity, and social justice. Access equals influence, so the development and use of social and professional networks, connectivity, and

You must learn to analyze your world through many different viewpoints so that when you are helping clients, you can more easily see into theirs.

collaborative approaches to planning and problem solving are important. Service learning, community service, and other community-focused agendas are also used. This paradigm could also simply be considered a grassroots or political approach (Bennett, 1999; Dustin, 1993; Putnam, 2000; Putnam & Feldstein, 2003; Veblen, 1899).

Consumer or Economic Paradigm

An alternative approach is to view the dynamics of our world within the context of economic models (i.e., supply and demand, cost–benefit modeling, profit generation, market-share value, cost recovery), which typically assert that decisions are money driven and made from either a micro- or macroeconomic perspective. This perspective may entail simple supply versus demand approaches, market-share value versus market-share total approaches, or value-added approaches. Potential issues from this perspective might include the effect of minimum wage on industry, education, and employment rates. This perspective might also look at the effects of collective bargaining (unions) on profit margins, general productivity, salary or position compression, merit pay versus raises based on cost of living, investment strategies, wealth management, and wealth protection. In this "you get what you pay for" approach, margins and volumes are critical. This approach can be referred to as a marketing approach or the Wal-Mart versus Versace approach (Bennett, 1999; Putnam, 2000; Putnam & Feldstein, 2003; Kelly & Warnick, 1999; Veblen, 1899).

Quality Management, or Mission and Vision, Paradigm

This perspective is based on the use of core values to shape the decision-making process. Under this philosophy, those involved in achieving the mission must believe in the values of the group that they are working with and use those shared values as a beacon to guide their work. Values are often prioritized, and strategic planning is used to achieve missions or visions. Leaders who implement such a philosophy often work hard to model agency or organizational values and the associated desired behavior. Also critical is recognizing and rewarding value-congruent behavior demonstrated by team members. This approach could be viewed as either a ritualistic approach or a humanistic approach (Covey, 2005; Holtz, 1998; O'Neill & Conzemius, 2006; Loher & Schwartz, 2003).

Behavioral or Outcomes Paradigm

Focusing on the end product, this approach is often data driven. It could involve a combination of organizational management and marketing strategies, as well as use of the scientific method as a forecasting tool. Examples within our profession might include issues of time on task, scope and sequence, billable time versus downtime, standard operating procedures (SOP), **diagnostic related groups** (DRGs), **risk pool insurance** systems, optimization of resources, and market share or niche approaches. The outcome is sometimes more important than the means of getting there. This approach could also simply be viewed as the segmentation–sterilization or specialization approach (Hubbard, 1993; Leavitt, 2006; O'Neill & Conzemius, 2006).

Change Theory Paradigm

Change theory can involve a mathematical or theoretical examination for patterns, interventions, issues, perspectives, and outliers. It can also focus on abstract or obtuse issues and the expected versus the unexpected. This approach could be viewed simply as the mathematical, experimental, or systematic pattern and outlier approach. Change theory projects futures based on trends of the past (Blanchard, Lacinak, Tompkins, & Ballard, 2002; Buckingham & Clifton 2001; Covey, 2005; Hutchens, 2000; Johnson, 1998; Senge et al., 1999).

Spirituality or Religious Systems Paradigm

This paradigm acknowledges the influence of religious systems on the world in which we live. Belief can be in a higher power (Buddhism, Christian, Judaism, Muslim), within oneself (self-reverent thought, self-determination, self-control), or in many things (Christian Science, holistic health, new age beliefs). Belief may not exist or may be of an undetermined nature (agnostic, atheist, not exposed to belief systems or have not thought about it). Faith or hope issues as well as rituals or beliefs about birth, illness, disability, gender, purpose in life, roles, families, relationships, lifestyle issues, and death all influence our world, how it works, and how we work within it (Aburdene, 2005; Buckingham & Clifton, 2001; Holtz, 1998; Lipson, Dibble, & Minarik, 1996; Zander & Zander, 2000).

Summary

National Geographic photographer Dewitt Jones has spent years finding beauty in places where most of us would never think to look. His name may not be familiar, but you probably know him through his work. I mention Dewitt here because he has realized that his ability to find what is right with the world can serve as a template for many of life's challenges. He now spends much of his time sharing this message with people, talking about how perspective is important to finding our way in life. Moving a short distance or waiting a few seconds can make a world of difference in both photography and in how we see problems, opportunities, one another, and the world in general. The six paradigms serve as examples of how different perspectives suggest different pathways to the future. Each of these paradigms can be used to solve a single problem, but in very different ways and often with far different results. Within the world of therapeutic recreation, we must learn to examine, critique, and apply these and other viewpoints available to us when venturing into our professional futures, as individuals and as a collective.

DISCUSSION QUESTIONS

1. How does knowing and understanding the past help improve the future? How does it prevent or hinder improvement or change?

2. Identify the primary elements of the professional development model and discuss which element (spoke, hub, tire, etc.) will be the most challenging for you and why.

3. Create a plan to help you work on this element both before and after you graduate. Share this with at least one other person.

4. Identify at least three trends (social, economic, cultural, etc.) that could affect the future of this profession and your potential for becoming a practicing professional.

5. Please identify one new trend (technology, economic, social, etc.) that is changing the way that you or those around you complete (or not) a routine task. Describe it to someone else and then identify how this could be used (positively or negatively) within this profession as you know it.

6. Identify by name or description the six different paradigms presented and then identify how each could be used to better assure or eliminate services to those you work with and why.

Appendix A
National Therapeutic Recreation Society Standards of Practice

This publication represents the work of numerous persons over many years, with significant input from the NTRS membership. The Standards of Practice are designed to serve as a basic framework relative to the practice of therapeutic recreation services regardless of setting.

It is hoped this document will be relevant, useful, and changing and growing as our practice evolves, and the beginning of a dynamic process that creates dialogue amongst colleagues. It is intended that this document be used in conjunction with the Guidelines for the Administration of Therapeutic Recreation Services and the Code of Ethics and Interpretive Guidelines. [Note: Visit www.nrpa.org for the most up-to-date standards and descriptions.]

Standard I - Scope of Service

- Treatment services are available which are goal-oriented and directed toward rehabilitation, amelioration and/or modification of specific physical, emotional, cognitive, and/or social functional behaviors. Therapeutic recreation intervention targeting these functional behaviors is warranted when the behaviors impede or otherwise inhibit participation in reasonable and customary leisure participation. (Note: This may not apply to all therapeutic recreation settings for all clients.)

- Leisure education services are available which are goal-oriented and directed toward the development of knowledge, attitudes, values, behaviors, skills, and resources related to socialization and leisure involvement. (Note: This may not apply for all clients.)

- Recreation services are available that provide a variety of activities designed to meet client needs, competencies, aptitudes, capabilities and interest. These services are directed toward optimizing client leisure involvement and are designed to promote health and well-being, and improve the quality of life.

Standard II - Mission and Purpose, Goals and Objectives

Mission, purpose, goals and specific objectives are formulated and stated for each type of therapeutic recreation service based upon the philosophy and goals of the agency. These are then translated into operational procedures and serve as a blueprint for program evaluation.

Standard III - Individual Treatment/Program Plan

The therapeutic recreation specialist develops an individualized treatment/program plan for each client referred to the agency for therapeutic recreation services.

Standard IV - Documentation

The therapeutic recreation specialist records specific information based on client assessment, involvement, and progress. Information pertaining to the client is recorded on a regular basis as determined by the agency policy and procedures, and accrediting body standards.

Standard V - Plan of Operation

Therapeutic recreation services are considered a viable aspect of treatment, rehabilitation, normalization and development. Appropriate and fair scheduling of services, facilities, personnel and resources is vital to client progress and the operation of therapeutic recreation services. See the NTRS Guidelines for the Administration of Therapeutic Recreation Services (1990) for additional reference information.

Standard VI - Personnel Qualifications

Therapeutic recreation services are conducted by therapeutic recreation specialists whose training and experiences have prepared them to be effective at the functions they perform. Therapeutic recreation specialists have opportunities for involvement in professional development and life-long learning.

Standard VII - Ethical Responsibilities

Professionals are committed to advancing the use of therapeutic recreation services in order to ensure quality, protection, and to promote the rights of persons receiving services.

Standard VIII - Evaluation and Research

Therapeutic recreation specialists implement client and service-related evaluation and research functions to maintain and improve the quality, effectiveness, and integrity of therapeutic recreation services.

Reprinted, by permission, from NTRS.

Appendix B
American Therapeutic Recreation Association Standards for the Practice of Therapeutic Recreation

The Standards for the Practice of Therapeutic Recreation, developed by the American Therapeutic Recreation Association, reflect standards for the quality of therapeutic recreation practice by therapeutic recreation professionals and paraprofessionals in a variety of settings. The standards are divided into two distinct areas: Direct Practice of Therapeutic Recreation; and Management of Therapeutic Recreation Practice. The standards, originally released in 1991, revised in 1994 and again in 2000 reflect state of the art practice in therapeutic recreation.

The standards as listed in this appendix do not stand-alone and should not be used without the measurement criteria of structure, process and outcome provided in the manual. For instance, the following examples illustrate the use of the measurement criteria to aid in interpretation and evaluation of each standard.

The Self Assessment Guide (includes useful worksheets on standards scoring, documentation audit, management audit, outcome assessment, competency assessment and clinical performance appraisals).

Standard 1—Assessment

The therapeutic recreation specialist conducts an individualized assessment to collect systematic comprehensive and accurate data necessary to determine a course of action and subsequent individualized treatment plan. Under the clinical supervision of the therapeutic recreation specialist, the therapeutic recreation assistant aids in collecting systematic, comprehensive and accurate data necessary to determine a course of action and subsequent individualized treatment plan.

Example: **Structure Criteria** 1.1.2. The assessment process generates culturally appropriate baseline data that identifies the patient's/client's strengths and limitations in the following functional areas: physical, cognitive, social, behavioral, emotional and leisure/play.

Example: **Process Criteria**

- **The therapeutic recreation specialist—**1.2.3. Provides a summary of the assessment process that contains information relative to the patient's/client's strengths, patient's/client's limitations, analysis of assessment data, and summary of functional status.

- **The therapeutic recreation assistant—**1.2.3.1. Provides a summary of assessment information relative to the patient's/client's strengths and weaknesses, to the therapeutic recreation specialist.

Example: **Outcome Criteria The patient/client, family and/or significant other(s)—**1.3.3. Benefits from the assessment process and does not incur adverse consequences due to participation in the assessment.

Standards for the Practice of Therapeutic Recreation*

Direct Practice of Therapeutic Recreation	Management of Therapeutic Recreation Practice
Standard 1. Assessment	Standard 8. Written Plan of Operation
Standard 2. Treatment Planning	Standard 9. Staff Qualifications and Competency Assessment
Standard 3. Plan Implementation	Standard 10. Quality Management
Standard 4. Re-Assessment and Evaluation	Standard 11. Resource Management
Standard 5. Discharge and Transition Planning	Standard 12. Program Evaluation and Research
Standard 6. Recreation Services	
Standard 7. Ethical Conduct	

*Please note: The standards as listed in this appendix do not stand alone and should not be used without the measurement criteria of structure, process and outcome provided in the manual.

To order the ATRA Standards for the Practice of Therapeutic Recreation and Self Assessment Guide, visit the online bookstore at www.atra-tr.org or call (703) 683-9420 or fax (703) 683-9431. Price for members is $20.00 plus shipping and handling, non-members $40.00 plus shipping and handling.

Reprinted, by permission, from ATRA.

Glossary

accommodation—Altering playful thoughts and behaviors to fit the demands of society (Piaget).

accreditation—Credentialing of an academic institution and specific curriculum that meets or exceeds prescribed criteria of educational quality with regard to professional preparation curricula.

achievement behavior—Action oriented to changing what we do, solving problems, and scheduled terminations of behavior.

active treatment—Services designed to promote the achievement of specific therapeutic outcomes directly related to illness or disability.

activity—WHO indicator of being able to execute and complete tasks (e.g., reading, thinking, walking, dressing, voiding, solving problems, having basic interpersonal interactions, making decisions).

activity analysis—The process of breaking down an activity into the various skills and requirements (equipment, setting) necessary for successfully doing the activity.

activity limitation—WHO indicator of difficulties experienced when attempting to perform tasks.

acute care hospital—Large health care facility that provides a variety of services to people with acute conditions requiring immediate medical attention.

adaptive skills—Daily living skills needed to live, work, and play in the community. These are often classified into 10 areas: communication, self-care, home living, social skills, leisure, health and safety, self-direction, functional academics, community use, and work.

adult day program—Program in which care is provided during day hours to older adults, often with physical or intellectual impairment.

Alliance for Therapeutic Recreation—Board members of both ATRA and NTRS who meet to communicate and work in partnership on certain issues.

allied health profession—A profession made up of formally trained and credentialed health care providers who assist physicians and other members of the treatment team in providing services relevant to their expertise.

ALS—A progressive, and usually fatal, disease in which upper and lower motor neurons die, resulting in the loss of voluntary movement.

alternate formats—Adapted materials that are usable by people with disabilities.

ambulation—Walking.

amendatory veto—Action by a governor or chief executive, after a bill passes the legislative body, that changes the wording or money amounts of a piece of legislation rather than rejects it completely or adopts it fully.

American Therapeutic Recreation Association (ATRA)—Created in 1984. A therapeutic recreation professional organization that separated from NTRS and NRPA, which emphasizes that therapeutic recreation is treatment for therapeutic change. Further, ATRA separates its therapeutic recreation historical roots and alignment to parks and recreation and its distinct association with leisure.

Americans with Disabilities Act (ADA)—Federal legislation passed in 1990 and effective in 1992 that made it illegal to discriminate against a person based on the existence of a disability.

aneurism—Dilation, or ballooning, of a blood vessel by more than 50% of its normal diameter, sometimes resulting in bursting and internal bleeding.

anhedonia—The inability to experience pleasure from normally pleasurable life events.

anomie—A dysfunctional state of alienation and isolation from economic, cultural, political, and primary socialization group systems.

aphasia—Impairment or inability to speak, comprehend, read, or write, resulting from damage to the brain.

apraxia—Inability to perform common expressive gestures on request due to a motor planning disturbance associated with thought organization.

art therapists—Master's-level psychotherapists who are trained in both psychology and art.

assessment—The process of determining current level of functioning of a client or participant.

assessment report—A document summarizing results and recommendations from a completed assessment.

assimilation—Egocentric playful behavior (Piaget).

assisted-living facility—Nonmedical living facilities for people who are unable to live on their own but who do not need continuous nursing care.

athletic trainer—A medical professional who provides injury prevention, evaluation of athletic injury, immediate care, and rehabilitation services.

atlantoaxial instability—Laxity between the ligaments and muscles surrounding the joint between vertebrae C1 and C2 that may slip out of alignment and result in spinal cord injury.

at risk—Refers to a set of presumed cause–effect dynamics that place a child or adolescent in danger of future negative outcomes.

audiologist—Professional trained in the area of hearing processes and hearing loss who assesses hearing loss and recommends hearing aids or other assistive listening devices.

autism—A neurological disorder that affects a person's ability to communicate, to understand language, to play, and to relate to others. A diagnosis of autism is given when a person exhibits 6 or more of 12 symptoms listed across three major areas: social interaction, communication, and behavior.

autonomic dysreflexia—An excessive rise in blood pressure that could be life threatening.

behavioral modification—The use of positive and negative reinforcers to reduce negative behaviors and increase positive behaviors.

bibliotherapy—Uses reading materials such as novels, plays, short stories, booklets, and pamphlets to help clients (1) become aware that other people have similar problems, (2) become aware of new insights, and (3) structure their lives.

bill—Legislation introduced by a member of the legislative body to cause something to happen, stop something from happening, or change the way in which something happens.

biofeedback—Involves measuring body functions such as heart rate or temperature and then using this information to master conscious control of the associated function.

blood pressure—A measure of the pressure of the blood on the arterial walls that consists of two values: systolic blood pressure, as the heart contracts or pumps the blood to the circulatory system (90 to 140 mmHg), and diastolic blood pressure, as the heart fills up with blood following a contraction (60 to 90 mmHg).

briefing—The process of providing information related to goals, expectations, and events of an upcoming therapeutic recreation session.

Canadian federalism—Refers to Canadian political ideology that emphasizes expression of both diversity and unity.

capacity qualifier—WHO indicator of a person's highest probable level of functioning can be indicated and differentiated depending on whether activity and participation are occurring with or without assistance.

capitalism—Economic system characterized by a free market and private and corporate business ownership.

cardiovascular—Refers to the circulatory system: heart, arteries, veins.

cardiovascular dysautonomia—Irregular function of the autonomic nervous system (ANS) that leads to a blunted heart rate and decreased blood pressure in response to exercise.

cardiovascular exercise—Exercise essential to maintaining a healthy heart and having endurance to perform activities of daily living.

career—An occupation or profession followed as a life's work.

career resilience—Taking control of one's own future by taking responsibility to seek out appropriate training, at one's own expense if necessary, to position oneself for a desired career track; to promote oneself.

causal attributions—Beliefs held about the causes of the events that occur in life.

cerebral palsy (CP)—A group of disorders characterized by an inability to control muscular and postural movements resulting from damage to the brain before age 12.

cerebral vascular accident—An acute neurological injury resulting from disruption of blood flow to the brain because of blockage or bleeding of blood vessels.

certification—A form of voluntary credentialing that ensures that a person has met specific standards or criteria with regard to education, experience, and continuing professional development through an application process and required exam.

chaining—Teaching small parts or simplified versions of a behavior by having each lesson build on the previously taught information.

change theory—The examination of data (behavioral, numeric, thematic, logical, or philosophical) for patterns, changes in patterns, normalcy and abnormality, and causes of patterns, followed by the real, perceived, or theoretical understanding of the cause of the pattern, and finally the knowledge of how to change said pattern.

charitable solicitation—Seeking funds from private or nonprofit sources, often done to support the activities of governmental organizations such as community recreation programs conducted by local governments.

child life specialists—Professionals specially trained to help both children and their families understand and manage stressful health care experiences and challenging life events.

chronic—A persistent or lasting medical condition or disease.

clinical pathways—A standardized process used to direct patient care within the health care system, specifying the role of various professionals at various levels and stages of care.

code of ethics—The official moral ideology of the professional group; within helping professions, a code of ethics is a basic requirement for recognition as a professional body.

community development—The collaborative process of improving the social, economic, and cultural conditions within a community.

compulsions—Repetitive behaviors or mental acts performed to prevent or reduce anxiety or distress.

congenital—A condition present at birth.

construct—A nonobservable trait that cannot be directly measured, such as happiness or satisfaction.

constructivism—Learning theory that focuses on the importance of learning through experience rather than lecture and memorization.

contracture—Permanent shortening of muscle groups and connective tissues surrounding the joint.

contraindication—A condition or indication against a particular line of treatment or activity.

cost-only condition—A narrow achievement outcome that can ignore issues of quality and the process of experience.

countertransference—Situation in which a therapist begins to associate his or her own feelings, sometimes repressed, toward a client.

crisis care—Level of psychiatric care in which a client receives supervision 24 hours a day for a short time, typically 30 days or less.

critical force—A factor that can influence the entire experience.

day treatment—Level of care in which a client resides at home but attends treatment-related activities at a treatment facility throughout the day.

debriefing—Skillful questioning of a client or group of clients to enhance understanding, learning, or insight.

defense mechanisms—Unconscious behaviors aimed at reducing anxiety.

degenerative—Refers to a condition in which tissues or organs progressively deteriorate over time.

degree—The dynamic nature of experience.

delusions—False beliefs related to one's perceptions or experiences.

dementia—Progressive decline in cognitive function characterized by disturbances in memory, attention, language, and problem solving.

demyelinating disease—Disease that affects the myelin sheath of nerves, which insulates them and allows them to conduct impulses or signals to and from the brain.

developmental disabilities (DD)—Severe, chronic disabilities originating before age 22 and resulting in substantial functional mental or physical impairments in two or more of the following areas of major life activity—self-care, receptive and expressive language, learning, mobility, self-direction, capacity for independent living, and economic self-sufficiency.

diagnostic related groups—A hospital classification system developed by the Center for Medicare and Medicaid Services that categorizes patient cases based on expected resource use.

dietitian—A professional who promotes health through sound eating habits by assessing the nutritional needs of clients and planning and managing dietary intake.

Down syndrome—A chromosomal developmental disability and a form of intellectual impairment resulting from the production of an extra chromosome during cell development.

dysarthria—Neurologically based disruption of tongue, throat, lip, or lung function that affects speech.

echolalia—Repetitive use of language.

ecological model of disability—A view of disability as being reciprocal in nature; a change that occurs within the community will change not only that system but also the individuals, directly or indirectly.

ecological system—The interaction between people (including personal characteristics, behaviors, and physiological factors) and their environments. The environment encompasses immediate settings or people (home, classroom, neighborhood, family, teacher, counselor, and peer groups) as well as larger contexts in which these settings or people are embedded (cultural, political, educational, and community institutions).

Eden Alternative—Philosophy that advocates for the creation of homelike environments in long-term care facilities that encourage continued growth and achievement among residents.

elastic tubing—A stretchy band or tube that is used to strengthen muscle groups by offering resistance.

ethics—Deals with the duties and obligations of professionals to their consumers (service recipients), the profession, and the wider public.

etiological—Refers to the cause or the source of a disease or disability.

evaluation—The process of determining the effectiveness of therapeutic recreation programs in addressing client goals.

exacerbation—Flare-up in which symptoms deteriorate in a particular condition.

expressive arts—The employment of visual arts, music, dance, or drama techniques with the intent to produce and achieve a final product.

facilitation skills—Related to the interpersonal interactions that the therapist has with clients; sometimes referred to as soft skills.

fact sheet—Concise summary of proposed or existing legislation used to explain the nature and benefits of a bill or law.

flexibility—Ability to move joints through a range of motion; helps maintain or improve range of motion and avoid spasticity and contractures.

Florence Nightingale—Cited as an early medical expert (nurse) who highlighted the therapeutic effects of recreation while working in British hospitals during the Crimean War (1854-1856).

forensic—Indicates that a treatment program is somehow related to the legal system, typically because of the influence of a mental condition on a person's criminal behavior or ability to stand trial.

fraud—Resulting inequity that describes leisure for people with different abilities or opportunities.

functional intervention (FI)—Component that focuses on correcting functional deficits in the physical, mental, emotional, and social domains.

gerontologist—Person who studies the elderly, the aging process, and associated phenomena.

Glasgow coma scale—A scale used to determine the conscious state of a person.

global assessment of functioning (GAF)—A rating system associated with psychological assessment used to indicate a client's overall level of functioning. GAF scores range from 0 to 100, with higher scores indicating higher functioning.

goal—General outcomes expected to result from participation in a therapeutic recreation program.

Guillian Barre syndrome—An autoimmune disorder affecting the peripheral nervous system that can affect motor, sensory, or autonomic functions (internal organs).

Halliwick method—A 10-step process for teaching swimming to people with significant physical disabilities with the primary goal of achieving total client independence in the water.

hallucinations—Perceived sensory experiences that do not really exist.

health—A state of complete physical, mental, and social well-being and not merely the absence of disease or infirmity.

health condition—The current health status of a person, regardless of whether a disease, disorder, or trauma exists.

health protection–health promotion model—A practice model meant to be used to guide therapeutic recreation clients toward achieving health and self-actualization; contains three components: prescribed activities, recreation, and leisure.

hemiplegia—Paralysis of one vertical half of the body.

hippotherapy—A form of animal-assisted therapy in which the movement created by the gait of a horse is used as a therapeutic tool for a variety of orthopedic conditions; requires extensive training and is typically conducted by a physical therapist.

HMO—A comprehensive health care funding system (health care maintenance organization) that contracts with health care providers for services at preestablished costs, which are then provided to HMO members based on a fixed rate. The HMO serves as a gatekeeper for what services are provided and at what cost.

holistic—Considering all aspects or properties of a given phenomenon, system, situation, or problem.

hospital recreation—Antecedent term to therapeutic recreation. The Red Cross hired recreation workers in hospital settings during both world wars. Further, hospital recreation had a specific section in the American Recreation Society (1938–1965).

Hull-House—A settlement house in a poor district of Chicago, which was established by Jane Addams, Ellen Gates Starr, and Mary Keyser in September 1889. Hull-House established agencies in the worst slums of Chicago (13th Ward), where Hull-House residents provided human services and engaged in social action on behalf of people with special needs (e.g., art, education, citizenship classes, community development, immigration protection, recreation programming).

human development index—A comparative measure of life expectancy, literacy, education, and standards of living for countries worldwide.

humanitarian treatment movement—A social movement that swept through Europe in the late 1700s and early 1800s regarding the treatment of people with special needs (e.g., people with mental illness, people with disabilities). Paramount aspects to this movement were removing patients from dungeons and allowing them to move freely on hospital grounds outside mainstream communities.

hydrocephalus—A condition resulting in an enlarged head that is caused by an abnormal accumulation of cerebrospinal fluid.

hypertension—High blood pressure.

hypertonia—Increased amount of tone in a muscle group.

hypotonia—Decreased amount of tone in a muscle group.

impairment—A significant deviation, loss, or problem in a body function or structure.

inclusive recreation—Recreation opportunities designed so that people with disabilities can experience leisure in mainstream society. Three venues of inclusive recreation are community reintegration programs, community integration programs, and community development programs.

income growth—Increase in one's income over time, often related to changing to a higher-wage job or position.

individualized educational program (IEP)—A legal document created for a child with a disability that outlines the educational and related service goals including evaluation of those services. It is reviewed and updated once a year.

individualized program plan (IPP)—A plan of action regarding the provision of services to a particular therapeutic recreation client, also known as a treatment plan or a care plan.

Individuals with Disabilities Education Act (IDEA)—Federal law passed in 1974 that requires free and appropriate education of all children, regardless of disability, and provides about 10% of the annual cost of educating a child with a disability.

Inkerman Cafe—Created by Florence Nightingale in September 1855 as a small wooden hut that was located at the center of the hospital complex. The structure had a recreation room and a coffeehouse. The cafe provided a safe place where soldiers could escape their problems and find friendship.

instrumental values—A perspective used when acting to apply measurement and analysis to permit individual negotiation.

intellectual impairment—Having significantly lower intellectual functioning (70 or below IQ), concurrent with limitation in at least two adaptive skill areas, and having an onset before age 18.

interdependence—Participation that involves reciprocal interaction between people.

interorganizational networking—An aspect of organizational networking that refers to the networking between organizations with similar characteristics.

intraorganizational networking—An aspect of organizational networking that focuses on the networks that operate, individually and collectively, within an organization for a shared goal and ultimately the betterment of the organization.

job—A regular remunerative position.

kinesiotherapy—The application of therapeutic exercise to improve strength, endurance, and mobility of people with physical injuries or limitations.

Labor Museum—A community leisure education program developed at Hull-House that provided a developmental process in which groups of people increased their understanding of leisure and the relationship among leisure, lifestyle, culture, and society. The Labor Museum developed from Jane Addams' concern for (1) the disdainful attitudes that immigrant children had toward their parents' old-world traditions and culture and (2) the contemptuous attitudes that Americans had toward poverty-stricken immigrants living in Chicago.

law—Refers to a legislative bill that has been approved by both houses and signed by the governor or president.

learning disability—A general classification given for significant problems with language or mathematical calculations not related to intellectual impairment or emotional or psychological problems in children.

least restrictive environment—A setting that allows maximum integration with the larger community. In the case of children with developmental disabilities, this includes educating and providing services in the same setting with children without disabilities.

legislative process—The process through which proposed bills are introduced, evaluated, and rejected or approved by the relevant legislative bodies.

legislator—Elected official representing a particular district or state in the state or federal Senate or House of Representatives.

leisure ability model—A practice model that describes the ultimate goal of therapeutic recreation services to be an enhanced leisure lifestyle and that includes three components: functional intervention, leisure education, and recreation participation.

leisure behavior—Action oriented to choice, passion (positive affect), and continuation of behavior.

leisure education—A developmental process through which a person or group of people increase their understanding of leisure and the relationship among leisure, lifestyle, and society.

leisure orientation to therapeutic recreation—Belief that the distinctness of therapeutic recreation is its clear association with programming recreation and leisure services. As such, leisure is an end unto itself, which creates freedom and choice among people with special needs.

licensure—A form of professional credentialing required by state law. Anyone wishing to practice the profession within the given state must be licensed.

life-span development—The study of growth over the entire life of a person.

long-term care facilities—A variety of residential facilities that provide different levels of care to people with illnesses and disabilities. Types of long-term care facilities include nursing homes, skilled nursing facilities, and custodial care facilities.

manic (mania)—Elevated level of mood involving symptoms such as distractibility, indiscretion, grandiosity, flight of ideas, increased activity, sleep deficit, and talkativeness.

maximal heart rate—Defined as a person's age subtracted from 220. For example, a 40-year-old person would have a maximum heart rate of 180 (220 − 40 = 180).

Medicaid—Insurance program sponsored by the federal government for people with disabilities. Each state sets its own guidelines for, administers, and partly funds Medicaid.

Medicaid waiver—A process that waives the patient's rights to institutional care and allows for use of Medicaid funds to pay for community-based care for a designated period. Medicaid waivers are designed to prevent unnecessary institutionalization and are allowed only for services approved by the governing state, which may include therapeutic recreation.

medical model of disability—A perspective that views disabilities as being physiological, cognitive, social, or psychological and in need of remediation.

medicalization of spas and thermal baths—The use of medical authority to justify leisure experiences during a time when leisure was not justified (1800s–mid-1900s).

meditation—The practice of focusing the mind.

moral character—What sort of person one ought to be.

moral community—How society should be constructed to enable ethical people to act ethically.

moral conduct—How one should act.

multi-infarct dementia—Refers to a group of syndromes caused by different mechanisms all resulting in vascular lesions in the brain.

municipal therapeutic recreation settings—Therapeutic recreation services provided in community settings such as public parks and recreation departments.

music therapy—Use of music as a modality to treat the health needs and improve the quality of life of well people and people with illnesses and disabilities.

National Association of Recreation Therapists (NART)—Created in 1953 so that (1) the therapy orientation to therapeutic recreation would have even greater distance from the recreation and physical education curriculum of AAHPER and (2) to bring greater importance to clinical outcomes and the role of recreation in bringing functional improvements in clients. NART eventually merged with three other professional organizations to develop the National Therapeutic Recreation Society, a branch of the National Recreation and Park Association, in 1966.

National Council for Therapeutic Recreation Certification (NCTRC)—An independent credentialing agency created in 1981 that oversees the national certification program in therapeutic recreation in the United States.

National Recreation and Park Association (NRPA)—Made up of five recreation and leisure professional organizations that merged in 1966. Today NRPA is a parks and recreation professional organization with a mission to advance parks, recreation, leisure, and environmental conservation.

National Therapeutic Recreation Society (NTRS)—A branch of the NRPA created in 1966 to enhance the competencies of therapeutic recreation specialists. Four therapeutic recreation professional organizations merged to form NTRS (Hospital Recreation Section of the American Recreation Society; Recreation Therapist Section of the American Association of Health, Physical Education, Recreation, and Dance; National Association of Recreation Therapists; and Recreation Services for the Handicapped Section of the National Recreation Association).

networking—The ability to create and maintain an effective and diverse system of resources, made possible by using relevant information, having good working relations, and maintaining and communicating a good track record.

normalization principle—A theoretical framework developed by the Scandinavian academic Bengt Nirje to help people with disabilities become included in mainstream society. Makes available to persons with disabilities patterns of life and conditions of everyday living that are as close as possible or indeed the same as the regular circumstances and ways of life of their communities.

nurse—A licensed medical professional who assists individuals, families, and communities to attain, re-attain, and maintain optimal health and functioning by observing patients, assessing symptoms, and documenting progress.

nursing home—Residential facility for people who require constant nursing care.

objectives—Specific indicators of goal achievement, characterized by identification of an expected behavior, a condition under which the behavior will occur, and a criteria for determining whether the behavior has occurred.

obsessions—Persistent thoughts, ideas, impulses, or images that are experienced as intrusive and inappropriate and that cause marked anxiety or distress.

occupational therapy—The use of purposeful activity and interventions to achieve functional outcomes such as pain reduction, improved strength and mobility, and prevention or treatment of permanent physical disabilities.

orientations to motivation—Acquisition, prevention, maintenance, and serendipity.

orthopedic impairment—Condition caused by disruption of the skeletal–muscle system.

orthostatic hypotension—A decrease or drop in blood pressure because of the pooling of blood in the lower extremities and abdominal area.

osteoarthritis—Arthritis that results from wear and tear on joints over a person's life span.

outcome—Observed change in client's status as a result of intervention or interaction.

outpatient care—Level of care in which clients reside at home but attend regular therapy sessions at the care facility.

outpatient services—A level of service in which clients do not check in or receive full-time care during the day but periodically visit the service provider for therapy sessions, typically for no more than 1 to 2 hours.

outsourcing—Delegating non-core business operations to outside agencies, sometimes across national boundaries (offshore outsourcing).

paradigm—A thought pattern, set of practices, or conceptual model for explanation.

paradox—A situation or perspective that links contradictory ideas or feelings to provide an explanation.

paralysis—Impairment often related to nerve damage, resulting in loss of sensation and motor function.

paraplegia—Complete or partial impairment of movement or sensation affecting the involvement of both legs.

paresis—Partial weakness to one or more limbs.

Parkinson's disease—A central nervous system disorder that affects muscle control.

participation—WHO indicator of involvement in meaningful life situations (e.g., going shopping, spending time on a hobby, dating, completing work tasks, volunteering, attending sporting events).

pathological reflex—Reflex responses that persist beyond the normal developmental time period.

performance qualifier—WHO indicator of what a person does in his or her current environment.

pericarditis—Inflammation of the lining of the heart.

person-first terminology—Language that refers to all people as individuals first and as personal characteristics second.

pervasive developmental disorder (PDD)—A neurological disorder that affects a person's ability to communicate, to understand language, to play, and to relate to others. The diagnosis of NOS PDD is given when a child displays behaviors similar to autism but to a lesser extent.

physical activity—All forms of bodily movement produced by the contractions of skeletal muscles that substantially increase energy expenditure.

physical fitness—The ability to perform daily activities with vigor and to be at low risk of premature development of the hypokinetic diseases or conditions associated with sedentary behavior.

physical therapy—Therapy designed to reduce pain, improve strength and mobility, and prevent or treat permanent physical disabilities.

politics—Social relations involving authority or power.

positive youth development—A service approach focusing on youth's unique talents, strengths, interests, and potential.

positive-order behaviors—Behaviors that are reinforced and have consensus value (e.g., work behaviors).

precaution—Measure taken to avoid injury or a potential problem.

presenting problem—A client's primary reason for receiving treatment.

pressure ulcers—Damage to the skin and possibly underlying tissues resulting from prolonged pressure on bony weight-bearing areas of the body, or excessive sweating or pressure on an area of the body during a fall.

primary prevention—The reduction of the number of new cases of identified problems or conditions occurring within a population; targets the promotion of health and development.

problatunity—Refers to a perspective that problem and opportunity can reside in the same time and space, essentially one and the same.

profession—Efforts of the person are directed toward service rather than simply financial remuneration.

professional authority—The ability of a profession to hold one another accountable.

professional credentialing—Evidence that a professional has acquired a body of knowledge that includes theory, philosophy, and practice within a given field.

professional culture—Made up of the customary beliefs, norms, or traits of the profession; often defined by professional associations.

professional development—The exchange and transmission of professional knowledge through professional associations' conferences, workshops, and publications.

professionalism—The conduct, aims, or qualities that characterize a profession or professional person and includes both professional and personal advocacy.

progress notes—Formal documentation procedure for recording the progression or regression of clients over time.

progressive relaxation—Stress management technique involving progressive tensing and relaxing of muscles throughout the body.

prosthetic device—Artificial limb designed for an amputated extremity.

prosthetist—A professional who designs and fits prostheses, or artificial limbs, to amputated extremities.

psychiatrist—Medical doctor who prescribes medications to treat various forms of mental illness and is extensively trained in diagnosis and treatment modalities for mental illness.

psychologist—A social scientist who studies psychology, which is the study of the human mind, thought, and human behavior.

pulmonary—Refers to the lungs.

quadriplegia (or tetraplegia)—Complete or partial impairment of movement or sensation affecting the involvement of all four limbs.

rating of perceived exertion (RPE)—A scale of how hard a person feels that he or she is exercising. The Borg scale ranges from 6 to 20. To use the scale, the person monitors how he or she feels while exercising, with a general goal of 12 to 13 RPE.

recreation service model—A practice model based on a World Health Organization model that describes therapeutic recreation services across the following levels of care: disease, impairment, disability, handicap, education, organized recreation services, and independent activities.

recreation therapy—The purposeful use of leisure-based interventions to improve functional abilities.

registration—A form of professional credentialing that is voluntary and generally provides a list of people who have met a minimum standard with regard to education and experience within a specific field.

rehabilitation hospital—Health care facility that specializes in longer-term treatment of medical conditions, often after clients have already received treatment from acute care facilities.

residential care—Level of care in which clients reside at the treatment facility.

rest cures—The use of rest and recreation to help restore mental health. Used as a medical strategy during the medicalization of spas and thermal baths (1800–mid-1900s).

rheumatism—An older term used for arthritis.

rheumatoid arthritis—Involves inflammation of the lining of joints and is believed to be related to an attack on the body by the immune system.

risk pool insurance—Partnerships, or pools, formed by insurance companies to reduce potential risk of catastrophic events.

scoliosis—Curving of the spine.

secondary conditions—Medical, social, emotional, family, or community problems that a person with a primary disabling condition likely experiences.

secondary prevention—The reduction of the number of existing problem cases and lowering the prevalence of the manifested problems or conditions in the population.

seizure—An abnormality in the electric activity in the brain.

self-advocacy—The ability of people with disabilities to promote for their own rights.

self-efficacy—The belief that one has about his or her capabilities to perform a particular task or manage a situation successfully.

sensory integration—The process by which the brain organizes and interprets sensory information.

separatist mentality (in therapeutic recreation)—Members of the NTRS in the early 1980s who separated themselves from NTRS and NRPA so that they could follow a therapy orientation to therapeutic recreation. This group eventually created the American Therapeutic Recreation Association.

sequencing—Arranging the elements of a therapeutic recreation session or series of therapeutic recreation sessions in an order that facilitates successful performance.

settlement house—Established human service agency developed purposely in city slums where human service workers provided human services (e.g., education, citizenship classes, community development, immigration protection, recreation) and engaged in social action on behalf of the poor living in the area.

shaping—Teaching small parts or simplified versions of a behavior with each lesson slightly modifying the previously taught information.

shunt—A surgically implanted device to drain cerebral spinal fluid.

social capital—The collective value of all social networks and the tendencies that arise from these networks to do things for each other. Networks that build social capital are characterized by reciprocity and trust.

social inclusion—Valuing the participation of all people in social aspects of community activities.

social model of disability—A perspective of disability that focuses on barriers being attributed to physical, cognitive, social, or emotional aspects of a society.

social worker—A professional who helps people function in the healthiest way possible in the environment, manage their relationships, and solve personal and family problems.

spasticity—Involuntary increase in muscle tone.

speech-language pathologists—Professionals trained in disorders related to speech, language, cognitive communication, and swallowing skills.

spina bifida—A condition in which the spinal column does not close during gestation.

spiral goals—Goals that are expressed outside the group in the real world.

stages of playful behavior—Suggested by Paiget; include sensorimotor play, symbolic play, and cooperative play.

strength training—Exercise or activity that maintains or improves skeletal muscle strength and endurance.

strength-based approach—Approach that focuses first on capabilities when working with a client.

stroke—See cerebral vascular accident.

syndrome—A group of symptoms or abnormalities that indicates a particular trait or disease.

systematic desensitization—A therapy technique in which the client maintains a relaxed state while being subjected to a hierarchy of fear- or anxiety-producing stimuli.

task analyst—The breaking down of a specific skill into its component parts.

technical skills—Tasks of a non-interpersonal nature associated with job responsibilities, such as completing documentation or preparing equipment, sometimes referred to as hard skills.

terminal—A progressive disease expected to cause death.

terminal values—A perspective used to generalize a feeling and affiliate people for group action.

tertiary prevention—The reduction of harmful effects and complications that occur within an existing disorder and identified condition; may also be referred to as treatment or rehabilitation.

therapeutic recreation—The purposeful enhancement or exercising of leisure as a means of maximizing a person's overall health, well-being, and quality of life.

therapeutic recreation process—The overall process of assessing, planning, implementing, and evaluating therapeutic recreation programs.

therapeutic recreator's dilemma—Programmed recreation behavior involving choice but with attention to normalcy.

therapeutic riding—Use of horseback riding as an alternative therapy for a variety of psychological, social, or physical conditions.

therapy orientation of therapeutic recreation—Belief that the essence of therapeutic recreation is to use or prescribe recreation and leisure for medical purposes. As such, recreation and leisure is a means to an end (treatment).

thermal injuries—Injuries resulting from exposure to temperature extremes.

thermoregulation—Regulation of body temperature.

transference—Unconscious redirection of feelings from one person to another, often occurring in therapy when client redirects feelings toward the therapist.

transient ischemic attack—Temporary disturbance of blood flow to brain, resulting in short-term neurological dysfunction; also known as ministrokes.

treatment modality—Activities used to help clients meet therapeutic goals.

treatment protocols—A standardized process for providing consistent treatment for a particular client group or within a particular form of treatment.

unconditional positive regard (UPR)—Accepting a client as worthy and capable, although the client may not act or feel that way. UPR is one of the three necessary conditions for positive change in therapy, along with genuineness and empathy.

utopian years of therapeutic recreation—A social movement that began in the early 1960s to unite all leisure-oriented professionals and therapeutic recreation organizations together into one loosely structured organization.

values clarification—Technique that can help clients examine their personal behavior, identify the values that are driving this behavior, determine whether these values are in line with their core personal values, and shift behavior to be congruent with personal core values.

veto—Rejection of a bill by a governor or president after the bill has passed both houses and been reconciled. Veto can be overturned by a vote that requires more than a simple majority, in most cases.

worldview—The lens, or perspective, through which one sees the world and interacts with it.

zero-order behaviors—Behaviors that receive attention only when they are absent.

References

Abrahmson, L.Y., Seligman, M.E. & Teasdale, J.D. (1978). Learned helplessness in humans: Critique and reformulation. *Journal of Abnormal Psychology, 87,* 49–74.

Aburdene, P. (2005). *Megatrends 2010: The rise of conscious capitalism.* Charlottesville, VA: Hampton Roads Publishing.

Addams, J. (1895/1990). Art work. In M.L. McCree Bryan & A.F. Davis (Eds.), *100 years at Hull-House* (pp. 39–41). Bloomington: Indiana University Press. (Reprinted from *Forum,* July 1895, pp. 614–617).

Addams, J. (1905/1990). Hull-house woman's club anthem. In M.L. McCree Bryan & A.F. Davis (Eds.), *100 years at Hull-House* (p. 108). Bloomington: Indiana University Press. (Reprinted from *The Commons,* April 1905, p. 225).

Addams, J. (1909/1972). *The spirit of youth and the city streets.* Urbana: University of Illinois Press.

Addams, J. (1910/1981). *Twenty years at Hull-House.* New York: Signet.

Administration on Aging, U.S. Department of Health and Human Services. (2004). *A Profile of Older Americans: 2003.*

Allen, B. & Allen, S. (1995). The process of a social construction of mental retardation: Toward value-based interaction. *The Journal of the Association for Persons With Severe Handicaps, 20,* 158–160.

Allen, L.R., Paisley, K., Stevens, B. & Harwell, R. (1998). The top 10 ways to impact at-risk youth in recreation programming. *Parks and Recreation, 33*(3), 80–85.

Alzheimer's Association. (2005). *Statistics about Alzheimer's disease.* Retrieved July 2005, from www.alz.org/AboutAD/Statistics.htm.

American Alliance for Health, Physical Education, Recreation and Dance (2006). *About AAHPERD.* Retrieved December 5, 2006 from http://www.aahperd.org/aahperd/template.cfm?template=aahperd_about.html.

American Association of Retired Persons. (2005). *Retired living.* Retrieved June 1, 2005, from www.aarp.org.

American Association on Mental Retardation. (1992). *Mental retardation: definition, classification, and systems of supports.* Washington, DC: Author.

American Board of Psychiatry and Neurology, Inc. (2005). *What is an ABPN board-certified psychiatrist?* Retrieved October 29, 2005, from www.abpn.com/geninfo/what_psychiatrist.html.

American Hospital Association. (2005). *Fast facts on U.S. hospitals.* AHA hospital statistics. Retrieved on July 18, 2005, from http://www.aha.org/aha/resource-center/Statistics-and-Studies/fast-facts.html.

American Kinesiotherapy Association. (2005). *Kinesiotherapy is . . .* Retrieved November 1, 2005, from http://akta.org/.

American Medical Association. (2004a). Art therapist. In *Health professions career and education directory, 2004–2005* (32nd ed., pp. 5–7). Chicago: AMA Press.

American Medical Association. (2004b). Kinesiotherapist. In *Health professions career and education directory, 2004–2005* (32nd ed., pp. 227–228). Chicago: AMA Press.

American Medical Association. (2004c). Music therapist. In *Health professions career and education directory, 2004–2005* (32nd ed., pp. 267–271). Chicago: AMA Press.

American Medical Association. (2004d). Occupational therapy. In *Health professions career and education directory, 2004–2005* (32nd ed., pp. 280–291). Chicago: AMA Press.

American Medical Association. (2004e). Physical therapy. In *Health professions career and education directory, 2004–2005* (32nd ed., pp. 323–336). Chicago: AMA Press.

American Medical Association. (2004f). Audiology and speech pathology. *In Health professions career and education directory, 2004–2005* (32nd ed., pp. 22–35). Chicago: AMA Press.

American Music Therapy Association. (1999). *Frequently asked questions about music therapy.* Retrieved November 19, 2005, from www.musictherapy.org/faqs.html.

American Occupational Therapy Association. (2005). *Consumer information: What is occupational therapy?* Retrieved October 20, 2005, from www.aota.org/featured/area6/index.asp#what.

American Physical Therapy Association. (2005). *About APTA.* Retrieved November 15, 2005, from www.APTA.org/AM/template.cfm?section=About_APTA.

American Psychiatric Association. (2000). *Diagnostic and statistical manual of mental disorders-IV-TR* (4th ed.). Washington, DC: Author.

American Psychiatric Association. (2005a). *Diagnostic and statistical manual of mental disorders-IV-TR* (5th ed.) Washington, DC: Author.

American Psychiatric Association. (2005b). *Let's talk facts about psychiatric hospitalization*. Retrieved July 19, 2005, from http://healthyminds.org/psychiatrichospitalization.cfm.

American Psychological Association. (2003). *Psychology: Scientific problem solvers*. Retrieved October 29, 2005, from www.apa.org/students/brochure/brochurenew.pdf.

American Speech-Language-Hearing Association. (2005a). *Frequently asked questions about the profession*. Retrieved November 16, 2005, from www.asha.org/students/professions/overview/.

American Speech-Language-Hearing Association. (2005b). *Employment settings*. Retrieved November 16, 2005, from www.asha.org/students/professions/settings.

American Speech-Language-Hearing Association. (2005c). *Academic, clinical, and exam standards for the certificate of clinical competence (CCC)*. Retrieved November 16, 2005, from www.asha.org/public/cert.

American Therapeutic Recreation Association. (2005). *ATRA affirms support for ICF* (News Release). Alexandria, VA. Retrieved February 1, 2006, from http://ww.atra-tr.org/Press%20releases/ATRA%20ICF%20statement%20Newsrelease%20.pdf.

American Therapeutic Recreation Association. (2006). *Definition, mission & vision statements*. Retrieved December 20, 2006, from www.atra-tr.org.

Americans with Disabilities Act of 1990, Pub. L. No. 101-336.

Anderson, S.C. & Stewart, M.W. (1980). Therapeutic recreation education: 1979 survey. *Therapeutic Recreation Journal, 14*(3), 4–10.

Answers.com. (2005). *Nursing*. Retrieved October 29, 2005, from www.answers.com/definition%20of%20nursing.

Archie, V.W. & Sherrill, C. (1989). Attitudes toward handicapped peers of mainstreamed and nonmainstreamed children in physical education. *Perceptual and Motor Skills, 69*, 319–322.

Arizona State University. (2005). *Department of Psychology*. Retrieved November 20, 2005, from www.asu.edu/clas/psych/gprogram/.

Association Task Force on Consent to Voluntary Hospitalization. (1992). *Consent to voluntary hospitalization*. Washington, DC: American Psychiatric Press.

Atchley, R.C. (1989). A continuity theory of normal aging. *The Gerontologist, 29*(2), 183–190.

Austin, D.R. (1997). *Therapeutic recreation: Processes and techniques* (2nd ed.). Champaign, IL: Sagamore.

Austin, D.R. (1998). The health protection/health promotion model. *Therapeutic Recreation Journal, 32*(2), 109–117.

Austin, D.R. (2001). *Glossary of recreation therapy and occupational therapy*. State College, PA: Venture.

Austin, D.R. (2002). A third revolution in therapeutic recreation. In D.R. Austin, J. Dattilo, & B.P. McCormick (Eds.), *Conceptual foundations for therapeutic recreation* (pp. 273–288). State College, PA: Venture.

Austin, D.R. (2004). *Therapeutic recreation: Processes and techniques* (5th ed.). Champaign, IL: Sagamore.

Australian Institute of Health and Welfare. (2000). *Australia's health 2000*. Canberra: Author.

Australian Sports Commission. (2005). *Active Australia*. Retrieved November 29, 2005, from www.ausport.gov.au/schools/about.asp.

Autry, C.E. (2001). Adventure therapy with girls at-risk: Responses to outdoor experiential activities. *Therapeutic Recreation Journal, 35*(4), 289–306.

Auxter, D., Pyfer, J. & Huettig, C. (2005). *Principles and methods of adapted physical education and recreation (10th ed.)* New York: McGraw-Hill.

Avedon, E.M. (1974). *Therapeutic recreation services: An applied behavior science approach*. Englewood, NJ: Prentice Hall.

Ayllon, T. (1999). *How to use token economy and point systems* (2nd ed.). Austin, TX: PRO-ED.

Azrin, N.H. & Besalel, V.A. (1999). *How to use positive practice, self-correction, and overcorrection* (2nd ed.). Austin, TX: PRO-ED.

Bailey, A., Le Couteur, A., Gottesman, I., Bolton, P., Simonoff, E., Yuzda, E. & Rutter, M. (2005). Autism as a strongly genetic disorder evidence from a British twin study. *Psychological Medicine, 25*, 63–77.

Baltes, P.B. & Baltes, M.M. (1990). *Successful aging: Perspectives from the behavioral sciences*. Cambridge: Cambridge University Press.

Bandura, A. (1986). *Social foundations for thought and action: A social cognitive theory*. Englewood Cliffs, NJ: Prentice Hall.

Barba, B., Tesh, A.S. & Courts, N.F. (2002). Promoting thriving in nursing homes: The Eden Alternative. *Journal of Gerontological Nursing, 28* (3), 7–13.

Bartko, W.T. & Eccles, J.S. (2003). Adolescent participation in structured and unstructured activities: A person-oriented analysis. *Journal of Youth and Adolescence, 32*(4), 233–241.

Beckett, L., Yu, Q. & Long, A.N. (September, 2005). The impact of fragile X: Prevalence, numbers affected, and economic impact. *National Fragile X Foundation Quarterly Journal, 2*, 18–21. Retrieved on-line June 12, 2006, from http://www.fragilex.org/html/prevalence.htm.

Bedini, L.A. (1995). The "Play Ladies"—The first therapeutic recreation specialists. *Journal of Physical Education, Recreation and Dance, 66*(8), 32-35.

Bedini, L.A. (2000). "Just sit down so we can talk": Perceived stigma and community recreation pursuits by people with disabilities. *Therapeutic Recreation Journal, 34*, 55–68.

Bedini, L.A. & Henderson, K.A. (1994). Women with disabilities and the challenges to leisure service providers. *Journal of Park and Recreation Administration, 12*(1), 17–34.

Bennett, W.J. (1999). *The index of leading cultural indicators: American society at the end of the twentieth century.* New York: Random House.

Blanchard, K., Lacinak, T., Tompkins, C. & Ballard, J. (2002). *Whale done! The power of positive relationships.* New York: Simon and Schuster.

Board of Certification. (2004). *Role delineation study for the entry level certified athletic trainer* (5th ed.). Omaha, NE: National Athletic Trainers' Association Board of Certification.

Boccaro, J. & Outley, C. (2005, October). *Developing effective relationships in recreation youth programs.* Paper presented at the National Recreation and Park Association Annual Congress, San Antonio, TX.

Bogdan, R. & Taylor, S.J. (1992). The social construction of humanness. In P.M. Ferguson, D.M. Ferguson, & S.J. Taylor (Eds.), *Interpreting disability* (pp. 275–296). New York: Teachers College Press.

Broida, J.K. (2000). *Therapeutic recreation—the benefits are endless.* Ashburn, VA: National Recreation and Park Association.

Bronfenbrenner, U. (1989). Ecological systems theory. In R. Vasta (Ed.), *Annals of child development: Vol. 6. Six theories of child development: Revised formulations and current issues* (pp. 187–249). Greenwich, CT: Jai Press.

Brooks, S. (2000). *Canadian democracy: An introduction* (3rd ed.). Don Mills, ON: Oxford University Press.

Brown, L.J. & Sevcik, K. (1999). TR for youth at risk. *Illinois Parks and Recreation, 20*(4), 31–33.

Bryan, M.L.M. & Davis, A.F. (Eds.). (1990). *100 years at Hull-House.* Bloomington: Indiana University Press.

Buckingham, M. & Clifton, D. (2001). *Now, discover your strengths.* New York: Simon and Schuster.

Bucolo, J.A. (2003). *Re-inventing yourself: The key to today's career success.* Paper presented at the Life Services Network 2003 Annual Convention and Expo. Chicago, IL.

Buettner, L. & Fitzsimmons, S. (2003). *Dementia practice guidelines for recreational therapy: Treatment of disturbing behaviors.* Alexandria, VA: American Therapeutic Recreation Association.

Bullock, C.C. & Mahon, M.J. (2000). *Introduction to recreation services for people with disabilities: A person-centered approach* (2nd ed.). Champaign, IL: Sagamore.

Burgstahler, S. & Doe, T. (2006). Improving postsecondary outcomes for students with disabilities: Designing professional development for faculty. *Journal of Postsecondary Education and Disability, 18*(2), 135–145.

Burlingame, J. (1998). Clinical practice models. In F.M. Brasile, T. Skalko & J. Burlingame (Eds.), *Perspectives in recreational therapy* (pp. 83–106). Ravensdale, WA: Idyll Arbor.

Burlingame, J. & Blaschko, T.M. (2002). *Assessment tools for recreational therapy and related fields* (3rd ed.). Ravensdale, WA: Idyll Arbor.

Caldwell, L.L., Adolph, S. & Gilbert, A. (1989). Caution! Leisure counselors at work: Long term effects of leisure counseling. *Therapeutic Recreation Journal, 25*(3), 41–49.

California State University at Northridge. (2005). *Department of Child and Adolescent Development.* Retrieved November 20, 2005, from http://hhd.csun.edu/cdev/.

Cameron, D. & Valentine, F. (2001). *Disability and federalism: Comparing different approaches to full participation.* Montreal, QC, and Kingston, ON: McGill-Queen's University Press.

Campbell, C. (2002). *The wealthy spirit.* Naperville, IL: Sourcebooks.

Campbell, W.J. (1997). *The book of great books: A guide to 100 world classics.* New York: Metrobooks.

Carruthers, C.P. & Busser, J.A. (2000). A qualitative study of boys and girls club program leaders, club members, and parents. *Journal of Park and Recreation Administration, 18*(1), 50–67.

Carruthers, C., Hawkins, B. & Voelkl, J. (1998). Introduction to the TRJ Special Series on Practice Models. *Therapeutic Recreation Journal, 32*(2), 80.

Carstensen, L.L. (1991). Selectivity theory: Social activity in life-span context. *Annual Review of Gerontology and Geriatrics, 11,* 195–217.

Carstensen, L.L. (1995). Evidence for a life-span theory of socioemotional selectivity. *Current Directions in Psychological Science, 4,* 151–156.

Carter, M.J. & LeConey, S.P. (2004). *Therapeutic recreation in the community: An inclusive approach* (2nd ed.). Champaign, IL: Sagamore.

Carter, M.J., Van Andel, G.E. & Robb, G.M. (2003). *Therapeutic recreation: A practical approach* (3rd ed.). Prospect Heights, IL: Waveland Press.

Caspersen, C.J., Powell, K.E. & Christensen, G.M. (1985). Physical activity, exercise, and physical fitness: Definitions and distinctions for health-related research. *Public Health Reports, 100*(2), 126–131.

Centers for Disease Control and Prevention. (1996). *At-a-glance.* Retrieved April 25, 2005, from www.cdc.gov/nccdphp/sgr/ataglan.htm.

Centers for Disease Control and Prevention. (2004a). *What causes mental retardation? Can it be prevented?* Retrieved September 15, 2005, from www.cdc.gov/ncbddd.ddmr.htm.

Centers for Disease Control and Prevention. (2004b). Suicide attempts and physical fighting among high school students—United States 2001. *Morbidity and Mortality Weekly Report, 52*(22), 474–476.

Centers for Disease Control and Prevention. (2007). *Prevalence of autism spectrum disorders.* Retrieved February 28, 2007, from http://www.cdc.gov/ncbddd/autism/faq_prevalence.htm#whatisprevalence.

Centers for Disease Control and Prevention and the National Institute on Disability and Rehabilitation. (n.d.). *Disability and secondary conditions.* Retrieved April 25, 2005, from www.healthypeople.gov/document/html/volume1/06disability.htm.

Centers for Medicare and Medicaid Glossary. (n.d.). Retrieved July 1, 2006, from http://www.cms.hhs.gov/apps/glossary/default.asp.

Chamberlin, R.W. (1994). Primary prevention: The missing piece in child development legislation. In R.J. Simeonsson (Ed.), *Risk, resilience and prevention: Promoting the well-being of all children* (pp. 33–52). Baltimore: Brooks.

Child Development Institute. (2000). *Facts about fragile X syndrome.* Retrieved June 13, 2006, from childdevelopmentinfo.com/disorders/facts_about_fragile_x_syndrome.htm.

Child Life Council. (2005a). *What is a child life specialist?* Retrieved November 19, 2005, from www.childlife.org/About/what_is_specialist.htm.

Child Life Council. (2005b). *Overview of Child Life Council.* Retrieved November 19, 2005, from www.childlife.org/index.htm.

Chubb, M. & Chubb, H. (1981). *One third of our time.* New York: Wiley.

City of Phoenix. (2004). *Juvenile diversion programs.* Retrieved November 12, 2005, from www.phoenix.gov/PRL/arythjv.html.

CNN. (2005). World's oldest person dead at 122. Retrieved September 13, 2005, from www.cnn.com/WORLD/9708/04/obit.oldest/ (originally posted on August 4, 1997).

Cohen, R. (2004). *Blindsided.* New York: HarperCollins.

Compton, D.M. (1997). Where in the world are we going? Armageddon and utopia revisited. In D.M. Compton (Ed.), *Issues in therapeutic recreation: Toward the new millennium* (pp. 39–50). Champaign, IL: Sagamore.

Conzemius, A. & O'Neill, J. (2002). *The handbook for SMART school teams.* Bloomington, IN: National Education Services.

Cordes, K. & Ibrahim, H. (2003). *Applications in recreation and leisure* (3rd ed.). Boston: McGraw-Hill.

Corey, G. (2004). *Theory and practice of counseling and psychotherapy* (7th ed.). Pacific Grove, CA: Wadsworth.

Covey, S.R. (2005). *The 8th habit: From effectiveness to greatness* (book and corresponding DVD). New York: Simon and Schuster.

Coyle, C., Kinney, W., Riley, B. & Shank, J. (Eds.). (1991). *Benefits of therapeutic recreation: A consensus view.* Ravensdale, WA: Idyll Arbor.

Crawford, M.E. (2001a). Organization and formation of the profession. In D.R. Austin & M.E. Crawford (Eds.), *Therapeutic recreation: An introduction* (2nd ed.) (pp. 22–44). Boston: Allyn & Bacon.

Crawford, M.E. (2001b). Issues and trends. In D.R. Austin & M.E. Crawford (Eds.), *Therapeutic recreation: An introduction* (2nd ed.) (pp. 333–359). Boston: Allyn & Bacon.

Csikszentmihalyi, M. (1993). *The evolving self.* New York: HarperCollins.

Csikszentmihalyi, M. & Larson, R. (1984). *Being adolescent: Conflict and growth in the teenage years.* New York: Basic Books.

CSWE Online. (2005). *About CSWE.* Retrieved on October 31, 2005, from www.cswe.org/.

CtArtTherapy.org. (2005). *Some facts about art therapy.* Retrieved November 19, 2005, from www.ctarttherapy.org/information/index.html.

Cullen, F.T. & Wright, J.P. (1997). Liberating the anomie-strain paradigm: Implications from social support theory. In N. Passas & R. Agnew (Eds.), *The future of anomie theory* (pp. 187–206). Boston: Northeastern University Press.

Cumming, E. & Henry, W.E. (1961). *Growing old.* New York: Basic Books.

Damon, W. (2004). What is positive youth development? *The Annals of the American Academy of Political and Social Science, 591,* 13–24.

Datillo, J. (2000). *Facilitation techniques in therapeutic recreation.* State College, PA: Venture.

Dattilo, J. (2002). *Inclusive leisure services: Responding to the rights of people with disabilities* (2nd ed.). State College, PA: Venture.

Davis-Berman, J. & Berman, D. (1999). The use of adventure-based programs with at-risk youth. In J.C. Miles & S. Priest (Eds.), *Adventure programming.* State College, PA: Venture.

Davison, G.C. & Neale, J.M. (1990). *Abnormal psychology* (8th ed.). New York: Wiley.

DeBord, K. (1996). *Childhood years: Ages six through twelve.* Raleigh, NC: North Carolina Cooperative Extension Service.

Department of Health and Ageing. (2003). *Aged care in Australia.* Canberra: Author.

Devine, M.A. (2004). From connector to distancer: The role of inclusive leisure contexts in determining social acceptance for people with disabilities. *Journal of Leisure Research, 35,* (2).

Devine, M.A. & Dattilo, J. (2000). Expressive arts as therapeutic media. In J. Dattilo (Ed.), *Facilitation techniques in therapeutic recreation* (pp. 133–164). State College, PA: Venture.

Devine, M.A. & Lashua B. (2002). Constructing social acceptance in inclusive leisure contexts: The role of individuals with disabilities. *Therapeutic Recreation Journal, 36,* 65–83.

Devine, M.A. & McGovern, J. (2001). Inclusion of individuals with disabilities in public park and recreation programs: Are agencies ready? *Journal of Park and Recreation Administration, 19*(4), 60–82.

Devine, M.A. & Sylvester, C. (2005). Disabling defenders? The social construction of disability in therapeutic recreation. *Philosophy of therapeutic recreation: Ideas and issues, Vol. III.* National Therapeutic Recreation Society: Ashburn, VA.

Devine, M.A. & Wilhite, B. (2000). The meaning of disability: Implications for inclusive leisure services for youth with and without disabilities. *Journal of Park and Recreation Administration, 18*(3), 35–52.

Dieser, R.B. (2002a). A personal narrative of a cross-cultural experience in therapeutic recreation: Unmasking the masked. *Therapeutic Recreation Journal, 36*(1), 84–96.

Dieser, R.B. (2002b, May). Accreditation, certification, registration—What should we do? Outlining a Canadian vision for therapeutic recreation professionalism. Keynote address at the Canadian Therapeutic Recreation Association Annual Conference, Calgary, AB, Canada.

Dieser, R.B. (2004a, September). *Jane Addams and Hull-House programs: Forgotten pioneers in therapeutic recreation.* Paper presented at the American Therapeutic Recreation Association Research Institute, Kansas City, MO.

Dieser, R.B. (2004b, Fall). Outlining a Canadian framework for therapeutic recreation professionalism: A mosaic certification framework part I. *Tribune,* 6–7. [Newsletter of the Canadian Therapeutic Recreation Association]

Dieser, R.B. (2005a). A genealogy of the United States therapeutic recreation certification framework. *Leisure Studies, 24*(1), 61–79.

Dieser, R.B. (2005b, Winter). Outlining a Canadian framework for therapeutic recreation professionalism: A mosaic certification framework part II (planting seeds). *Tribune,* 7–9. [Newsletter of the Canadian Therapeutic Recreation Association]

Dieser, R.B. (2005c). Understanding how Jane Addams and Hull-House programs bridged cross-cultural differences: Leisure programs and contact theory. *Human Service Education, 25*(1), 53–63.

Dieser, R.B. (in press). Outlining a Canadian framework for therapeutic recreation professionalism: A mosaic certification framework. Manuscript accepted for publication in *Annual in Therapeutic Recreation.*

Dieser, R.B., Fox, K. & Walker, G. (2002). Recognizing the fundamental attribution error in leisure education research. *Annual of Therapeutic Recreation, 11,* 77–96.

Dieser, R.B., Harkema, R.P., Kowalski, C., Ijeoma, O. & Poppen, L.L. (2004). The portrait of a pioneer: A look back at 115 years of Jane Addams' work at Hull-House—her legacy still lives on. *Parks and Recreation, 39*(9), 128–137.

Dieser, R.B., Magnuson, D. & Scholl, K. (2005). Questioning the dominant beneficial outcome approach in therapeutic recreation and leisure service delivery: The need for a critical thinking extension. In C. Sylvester (Ed.), *Philosophy of therapeutic recreation: Ideas and issues, Volume III* (pp. 59–72). Ashburn, VA: National Recreation and Park Association.

Dieser, R.B. & Peregoy, J.J. (1999). A multicultural critique of three therapeutic recreation service models. *Annual in Therapeutic Recreation, 8,* 56–69.

Discovernursing.com. (2005). *Nursing the basics.* Retrieved on October 29, 2005, from www.discovernursing.com/jnj-sectionID_2-pageID_8-dsc-landing.aspx.

Diversional Therapy Association of Australia (DTAA). (2003). *25th annual convention workbook and DTAA history.* Sydney: Author.

Diversional Therapy Association of Australia (DTAA). (2005). *The Diversional Therapy Association of Australia 1976–1996.* Retrieved November, 29, 2005, from www.diversionaltherapy.org.au/h.htm.

Dixon, J. (1984). Research on teaching recreation skills to adults labeled mentally retarded. *Society and Leisure, 7,* 259–268.

Dixon, J. (1995). Task-oriented versus activity-oriented intervention in therapeutic recreation. *Expanding Horizons in Therapeutic Recreation, 16,* 55–70.

Duncan, M. (1991). Back to our radical roots. In T.L. Goodale & P.A. Witt, *Recreation and leisure: Issues in an era of change* (3rd ed., pp. 331–338). State College, PA: Venture.

Durstine, J.L. & Moore, G.E. (2003a). Mental retardation. In *ACSM's exercise management for persons with chronic diseases and disabilities* (2nd ed., pp. 304–310). Champaign, IL: Human Kinetics.

Durstine, J.L. & Moore, G.E. (2003b). Spinal cord disabilities: Paraplegia and tetraplegia. In *ACSM's exercise management for persons with chronic diseases and disabilities* (2nd ed., pp. 247–253). Champaign, IL: Human Kinetics.

Dustin, D. (Ed.). (1993). *For the good of the order: Administering academic programs in higher education.* San Diego: Institute for Leisure Behavior, San Diego State University.

Edginton, C.R., Compton, D.M. & Honson, C.J. (1989). *Recreation and leisure programming: A guide for the professional.* Dubuque: WM. C. Brown Publishers.

Ellis, M. (August, 1971). Play and its theories re-examined. *Parks & Recreation,* pp. 51–57.

Ellis, M. (1973). *Why people play.* Englewood Cliffs, NJ: Prentice Hall.

Ellis, G., Morris, C. & Trunnell, E. (1995). Engineering experiences: The COMPLEX Model of recreation leadership. *World Leisure and Recreation, 37*(4), 37–43.

Elshtain, J.B. (2002). *Jane Addams and the dream of American democracy.* New York: Basic Books.

Esveldt-Dawson, K. & Kazdin, A. E. (1998). *How to maintain behavior.* Austin, TX: PRO-ED.

Farmer, J.E. (1997). Epilogue: An ecological systems approach to childhood traumatic brain injury. In E.D. Bigler, E. Clark, & J.E. Farmer (Eds.), *Childhood traumatic brain injury: Diagnosis, assessment, and intervention.* Austin, TX: PRO-ED.

Fine, M. & Asch, A. (1988). Disability beyond stigma: Social interaction, discrimination, and activism. *Journal of Social Issues, 44*(1), 3–21.

Fischer, M. (2004). *On Addams.* Toronto, ON: Thomson Wadsworth.

Fonagy, P. & Target, M. (2003). *Psychoanalytic theories: Perspectives from developmental psychopathology.* London: Whurr.

Fosnot, C.T. (1996). Constructivism: A psychological theory of learning. In C.T. Fosnot (Ed.), *Constructivism: Theory, perspectives, and practice* (pp. 8–33). New York: Teachers College Press.

Foucault, M. (1965). *Madness and civilization: A history of insanity in the age of reason.* (R. Howard, Trans.). London: Tavistock.

Fritz, R. (1991). *Creating.* New York: Fawcett Columbine.

Frye, V. & Peters, M. (1972). *Therapeutic recreation: Its theory, philosophy, and practice.* Harrisburg, PA: Stackpole Books.

Gagnon, A.G. (1995). The political uses of federalism. In F. Rocher & M. Smith (Eds.), *New trends in Canadian federalism* (pp. 23–44). Toronto, ON: Broadview Press.

Galbraith, J. (2004). *The economics of innocent fraud.* Boston: Houghton Mifflin.

Germain, C.B. (1991). *Human behavior in the social environment: An ecological view.* New York: Columbia University Press.

Gilchrist, R. (2001). Settlements and the arts. In R. Gilchrist & T. Jeffs (Eds.), *Settlements, social change and community action: Good neighbours* (pp. 173–193). Philadelphia: Jessica Kingsley.

Gist, Y.J. & Hetzel, L.I. (2004). *We the people: Aging in the United States.* Census 2000 Special Reports. U.S. Census Bureau. Retrieved January 5, 2005, from www.census.gov/prod/2004pubs/censr-19.pdf.

Gold, M. (1980). *Try another way training manual.* Champaign, IL: Research Press.

Goodwin, D. (2003). The meaning of social experiences in recreation settings. *Impact, 16*(2), 4–5.

Gordon E. & Yowell, C. (1994). Cultural dissonance as a risk factor in the development of students. In R. Rossi (Ed.), *Schools and students at risk* (pp. 51–69). New York: Teachers College Press.

Grulke, W. (2000). *Ten lessons from the future: Tomorrow is a matter of choice – make it yours.* Englewood Cliffs, NJ: Financial Times/ Prentice Hall.

Guiness World Records (50th ed.). (2005). London: Guinness World Records Limited.

Gunn, S.L. & Peterson, C.A. (1978). *Therapeutic recreation program design: Principles and procedures.* Englewood Cliffs, NJ: Prentice Hall.

Guralnik, D. (Ed.). (1975). *Webster's new world dictionary.* New York: World.

Gustaferre, C. (1914/1990). What kind of a home I would like to have. In M.L. McCree Bryan & A.F. Davis (Eds.), *100 years at Hull-House* (pp. 132–133). Bloomington: Indiana University Press. (Reprinted from *Survey*, July 1914, p. 420).

Hackett, F. (1925/1990). Hull-House—A souvenir. In M.L. McCree Bryan & A.F. Davis (Eds.), *100 years at Hull-House* (pp. 67–73). Bloomington: Indiana University Press. (Reprinted from *Survey*, July 1925, p. 275–279).

Hagan, J. & McCarthy, B. (1997). Anomie, social capital, and street criminology. In N. Passas & R. Agnew (Eds.), *The future of anomie theory* (pp. 124–141). Boston: Northeastern University Press.

Hahn, H. (1988). The politics of physical differences: Disability and discrimination. In M. Nagler (Ed.), *Perspectives on disability* (2nd ed., pp. 37–42). Palo Alto, CA: Health Markets Research.

Halberg, K.J. (1997). Community-based therapeutic recreation: Past, present, and future. In D.M. Compton (Ed.), *Issues in therapeutic recreation: Toward the new millennium* (pp. 507–537). Champaign, IL: Sagamore.

Hall, V.R. (1975). *Managing behavior 2: Behavior modification—basic principles.* Lawrence, KS: H & H Enterprises.

Hall, V.R. & Hall, M.L. (1998a). *How to use planned ignoring (extinction)* (2nd ed.). Austin, TX: PRO-ED.

Hall, V.R. & Hall, M.L. (1998b). *How to use time out* (2nd ed.). Austin, TX: PRO-ED.

Hauser, S.T. (1991). *Adolescents and their families: Paths of ego development.* New York: Free Press.

Health Canada (2004). *Canada Health Act annual report for 2002–2003.* Retrieved December 10, 2004, from www.hc-sc.gc.ca/medicare/annualreports.htm.

HealthyMinds.org. (2005). *What is a psychiatrist?* Retrieved October 30, 2005, from www.healthyminds.org/whatisapsychiatrist.cfm.

Henry, R.S., Cox, N.J., Reifler, B.V. & Asbury, C. (2000). *Adult day centers.* Robert Wood Johnson Foundation. Retrieved February 1, 2006, from www.rwjf.org/files/publications/books/2000/chapter_05.html.

Holtz, L. (1998). *Winning every day.* New York: HarperCollins.

Howard, D. (2006, June 5–7). *The significance of environmental factors for older men diagnosed with prostate cancer.* Paper presented at the 12th Annual North American Collaborating Center Conference on *ICF,* Vancouver, BC.

Howe-Murphy, R. & Charboneau, B.G. (1987). *Therapeutic recreation intervention: An ecological perspective.* Englewood Cliffs, NJ: Prentice Hall.

Hubbard, D. L. (Ed.). (1993). *Continuous quality improvement: Making the transition to education.* Maryville, MO: Prescott Publishing.

Hunnicutt, B.K. (1980). To cope in autonomy: Therapeutic recreation and the limits to professionalization and intervention. In G. Hitzhusen, J. Elliott, D.J. Szymanski, and M.G. Thompson (Eds.), *Expanding horizons in therapeutic recreation VII* (pp. 121–134). Columbia: University of Missouri.

Hutchens, D. (2000). *Out learning the wolves: Surviving and thriving in a learning organization* (2nd ed.). Williston, VT: Pegasus Communications.

Hutcheon, L. (1989). *The politics of postmodernism.* New York: Routledge.

Hutchison, P. & McGill, J. (1998). *Leisure, integration, and community*. (2nd ed.). Toronto, ON: Leisurability Publications.

Isaac, S. & Michael, W. (1971). *Handbook in research and evaluation*. San Diego: Knapp.

Jacobs, J. (2000). *The nature of economies*. New York: The Modern Library.

Jacobson, M. & Ruddy, M. (2004). Open to outcome: A practical guide for facilitating and teaching experiential reflection. Oklahoma City, Oklahoma: Wood N. Barnes.

James, A. (1998). The conceptual development of recreational therapy. In F. Brasile, T.K. Skalko, & J. Burlingame (Eds.), *Perspectives in recreational therapy: Issues of a dynamic profession* (pp. 7–38). Ravensdale, WA: Idyll Arbor.

Jewel, D.L. (1999). *Confronting child maltreatment through recreation* (2nd ed.). Springfield, IL: Charles C Thomas.

Johnson, S. (1998). *Who moved my cheese?* New York: Penguin Putnam.

Jones, A. (2002). *The National Nursing Home Survey: 1999 summary*. National Center for Health Statistics. Vital Health, Stat, 13 (152).

Kane, R., Kane, R. & Ladd, R. (1998). *The heart of long-term care*. New York: Oxford University Press.

Kelly, J.R. (1995). *Leisure (2ⁿᵈ ed.)*. Englewood Cliffs, NJ: Prentice Hall.

Kelly, J. (1982). *Leisure*. Englewood Cliffs, NJ: Prentice Hall.

Kelly, J.R. & Godbey, G. (1992). *The sociology of leisure*. State College, PA: Venture.

Kelly, J.R. & Warnick, R.B. (1999). *Recreation trends and markets*. Champaign, IL: Sagamore.

Kelly, K. (2000). *Mary Shelley's Frankenstein*. Portland, ME: Research and Education Association.

Kennedy, B.S. & Montgomery, N.D. (1998). Recreational therapy in the community. In F. Brasile, T.K. Skalko, & J. Burlingame (Eds.), *Perspectives in recreational therapy: Issues of a dynamic profession* (pp. 125–140). Ravensdale, WA: Idyll Arbor.

Kentucky Department of Education (2005). *Kentucky emotional–behavioral disability: Technical assistance manual: Behavioral examples*. Retrieved July 2005, from www.state.ky.us/agencies/behave/bi/ebdex.html.

Kim, O-J. (2000). *Introduction of leisure and recreation*. Seoul, South Korea: Taekyung Books.

Kinney, J.S., Kinney, T. & Witman, J. (2004). Therapeutic recreation modalities and facilitation techniques: A national study. *Annual in Therapeutic Recreation, 13*, 59–79.

Kirby, D. (2001). *Emerging answers: Research findings on programs to reduce teen pregnancy*. Washington, D.C.: National Campaign to Prevent Teen Pregnancy.

Kiresuk, J. & Sherman, R. (1968). Goal attainment scaling: A general method for evaluating comprehensive community mental health programs. *Community Mental Health Journal, 4*(6), 443-453.

Kiresuk, J., Smith, A. & Cardillo, J. (Eds.). (1994). *Goal attainment scaling: Applications, theory, and measurement*. Hillsdale, NJ: Lawrence Earlbaum Associates.

Kloseck, M. & Crilly, R.G. (1997). *Leisure competence measure: Professional manual and user's guide*. London, ON: Leisure Competence Measure Data System.

Koch, L. (2001). Disability and difference: Balancing social and physical constructions. *Journal of Medical Ethics, 27*, 370–376.

Kolaski, K. (2006). *Myelomeningocele*. Retrieved June 9, 2006, from www.emedicine.com/pmr/topic83.htm.

Korean Therapeutic Recreation Association. (2006). *Korean Therapeutic Recreation Association: Introduction, history, and education*. Retrieved on April 2, 2006, from www.ktra.com.

Kraus, R. & Shank, J. (1989). *Therapeutic recreation services* (4th ed.). Dubuque, IA: Brown.

Kronick, R.F. (Ed.). (1997). *At-risk youth: Theory, practice, reform*. New York: Garland.

Lammel, J. & Emmerichs, J. (1992). The state of therapeutic recreation in German speaking Switzerland. In G.L. Hitzhusen and L.T. Jackson (Eds.), *Global TR II* (pp. 105–112). Columbia, MO: University of Missouri.

Lang & Carstensen (1994). Close emotional relationships in late life: Further support for proactive aging in the social domain. *Psychology and Aging, Vol 9*(2). 315-324 .

Lang, F.R., Rieckmann, N. & Baltes, M.M. (2002). Adapting to aging losses: Do resources facilitate strategies of selection, compensation, and optimization in everyday functioning? *Journal of Gerontology: Psychological Sciences, 57B*(6), P501–P509.

Larson, R., Csikszentmihalyi, M. & Freeman, M. (1992). Alcohol and marijuana use in adolescents' daily lives. In M.W. deVries (Ed.), *The experience of psychopathology: Investigating mental disorders in their natural settings* (pp. 180–192). New York: Cambridge University Press.

Larson, R. & Richards, M.H. (1991). Boredom in the middle school year: Blaming schools versus blaming students. *American Journal of Education, 99*, 418–443.

Laselva, S.V. (1996). *The moral foundations of Canadian federalism: Paradoxes, achievements, and tragedies of nationhood*. Kingston, ON: McGill-Queen's University Press.

Leavitt, P. (2006, November 10). Norway best place to live, according to U.N. *USA Today*, p. 7A.

Lemon, B.W., Bengston, V.L. & Peterson, J.A. (1972). An exploration of the activity theory of aging: Activity types and life satisfaction among in-movers to a retirement community. *Journal of Gerontology, 27*(4), 511–523.

Lewinsohn, P.M., Hops, H., Roberts, R. & Seeley, J.R. (1993). Adolescent psychopathology: I. Prevalence and incidence of depression and other *DSM-III-R* disorders in high school students. *Journal of Abnormal Psychology, 102,* 110–120.

Lewis, D. & Bridger, D. (2000). *The soul of the new consumer.* London: Nicholas Brealy.

Lipson, J.G., Dibble, S.L. & Minarik, P.A. (1996). *Culture & nursing care: A pocket guide.* San Francisco: University of California at San Francisco Nursing Press.

Loher, J. & Schwartz, T. (2003). *The power of full engagement: Managing energy, not time, is the key to higher performance and personal renewal.* New York: Simon and Schuster.

Lokerson, J. (1992). *Learning disabilities.* Retrieved June 10, 2006, from http://ericec.org/digests/e516.html.

Lollar, D. & Simeonsson, R.J. (2005). Diagnosis to function: Classification for children and youth. *Developmental and Behavioral Pediatrics, 26*(4), 323–330.

Long, T.D. (2000). *An ethical decision making model for therapeutic recreation.* Unpublished manuscript.

Lugalia, T.A. (2003). *A child's day: 2000 (selected indicators of child well-being).* Retrieved July 20, 2005, from www.census.gov/prod/2003pubs/p70-89.pdf.

Mackaman, D.P. (1998). *Leisure settings: Bourgeois culture, medicine, and the spa in modern France.* Chicago: University of Chicago Press.

Malkin, M.J., Coyle, C.P. & Carruthers, C. (1998). Efficacy research in recreational therapy. In F. Brasile, T.K. Skalko, & J. Burlingame (Eds.), *Perspectives in recreational therapy: Issues of a dynamic profession* (pp. 141–164). Ravensdale, WA: Idyll Arbor.

Maton, K. (2000). Making a difference: The social ecology of social transformation. *American Journal of Community Psychology, 28,* 25–58.

McBride, P. (1989). Jane Addams. In H. Ibrahim (Ed.), *Pioneers in leisure and recreation.* Reston, VA: American Alliance for Health, Physical Education, Recreation and Dance.

McCormick, B., Lee, Y. & Jacobson, J. (2004, June 1–4). *Operationalizing community integration via the ICF.* Paper presented at the 10th Annual North American Collaborating Center Conference on *ICF,* Halifax, NS.

McWhirter, J.J., McWhirter, B.T., McWhirter, E.H. & McWhirter, R.J. (2004). *At-risk youth: A comprehensive response.* Belmont, CA: Thomson Brooks/Cole.

Medical-Central.org. (2005). *Nurses.* Retrieved October 30, 2005, from www.medical-central.org/nurses.htm.

MedicineNet.com. (2005). *Definition of psychiatrist.* Retrieved October 29, 2005, from www.medterms.com/script/main/art.asp?articlekey=5107.

Menninger, W.C. & McColl, I. (1937). Recreational therapy as applied in a modern psychiatric hospital. *Occupational Therapy and Rehabilitation, 16,* 15–23.

Meyer, L.E. (1980). *Philosophical alternatives and the professionalization of therapeutic recreation.* Arlington, VA: National Recreation and Park Association.

Minnesota Governor's Council on Developmental Disabilities. (1998). *Parallels in time* [CD ROM]. St. Paul: Author.

Mitroff, I. (1998). *Smart thinking for crazy times.* San Francisco: Berrett Koehler.

Mobily, K. (1999). New horizons in models of practice in therapeutic recreation. *Therapeutic Recreation Journal, 33*(3), 174–192.

Mobily, K.E. & MacNeil, R.D. (2002). *Therapeutic recreation and the nature of disabilities.* State College, PA: Venture.

Mobily, K.E. & Ostiguy, L.J. (2004). *Introduction to therapeutic recreation: US and Canadian perspectives.* State College, PA: Venture.

Monroe, H. (1912/1990). The working girl's song. In M.L. McCree Bryan & A.F. Davis (Eds.), *100 years at Hull-House* (pp. 119–120). Bloomington: Indiana University Press. (Reprinted from *Life and Labor,* July 1912, p. 236).

Mundy, J. (1998). *Leisure education: Theory and practice* (2nd ed.). Champaign, IL: Sagamore.

Muscular Dystrophy Association. (2005). *Neuromuscular disease in the MDA program.* Retrieved May 27, 2005, from www.mdausa.org/disease/index.html.

Myer D.G. & Diener E. (1995). Who is happy? *Psychological Science, 6*(1), 10–19.

Nachmanovitch, S. (1990). *Free play.* New York: Putnam.

National Center for Health Statistics. (2005). *Hospital utilization.* Retrieved July 18, 2005, from www.cdc.gov/nchs/fastats/hospital.htm.

National Center on Physical Activity and Disability. (2005a). *Amputation.* Retrieved May 15, 2005, from www.ncpad.org/disability/fact_sheet.php?sheet=324&view=all.

National Center on Physical Activity and Disability. (2005b). *Stroke.* Retrieved May 15, 2005, from www.ncpad.org/disability/fact_sheet.php?sheet=132&view=all.

National Center on Physical Activity and Disability. (2005c). *Acquired brain injury.* Retrieved May 15, 2005, from www.ncpad.org/disability/fact_sheet.php?sheet=111&view=all.

National Center on Physical Activity and Disability. (2005d). *Multiple sclerosis: Designing an exercise program.* Retrieved May 20, 2005, from www.ncpad.org/disability/fact_sheet.php?sheet=187&view=all.

National Center on Physical Activity and Disability. (2005e). *Resistance training for persons with physical disabilities.* Retrieved May 27, 2005, from www.ncpad.org/exercise/fact_sheet.php?sheet=107&view=all.

National Center on Physical Activity and Disability. (2005f). *Autism.* Retrieved May 15, 2005, from www.ncpad.org/disability/fact_sheet.php?sheet=366&view=all.

National Council for Assisted Living. (2001). *Assisted living: Independence, choice and dignity.* Retrieved July 5, 2005, from www.ncal.org.

National Council for Therapeutic Recreation Certification (2004). *Why hire a CTRS?* [Brochure]. New York: Author.

National Council for Therapeutic Recreation Certification. (n.d.) Pocket profile of the Certified Therapeutic Recreation Specialist [Brochure]. New York City, NY: Author.

National Dissemination Center for Children with Disabilities (NICHCY). (2004a). *Down syndrome: Disability fact sheet, No. 4.* Retrieved September 12, 2005, from www.nichcy.org/pubs/factshe/fs4.pdf.

National Dissemination Center for Children with Disabilities (NICHCY). (2004b). *Cerebral palsy: Disability fact sheet, No. 2.* Retrieved September 12, 2005, from www.nichcy.org/pubs/factshe/fs2.pdf.

National Dissemination Center for Children with Disabilities (NICHCY). (2004c). *Spina bifida: Disability fact sheet, No. 12.* Retrieved September 12, 2005, from www.nichcy.org/pubs/factshe/fs12.pdf.

National Dissemination Center for Children with Disabilities (NICHCY). (2006). *Autism and pervasive developmental disorders: Disability fact sheet, No. 1.* Retrieved May 24, 2006, from www.nichcy.org/pubs/factshe/fs1.pdf.

National Institute of Neurological Disorders and Stroke (NINDS). (2006). *Muscular dystrophy: Hope through research.* Retrieved June 13, 2006, from www.ninds.nih.gov/disorders/md/md.htm.

National Institutes of Health Consensus Development Statement. (2000). *Phenylketonuria: Screening and management.* Washington, DC, October 16–18. Retrieved May 2006, from www.nichd.nih.gov/publications/pubs/pku/index.htm.

National Institutes of Health. (1995, December 18–20). Physical activity and cardiovascular health. *NIH Consensus Statement Online, 13*(3), 1–33.

National Multiple Sclerosis Society. (2005). *Diagnosis: The basic facts.* Retrieved May 20, 2005, from www.nationalmssociety.org/Brochures-On%20Diagnosis.asp.

National Therapeutic Recreation Society. (1996). *NTRS philosophical position statement.* Retrieved July 21, 2005, from http://www.nrpa.org/content/default.aspx?documentId=871.

National Therapeutic Recreation Society. (2005). *NTRS vision and mission.* Retrieved on February 1, 2007, from www.nrpa.org/ntrs.

Negley, S.K. (1994). Recreation therapy as an outpatient intervention. *Therapeutic Recreation Journal, 28* (1), 35–41.

Negley, S.K. (1997). *Crossing the bridge: A journey in self-esteem, relationships, and life balance.* Emsumclaw, WA: Idyll Arbor.

Nesbitt, J.A. (1984). The new/old American TR Association Inc.: Heroic or foolish. *Journal of Iowa Parks and Recreation, 10*(4), 14–15.

Neugarten, B.L., Havighurst, R.J. & Tobin, S.S. (1968). Personality and patterns of aging. In Neugarten, B.L. (Ed.), *Middle age and aging.* Chicago, IL: University of Chicago Press.

Nice, C.J. (1948). Recreation is not therapy. *The Journal of Health and Physical Education, 19,* 642–643.

Nirje, B. (1992). *The normalization principle paper.* Uppsala, Sweden: Centre for Handicapped Research.

Noh, Y. & Lee, Y. (2004). Development of professional identity in therapeutic recreation: Suggestions for Korean therapeutic recreation profession. *Korean Therapeutic Recreation Journal, 3,* 1–28.

North Carolina Office on Disability and Health. (2001). *Removing barriers to health clubs and fitness facilities.* Chapel Hill, NC: Frank Porter Graham Child Development Institute.

Northern Illinois Special Recreation Association. (2005). *Programs.* Retrieved November 13, 2005, from www.nisra.org/.

OccupationalTherapist.com. (2005). *Frequently asked questions.* Retrieved October 31, 2005, from www.occupationaltherapist.com/faq.html.

O'Connor, T. (2004). *An overview of juvenile justice.* Retrieved November 17, 2005, from http://faculty.ncwc.edu/toconnor/111/111lect14.htm.

Oliver, M. (1996). *Understanding disability: From theory to practice.* London: MacMillan Press.

O'Morrow, G.S. & Reynolds, R.P. (1989). *Therapeutic recreation: A helping profession* (3rd ed.). Englewood Cliffs, NJ: Prentice Hall.

O'Neill, J. & Conzemius, A. (with Commadore, C., & Pulfus, C.). (2006). *The power of SMART goals: Using goals to improve student learning.* Bloomington, IN: The Solution Tree.

O'Neill, J. & Conzemius, A. (2001). *Building shared responsibility for student learning.* Alexandria, VA: Association for Supervision and Curriculum Development.

Orrù, M. (1987). *Anomie: History and meanings.* Winchester, MA: Allen & Unwin.

Ostiguy, L. & Dieser, R. (2004). Developing a framework for therapeutic recreation certification in Canada. *Expanding Horizons in Therapeutic Recreation, 21,* 21–26.

O'Sullivan, E. (2001). Repositioning parks and recreation as essential to well-being. *Parks and Recreation, 36*(10), 89–94.

Papert, S. (March 29, 1999). Jean Piaget. *Time,* pp. 105–107.

Parliament of Australia Senate. (2006). *A national approach to mental health—from crisis to community.* Canberra: Author.

Passas, N. (1997). Anomie, reference groups, and relative deprivation. In N. Passas & R. Agnew (Eds.), *The future of anomie theory* (pp. 27–51). Boston: Northeastern University Press.

Paul, J.L. & Epanchin, B.C. (1991). *Educating emotionally disturbed children and youth: Theories and practices for teachers* (2nd ed.). New York: Macmillan.

Paulsen-Hughes, P. & Sherrill, C. (2004). Les autres conditions and amputation. In C. Sherrill, *Adapted physical activity, recreation, and sport: Crossdisciplinary and lifespan* (6th ed., pp. 643–672). New York, NY: McGraw-Hill.

Pawelko, K.A., & Magafas, A.H. (1997). Leisure well being among adolescent groups: Time, choices and self-determination. *Parks and Recreation, 32*(7), 26–39.

Pedlar, A. (1996). Community development: What does it mean for recreation and leisure? *Journal of Applied Recreation Research, 21*(5), 5–23.

Pedlar, A. & Gilbert, A. (1997). Normalization and integration: The Canadian experience. In D.M. Compton (Ed.), *Issues in therapeutic recreation: Toward the new millennium* (pp. 489–506). Champaign, IL: Sagamore.

Perkins, D.F. & Caldwell, L.L. (2005). Resiliency, protective processes, promotion, and community youth development. In P.A. Witt & L.L. Caldwell (Eds.), *Recreation and youth development* (pp. 149–167). State College, PA: Venture Publishing.

Peterson, C. (2000). The future of optimism. *American Psychologist, 55*(1), 44–55.

Peterson, C.A. (1984). A matter of priorities and loyalties. *Therapeutic Recreation Journal, 18*(3), 11–16.

Peterson, C.A. & Gunn, S.L. (1984). *Therapeutic recreation program design: Principles and procedures* (2nd ed.) Englewood Cliffs, NJ: Prentice Hall.

Phillips, B.E. (1952a). Recreation therapy. *Journal of the American Association for Health, Physical Education and Recreation, 23*(6), 23–24.

Phillips, B.E. (1952b). Hospital recreation is unique. *Journal of the American Association for Health, Physical Education and Recreation, 23*(5), 29–30, 35.

Physical-Therapist.com. (2005). *Welcome to physical therapist.* Retrieved November 15, 2005, from www.physical-therapist.com/.

Piaget, J. (1970). *Genetic epistemology.* New York: Columbia University Press.

Pioneer Network. (2005). *Stories from the field.* Retrieved July 5, 2005, from www.pioneernetwork.net.

Polacheck, H.S. (1989). *I came a stranger: The story of a Hull-House girl.* Urbana: University of Illinois Press.

Potts, M.K. (1997). Social support and depression among older adults living alone: the importance of friends within and outside of a retirement community. *Social Work, 42*(4), 348–362.

Prader Willi Syndrome Association. (2005). *Basic facts on Prader Willi.* Retrieved May 29, 2005, from http://www.pwsausa.org/syndrome/basicfac.htm.

Putnam, R.D. (2000). *Bowling alone: The collapse and revival of American community.* New York: Touchstone.

Putnam, R.D. & Feldstein, L.M. (2003). *Better together: Restoring the American community.* New York: Simon and Schuster.

Rappaport, J. (1987). Terms of empowerment/exemplars of prevention: Toward a theory for community psychology. *American Journal of Community Psychology, 15*, 121–147.

Reddick, P.J. (2000, Spring). History of the Canadian Therapeutic Recreation Association. *Tribune*, 1–2. [Newsletter of the Canadian Therapeutic Recreation Association]

Reed, G. & Bufka, L. (2005, March 9). *Implementing the ICF in health care delivery.* Paper presented at the American Therapeutic Recreation Association Mid-Year Professional Issues Forum, Arlington, VA.

Reid, D. & van Dreunen, E. (1996). Leisure as a social transformation mechanism in community development practice. *Journal of Applied Recreation Research, 21*(1), 45–65.

Rimmer, James H. (2005a). *Introduction to achieving a beneficial fitness for persons with developmental disabilities.* Retrieved May 29, 2005, from www.ncpad.org/disability/fact_sheet.php?sheet=117.

Rimmer, James H. (2005b). *Spinal cord injury.* Retrieved April 25, 2005, from www.ncpad.org.

Robertson, T. (1993). *The wheel of fortune or the wheel of torture: Professional development.* Midwest Symposium on Therapeutic Recreation, St. Charles, IL.

Rodreguez-Hanley, A. & Snyder, C.R. (2000). The demise of hope: On losing positive thinking. In C.R. Snyder (Ed.), *Handbook of hope: Theory, measures, and applications* (pp. 39–54). San Diego: Academic Press.

Rojek, C. (1985). *Capitalism and leisure theory.* London: Tavistock.

Rojek, C. (1995). *Decentering leisure: Rethinking leisure theory.* Thousand Oaks, CA: Sage.

Romney, G.O. (1945). *Off the job living.* Washington, DC: McGrath and National Recreation and Park Association.

Ross, J.E. (1998). Critique of Austin's Health Protection/Health Promotion Model. *Therapeutic Recreation Journal, 32*(2), 124–129.

Rubin, H.J. & Rubin, I.S. (2001). *Community organizing and development* (3rd ed.). Needham Heights, MA: Allyn & Bacon.

Russell, K. (2002). *A longitudinal assessment of treatment outcomes in outdoor behavioral healthcare.* (Technical Report 28). Moscow, ID: Idaho Forest, Wildlife, and Range Experiment Station, University of Idaho—Wilderness Research Center.

Sampson, R.J. (2001). How do communities undergird or undermine human development? Relevant contexts and social mechanisms. In A. Booth & A.C. Crouter (Eds.), *Does it take a village?* (pp. 3–30). Mahwah, NJ: Lawrence Erlbaum Associates.

Schaie, K.W. & Willis, S. (2002). *Adult development and aging.* Upper Saddle River, NJ: Prentice Hall.

Schoel, J., Prouty, D. & Radcliffe, P. (1988). *Islands of healing: A guide to adventure based counseling.* Hamilton, MA: Project Adventure.

Scholl, K.G., Smith, J.G. & Davison, A. (2005). Agency readiness to provide inclusive recreation and after-school services for children with disabilities. *Therapeutic Recreation Journal, 39*(1), 47–62.

Schram, B. & Mandell, B.R. (2000). *An introduction to human services: Policy and practice* (4th ed.). Boston: Allyn and Bacon.

Schroeder, S.R., Gerry, M., Getz, G. & Valazquez, F. (2002). *Usage of the term "mental retardation": Language, image, and public education.* Retrieved September 12, 2005, from www.ssa.gov/disability/MentalRetardationReport.pdf.

Schroots, J. F. (1996). Theories of aging: psychological. In J. E. Birren (Ed.), *Encyclopedia of Gerontology, vol. 2* (pp. 557–567). New York, NY: Academic Press.

Schwartz, B. (2004). *The paradox of choice.* New York: HarperCollins.

Schwartz, P. (1996). *The art of the long view.* New York: Doubleday.

Scott, D., Witt, P.A. & Foss, M.G. (1996). Evaluation of the impact of the Dougherty Arts Center's club on children at-risk. *Journal of Park and Recreation Administration, 14*(3), 41–59.

Search Institute. (2007). *The 40 developmental assets for adolescents.* Retrieved February 28, 2007, from http://www.search-institute.org/assets/.

Searle, M.S., Mahon, M.J., Iso-Ahola, S.E., Sdrolias, H.A. & van Dyck, J. (1995). Enhancing a sense of independence and psychological well-being among the elderly. *Journal of Leisure Research, 27*(2), 107–124.

Searle, M.S., Mahon, M.J., Iso-Ahola, S.E., Sdrolias, H.A. & van Dyck, J. (1998). Examining the long term effects of leisure education on a sense of independence and psychological well-being among the elderly. *Journal of Leisure Research, 30*(3), 331–340.

Seligman, A.B. (1997). *The problem of trust.* Princeton, NJ: Princeton University Press.

Senge, P., Kleiner, A., Roberts, C., Ross, R., Roth, G. & Smith, B. (1999). *The dance of change: Challenges to sustaining momentum in learning organizations.* New York: Random House.

Shank, J. & Coyle, C. (2002). *Therapeutic recreation in health promotion and rehabilitation.* State College, PA: Venture.

Shank, J.W., Kinney, W.B. & Coyle, C.P. (1993). Efficacy studies in therapeutic recreation research: The need, the state of the art, and future implications. In M.J. Malkin & C.Z. Howe (Eds.), *Research in therapeutic recreation: Concepts and methods* (pp. 301–335). State College, PA: Venture.

Sharp, L. (2005). *Occupational therapist.* Retrieved November 1, 2005, from www.medical-central.org/occupational-therapist.htm.

Sheldon, K. & Mendenhall, D. (1995). Therapeutic recreation techniques for participation in a summer day camp arts and crafts program. *Therapeutic Recreation Journal, 29* (4), 289–293.

Shelley, M. (1818/2003). *Frankenstein.* New York: Bantam.

Sherrill, C. (2004). *Adapted physical activity, recreation, and sport: Crossdisciplinary and lifespan* (6th ed.). New York, NY: McGraw-Hill.

Shivers, J. & Fait, H. (1985). *Special recreation services: Therapeutic and adapted.* Philadelphia: Lea & Febiger.

Shore, B.A., Lerman, D.C., Smith, R.G., Iwata, B.A. & DeLeon, I.G. (1995). Direct assessment of quality of care in a geriatric nursing home. *Journal of Applied Behavior Analysis, 28*, 435–448.

Shorter, E. (1997). *A history of psychiatry: From the era of the asylum to the age of Prozac.* New York: Wiley.

Shulewitz, R. & Zuniga, S. (1999). NISRA teams with community health providers for at risk youth. *Illinois Parks and Recreation, 20*(4), 33.

Shultz, L.E., Crompton, J.L. & Witt, P.A. (1995). A national profile of the status of public recreation services for at-risk children and youth. *Journal of Park and Recreation Administration, 13*(3), 1–25.

Silver, R.A. (1989). *Developing cognitive and creative skills through art.* Mamaroneck, NY: Albin Press.

Simeonsson, R.J. (1994). *Risk, resilience, and prevention: Promoting the well-being of all children.* Baltimore: Brooks.

Simon, S.B. & Olds, S.W. (1977). *Helping your children learn right from wrong. A guide to values clarification.* New York: McGraw-Hill.

Skalko, T.K. (1997). Therapeutic recreation in health care reform. In D.M. Compton (Ed.), *Issues in therapeutic recreation: Toward the new millennium* (pp. 1–16). Champaign, IL: Sagamore.

Sklar, S.L. (2005). *Positive youth development: The case of a wilderness challenge intervention.* Unpublished doctoral dissertation, University of Florida, Gainesville, FL.

Smith, S.H. (1976). Practitioners' evaluation of college courses, competencies, and functions in therapeutic recreation. *Therapeutic Recreation Journal, 10*(4), 152–156.

Snyder, C.R. (2000). Hypothesis: There is hope. In C.R. Snyder (Ed.), *Handbook of hope: Theory, measures, and applications* (pp. 3–21). San Diego: Academic Press.

Spangler, K. (2005). *NRPA efforts to support youth development in parks and recreation: 2005 executive summary and timeline.* Ashburn, VA: National Recreation and Park Association.

Sprouse, J.K., Klitzing, S.W. & Parr, M. (2005). Youth at risk: Recreation and prevention. *Parks and Recreation, 40*(1), 16–21.

Starr, E.G. (1896). Settlements and the church's duty. *The Church Social Union, 28*, 1.

Statistics Canada. (2004). *2001 census.* Retrieved on January 20, 2005, from http://statcan.ca.

Stein, T.A. (1970). Therapeutic recreation education: 1969 survey. *Therapeutic Recreation Journal, 4*(2), 4–7, 25.

Steinberg, L. (2002). *Adolescence* (6th ed.). Boston: McGraw-Hill.

Steinmetz, E. (2006). *Americans with disabilities: 2002.* (Current Population Reports, P70–107). Washington, DC: U.S. Census Bureau.

Stivers, C. (2000). Bureau men and settlement women: Constructing public administration in the progressive era. Lawrence: University Press of Kansas.

Streifel, S. (1998). *How to teach through modeling and imitation* (2nd ed.). Austin TX: PRO-ED.

Stumbo, N.J. (1986). A definition of entry-level knowledge for therapeutic recreation practice. *Therapeutic Recreation Journal, 20*(4), 9–19.

Stumbo, N.J. (2002). *Client assessment in therapeutic recreation services.* State College, PA: Venture.

Stumbo, N. J. & Folkerth, J. E. (2005). *Study guide for the therapeutic recreation specialists certification examination* (3rd ed.). Champaign, IL: Sagamore.

Stumbo, N., Martin, L. & Ogborne, V. (2004). Collective voices, shared wisdom: On the need for a professional association to represent therapeutic recreation in Australia. *Annals of Leisure Research, 7*(2), 85–94.

Stumbo, N.J. & Peterson, C.A. (1998). The leisure ability model. *Therapeutic Recreation Journal, 32*(2), 82–96.

Stumbo, N.J. & Peterson, C.A. (2004). *Therapeutic recreation program design: Principles and procedures* (4th ed.). San Francisco: Benjamin Cummings.

Sylvester, C. (1989). Therapeutic recreation and the practice of history. *Therapeutic Recreation Journal, 23*(4), 19–28.

Sylvester, C., Voelkl, J.E. & Ellis, G. (2001). *Therapeutic recreation programming: Theory and practice.* State College, PA: Venture.

The ARC (1997). *Phenylketonuria (PKU).* Retrieved May 2006, from www.thearc.org/faqs/pku.html.

Thibadeau, S.F. (1998). *How to use response cost.* Austin, TX: PRO-ED.

Thomas, W. (1996). *Life worth living: How someone you love can still enjoy life in a nursing home—The Eden Alternative in action.* Acton, MA: Vanderwyk & Burnham.

Tiffany Court. (2005). *Activities calendar.* Retrieved July 5, 2005, from www.tiffanycourt.com/activities.html.

Tiger, L. (1979). *Optimism: The biology of hope.* New York: Simon & Schuster.

Trowbridge, R. (1988). *Therapy and recreation.* Melbourne: Centre for Continuing Education, Monash University.

Twenge, J.M. (2000). The age of anxiety? Birth-cohort change in anxiety and neuroticism, 1952–1993. *Journal of Personality and Social Psychology, 79,* 1007–1021.

United States Department of Health and Human Services (2000). *Healthy people 2010.* Washington, DC: United States Government Printing Office.

United States Department of Justice. (1991). *Americans with Disabilities Act.* (P.L. 101-336).

United States Department of Labor, Bureau of Labor Statistics. (2004a). Dieticians and nutritionists. In *Occupational outlook handbook.* Retrieved October 29, 2005, from www.bls.gov/oco/ocos077.htm.

United States Department of Labor, Bureau of Labor Statistics. (2004b). Occupational therapists. In *Occupational outlook handbook.* Retrieved November 19, 2005, from http://www.bls.gov/oco/ocos078.htm.

United States Department of Labor. Bureau of Labor Statistics. (2004c). Physicians and Surgeons in the Bureau of Labor Statistics. In *Occupational outlook handbook.* Retrieved on June 20, 2006, from http://www.bls.gov/oco/ocos074.htm.

United States Department of Labor, Bureau of Labor Statistics. (2004d). Psychologists. In *Occupational outlook handbook.* Retrieved on November 19, 2005, from http://www.bls.gov/oco/ocos056.htm.

United States Department of Labor, Bureau of Labor Statistics. (2004e). Registered nurses. In *Occupational outlook handbook.* Retrieved October 29, 2005, from http://www.bls.gov/oco/ocos083.htm.

United States Department of Labor, Bureau of Labor Statistics. (2004f). Social Workers. In *Occupational outlook handbook.* Retrieved on June 24, 2006, from http://www.bls.gov/oco/ocos060.htm.

United States Department of Labor, Bureau of Labor Statistics. (2005). Recreational therapists. In *Occupational outlook handbook.* Retrieved September 26, 2005, from www.bls.gov/oco/ocos082.htm.

United States Public Health Service. (2002). *Closing the gap: A national blueprint for improving the health of individuals with mental retardation, Report of the Surgeon General's Conference on Health Disparities and Mental Retardation, February 2001.* Washington, DC. Retrieved September 15, 2005, from www.surgeongeneral.gov/topics/mental-retardation/retardation.pdf.

Van der Smissen, B. (2005). *Recreation and parks the profession: A comprehensive resource for students and professionals.* Champaign, IL: Human Kinetics.

Veblen, T. (1899). *The theory of the leisure class: An economic study of institutions.* New York: Macmillan.

Velde, B.P. & Murphy, D. (1994). The therapeutic recreation (TR) profession in Canada. Where are we now and where are we going? In G.L. Hitzhusen, L. Thomas, & N. Frank (Eds.), *Global Therapeutic Recreation III: 3rd International Symposium on Therapeutic Recreation* (p. 108). Columbia: University of Missouri at Columbia.

Vipond, R. (1991). *Liberty and community: Canadian federalism and the future of the constitution.* Albany: State University of New York Press.

Vladeck, B. (1980). *Unloving care: The nursing home tragedy.* New York: Basic Books.

Voelkl, J.E., Fries, B. & Galecki, A. (1995). Predictors of nursing home residents' participation in activity programs. *The Gerontologist, 35,* 44–51.

Voight, A. (1988). The use of rope courses as a treatment modality for emotionally disturbed adolescents in hospitals. *Therapeutic Recreation Journal, 22*(2), 57–64.

Wake Forest University Baptist Medical Center. (2003). *National Census finds most US counties don't have enough adult day centers.* Retrieved March 20, 2005, from http://www.eurekalert.org/pub_releases/2003-03/wfub-ncf031003.php.

Washburne, M.F. (1904/1990). The labor museum. In M.L. McCree Bryan & A.F. Davis (Eds.), *100 years at Hull-House* (pp. 74–81). Bloomington: Indiana University Press. (Reprinted from *Craftman,* September 1904, pp. 570–579).

Wehman, P. (2001). *Supported employment in business: Expanding the capacity of workers with disabilities.* St. Augustine, FL: Training Resources Network.

Weil, E.F. (1913/1990). The Hull-House players. In M.L. McCree Bryan & A.F. Davis (Eds.), *100 years at Hull-House* (pp. 92–95). Bloomington: Indiana University Press. (Reprinted from *Theatre Magazine,* September 1913, pp. xix–xxii).

Wenzel, K. (1998, May/June/July). President's message. *NTRS Report, 23*(3), 1–5.

West, P.C. (1984). Social stigma and community recreation participation by the physically and mentally handicapped. *Therapeutic Recreation Journal, 26*(1), 40–49.

White, F. (1997). Wilderness therapy programs: What skills are needed to conduct therapy without serious injury. In D.M. Compton (Ed.), *Issues in therapeutic recreation: Toward the new millennium* (pp. 559–576). Champaign, IL: Sagamore.

Whorf, B. (1956). *Language, thought, and reality.* New York: Wiley.

Wilhite, B., Devine, M.A. & Goldenberg, L. (1999). Self-perceptions of youth with and without disabilities: Implications for leisure programs and services. *Therapeutic Recreation Journal, 33*, 15–28.

Wilhite, B., Keller, M.J. & Caldwell, L.L. (1999). Optimizing lifelong health and well-being: A health enhancing model of therapeutic recreation. *Therapeutic Recreation Journal, 33*, 98–108.

Winnick, J. (2005a). Spina bifida in *Adapted physical education and sport* (4th ed., pp. 287–290). Champaign, IL: Human Kinetics.

Winnick, J. (2005b). Traumatic brain injury in *Adapted physical education and sport* (4th ed., pp. 240–242). Champaign, IL: Human Kinetics.

Witt, P.A. (2001). Re-examining the role of recreation and parks in after-school programs. *Parks and Recreation, 36*(7), 20–28.

Witt, P.A. & Caldwell, L. (2005). Principles of youth development. In P.A. Witt and L.L. Caldwell *Recreation and youth development.* State College, PA: Venture.

Witt, P.A. & Crompton, J.L. (1996). The at-risk youth recreation project. *Journal of Park and Recreation Administration, 14*(3), 1–9.

Witt, P.A. & Crompton, J.L. (2002a). *Best practices in youth development in public parks and recreation settings.* Ashburn, VA: National Recreation and Park Association.

Witt, P.A. & Crompton, J.L. (2002b). Programming for the future. *Parks and Recreation, 37*(12), 64–68.

Witt, P.A. & Ellis, G.D. (1989). *The leisure diagnostic battery: Users manual.* State College, PA: Venture.

Wolf, M. (1999). *The entertainment economy: How megamedia forces are transforming our lives.* New York: Times Books.

Wolfensberger, W. "The Normalization Principle, and Some Major Implications to Architectural Environmental Design." in Bedner, M. *Barrier Free Environments.* Stroudsburg, PA: Dowden, Hutchinson & Ross, Inc. 1977. pg. 135.

Woodham-Smith, C. (1951). *Florence Nightingale: 1820–1910.* New York: McGraw-Hill.

Woods, R.A. & Kennedy, A J. (1970). *The rise of urban America: Handbook of settlements.* New York: Charities Publication.

World Health Organization. (1989). *History of the development of the ICD.* Geneva, Switzerland: Author.

World Health Organization. (1992). *International classification of functioning, disability and health* (10th ed.). Geneva, Switzerland: Author.

World Health Organization. (2001). *International classification of functioning, disability and health.* Geneva, Switzerland: Author.

Worthington, C., Myers, T., O'Brien, K., Nixon, S. & Cockerill, R. (2005). Rehabilitation in

Yaffe, R. M. (1998). The Leisure Ability Model: A response from a service perspective. *Therapeutic Recreation Journal, 32*(2), 103-108.

Zander, R.S. & Zander, B. (2000). *The art of possibility: Transforming professional and personal life.* Boston: Harvard Business School Press.

Index

Note: The letters *f* and *t* after page numbers indicate figures and tables, respectively.

About the Editors

Editors Terry Long and Terry Robertson with their wives and friend at the 2005 World Leisure Symposium in Brisbane, Australia. Pictured from left to right, Anne and Terry Long, Shelly and Terry Robertson, and John Chambers.

Terry Robertson, PhD, is an associate professor and department chair in the department of health, physical education, recreation, and dance at Northwest Missouri State University. He has worked in therapeutic recreation for over 30 years as a practitioner, consultant, and educator.

Dr. Robertson is a past president of the National Therapeutic Recreation Society, the regional independent living center, the Missouri Therapeutic Recreation Society, and the Nevada Therapeutic Recreation Society. He also served on the Utah Therapeutic Recreation Licensure for 6 years and was the director of CEUs for the Midwest Symposium on Therapeutic Recreation for over 20 years. Dr. Robertson is currently serving a 4-year, publicly elected term on his county's health board and has served on numerous other boards and in other leadership capacities for related organizations. He is currently serving locally on his county's

organization for group homes. Dr. Robertson was also a codeveloper of the Case Histories section of the Therapeutic Recreation Journal. Currently known as Practice Perspectives, this section helps the profession examine individual and group interventions and contributes information on best practices, interventions, and treatment concerns to research literature.

Terry Long, PhD, is an associate professor in the department of health, physical education, recreation, and dance at Northwest Missouri State University, where he has coordinated the therapeutic recreation curriculum since 2000. He is also the director of the HPERD Abilities Laboratory. His specialty is applications of therapeutic recreation in the mental health realm, particularly in the area of behavior disorders. Dr. Long also has a master's degree in clinical psychology and worked with various mental health agencies and facilities over the past 10 years in both clinical and outdoor settings.

Dr. Long is an associate editor for *Therapeutic Recreation Journal* and an associate editor for *SCHOLE*. He is past president of the Missouri Therapeutic Recreation Society, at-large director for the National Therapeutic Recreation Society Board of Directors (2006-2008 term), and the board president for the independent living center serving the Northwest Region of Missouri. He is past president of the Missouri Park and Recreation Association Educators Section.

About the Contributors

Patricia Ardovino

Patricia Ardovino, PhD, CTRS, CPRP, is an associate professor at the University of Wisconsin, La Crosse. She received her undergraduate and master's degrees in Physical Education and Adapted Physical Education from Ohio State University, and her PhD from Indiana University. Before receiving her doctorate, Dr. Ardovino spent 22 years working with people with disabilities as an instructor in an institution for people with intellectual impairments, as the program director of a sheltered workshop, coordinator of a respite program, and director of a community-based therapeutic recreation/special recreation center for the Memphis Park Commission. At the University of Wisconsin, La Crosse, she has led 4 study tours of Italy which focused on leisure in the Roman Empire and accessibility for tourists with disabilities. Her teaching and research interests include therapeutic recreation in correctional settings, inclusive recreation, and the impact of the war in Iraq on recreation and therapeutic recreation.

Cari E. Autry

Cari Autry, PhD, CTRS, is an assistant professor in the Department of Recreation and Tourism Management at Arizona State University where youth development is the primary focus of her research, teaching, and service. She earned her PhD in Health and Human Performance with a concentration in Therapeutic Recreation from the University of Florida and her MS in Recreation Administration with an emphasis in therapeutic recreation from the University of North Carolina at Chapel Hill. Cari's research interests include recreation as a means for community development and prevention in relation to youth development. She is interested in the theoretical frameworks of the ecological perspective and social capital. Her research has been presented at national and international conferences related to youth development, leisure, and social capital. Cari is published in many professional journals such as the *Therapeutic Recreation Journal,* and she serves as an associate editor of the *Therapeutic Recreation Journal.*

Begum Aybar-Damali

Begum Z. Aybar-Damali, MS, is a PhD candidate in Parks, Recreation, and Tourism Management at Clemson University. She completed her BS in Psychology at Middle East Technical University in 1999 and her MS in Industrial Management at Clemson University. In 2005, she was awarded the Graduate Student Certificate for Excellence in the Department of Parks, Recreation, and Tourism Management by the College of Health, Education, and Human Development, Clemson University. Currently, she is serving as a graduate assistant of the Institute for Engaged Aging at Clemson University. In particular, she is interested in leisure in human development, therapeutic recreation, and aging. Her leisure interests include socializing with family and friends, cooking, swimming, rollerblading, skiing, and making ceramic sculptures.

Mary Ann Devine

Dr. Mary Ann Devine, CTRS, is an associate professor in Recreation, Park, and Tourism Management at Kent State University. She received her doctoral degree from the University of Georgia in Recreation and Leisure Studies. Her research interests are in the area of inclusion of individuals with disabilities in recreation, sport, and leisure services. Dr. Devine has conducted numerous studies examining aspects of the inclusion process such as social acceptance, social construction of disability, best practices, stigma, attitudinal barriers, and the application of the ADA in leisure settings. Most recently, Dr. Devine has begun examining the role of therapeutic recreation in promoting healthy, active living with individuals with disabilities.

Rodney Dieser

Rodney Dieser, PhD, is a faculty member at the University of Northern Iowa in the School of Health, Physical Education, and Leisure Services. His research and teaching interests include cross-cultural therapeutic recreation and leisure practice; therapeutic recreation as an adjunctive therapy in mental illness; historical and philosophical foundations of leisure, youth, and human services; historical research on leisure, youth, and human services provided at Hull-House, 1889–1953; representations of health in popular culture; and hegemonic masculinity in leisure and physical activities.

Dr. Dieser has served as an associated editor for the *Therapeutic Recreation Journal* and as an editor for the academic newsletter the *SPRE Professor*. In 2006 he received the Outstanding Professional Research Award by the National Therapeutic Recreation Society. He has also received outstanding research and writing awards from the Alberta Therapeutic Recreation Association, and the Canadian Therapeutic Recreation Association, respectively. Dr. Dieser's academic writings have appeared in various academic journals and he has co-authored two textbooks in leisure studies.

Jesse Dixon

Jesse Dixon completed his PhD in 1977 at the University of Illinois at Urbana-Champaign and is currently a professor at San Diego State University in the Department of Recreation, Parks, and Tourism. His teaching interests include therapeutic recreation, concepts of leisure, community benefits from recreation services, accessible park planning, economics for leisure/recreation, future leisure experiences with technology, and community tourism.

He has been recognized for his teaching with numerous awards from the university, the College of Professional Studies, and the California Park and Recreation Society and received formal "Service Recognition" for his work with the Santee Lakes Recreation Preserve, as a commissioner on the San Diego Metro Commission, and as a director on the San Diego County Water Authority.

Professor Dixon has written for more than 70 publications and has also served as a reviewer for a wide variety of professional journals. He was "qualified" with both the National Council on Therapeutic Recreation Certification and the California Board of Park and Recreation Personnel.

Frederick P. Green

Frederick "Rick" Green, PhD, is a professor in Therapeutic Recreation at the University of Southern Mississippi. Rick began working in recreation with people with disabilities in 1976, and began advocating and programming for inclusive recreation services in the early 1980s. His professional experience includes seven summers of summer camp work experience in Illinois, several as camp director, and five years as coordinator of recreational sports at Southern Illinois University where he coordinated recreation programs for college students with disabilities.

Rick is a current member of NRPA and serves as an accreditation visitor for the Council on Accreditation. He is a founding member and past president of the Mississippi Therapeutic Recreation Alliance. He is currently the project director for *ACCESS-Recreation*, an award-winning service learning program that promotes access to the community for people with disabilities and experiential learning experiences for students in recreation.

Alice Foose

Alice Foose is an assistant professor at Northwest Missouri State University. She has worked with children and adults with developmental disabilities (DD) in various community settings. During her graduate work at Indiana University, she assisted with several research projects involving children and adults with DD, including the final 5 years of a longitudinal study on the aging process of adults with DD. This project led to the development of the Leisure Assessment Inventory and several new models of aging. Her current interests are social networks, leisure over the life span, and social advocacy.

David Howard

Dr. David Howard is an assistant professor in the College of Health and Human Performance at Indiana State University. He received his PhD in Rehabilitation Science from the University of Florida and earned a master's in Clinical Social Work and an undergraduate degree in Recreation and Leisure Studies from the University of Utah. David is a member of the American Therapeutic Recreation Association and has served as the chair of the ATRA Public Health—WHO/*ICF* team and ATRA Public Health—*Healthy People 2010* committee. At Indiana State University, his scholarly interests include utilization of the WHO *International Classification of Functioning, Disability, and Health (ICF)* in clinical practice and health promotion; psychosocial factors related to coping after cancer diagnosis and treatment; complementary and alternative medicine; and sexuality and intimacy issues related to disability. As a practitioner, David has experience in mental health, substance abuse, and corrections settings.

Julie Lammel

Julie Lammel, PhD, is an assistant professor in Recreation Management at Lock Haven University of Pennsylvania. Julie serves as the therapeutic recreation track coordinator for the department. Julie spent 10 years working in acute care physical rehabilitation prior to returning to graduate school to complete her advanced degrees. While her primary job responsibility is teaching, she is involved in research efforts that explore the influence of leisure and recreation on wellness and health behavior. Additionally, she is involved in community service efforts at the university and exploring the effect of community service on students' attitudes toward civic involvement and in understanding cultural differences. Julie spends time away from work volunteering with a local animal rescue, walking her dogs, spending time with friends, gardening, and traveling.

Michal Anne Lord

Michal Anne Lord, PhD, is the executive director of the Texas Recreation and Park Society (TRAPS). She is a Certified Parks and Recreation Professional and is state TR certified. She taught for 13 years at Southwest Texas State University in the Department of Health, Physical Education, Recreation, and Dance and was the division coordinator of Recreation Administration, including the Therapeutic Recreation emphasis. She also has worked in community recreation for nearly 25 years.

She has served on the NRPA Board of Trustees and as past president of the NTRS and the Therapeutic Recreation Branch of TRAPS. She currently serves on the Board of Directors of Special Olympics Texas and has chaired the National Advisory Council of Very Special Arts. Michal Anne has received the Fellow Award from the Texas Recreation and Park Society and the TR Professional of the Year Award from the TRAPS' TR Branch; the Fellow Award from the NRPA Southwest Regional Council; and NTRS' Distinguished Service Award.

Chris Mackey

For 6 years, Chris Mackey has been the physical activity and recreation initiative coordinator for the North Carolina Office on Disability and Health (NCODH), a CDC-funded project that works to promote the health of persons with disabilities throughout North Carolina. His work has involved training fitness and other health promotion professionals about inclusion of persons with disabilities, the Americans with Disabilities Act, and universal design. In September 2003 he was named to the regional training team for the Southeast Disability and Business Technical Assistance Center. In 2003, he was named a national youth leader for the Healthy and Ready to Work initiative of the federal Maternal and Child Health Bureau. A North Carolina native, Chris was born with spina bifida and graduated from East Carolina University with a BS in Therapeutic Recreation. He has participated in wheelchair basketball and swimming at both a regional and national level and is studying to become a Certified Fitness Trainer.

Tanya E. McAdory-Coogan

Tanya McAdory-Coogan is currently the director of chapter services for the Spina Bifida Association (SBA) in Washington DC. Prior to her work with SBA, Tanya worked at NRPA for 3 years as the therapeutic recreation manager and staff liaison to NTRS. She has 3 years of experience in municipal parks and recreation and 5 years in higher education. She served on the board of directors for the Mississippi Recreation and Park Association and is a former president of the Mississippi Therapeutic Recreation Alliance. Her previous work experience includes working with persons with disabilities in community-based settings, transitioning segregated programs to inclusive programs, and coaching university wheelchair sports teams. Tanya holds a BS in Health, Physical Education and Recreation and an MS in Therapeutic Recreation. She is a member of NRPA as well as a Certified Therapeutic Recreation Specialist (CTRS) and a Certified Park and Recreation Professional (CPRP).

John McGovern

John N. McGovern, JD, is the executive director of the Northern Suburban Special Recreation Association (NSSRA) in Northbrook, Illinois. NSSRA is a partnership of 13 local governments providing community-based TR services to people who live in the partner communities. He has more than 30 years' experience as a supervisor and administrator in community-based TR.

He complemented his education in Recreation Administration with a law degree from Loyola University of Chicago. He writes, speaks, and consults frequently about the application of the Americans with Disabilities Act to public parks and recreation. McGovern is a very active member of the National Recreation and Park Association, National Therapeutic Recreation Society, and the Illinois Park and Recreation Association, and is very involved in legislative issues affecting parks and recreation in Illinois.

Shane Pegg

Shane Pegg, PhD, is a senior lecturer with the School of Tourism in the faculty of Business, Economics and Law at The University of Queensland. He is a past recipient of the Future Scholars Award from the Academy of Leisure Sciences and a current member of the World Leisure Commission on Access and Inclusion. He has been involved in a wide array of research projects related to service evaluation, therapeutic recreation, tourism access and inclusion issues, and the tourism and leisure behavior of people with disabilities. More recently, this has included a study of the links between leisure, boredom, alcohol use, and levels of self-determination of rural and urban youth in Australia; the risk-taking behavior of Gold Coast Schoolies Week participants and the effective management of such tourism events; and satisfaction with volunteer engagement in community events, as well as an investigation of the key motivators for engagement of young adults in sport tourism.

Sydney L. Sklar

Sydney Sklar, PhD, CTRS, is an assistant professor in the Department of Recreation, Sport, and Tourism Management at the University of St. Francis in Joliet, Illinois, where he coordinates the Therapeutic Recreation concentration. Syd earned his PhD in Health and Human Performance from the University of Florida and an MS in Recreation Administration from Aurora University. He has served as a mental health practitioner at Shands Healthcare, Gainesville, Florida, and provided community-based therapeutic recreation services at Fox Valley Special Recreation Association, Aurora, Illinois. His research includes the impacts of therapeutic wilderness programming and social capital on youth development. Syd serves on the boards of directors for the NTRS (2004–2007) and the Illinois Recreation Therapy Association (2005–present). He has chaired the NTRS Poster Session for 5 consecutive years and twice received the NTRS Presidential Citation. He enjoys camping and hiking with his wife, Bev, and his children, Frank and Etta.

Sheila Swann-Guerrero

Sheila Swann-Guerrero, CTRS, is an information specialist with the National Center on Physical Activity and Disability at the University of Illinois, Chicago. As an NCPAD information specialist, Sheila provides information and resources on physical activity, recreation, sports, and health promotion to help people who have a disability or chronic condition lead physically active lifestyles. She has more than 20 years of experience in therapeutic recreation. She is a co-author of *Autism and Considerations in Recreation and Physical Activity Settings*, an NCPAD fact sheet that serves as a practical overview of how to incorporate individuals with autism into recreation and physical activity to lead healthy, active lifestyles. Sheila serves on the Illinois Recreation Therapy Association board of directors and is the ILRTA president for 2007. Sheila is the Sibshop coordinator for Advocate Illinois Masonic Pediatric Developmental Center, providing family support services to siblings of children with a disability or chronic condition and their families.

Judith E. Voelkl

Judith Voelkl, PhD, CTRS, is a professor of Therapeutic Recreation in the Department of Parks, Recreation, and Tourism Management at Clemson University in Clemson, South Carolina. Voelkl has conducted numerous research studies investigating the quality of life of nursing home residents in relation to recreation therapy services. From this research she has published articles in journals such as *Therapeutic Recreation Journal, Annual in Therapeutic Recreation,* and *The Gerontologist.* Voelkl was awarded the Scholarly Achievement Award from the American Therapeutic Recreation Association in 2005 and was inducted as a Fellow in the Academy of Leisure Sciences in 2006. She is currently serving on the board of directors of the American Therapeutic Recreation Association. In her free time she enjoys walking her dog, reading, meditating, spending time with friends, and going to auctions.

Richard Williams

Richard Williams is an associate professor in the Department of Recreation and Leisure Studies at East Carolina University in Greenville, North Carolina. He is a Certified Therapeutic Recreation Specialist and a Licensed Recreational Therapist (NC). Dr. Williams received a Bachelor of Science degree from Virginia Commonwealth University and Bachelor of Arts, Master of Arts, and Doctorate of Education degrees from the University of Georgia. He is currently the co-chair of the research team of the American Therapeutic Recreation Association and an associate editor of the *Therapeutic Recreation Journal.*

Heewon Yang

Heewon Yang, PhD, CTRS, is an assistant professor in the Department of Health Education and Recreation at Southern Illinois University (SIU), Carbondale, Illinois. Heewon teaches both general recreation and therapeutic recreation courses. He is interested in aggressive behaviors among adolescents and the development of therapeutic treatment programs for the population. He is a co-leader of the international relations team at American Therapeutic Recreation Association (ATRA) and serves as an exam management committee member for the National Council for Therapeutic Recreation Certification (NCTRC).

*You'll find
other outstanding
recreation resources at*

www.HumanKinetics.com

In the U.S. call

1-800-747-4457

Australia...08 8372 0999
Canada 1-800-465-7301
Europe.......................................+44 (0) 113 255 5665
New Zealand.......................................0064 9 448 1207

HUMAN KINETICS
The Information Leader in Physical Activity
P.O. Box 5076 • Champaign, IL 61825-5076 USA